The Survivors Mode

The Survivors Mode

Anthony McMaryion

Copyright © 2018 by Anthony McMaryion.

Library of Congress Control Number:		2018907132
ISBN:	Hardcover	978-1-9845-3572-6
	Softcover	978-1-9845-3571-9
	eBook	978-1-9845-3570-2

All rights reserved. No part of this book may be reproduced or transmitted in any form or by any means, electronic or mechanical, including photocopying, recording, or by any information storage and retrieval system, without permission in writing from the copyright owner.

This is a work of fiction. Names, characters, places and incidents either are the product of the author's imagination or are used fictitiously, and any resemblance to any actual persons, living or dead, events, or locales is entirely coincidental.

Scripture taken from the Holy Bible: International Standard Version® Release 2.0. Copyright © 1996-2012 by the ISV Foundation. ALL RIGHTS RESERVED INTERNATIONALLY.

Scripture taken from the Holy Bible, NEW INTERNATIONAL VERSION®. Copyright © 1973, 1978, 1984, 2011 by Biblica, Inc. All rights reserved worldwide. Used by permission. NEW INTERNATIONAL VERSION® and NIV® are registered trademarks of Biblica, Inc. Use of either trademark for the offering of goods or services requires the prior written consent of Biblica US, Inc.

Scripture quotations taken from the Holy Bible, New Living Translation, Copyright © 1996, 2004. Used by permission of Tyndale House Publishers, Inc., Wheaton, Illinois 60189. All rights reserved.

Any people depicted in stock imagery provided by Getty Images are models, and such images are being used for illustrative purposes only.
Certain stock imagery © Getty Images.

Print information available on the last page.

Rev. date: 08/08/2018

To order additional copies of this book, contact:
Xlibris
1-888-795-4274
www.Xlibris.com
Orders@Xlibris.com
779561

CONTENTS

Introduction vii

Chapter 1   Living in the U's 1

Chapter 2   Fathers and Daughters 32

Chapter 3   Survivor's Mind and Mentals 47

Chapter 4   The Seduction of Your Mind 53

Chapter 5   Survivor's Thoughts and Thinking 62

Chapter 6   Survivor Mind-Set and Mentality 71

Chapter 7   Survivor Mode 85

Chapter 8   The Survivor-Survival Journey 99

Chapter 9   The Next Chapter in Your Journey 114

Chapter 10   The Survivor Mode Danger Zone 123

Chapter 11   Unmasking the Masquerade 132

Chapter 12   Mollie: Surviving the Journey 145

Chapter 13   Rose: The Journey of a Survivor 172

Chapter 14   Drifting into Darkness 226

Chapter 15   Traps, Triggers, and Trespassers 238

Chapter 16   Sense and Reason 252

Chapter 17   Appetites and Impulses 282

Chapter 18   Sensual Survivors 293

Chapter 19   Self-Deception 302

Chapter 20   Accountability and Responsibility 324

Chapter 21 Secular Sense and Reason Ministers............................ 340

Chapter 22 Secular World Ministers' Healing Solutions...............350

Chapter 23 Secular Ministers' Healing Facts................................357

Chapter 24 Overpower, Overtake, Overthrow 360

Chapter 25 Take down, Take over, and Take out..........................398

Chapter 26 Run for Your Life...425

INTRODUCTION

HIS IMAGE IS in her eyes, and her little eyes would light up like a bright gleaming light. She was taking in the total essence of who he was, is, and would be to her, and every time he would talk to her, everything inside of her would jubilantly respond. Even though she just came into this world, it's like she already knows him and she can feel him. Even though she came out, exited out of the safety and the security of her mother's womb, it would be all right because she entered right into the safety and the security of her father's world. Everything that he said or did brought a smile and laugh to her face. She is her daddy's baby girl, and the only thing she ever wanted was to be a daddy's girl, his little princess, the apple of his eye.

When she heard his voice or saw him coming, she would run to him; and with all the baby and childlike faith and trust a little girl could and would have, she would thrust herself toward him somehow knowing that he wasn't going to let her hurt herself and just innocently knowing, anticipating, and expecting him to open up his arms and scoop her up.

When he did, she could and would feel all the love he had for her, and she felt safe and secure in his arms, and she somehow would know she was daddy's little girl. He made her feel loved, protected, and cared for, and more importantly, he made her feel like she was the most important little girl in the whole wide world.

Every day, she waited to repeat the same scene, and she got to the point where she would hold on to him and cling to him, and she followed him around. She would climb up in his arms and make that cuddling moment they would have; her safe haven. Not only had she taken in the fullness of his essence, but as she would grow up, she would also begin to take in and be consumed with his aura.

He was her daddy, her father, and she was his little girl, a daddy's girl, and not only did his aura fill the room that she shared with him but his aura also filled up her easily excited little heart. He was larger than life to her, and he was not only her provider but also her protector.

It would be because of him, her daddy, that she could go about being the little girl that she was, and it was because of him, her daddy, and the comforting presence he had in her life that allowed her to just "be." No one could have told her that, one day, all of what he gave her would change and he would end up rationing out his love, affection, and attention between her and her other siblings.

No one told her that, one day, she would end up feeling like she had to compete with her other siblings for what she had become accustomed to receiving from him. No one ever warned her that, one day, she would end up getting the leftovers from her daddy's love, affection, and attention.

Why didn't someone tell her she, one day, would have to compete for his time and attention and she would one day end up being compared to her other siblings, and what she thought and felt made her special to him and the center of his attention ended up making her feel different and not the same as her other siblings? She is just one of other siblings, and for years, she had waited for that one moment when she could have him all to herself; and just when she thought that was about to happen, something else would happen (divorce and/or another sibling was born). She felt like she would never have him, her daddy, to herself, and the daddy-daughter life as she once knew, it would change and it would be forever changing. What you have to understand is this: that from the moment a baby girl is born into the world, her father can have an amazing impact on her life.

From the first time she wraps her tiny little hand around his finger to the time he walks her down the aisle and beyond, his presence, involvement, and character will help mold and shape her into the woman she will become. She will look to this man with wonderment, and she has certain needs that only he can fulfill. Through all the many interactions and experiences she had with him, incredible things are developing inside of her.

Some very powerful and profound things are taking place in her mind, emotions, and psyche through the powerful dynamics that occur between a father and a daughter. As her daddy-daughter world began to change, life, as she once knew it, would never be the same. Those days and times when life was so simple and so easy would never be that way again. She is grown now, and she walked away from her childhood with wounds, voids, and emptiness.

She's having a hard time just finding her way, and from time to time, she reflects back on her childhood days, and she would remember the times when her daddy wasn't there to do just the simple and easy things with her and for her. Her life is different, and she is different, and she often feels like it is not up to her to choose whether she will win or lose.

Somewhere along the way from babyhood to childhood to teenhood to adulthood, a daddy-daughter disconnection happened, and she went looking for what she did not get from her daddy, her father, in the relationships she got into. She was just trying to fill that emptiness, those voids, and close up the wounds she didn't even know she had.

She just wanted to be her father's little girl, and she waited for the moment when she could, and she would take pride when others would look at her and them together and say to her, "You are a daddy's girl, aren't you?" Her other siblings received from him what she desperately needed and wanted and thought, felt, and believed she would also receive, and when that didn't happen, it left something missing between them, and she ended up not being as close to them as she is supposed to be. Now, don't get me wrong, they do love each other.

Her life is not like theirs. The rejection she feels (she didn't even know she had) has kept her making choices and decisions that have left her struggling, straining, and trying to survive and trying to make it through all the challenges, tests, trials, tribulations, and temptation that have come her way that she had never seen coming.

Is this story really *her* truth? Is it really *your* reality? Or is it just a daddy-daughter story that looks like, feels like, sounds like, and was imagined to be right; but when all the facts and all the factors and when fate showed up, it made her daddy-daughter story all wrong, and it left *her*, *you*, or *someone* once again in the mode where they are trying to find a way to survive and make it through?

The truth be told; this story is about some little girl's truth. It's about some little girl's reality, some little girl's real-life story, about some little girl's wish, want, fantasy, dream, and desire.

But most of the time, it is the true story about some little girl who is now a full-grown woman, and the little girl inside of her (when she is not afraid and comes out to play) still calls for and still craves for a daddy-to-daughter love, and she still remembers and still relives and still have sudden moments with how she grew up without and never knowing, grew up with and one day lost, grew up with and was in the same space with but was still was a stranger to, and grew up and was rejected, neglected, overlooked, abandoned, or abused by the daddy that she always wanted to be a daughter to.

The one that she was never validated by, that she never felt good enough for and she never felt pretty enough to be called "a daddy's girl," her daddy's baby girl.

So come with me as I take you on a journey into the life and lives of what was supposed to be so simple and so easy for a daddy's girl. Come with me as I take you on a behind-the-scenes look at what happens when a daddy's girl's life ends up being filled with fighting to survive and filled with fighting for survival.

CHAPTER ONE

Living in the U's

Prelude: Simple and easy

A TIME OF innocence and love, could we go back to the way it was? I remember when life was so simple you did or you didn't, you would and you wouldn't, but it ain't like that anymore. I remember when life was so easy people said what they meant; they were either for it or against, but it ain't like that anymore. I am talking about those days when we could clearly see the way and when it was up to us to choose whether to win or lose. I'm talking about those times when it was up to us to see what it was we were to be. Somehow, along the way, we got caught up in the mix of complexity.

I remember when life was so simple parents were a light, and through them, we saw what was right, but it ain't like that anymore. I remember when life was so easy little boys grew into men and little girls into women, but it ain't like that anymore. We knew where we belong, and we knew what was right and wrong. We need a simple yes or no. The question now is should I stay or should I go? Life has become so advanced, and I wish I had a second chance to go back if I could and see what was bad and what was good. Now, I'm here, and what I fear the most have come upon me. And now, here I stand, and I want for the opportunity once again to say yea and nay. I guess I will search until I find it . . . I'm looking for my yea or nay.

Growing up

Somewhere down in the southern part of a place that only you know about in a city, state, and town no one probably have heard of and knew of unless you lived there or you drove by that way, there was this little girl who, in her own way, was dreaming of a simple and easy life. Her name was Sarai, and not only was she born in that place that only you or someone like you and her would know about, but also she had lived in that place all her life. The town she grew up in was a farming community. She was no different than most little girls and kids her age, running around and enjoying a simple and easy life, no cares and no worries and no concerns. She had only one focus, and that was to be Sarai and to enjoy being Sarai. She, like most girls her age, was enjoying her age of innocence, and she was enjoying the freedom she had to be herself. She enjoyed her simple life, and she enjoyed looking up to those who were larger than life to her.

Everything for this little girl was so simple. The end of her days was just like the middle and the beginning of her days, and she had nothing to stress her out, and she had nothing to be fearful of. She had her support system, and she had her safety zones, and she had her secret places. Times were so simple and times were so easy, and there wasn't anything that was complicated or complex for Sarai. She could just wake up and go about her day-to-day life and just "be." Like most families during those days, they had their good times and their tough times; but in the midst of whatever times they had, they remained a family, and she had people in her life that, to the best of their ability, kept her connected to family values.

When she was just a kid growing up, her mom worked in a neighboring state at the local plant like most of the people who lived in and around the plant. After leaving the plant, her mom would do one of the things she had always wanted to do, and that was to do substitute teaching. Because she was trying to provide for her family, Sarai's mom not only would substitute teach but would also work at the local mill. It was hard for her mom to balance the two, but her mom knew she had to. Sarai's grandfather, or "paw" as she passionately called him, once sold jeeps and then anhydrous ammonia to farmers, and when he wasn't doing that, he was doing the other thing that he loved doing, which was planting gardens and doing his gardening.

Her grandma was what most women back in those days and times were, and that was a homemaker. Sarai learned from her grandma what women should do in a home. She learned from her grandma how to cook and clean, how to do household budgets, how to treat people, and how to be respectable and to always be well mannered, and how to entertain guests, and many other things. But what her grandma made sure she understood was what women did in the home and how they were to go about being responsible for their home. Sarai was given the daily responsibility of making and baking the bread and biscuits, which was something she, like any or like most and even all little girls her age, really loved doing and looked forward to doing. There was nothing that her grandma would teach her that would ever be complicated, complex, or hard or a challenge.

When you are and you were a little girl like Sarai and you had someone like the grandmother she had, quite naturally you would look up to her, respect her, and you looked forward to sitting at her feet and learning what women did and how they were supposed to take care of their husbands. Sarai admired her grandma's ability to manage a house so well, take care of her paw, and keep her faith and pray to the God that most did not see a need for. And as far as she could remember, she only saw her grandma get upset and fuss at her paw only one time.

Back then, parents didn't let their kids see them in disagreement. Those were simple times and easy times where little girls like Sarai were taught simple things like having social graces and manners, which is a lost art and a forgotten importance today. Because she grew up in a farming community, she had the whole farming countryside to use and utilize as her personal playground, and she could run and roam all over it without having the fear of something bad, wrong, negative, or ugly ever happening to her.

She could live in and out of her innocence, and she was surrounded by people who gave her all the love any little girl would need and want. She loved doing simple things like spending time on the lake, fishing, and going hunting with her friends and family members, and she enjoyed being around and with all the animals. But most of all, she just enjoyed the simple life and the easy times and the fact that she was free to live out of and see life and things and people out of her age of innocence. But her most precious and most unforgettable times and moments would be when she would dream.

Her dreams were not any different from most girls her age. She dreamed of having a home, a family, and being loved, needed, wanted, accepted, and being so happy. She dreamed of her prince charming one day showing up and taking her away and they would live happily ever after and he would love her for who and what she was. In the age of her innocence, she would just dream like that.

She could do that! Why? Because life was so easy and things were so simple, and nothing and no one was complex, and the people back then was for you or against you, and their yea was yea and their nay was just that, their nay. The simplicity of her life and things being so easy back then provided a protective and safe environment for her dreams, which prevented her innocence from being in harm's way and from being hindered in any way whatsoever. After all, she was just a little girl, and she had not said or done anything wrong that could or would compromise her innocence.

Life was just simple and times were just easy even when the time she grew up in wasn't the best of times. Simple times, simple people, simple moments, simple memories, simple matters, she conceived, birthed, born, and lived her dreams, hopes, and desires out of "simplicity." When she wasn't busy helping her grandfather, her paw, in the gardens or helping her grandma with the housework, she would climb one of her favorite trees that was by the house. There she would sit and talk to God and let her imagination wander, and she would imagine and she would see images of the way she wanted her life to be.

It would be in those times she could and would be able to clearly see her way, and because of the simplicity of her life, she could clearly see what it was she wanted to be. She was just a little girl, an innocent little girl, a simple little girl talking to and believing in a big God that she had never seen with her own physical eyes. But she knew He was there, and for some reason, she always knew He would meet her there in that secret place she had created for Him and her. She had that innocent childlike faith that kept her believing the God her grandma taught her about and prayed to and talked to would always be there and meet her there in the same place she would always go to so she could talk to Him.

How did she know, and why did she know, you ask? It was because her simple life and her simple innocence and life for her being so easy and simple made talking to God and meeting God at their secret place "simple and easy." Listen! Can't you hear her talking to God about the simple and easy things she wanted out of life? There was nothing that a little girl would say to a big God that was so complicated and complex; it was just a simple and easy yea-and-nay conversation. He was there and she was there, and simplicity was and would always be there to help her, a little girl, reach out to and touch the heart of a big God she had never seen but could, would, and did believe in out of her "simplicity" and out of her "innocence."

Sarai had a dog whose name was Misty, and Misty would rest at the base of the tree while she was in a simple personal meeting with God and wait on her. Can you imagine a dog, her dog, knowing what she was going to do when she climbed up into her favorite tree, and then she would sit down at the base of it, acting like she was the designated protector of her simplicity and her innocence and acting as if she was accountable and responsible for making sure nothing and no one interrupted her simple and innocent time with God?

Sometimes, Misty and she would roam down to the strawberry patch, and she would curl up with her, and they would do some cloud gazing after eating the strawberry vines bare. Misty was Sarai's only company, and when Misty passed, Sarai insisted on having a funeral for her.

That was a tough time for Sarai because Misty wasn't just a dog; she was Sarai's best friend and sometimes her only friend, and they spent so much time together doing simple and easy things. When it came time to say good-bye to Misty, Sarai remembered praying at that funeral, and everyone was crying. What can a little girl do when her simple and easy innocent life is suddenly and immediately hit with a loss that is not so simple and easy to accept and grasp and maybe even get past?

When you are a kid and you are enjoying what you know is a simple and easy life, you never think about death and people dying, and you

THE SURVIVORS MODE

never think or feel like some part of you dies when you lose something or someone and even your dog. That's when simple and easy becomes not so simple and not so easy, and a kid first gets his or her feel of things and life being complicated and complex.

We all have had something that happened to us when we were kids and we were living in and out of our simplicity and our easy that we didn't expect, anticipate, predict, plan and prepare for, believe could and would happen because we never think about such times and moments; we are too busy enjoying simplicity and easy.

And when our simplicity and our easy is suddenly and immediately challenged by whatever it is that challenges us, we can't help but be changed or crippled because we are just little kids, and no one had ever prepared us for the unexpected, the unplanned, the unknown, the unseen, the undetected, the unwanted, the unpleasant, the unbelievable, the things we are unaware of that become our undeniable and our unexplainable, our unthinkable, and our unforgettable that leave us simply and innocently feeling and thinking it's all unfair.

Because we are and were just kids living in and out of our simplicity, our easy, and our innocence, we end up in a place called the "unsure." Not because we want to; it happens that way because we were just plain ole simple, easygoing, innocent kids who never thought, felt, or believed something of that magnitude that is simple and easy within its own self should, could, and would happen to us and to what we love and cherish. We grow up in our simplicity and in our easy and in our innocence going about our childhood as if we are untouchable until we come in contact with our first unimaginable and our first unthinkable.

That should be our first indication that life changes, and life, love, and living are not always simple and easy and neither are always innocent. Well, Paw got Sarai another dog, and she named her Princess. And she went back to doing simple and easy things like sitting outside brushing her fur and eating ice cream on a hot day, and, yes, they even shared licking the ice cream; that's what most simple, easygoing, innocent kids do. Back to simple and easy and innocence.

Simple, easy, and innocent dreaming

Sarai, like most girls, spent a lot of time in her playhouse and dreaming of having a husband to take care of like her paw did with her grandma. She wanted a nice home with plenty of room, so when they would have kids, they could grow up and run all over the place like she did. She enjoyed having the opportunity to do what a lot of girls her age couldn't, wouldn't, and didn't get the opportunity to do, and that was to sit in her playhouse and make believe she was having his, her fairy-tale prince, meals ready when he came home.

Her grandparents were her relationship light, and she wanted her fairy-tale guy and herself to stand in the shadows of the kind of relationship they had. She knew and thought, felt, and really believed that it was up to her to choose what her life, love, and living could and would be like, because in her mind, it was simple and it was easy to arrive at that choice and decision. And that was because in her innocent, simple, and easy thoughts, train of thought, thinking, and way of thinking, she had the perfect relationship role models in her grandparents.

In her free time, she would sit among the beautiful lilies in the fields that surrounded her house and dream of one day touring with one of her favorite singing groups or being a solo singer and singing like one of her favorite gospel artists. She also dreamed of one day being on Broadway and being in musicals and being able to travel the world and see places that she had never seen before.

Sarai's biggest passion was her love for ballet and for tap dance; that is where she spent the majority of her dreaming time. Her simplicity and her easygoing spirit and her innocence kept her from being nervous whenever she as a kid would end up on some kind and type of stage. Sarai would dedicate and commit herself to dance lessons, piano lessons, and voice lessons all in the hopes of, one day, those dreams becoming her reality.

She would practice all day when she could, and she knew her grandma had gained patience while dealing with her. Sarai loved to write too, and she would write pages and pages of thoughts, poems, and short stories mostly because she loved to do so, but really and truly, it was how she used to express herself. While she was in high school, she wrote a lot of poems, but one of her poems was published in a book with many others poems, and because of that recognition, she was interviewed for the school paper.

Somewhere in the midst of her childhood days, in the midst of simplicity, in the midst of ease and innocence, in the midst of all those she looked up to, and right in the midst of everything that those who were close to her gave her, there was something still missing, something none of those who nurtured, cared for, watched over, and protected her ever saw.

In her little girl's heart, what was missing was just as simple and easy and innocent as her childhood days were growing up in that small farming community town she grew up in. Deep down within her, like in any child, there was a need, want, and desire to be somebody and to do something that was important, rewarding, fulfilling, and satisfying. She did what you and I and all of us do when we are kids; we dream and say what we are going to do when we grow up, what we are going to be, what we are going to have, and where we are going to go. We picture it all in our minds and plan, and we try to prepare and position ourselves for what we aspire to.

At some place, point, and time, Sarai still felt like she needed and wanted to be important even though she grew up in a safe, stable, and secure home life. To this very day, Sarai still wishes she still had that book with all her writings in them, but it, along with her personal and private journals, was tossed away by the man she would later marry and would become her husband. He didn't see them as important and valuable like she did, but that's another story. Sarai grew up knowing what it was she wanted to be and what she wanted to do with her life.

Seeing life right

It is through our parents' eyes that we as kids are able to clearly see what's wrong and what's right because they were and they are our light, am I right? Sarai's mom would eventually end up traveling with a group, singing, and began spreading the gospel. Church is where her mom really blossomed and grew and became a lot better person. As a result, Sarai would end up participating in the school musicals, and she sang in the adult choir and in the youth choir at the same time. It would be during those days that Sarai would meet someone who would step into some of those void and empty places in her life, and he would be a positive inspiration in her life.

In her eyes, he was an awesome person who was not just a leader and a teacher, but his image was that of a father figure. He would be the one who encouraged her to go for her dreams and to shoot for the stars and to never ever give up. Nobody knew what was going on with Sarai on the inside, and no one really knew how she really felt about her life and about herself. No one ever knew what she was still missing and what she had to go through. No one knew what she ended up collecting, carrying, and coming out with out of her simple, easygoing, innocent childhood life.

She didn't know what generationally she had inherited. And just like little boys growing into men, Sarai was a little girl growing into what, one day, would become a woman. No one knew what impact the not-so-good things that Sarai experienced from childhood to being a teen to being a young adult would have on her life; not even Sarai knew herself. That's how we grow up, and that is what we step over into, the unknown, and we, at some place, point, and time, come face-to-face with the unreal and the realities and truths about life and concerning ourselves, who we really are, what we are, where we are, what we as kids have been through, and where we really are in our life journey.

And we all have had that one someone who steps into our pathway and comes into our life while we are going from childhood to being a teen to being an adult and while we are still growing, developing, and maturing, and trying to find, figure out, and discover who we are and what our life is. It ends up being that someone we didn't expect and we didn't see or notice that ends up having a positive effect upon us and affects us in the right way when we needed it and him or her, when we least expected him or her to show up.

That someone ends up being there when we need him or her and being there even when we didn't know we needed or wanted someone. And that person seemingly just knows what to say and do and how to say and do what gets us through a time and a place and a point in our life when we would get stranded and stuck. He or she shows up when we don't even see it or know it, and we don't even realize it or recognize it, and we may even at the time, and because of what we are going through, reject, resist, and refuse to accept what we see and we have seen and what we know or have known.

Sarai had that one person who was there to help her, motivate her, and help her build momentum so that she could and would keep moving and would be able to move forward. She believed that she never would have made it through school without him. He kept her motivated and occupied with productive things that he didn't even know would help her and keep her mind off the changes that were going on that she was going through at home.

As her life and her home life continued to change and be challenged, music and travel would become, be, and end up being her escape from it all. Her days of life being so simple and easy and her days of innocence were slowly dwindling away, and she found herself having to grow up really fast, and she was developing in a lot of different ways and in a lot of different areas. There were some areas she was and had matured in, but there were still some simple and easygoing "innocence ignorance" areas that were still there within her. She loved going to see her favorite aunt and uncle in North Carolina, and whenever she was there, what she really and truly loved most were the mountain air, the hikes, and the feeling of God seemingly being at hand's reach.

She loved going on the mission trips because she could blend in and not have any attention drawn to what she was going through in getting to know others. In those times, she didn't feel like she was the different anymore, and she felt like she fit in and she was someone who was liked. It's amazing how things in a person's life change but stay the same.

She closed her eyes, and she went to sleep an innocent little girl with little girl's dreams, desires, hopes, expectations, fantasies, and fairy tales, and when she woke up, she's almost grown now, and those days of simplicity and being easy are and would be gone, and those days when life was so simple and your choices and decisions were clear, you did or you didn't, you would and you wouldn't, well, they have almost faded away.

And those days when Sarai and you and I could remember when life was so easy and the people you met and were in your life said what they meant, you knew they were either be for or against. Those simple, easygoing, and innocent summertime days, moments, and memories of growing up in that small farming community and town in Georgia has come and gone, and her fond childhood memories are and have slowly faded, and just the other day, she heard the voice of those days of her innocence calling.

She heard the voice of those who once made her life and childhood simple and easy also calling her. You see, they all went to sleep on this side, and some of them woke up in Beulah land, not all of them as she would have, out of her childlike faith, hoped. And some of those times and people Sarai, to this day, still miss; more than you will ever know just how much she misses them so. There were so many who protected her from danger, and there were those who loved her so much that they made sure she was safe and warm, and those are the ones she really does miss a lot.

Her headlines and story lines

Those she miss, well, they are not here in this life with Sarai anymore, and she is standing by herself. And her life, that simple, easy, and innocent life she once knew, she would not know anymore. Why? You see, the headlines and the story lines for life are scattered and filled with shattered images, shattered days, shattered times, shattered moments, shattered memories, and shattered matters that colored her world and her life with hopelessness.

The chapters and the pages in her life are filled with that day, that time, and that moment when she got involved with a guy who said all the right things to her and he did a lot of good things for her and with her, but he also did all the wrong things to her. The headlines for her life stated she was dominated, manipulated, and controlled by him. And the story lines for her life said she was battered, beaten, bruised, and almost broken, abused, abandoned, neglected, and rejected by him.

Her headlines and her story lines made it clear that he tried to destroy her dreams and her desires, and for years, she would live in a world and live in a life that she never asked for, begged for, pleaded for, prayed for, or asked for. She became a "hostage in and to her own hurt." The only thing she was guilty of was wanting someone to love her, need her, want her, respect her, appreciate her, believe in her, care for her, desire her, treasure and value her, protect her, provide for her, be there for her, and stand with her and never stand against her like her paw did for her grandmother.

She just wanted to be, and she wanted to have age of innocence happiness, life-so-simple and life-so-easy happiness. She married a man that did not treat her right; nor did he talk to her right. She never asked for much; she just wanted a man who would do what her paw would do, and that was to protect and provide for them and prevent things from happening to them that were bad. When he betrayed her heart, he also busted her belief in her dreams, and he broke her self-confidence and he also shattered her self-esteem.

Those who knew her and saw, knew, or heard about the way her life had turned out shook their head while she hung her head down. She could hear them asking, where was that little girl who would run wild in the strawberry patch, who climbed trees, loved the outdoors, and had big dreams, and somewhere from deep down within her, a small weak voice that only she could hear would say, "Here I am. Please help me," but no one could hear her saying it. She not only was a hostage in her own hurt but also had become a hostage in her own life. She married a man whose thoughts and thinking when it came to God, family, marriage, relationship, home, and children were tainted and twisted long before they met and were married.

She saw him and she saw them and she saw their life through her innocence and through her so easy and so simple. Every day of her life, fear, being scared and afraid, kept her drawn and driven, pulled and pushed, forced, seduced and enticed, and tricked and trapped into thinking, feeling, and believing she would not make it and she would not survive, and if she didn't, she would not be able to protect her kids; and that is when it happened, when she happened, and when it happened.

She decided and she determined and she said within herself she would no longer be "submissive" to another beating at the hands of the man she loved and married but didn't know was a batterer. And when it was time for it to go down, that being beaten and being battered, it became a fight and then her battle and then her war. When faith and favor and her willingness to fight gave her the upper hand, she hit him, and then she did something she had never done in her married life, and that was to grab what little she had left of herself and her dreams and grab her children and run for her life and run for their life.

The heart lines in her heart

Now that you know Sarai's headlines and story lines, it is also important that you know her heart lines. You see, Sarai and her mom never had the kind of relationship she wished they would have had, and the good times they had together were far and few. From as far back as she could remember, she has always had Jesus and He has always had her, and for that reason alone, she felt like she didn't need anyone else.

But there are those days when she would miss some parts of her mama, maybe more than she would ever know herself. The day her mama went to sleep on this side, she prayed, hoped, and believed God would be merciful and show her mercy and she would wake up in Jesus's arms; and they call it "childlike faith." And those good times they had and those days of simplicity and innocence, when she could clearly see the way and when she really felt and believed and knew it was up to her to choose whether she wanted to win or lose, they, too, are gone.

Oh, now that she has grown older, how she misses them so; like yesterday, she missed her mama and those days growing up in that farming community in Georgia . . . more than you will ever know. They say like mother like daughter, and that is where Sarai's heart do not have those lines flowing through it. You see, she knew of her mama and her mama at times was around, but her mama was never really there to tutor, train teach, talk to her, and tell her the secrets mamas know about life, love, little boys that grow up to be men, being a wife, and being a mother.

And now she is that mama that has been through things that she knows her mama went through that no one ever told her about. She knows her grandparents loved her and they were trying to protect her innocence and protect her yea and nay, and her life so simple and so easy, and her did and her didn't, her would and her wouldn't; they never did know she would grow up in a "her world's not like that" and her world is not and would not be like theirs.

She is older now, and when she dreams, she dreams of having the relationship she never had with her mom, and she dreams of hearing her mama telling her about having dreams that have no truth and having dreams that have no reality. Because what they all turn out to be are fantasies that lead to lies. Oh, how she misses her mama so, more than you will ever know!

Dare not dream

On the other side of the world and maybe even on the other side of our thoughts and thinking and on another continent and maybe even in another country and even maybe somewhere in a land we call Down Under, there is another little girl that had not been conceived, birthed, and born yet, but she still is important and she still matters and she is in her "one day I'm going to come alive and exist" condition and state. She may exist only in our imagination, in our minds, and in our thoughts, and maybe in our consciousness, in our subconsciousness, and at times even in our unconsciousness. But where she really does exist is in her dad and in her mum's yet-to-be-conceived, birthed, and born future.

No matter, she is still significant and she still has value. You and I and we may not ever get to meet her or get to know how or get to hear her, and maybe we may not ever know she has arrived in this world, in her world. But one day, she will make her innocent entrance into this world, and she will become someone's mother, sister, aunt, niece, wife, and best friend, this little girl whose life is and would be parallel to that of Sarai. Even though they had and would never meet each other and even though they were different in a lot of ways, they are and would be the same.

Like Sarai, her life will have a beginning, a middle, an end; a past, a present, and a future. Only God really and truly knows and knew what will happen in all those. But let us *dare to dream* and *imagine* and take a look into the life of this little girl, and let us make her someone that really and truly matters and important by giving her an identity and by giving her a name. This little girl's name is Rose. Why is her name Rose? It is because she was really beautiful just like the flower called a rose; but unlike the flower, she never learned how to open up and blossom and bloom and become the rose God created her to be. Now, let us sit back and let the life that Rose never knew she would end up living speak for her.

You see, life for Rose should have, could have, and would have been simple, easygoing, and innocent if someone would have taken the time to help Rose find out who she was and help her find her real true place in life, love, and living. Everything that could have and would have made Rose the rose she was would remain hidden in the shadows of her shyness and in the shadows of the shame she felt.

In fact, from the time she was a child up until that wonderful day in 2013, she would remain a rose that could not and would not and did not open up and show her real true inner beauty and reveal the true essence of who she really was and is and would, could, and should be. With this in mind, you can just say, although some may call her some other names, she chose the name Rose because that is what she really aspired to be; but she really didn't know how to become, be, and end up being that rose she had seen deep down on the inside of her where no one in her childhood, in her world, and in her life had dared to look and dig deep down inside to look for and discover.

Her story is about innocence and love and the lack thereof and how those in her childhood saw and interpreted both. Rose really couldn't remember a time in her life when things really were so easy and simple in her life. She grew up thinking, feeling, and believing her life was

THE SURVIVORS MODE

insignificant, and as a result of that, she felt she wasn't important and didn't matter.

Of innocence and love

Her story and her childhood would never reflect the person and the kind of person she wanted to be and the name she chose to use in the writing of her story. Her name is Rose, and she was born in Australia in the season of autumn in March 1961. And she grew up doing what most little girls do, and that would be to just be a little girl. She had her innocence, and she was an innocent little girl that could love and wanted to be loved. Her parents were dairy farmers, and they loved their children, and they were a very special family.

By the time Rose was born, she already had two older sisters, and twenty-one months later, her younger sister would be born. They were like most families in a lot of ways, and they were different from most families in some ways, but their parents managed to make things work for them. Rose's dad was a strong, prideful man who loved his family, and he made sure they were taken care of and provided for. It was at times hard for Rose to get the love, affection, and attention she needed because she had two older sisters who demanded and had her father's attention, and just when she thought she would get a chance to have him all to herself, a younger sister would be born.

That was a really hard and often difficult time in Rose's childhood, and it forced her to make and find her own way. It wasn't easy growing up in a house with all sisters who wanted, needed, demanded, expected, and anticipated the same things she did from her dad. At times, it felt like Rose was only getting what was left over after her dad had given what often seemed like and felt like the best part of his love to her two older sisters and her younger sisters. She knew her dad loved her, but there were those times when she wished and wanted him all to herself. Isn't that what most and all little girls want, and that is the love, affection, and attention of the first man that is in their life, who is their dad? And at times, that little girl would say and do anything to get his attention even if it meant saying or doing something that she knew was wrong. There is a special and unique bond that every little girl is to have with the first man in her life, who is her dad/father.

And when that bond is not safely and securely there and intact, and when that little girl doesn't feel her daddy-daughter bond and relationship is solid, safe, sound, secure, and stable, it will present a problem for that little girl. That little girl's childhood becomes shattered, and life ceases to be so simple, and that little girl spends her days and her time imagining, and she finds herself caught up in the "I did or the I didn't" and in the "I would and I wouldn't." She is Rose, a little girl, and her childhood is already caught up in an adult complexity, and in doing so, her innocence, without her knowing it and without the people who said the loved her knowing it, was placed in harm's way.

How could and would she feel complete when there is a "love" complexity? When a little girl can't and don't get the fulfilling love that she needs from the first man in her life, her father/dad, or she gets the love that is left over after everyone else have gotten the love they need first, that little girl is left with a love void and a love emptiness. And that love emptiness and love void will one day turn into a lust and a craving for the love she never received. Think about it, a little girl caught up in an adult complexity, and it wasn't because the adult(s) tried to do so. Imagine what it is like for a little girl to grow up being faced with what was supposed to be so simple and so easy becoming something that is so complex and she is caught up in the midst of that complexity.

Imagine what it is like growing up and having something you need to simply survive missing and you don't know it is missing, and the people who are supposed to know you and know who you are and what you are to be and what roads you are to take that would help you blossom and bloom into the person you are to be not knowing and not seeing something that is missing inside of you.

Childhood complexities

What I am talking about are childhood complexities that come out of love voids and love emptiness that a child, a little girl, is forced to live in and, out of that, takes away her innocence. Rose was supposed to be a "daddy's girl"; she was supposed to be daddy's little girl, the apple of his eye, her protector and not just her provider. And out of innocence, she needed and wanted and had to have and should have had the simplicity of it all, and her childhood and her life would have been easy, and she would have been able to grow, develop, and mature into a whole easygoing little girl.

Life for Rose would never be easy, and life for Rose would never be simple because he found herself surrounded by an atmosphere that is filled with childhood complexities. Her what was supposed to be simple and easy and innocent childhood would become intricate and complicated, and she would be constantly, continuously, and consistently drawn, driven, pulled, pushed, persuaded, tricked, trapped, seduced, enticed, entangled, and entrapped into that intricate and complicated state and quality.

Just to be a "daddy's girl" and to get the deserved love, affection, and attention to the degree that she really needed, it would get caught up in factors involved in a complicated process and situation. I'm talking about Rose and you, little girl, that is in the grown woman that is reading this book that found yourself caught up in a childhood complexity. Life was supposed to be so easy for you, and you could count on and believe what those in your life said to you because you were a little girl and you were innocent, and out of your innocence, you believe people said what they meant, and they were either for you or against you, but that all changed because of childhood complexities.

Her childhood went from simplicity and easygoing and innocence to being something that would have many parts and components, where those parts and components interact with each other in multiple ways. That's the way gaining and getting a fulfilling and satisfying dose of her daddy's love and the lack of it became and end up being. Like any little girl who finds herself in the midst of a childhood complexity, she would accept, adopt, and adapt to, and apply a thought, train of thought, thinking, and a way of thinking that would help her make it through those times and that would also protect the person she loved and would justify and make excuses for what she wasn't getting from the first man in her life, her father/dad.

Rose would say to herself and begin to think, feel, and believe she was strategically placed in her family and what she was receiving was a bit of this and a bit of that came from her parents' genes, her grandparents' genes. In her innocent little girl's mind and heart, thinking that way would make her the precious and unique little girl she was. Rose, the little girl, grew up knowing and feeling she was loved and cared for, and she was nurtured and protected from the influences of the world because she lived on a farm; all of which added to her childhood complexities without her even knowing it.

Her childhood should not have ever been clouded with something as simple as giving a daddy's girl the love she needed being made complicated and hard to understand. Why was Rose's life so complex, and why had her childhood become so filled with complexities? Those childhood complexities kept Rose in a place and at a point in her childhood where she couldn't clearly see the way, and that kept her feeling and thinking like it was not up to her to choose whether to win or lose.

Childhood innocence

Everything in her childhood and in her world was changing, and she often found herself wondering if it were really up to her to decide and to determine and would she be able to clearly see what it was she was to be, something she had never questioned before in her life until those childhood complexities showed up and she got caught up in the mix of them. With her childhood slowly changing, her thoughts, train of thought, thinking, and way of thinking no longer being innocent because of the childhood complexities she found herself involved, entangled, and entrapped in doing all things that was expected of her. Out of the need to gain her dad's/father's attention and gain more of his love and attention, she played sport, she went to Sunday school, and she aimed to please her parents.

But what she didn't know was everything she had never received from her father/dad, the first man, had left a scar and a wound and a void and an emptiness inside of her, and out of that would come a hole in her soul that would not heal, and there would be a rage and a pain that she would still feel, and even though she was no longer a child, a little girl, and she was into her teens and into her adulthood, she still didn't, doesn't, and never did understand what was happening to her and why. But please understand that's what happens when you don't have a father or you have a father who never validated you and does not give you the love you need for you to be the complete person you need and should be.

With her innocence, you know, the part of her that was once uncorrupted and pure and not responsible for or directly involved in an event but is yet suffering its consequences, being compromised and then taken without her even knowing it or wanting it to happen because of the childhood complexity and the fact she was often overlooked as a child a little girl, she found herself trapped into being shy and withdrawn and passive. She would never allow herself to be a part of the "cool group" at school, and she felt like she was not a physically attractive person. Who told her that she wasn't? Because she didn't get what she needed from her father, it left her feeling rejected and not good enough, and she would spend her life thinking, feeling, and believing she had to say something or do something to please others to make up for something she was led to believe she didn't have.

Leftover love

That's what comes out of childhood complexities. When a little girl doesn't get the right attention she needs from her father and she does not get his attention and gain his acceptance and approval and receive his validation, she will grow up feeling like she is incomplete, inadequate, has too many inabilities, and out of that will come a lot of insecurities about herself. That was the gift she was given, and that came out of not having the right relationship with her father, with herself, and with God. When a child's innocence is taken, like Rose's was, because of childhood complexities, that child, that little girl will go through her life with the words etched in her brain, "You are so stupid and ugly," and she will go through life thinking, feeling, and led to believe she's not important and she does not matter.

That's the message she believes her dad, the first man in her life, was sending her every time he overlooked her, gave her the leftover love, or rejected her in favor of her other siblings. He would never see Rose's value and importance, and he would never see, pay attention to, or celebrate her accomplishments and achievements because they were not equal to that of her siblings, and he would in his own way try to measure her accomplishments and achievements based on her other siblings' accomplishments and achievements. Every little girl and every kind needs to be loved, needed, wanted, accepted, and celebrated, and they should never be forced or led to believe they have to stand in anyone else's shadow to be somebody and be accepted and celebrated; this is especially true when it comes to their other siblings and even when it comes to the parents' successes.

When a person, especially a little girl like Rose, is not correctly validated and the right things and self-skills are not instilled in him or her and brought out of him or her by the one person or people who are accountable and responsible for doing so, he or she will grow up and go through life being squashed, and his or her voice will end up being squashed deep inside of him or her by someone who is physically and mentally stronger than they are. Rose knew what her life should look like, and she could at one time see what it was and what it would be like, and every time she thought about her childhood complexities and how they took away, stole, raped, robbed, and cheated her out of her innocence, and the roads she ended up going down were wrong, she wished she had a magic wand that she could wave just once like the fairy godmother did in Cinderella. She would wave her wand, and her life would be full of laughter, love, harmony, and happiness.

Isn't that what all little girls want as they grow up? Rose did not require fame or fortune, riches or prestige. She only wanted the simple things that are free, you know, the things that fill her heart and life with joy unspeakable. Life and childhood for Rose was supposed to be and should have been simple, and her innocence should have never been taken from her but something she of her own free will had given up knowing the consequences for doing so. Everything she never got of her relationship with the first man in her life, her father, she would go looking for in the relationship with the men she got involved in. And in doing so, that would put and keep her in harm's way.

Asking Rose what she wanted to be when she grew up, what she aspired to, and what was her dream wasn't an easy question for her to answer; in fact, it became a very sensitive question for her. There has only been one other person in her life who knew the difficulty of that word "dream." What she *aspired* to was to grow up and have a happy family and life, and if that was her dream, it was simple and it came out of innocence. Rose did not know of the big, wide world; what was out beyond the isolation and protection of "farm life." When what she aspired to failed, she dared not "dream" at all, for dreaming, according to her, was and would be futile.

Rose, like many little girls, one day woke up, and her childhood was gone and her innocence was gone and life was no longer easy, and love, well, it was just like her ability to dream and her freedom to aspire to something; she would have to wait for that to happen. In 2013, God would touch her and heal her, and that was the day her hope was revived. She knew she could not and would not ever be able to dream where there was no hope.

And because of the unexpected, the unplanned, the unknown, the unseen, the undetected, the unwanted, and the unbelievable childhood complexities that showed up on their own in her life, and the things she was unaware of that stole her simple life and the simplicity of her childhood and cheated her out of her innocence. And because of the way and how all of what happened to her one day became her undeniable and her unexplainable, her unthinkable and her unforgettable that left her feeling and thinking what happened to her was unfair; and because she was just a little girl and the only thing she wanted was to live in and out of her simplicity, her ease, and her innocence, she ended up in a place called the "unsure," and she dared not dream again while she was growing up.

Waking up in the U's

And the unseen and the unknown director in your life and for your life shouts out, "Lights, cameras, and action," and the curtains come up on your infant life. You were innocent, and you had no idea what your life would be like, whom you would meet, and you didn't know what type and kind of events would take place in your life. You had no clue as to what kind of generational cures you inherited, and you didn't know what would be said and done to you in your life. We all are conceived, birthed, and born, and grow up in the *unknown,* and we go through our life walking into the *unseen*. We spend our days trying to recover from the *unexpected*, things, moments, circumstances, situation, and confrontations no one prepared us for.

We grow up looking up to the people who are in our lives that we idolize and one day vow to be like just like them and try to pattern our life after that person we idolize, and we spend our days living in and out of great expectations and high hopes and living in and out of anticipation. No one could have told Sarai and Rose and you and me the bad, negative, wrong, and the ugly things that had happened to us would have taken place. After all, we were just innocent kids living in the age of innocence, and the things that have happened to us as we grew up and as we were growing up never should have happened to us. We didn't choose those hurtful, painful, and brokenness-filled events and moments that did and had showed up in our lives; it was as though they chose us.

No one when they are a kid says when they grow up they want to be someone who is abused, battered, beaten, degraded, victimized by OCD or PTSD, neglected, rejected, etc. That is not what we say, and that is not what we dream of, hope for, plan and prepare for, and try to position ourselves for. And so when events like that show up in our lives on their own *uninvited,* not only are we and were we left shocked, stunned, and speechless, but also we are and were left staring at and being face-to-face with the *unimaginable.*

THE SURVIVORS MODE

Let me paint the picture

We came into this world, and the only thing we have ever wanted was to live our life and be happy, but as we went along going from childhood, to teenhood, to adulthood, we quickly discovered that something in the unseen and someone that we would be unaware of that had the wrong spirit upon him or her and had the wrong motives and motivation would make his or her grand entrance into our day and into our lives, and from that day and moment, our innocent lives and innocent life would never be the same. Everything that has happened to Sarai, to Rose, to yourself, and to myself wasn't a accident; nor had it been and is it a coincidence. In fact, from the first day your mom and your dad got together and they one day had talked about having kids, planned it, or it just happened, or maybe you were an *unplanned* and even an *unwanted* pregnancy; it doesn't matter because Satan had made sure demonic fear and fate were behind the scenes watching and waiting for you.

When it was time for you to be conceived, fear and fate got together and decided they had to fight against faith because they did not want you to have any contact and communication and conversations with faith, and they did not want your mind, heart, thoughts, and feelings to have any contact with faith. When it came time for you to be birthed, fear and fate would step up their assault, attack, and assassination on faith so you would never want or desire it and the God of faith; so they put in place and put into effect a lot of *unforeseen, undesired, and undesirables* in between your dreams and your hopes.

Fear and fate were behind the scenes while you were being conceived, plotting and planning and positioning themselves and positioning everything and everyone that was and would be bad, wrong, negative, and ugly that could prevent you from "the thoughts that God could and would and still do think towards you, thoughts of peace, and not of evil, and disaster, plans to prosper you, not to harm you, plans for your welfare, not for disaster, plans to give you a future filled with hope, to give you an expected end" (Jer. 29:11).

Satanic and demonic fear and fate had to undo what God did and still do want to do in your life and what faith still will do and will bring forth a visible manifestation of. And the day you were born into this world, satanic and demonic fear and fate had already decided and determined they would create within you a craving for, a need and a want and fear filled need for "survival."

They wanted to make sure you lived your life scared and afraid, and in doing so, they would then easily be able to strongly suggest to you that you need to survive "by any means necessary," and if you took that suggestive "bait," your feelings, emotions, and desires would be influenced, drawn, driven, pulled, pushed, forced, seduced and enticed, entangled and entrapped into leaning on, relying on, depending on, and counting on survivor-survival urges, tendencies, inclinations, intuitions, impulses, impulsiveness, and instincts.

And from that, fear and fear would team up and make sure you had a clear, constant, continuous, and consistent connection, link, and tie to a survivor-survival mode. What I'm trying to get you to see and understand is what to Mollie and Rose and what has happened to you was carefully and meticulously planned and prepared and catered to you and your life.

Satan wasn't experimenting with what happened to you, and you were not randomly selected or picked. You were an intentional target, and you had been set up what would end up being painful, hurtful, and brokenness-filled *unforgettable* matters, memories, and moments that you "walked into." Those unforgettable that you woke up one day and walked into were designed to push you further away from faith and pull you into *unsure* feelings about yourself and about your life. And once fear had you feeling unsure, it would then persuade you into having and demonstrating *unsettled* emotions, and out of that would come nervous and erratic behavior and conduct that would drive and lead to *uncontrollable* survivor-survival desires.

You were set up for "failure" by fear long before you had flaws and long before you had ever fallen. Everything that happened to you Satan had set you up for so that you would be so overwhelmed you would be shocked, stunned, and end up standing still and shaking your head in disbelief because of the *unbelievable* and the *unexplainable* and the *unthinkable* things that have happened to. Because what has happened to you was not the way you saw happening and it was not the way you planned your life to be.

And while you are standing still, satanic and demonic fear once again suggested to you and influenced you into *unbelief,* and instead of you fighting for yourself, you would give in and give up and allow fear and fate to use you as a weapon formed against yourself. In doing so, fear would use you to cause, create the atmosphere for, and contribute to yourself being a slave to, yoked to, bound and limited by and in a stronghold to walking into and expecting, accepting, and adapting to the *unexpected.*

Satan and fear would use the *undeniable* that has happened to you as a hurdle, a hindrance, and a stumbling block that would hold you hostage to feeling sorry for yourself and a hostage to you being so emotional that you cannot and will not be able to focus. From that, you would end up being scared to talk about what has happened to you, and you would be afraid to release what you have been through.

When all the u's keep forcing their way into our lives, we are left questioning ourselves and blaming ourselves and asking ourselves what did we say and do wrong to deserve all the bad, wrong, negative, and ugly happening to us? And it seems like no matter what Sarai, Rose, your, and I tried or try to do to avoid all the hurtful and painful things that were happening or had happened to them, those same painful and hurtful events kept finding their way into their lives and our lives; or we kept finding our way back into their pathway.

Satanic and demonic fate, that hidden and undetected spirit, had kept forcing us into the pathway of someone who would tutor, teach, and train us to fear and how to live a fearful life and would tutor, teach, and train us how not to have faith and how to make sure faith doesn't have a hold on any part of our life and who we are.

Once all the u's make their way into your life and they etch out a place where they would fit and even belong in your thoughts, train of thought, thinking, and way of thinking and life, and they make the impression upon your mind, frame of mind, mental condition, and state of mind, you will spend your life constantly, continually, and consistently locked into being dominated, manipulated, and controlled by a survivor-survival mind-set, mentality, and locked into a survivor-survival mental state of being.

From the day you were conceived, birthed, and born into this world, you, like myself and like Sarai and Rose and so many others, have had so many things to happen to us that we didn't and don't understand and we spend our time trying to figure out. When you were a kid, you never pictured your life to be one great big puzzle where you would spend your time and your days trying to get the pieces of your shattered and shamed life to fit. And you do your very best to get yourself disconnected from those negatives, and you work hard at distancing yourself from what has happened, but it almost feels like what has happened to you and what you have been through have a hold on you.

Sometimes, it can almost feel like you are not living your own life, you know, the one you dreamed and hoped for and prayed for and had set out to have when you were a little kid, but you are living someone else's life. From the time you, like Sarai and Rose, were little kids, you had dreamed of the life you would have, the lifestyle you would have, and the love you would give and get from the relationship you dreamed of. No one ever told you would have to spend valuable time out of your life trying to overcome something that you never saw happening to you, time that you can't get back or replace. No one ever told Sarai, Rose, and you that you would end up trying to find ways to survive and you would end up in a survivor-survival mode.

It ain't like that anymore

Sarai and Rose went to sleep in a child's world and they woke up in an adult's world, and their life would never be the same anymore. They would never get to see and get to live in a time of innocence and love ever again. And if the both of them could and would get to meet and they would both sit down and talk about life and the way it once was and they would remember those days when they were just a kid, a little girl, I'm sure they would ask themselves what we would ask ourselves, and that is "Could we go back to the way it was?"

How often do we walk back down memory lane and we arrive at those "I remember when's"? How often do we, for just a moment, sit down and reflect on what we said we would do and we reflect back on those days when we could clearly see our way? Nothing was complicated, nothing was complex, and nothing was cloudy, and everything was clear and our life wasn't filled with all different kinds of chaos and confusion. But it ain't like that anymore! I know you are just trying to survive and everything in your life now is about survival, but let me ask you some questions:

A. Do you remember when life was so simple?
B. Do you remember when life was so easy?
C. Do you remember when you either did or you didn't or you would and you wouldn't?
D. Do you remember when people said what they meant they were either for it or against it?

The things that Sarai and Rose and even you have been through have forever changed your life, and it has forever changed life as you once knew it. They were forced to grow up faster than they wanted to. They went to sleep one night in a safe haven of childlike peace and woke up where there was so much grown-up pressure and pain.

They went to sleep and dreamed of being happy and being surrounded with happiness, and when they opened their eyes, there was adult hurt and humiliation. Every now and then, like most kids, they would accidentally fall and end up with a bruise, but no one ever told them they would grow up to be adults and there would be someone who would intentionally push them down, try to break them down, and beat them down until they accepted failure and defeat, being beaten and broken and filled with brokenness.

Because of what happened to them and what has happened to you, neither Mollie nor Rose nor you will never see those days of yea and nay again, and those times when they and you can and will clearly see the way have become cluttered with shades of shame, colored with shadows of "what doesn't make sense" and cloudy with adult cares and concerns. Sarai and Rose and even you one night closed your eyes at a point and at a place where you just knew it was up to you to choose whether you wanted to win or lose, and you just knew it was up to you to see what it was you were created to be.

And because of what happened to Sarai, to Rose, and to you, it ain't like that anymore. What I'm talking about are those times when it was up to us to decide and determine and to function and flow and to just "be." We were kids and we were innocent and we could do that. When we were kids, we could see what it was we were to be and we could see the path that we were to travel down, and the moment when we became adults, we got caught up in the mix of complexity, and we found ourselves caught up in the search for people who would simply say yea and nay, or yes and no. That's the way it was when Sarai and Rose grew up. That's what they will remember about their childhood and the people who just "let" them be kids.

But it ain't like that anymore. I know every day since what happened to you, just like what happened to Sarai and Rose, you were and are struggling and straining because you have been pulled, pushed, persuaded, and forced into trying to survive and be a survivor. And I know you never saw what happened to you coming, and that is because you were doing what you were supposed to be doing, and that was just "be" a kid. You were a child, and you were not supposed to see, hear of, and be caught up in growing up in grown-up matters, circumstances, and situations. You were just a child, and you should have never been seduced, tricked, enticed, and led into going from a little girl to a woman.

I know this may be hard for you, you know, reading this book about you and your life, and I know some parts or all of you and who you are may still be going through and still trying to make it to the place and point where you can finally get into your survivor mode so that you can get into that false sense of security survival mind-set and mentality and mental state of being. I do understand that, and I know it is so hard to let go of "the very things you feel you need to and should hold on to."

THE SURVIVORS MODE

I know that it is so hard for you right now to remember when life was so simple, and it's hard for you to recall when your parents were a light and through them you saw what was right. And what has happened to you has done what it has done to Sarai and Rose and to so many others, and that is to make it hard for them and for you to remember when life was so easy.

And because of the suddenly and immediate child-to-teen-to-adult path their life and your life has been on, when your life was finally *unveiled,* you would never get to see something so simple as a little boy growing into a man and a little girl just like what you once were growing into a woman. And as your life began to *unfold,* it became harder for you to know where you belonged, and when your life finally *unraveled,* you were left in a place where you had a hard time knowing what was right and wrong.

Sarai and Rose never knew their life would be unveiled in the way it was. And when their lives started to unfold or open or spread out from its safe and secure and protected folded childlike place, and reveal or disclose thoughts or information about itself and the sequence of events about their life that was to be revealed or disclosed finally manifested itself, what was uncovered was what they both needed out of love, life, and living was a simple yes or no, and what they never should have done was allowed themselves to get into and have the "should I stay or should I go" thoughts, train of thought, thinking, and way of thinking because their adult life had become so advanced.

And when their life finally unraveled or it finally came undone and begin to unwind, fail, and then collapse, they could only wish they had a second chance to go back and see what was bad and what was good, but that would not be something they would get a chance to do, and they would not get a chance to ponder on that thought for too long because where they have found themselves because of what they have been through is at a place and at a point with what they both fear. And they can only see and feel the need to survive and make it through. Fear won't let them see simple and easy because fear has them in a survivor-survival mind-set, mentality, and mental state of being.

Their mind and frame of mind, mental condition, and their state of mind tells them to stay alive long enough for them to "exist," and from just existing, they will have some kind of life and one day they can and will get the chance to come alive and be alive.

They are led to think, feel, and believe that it can and will happen as long as they keep living in and out of and functioning and flowing in and out of survivor-survival mode. And just like in the Charlie Brown cartoons, the character called Linus feels insecure and he feels he can't make it and survive without his blanket, fear has Sarai and Rose and even yourself relying on, depending on, and in need of their security blanket that is called a "survivor-survival mode."

CHAPTER TWO

Fathers and Daughters

The first man in your life

A FATHER-DAUGHTER RELATIONSHIP is one of the most important relationships, and a girl's father is one of the most valuable, important, and influential people in her life. From the time she is an infant and she grows to be a toddler and develops into a teen and matures into an adult, he has a lot of influence and input into how that happens for her. Every dad makes a big impression in his daughter's life, and he has a big impact on his little girl will grow, develop, and mature into a strong, confident woman.

Please understand that a father's influence in his daughter's life shapes her self-respect, her self-confidence, her self-esteem, her world, her self-image, her self-worth, and her opinions of men. How her dad approaches life will serve as an example for her to build off in her own life, even if she chooses a different view of the world.

What is important and what really matters the most in the father-daughter relationship is the dad recognizes and realizes and clearly understands he is the "first man" in her life, and with that in mind, he should seek to live a life of integrity and honesty, avoiding hypocrisy and admitting his own shortcomings. And when he does so, what she will gain and end up having is a realistic and positive example of how to deal with the world. Because he is the first man in her life, he should try to model a reflective approach to life's big questions so that she can seek to do the same without having to procrastinate, hesitate, question, and second-guess.

He is the first man in her life, and his involvement in his daughter's life is a crucial ingredient in the development of her self-esteem. Because he is the first man in her life, he should take a "common sense" approach to the way he parents her and protects her, and in doing so, he can help support his daughter's self-image and he can be instrumental in removing any possibility of her having low self-esteem. He should also make sure he is constant, continuous, and consistent in his verbal encouragement, is consistently present in her life, is alert and sensitive to her feelings, takes time to listen to her thoughts, and takes an active interest in her hobbies.

As the first man in her life, it is very important that he gives her all the love, affection, and attention she needs and he has direct involvement in her life. And each time that he offers and gives her encouragement, it will help diminish her insecurity and increase her confidence in her own abilities. When her father takes his role and importance as the first man in his daughter's life, the type of men that his daughter will end up dating and having long-term relationships with will be a direct reflection of and directly related to the kind of relationship she had with her him.

He is the first man in her life and she is his princess, and she will look to him to be an example of what kind of man she should choose, therefore everything he does should be aimed at skewing her opinions of men in a positive way. And the way he goes about doing that is he must, first and foremost, make sure he treats his daughter with respect and love. It doesn't matter if he is married to someone else or he is still together with his daughter's mom; showing respect to her mother is essential as well. He is the first man in her life, and he must also value women as human beings and not as persons to be used. His daughters will see what her dad believes about women by how he values and respects women, or by how he fails to do so.

Father and faith failure

She never thought the traumatic, troubling, and tragic events that have happened to her would have occurred, and the things she had to endure would have shown up in her life, and she never thought or felt her life would be the way it is and has been. Just like you, the only thing she ever wanted was to be loved, needed, wanted, cared for, accepted, and protected. When she was a child and a dreamer, no one could have told her she would one day go to sleep an innocent little girl and wake up a rejected and abused woman. Where did it all come from, and why did it happen to her, and why was she chosen for what she has had to endure? Sometimes, she just sits there in her place of brokenness feeling empty and all alone.

Everything within her is hurting, and everything she thinks and feels is also hurting. She is so distracted to the point where she is also disconnected. And she is home alone, and she just sits there in her silence and she starts to soul search. She starts to look within herself trying to find what she is looking for that will help her understand what has happened to her and why. Frantically, she searches within for what she needs because she needs it and she needs it now. But she can't find what she is looking for. In desperation, she does a second inner search, and she arrives at the same results.

What was so important that she would engage in a frantic and desperate search within herself? What is it that is and was so valuable and priceless that all her focus was directed on deep inner soul-searching? It had to be important to her, and she had to care about whatever it was that she was looking for. She even managed to push through and push away all the traumatic, troubling, and tragic hurt, pain, and brokenness she was feeling just so that she could look deep within herself to see if she could find whatever it was that she was looking for that she really needed for the moment that she found herself drawn, driven, pulled, pushed, persuaded, seduced, tricked, and forced into. She was looking for something that her daddy had said that could and would help her make it through her weeping that has endured for more than a night.

She went looking within herself for something that would help her understand why what has happened to her took place, and she was looking for what she was to do next that would help her make it through her nights when all she could do was weep. Nobody told her they would argue, fuss, and fight, and no one told her she would one day have an unfaithful heart, unfaithful thoughts, unfaithful feelings, and unfaithful emotions. She just wanted to be loved, needed, and wanted.

She just wanted to believe in her "always and forever," and she just wanted to believe in his "'cause I love you." In the midst of her feeling what she was feeling and thinking the way she was thinking and even in the midst of her believing the way she didn't want to believe, it felt like her father had failed her and her faith had failed her.

She'll never forget he wasn't there

She went looking for those two things her daddy had always told her and led her to believe, think, and feel in the way in which he treated and talked to her, and that was she absolutely knew for sure she was sent here from heaven and she was his little girl, a daddy's girl. She went looking for those moments when he would drop to his knees by her bed at night and she could and would feel his love for her and she felt and knew she was safe, secure, and stable. She will never forget that moment when she woke up and her life wasn't the same as it was. She still talks to Jesus, but it is not the same talks she used to have when she was in her innocence.

Her daddy, well, he is not there with her, and she feels like she is all alone. She wonders if he, her daddy, still closes his eyes and thanks God for all the joy she brought into his life and if he remembers those butterfly kisses she used to give him after bedtime prayer. She often remembers when he used to walk beside her when she was experiencing her "firsts," and she wonders if he remembers when she did her best and what she tried to do didn't turn out to be the way she wanted it to and it looked funny, but she sure tried. She wishes she could tell him that no matter what he had ever done wrong, he did something right to deserve a hug every morning and butterfly kisses at night.

Daddy once said

She remembers her last daddy-daughter date and how he looked at her with a look that she has never seen before, and he told her she has grown up and she was one part woman and one part girl. And she has gone to wearing perfume and makeup when she used to wear ribbons and curls. He knew that she was growing up and one day she would be trying her wings out in a great big world. She knew he had done his best to do what a father is supposed to do for his daughter, and that was to *protect* her and to *prevent* bad and wrong things from happening to her and to *provide* for her and to *prepare* her for a life and a world she knew nothing of.

She, while still sitting in her brokenness, hurt, and pain, will never forget the day when she said to him, "You know how much I love you, Daddy, but if you don't mind, I'm only gonna kiss you on the cheek this one last time." She knows he done his best and he gave her his best, and she never meant to hurt him. She never meant to bring him any pain, shame, and embarrassment, and the things that have happened to her are not his fault.

She falls to her knees and she cries, and her heart yearns deeply to just let him know that with all that she's done wrong, she must have done something right to deserve his unconditional love no matter what she has been through. She remembers the last words he said to her, and those words were "All the precious time, like the wind, the years go by, precious butterfly. Spread your wings and fly." Words that she has held on to and has hidden deep down in the treasure chest called her heart.

She wonders

It is her best friend's special day, and she once again is participating in someone else's happy day and happy moment, a scene she has repeated over and over again. It is a scene she had always hoped and prayed would one day be her story and be her scene. Sometimes, she struggles to express happiness for others, even for those who are close to her, and some days, she strains just to release the emotions that she really feels deep down on the inside of her. It's not because she doesn't want to; it's just because of her journey and it's because of her life and the way it has been.

She so desperately wants to be the bride she has never been, she so desperately wants to be the wife that she envisioned being, and she so desperately wanted to be the happy person that lives a happy life and that has someone in her life that not only "makes" her happy but also "adds" to her happiness. And she so desperately wants to be a mother, and she wants to have a strong, safe, secure, and stable home and a family; all of which have, for some reason or for reasons beyond her control, eluded her.

Why has this been and it is the story that her life is telling she has no idea, and why has she been forced to be different when all she ever wanted was to be the same as other little girls who woke up in a grown adult's world? Sometimes, when she is all alone, she wonders if God really loves her, sees her, knows her, understands her, and cares about her. She, from time to time, wonders if He hears and answers her prayers, and she often struggles and strains when it comes to feeling worthy of His love, care, concern, and compassion. Every now and then, she feels useless and worthless because of the bad, wrong, negative, and ugly choices and decisions she has made and mostly because of the traumatic, troubling, and tragic things that had happened to her; all of which have been and still is indescribable and unforgettable.

And there are those moments when she can only pray and ask God to give her something to hold on to, something that can comfort her. Can't you hear her, yourself, crying tears that are not wet, don't you hear her screaming with a voice that has no sound, and are you not able to feel her pain, a pain that has taken away her feelings and has made her numb to what her true feelings once was? I know she is not important to you, and I know she really doesn't matter to you because she may not be you and her story may not be yours. But it's a story, a true story, and it is her story. Can't you see her, don't you hear her, and can't you feel her? She is just like you, and maybe she is actually the real true you. Maybe she is someone you know, have known, are scared to know and you are afraid to get to know again.

She is just an everyday ordinary person, woman, little girl, and human being who has experienced and encountered extraordinary and unusual, unbelievable, undeniable, unwanted, and unplanned for circumstances, situations, confrontations, challenges, matters, and moments that is left with having to deal with and live through and live with often overwhelming and incredible terrorizing, tormenting, torturing, and traumatizing memories; all of which have caused, created the atmosphere for, and contributed to her struggling just to get up in the morning and straining to lie down and go to sleep at night because she is not only scared and not just afraid but also fearful of what lies in wait for her in the dark, in her darkness.

Sometimes, she just wishes, oftentimes she just wants, needs, and desires, but most of the time, she just sits and wonders . . . she wonders what her life could have, would have, and should have been "if" . . . that big two-letter little word that often haunts her and hurts her. She can't help but to wonder "when" . . . where and even how . . . you know, her life will one day turn around and what she feels will one day "never be again." And what about those days, those unseen and unknown and undetected days when she struggles and strains to just become, be, and end up being, what does she do with those days? Sometimes, she feels like she in a fast lane moving slow and she is in a slow lane running and moving really fast; and then there are those days when she can't, doesn't, and won't be able to distinguish between the two. On those days and in those moments, she does what she knows best to do, and that is to just "survive" and "exist" and try to make it through so she can get to the other side where her "I don't know who I am and where I am and I don't know what I am and I don't know where I am going" moments represent and have represented her place of safety, her safety zone.

I know you can't understand that, her, and I know you don't want to understand, and maybe you really don't understand that kind of thought, thinking, way of thinking, and train of thought, but she knows it, understands it, accepts it, adopts it, adapts to it, and embraces it. On most occasions, it is true that "she can't see for looking," and that is because she just keeps looking for the things she not only can't see but also has never seen in her life and day like you have.

You don't know what it's like to be disconnected from a memory and moment and a matter that you still feel you are somehow, in some way that boggles your mind, still connected to, and then the next time, you feel like you are still deeply connected to something and someone that you thought you were disconnected from. Is her mind, your mind, playing tricks on you? Is it all just an illusion, and is it all just a figment of your untamed and uncontrolled imagination, or is it all a reality, your reality?

She wonders if it is really OK for her to wonder, to wish, and to want without really ever needing. She even wonders if it is really all right for her to dream and desire but never hope for and to pray and have faith, have trust, have belief, have confidence, but never expect or anticipate. She often wonders, will there ever be a day in her life when she will ever wake up, and although she is different because of the traumatic, troubling, and tragic terrorizing, tormenting, torturing, and traumatizing events, moments, and matters that had taken place in her life without her permission, will she ever be different yet the same?

Her unfaithful and unfinished

She can't help but to wonder what will happen if her differences never become the same as yours and what would happen if what has made her different yet the same as you are never get linked, connected, and tied together and she leaves this life with unfinished dreams. She wonders what those who loved her, liked her, felt her, knew her, kinda liked her, or really didn't like her or care for her would say. Will that space or that dash (-) between the day she was born and the day she exited her life with unfinished dreams have a question mark (?) instead of that dash (-)?

She can't help but to sit and think and then think while she just sits. And she asks herself, who would ever miss her and know she was alive and living in life, her life, this life, and in her world if her differences and what made her different from you never met at those crossroads in life we all one day cross and made her the same as you are? What would she do with her unfinished dreams and desires that she never got a chance to "hope" for? She just dreamed and desired having what you are having and sharing and creating what you get a chance to share, have, and create that in being able to do so ends up making you feel like you are special and you not only "fit" in life but also absolutely "belong" in someone's life. She never wanted an unfaithful heart, unfaithful mind, unfaithful thoughts, unfaithful feelings, unfaithful

THE SURVIVORS MODE · 39 ·

emotions, unfaithful desires, unfaithful dreams, etc., because she knew they would produce, prepare, and present an unfinished dream(s). The things that were and have been traumatic, troubling, and tragic that keep terrorizing, tormenting, torturing, and traumatizing her had forced her into an unfaithful faith, unfaithful hope, unfaithful belief, unfaithful confidence, and unfaithful trust, and as a result, she can only demonstrate and deliver an unfaithful dream and unfinished dreams.

She fears leaving this life with unfinished dreams because some part of who she was and is had been unfaithful. Maybe it was her choices and decisions that were unfaithful, or maybe it was her truths and realities that were unfaithful; it doesn't matter because they all have left her feeling unfinished and unfulfilled. And when she feels that way, she once again finds herself being faced with being terrorized, tormented, tortured, and traumatized by a fear that draws, drives, pulls, pushes, persuades, tricks, seduces, and forces her into the unfaithful and then into the unfinished.

I know you don't want her at your wedding, and God forbid in your wedding! I know you don't want her to be your best friend, part of your family, or someone you know or have known or someone you want to get to know. It's all because of the unfaithful flaws, failures, falling times, and weaknesses that have exposed her life and keep doing so, and it is because of the unfinished insecurities, inadequacies, and inabilities that keep exploiting her. Maybe it's because she is like you once was and still is or she is just like you are trying not to be.

It really doesn't matter with you that she is still someone's sister, cousin, aunt, relative, and daughter, and even maybe she is someone's mother. It doesn't matter that she is a human being and she is God's creation, and she never set out on her journey into life seeking to struggle and strain, be forced to struggle and strain, and have to survive and be in a survivor-survival mind-set, mentality, mental state of being, and mode.

She never said when she grew up she wanted to be someone who would end up being in a traumatic, deeply troubling, and tragic circumstance, situation, confrontation, matter, and moment. I can tell you she never said when she left being an innocent child and she grew, developed, and matured in being a full-grown woman she wanted to be someone who would be constantly, continuously, and consistently terrorized, tormented, tortured, and traumatized by past and old bad, wrong, negative, and ugly memories and moments. I can assure you that person you are trying so hard to distance yourself from and disconnect yourself from and disguise yourself from is someone who had not at any moment and time in her life dreamed, hoped, desired, and prayed she would one day grow up and be someone who would be scared, afraid, and fearful.

And please believe me when I tell you that from the time she was an innocent little girl like yourself and she became a teen and then would become an adult, she never ever said, thought, felt, or believed or pursued after being someone who would eventually become, be, and end up being unfaithful and unfinished and unforgettable for all the wrong reasons. Her life has been different because everything that has shaped her life has been different.

She has not been the same as you are because her self-image, self-esteem, self-worth, self-confidence, self-respect, self-perception, self-will, her self-determination, and her confidence and opinions of men have not been the same as yours; and for the most part, it's still not even as you are reading this book. I know that you know she is disconnected, damaged, distraught, destitute, and she has been and maybe she still is detoured, dismantled in a lot of ways, delayed in some ways, and denied in most ways of the things, values, principles, standards, etc., that would make her just like you, "normal."

Imagined and wondering

And because she did have or didn't have or never had or never had to the degree you have had; she could have, should have, and would have had and maybe she even had the opportunity to have a father-daughter relationship but didn't, couldn't have, wouldn't have because of the things that had happened to her, that had happened in her childhood, teenhood, and adulthood that drastically challenged and changed her thoughts, feelings, emotions, desires, faith, hope, beliefs, confidence, opinions of men, and approach to life; she can only do what she does best, and that is to isolate and separate herself from something she desperately wants to be not only an active and willing "participant" in but also a happy and willing "partaker" of.

She can only stand on the outside looking in on what she had hopes and hoped would be her life's story line, as well as her future and her destiny. She does her best to hide how she really feels when it comes to herself. She doesn't want anyone to know she is still being terrorized, tormented, tortured, and traumatized by everything that was good, real, right, and positive that was supposed to happen to her, maybe even to you that never happened.

As you stand there looking at your best friend's special day, you can see all of what you thought you had and would have for yourself. Everyone is happy and smiling and laughing and enjoying the moment. Your best friend's dad is so happy, and he is maximizing the moment that he is having with your best friend, his daughter. You do your best to laugh to keep from crying. They don't know you feel like your father and your faith has failed you.

They don't know your faith has been overpowered, overtaken, and overthrown by fear, and they don't know you have to find a way to "survive" their happy moment. They don't know that you are there and you are in your survivor-survival mind-set, mentality, and mode. And somewhere in the midst of it all, her, your, mind and her and your thoughts drift off into another place where you would find yourself and she would find herself just wondering . . . she can't and won't stop wondering because she absolutely knew and knows she did have, she didn't have, or she never had or never had to the degree that you have had; she also knew and knows she could have, should have, and would have had and maybe she even had the opportunity to have a father-daughter relationship, but she didn't, she couldn't, and she wouldn't.

And that has left her wondering if it would have bothered her dad, her father, the one who was supposed to be the first man in her life, when she changed her last name, and would it have bothered him when she made a promise to another man and he had to give her away? She imagined her dad standing in the bride room and just staring at her.

She imagined asking him what he was thinking, and she imagined him saying, "I'm not sure," and under his breath, he says, "I'm losing my baby girl." And in that moment and with those words spoken, she imagines herself leaning over and she gives him one of her butterfly kisses with her mama standing there.

She then can't and won't stop wondering and imagining what it would have been like to say to him, "Walk me down the aisle, Daddy. It's just about time. And does my wedding gown look pretty, Daddy? Daddy, please don't cry!" And in her wondering and in her imagining, she pictures him being so happy for her that she can hear him when he says, "I couldn't ask God for more. I know this is what love is." She can see him and feel him as he struggles and strains to let her go.

For some reason, while she is sharing in on and being an important part of her best friend's special moment and special day, she finds herself staring at them, her best friend and her father, and she can't and won't stop wondering and imagining, would things be different for her and the same as her best friend's if she would fall to her knees and ask God if her daddy remembers every hug she gave him, and does he remember her butterfly kisses that she gave him on his cheek?

She wonders if in doing so what she is actually seeing and what she is imaging would suddenly, immediately, and quickly change and her best friend's moment would become and be and end up being her moment . . . she can only imagine. Since that day when all those traumatic, troubling, and tragic things happened to her, she has had no problem getting someone, him, to take her out; she had had a problem getting him to keep her.

Beat down to a breakdown

The first thing that I want to tell you is you are so important and you really matter, so much so that the Satan, the devil, has been after you long before you came into this world. He has been working behind the scenes in the shadows of your life stalking you and waiting for the moment when he could seize your faith and then begin to dominate, manipulate, and control you. The weapon he has formed against you and is using and has been using to carry out his master hostile takeover of your life, faith, future, and hope is called fear.

It has not been a coincidence, bad luck, etc., that the bad, wrong, negative, and ugly things that have happened to you and have been said and done to you and have taken place in your life; all of it was strategic, and you were being set up for failure. The fact that you did not have the right someone in your life to help you and talk you down and talk you through the things that happened to you and help you get free of, get past, and get over the weapon Satan formed against you starting from your childhood days to your teenage days and into your present day gave Satan the open door he needed.

The fact that you had the wrong person and people who supposedly were watching over you and supposedly were helping you and protecting you were the same person and people whom Satan used to expose your voids, empty places, lack, needs, and wants and then exploit them was no coincidence and it wasn't no accident.

Everyone that has caused, created the atmosphere for, and has contributed directly or indirectly, knowingly or unknowingly, willingly or unwillingly to the hurt, harm, humiliation, danger, and destruction you have been through and your life being the way it is and the choices and decisions being the ones they have been were all part of Satan's plan to dismantle, disconnect, and destroy your life. From the first day you were thought of, conceived, birthed, and born, Satan had set his evil sights on having you for his purposes and plan.

You couldn't and wouldn't and didn't see it and you couldn't and wouldn't and didn't know it because you were an innocent baby and you had no idea how your life would be and you had no idea "who" would come into your life and "what" would happen to you when they did. The way you are and the things you have been through that you still are fighting with and fighting to get over that seemingly can't and won't go away have come about because of the following words spoken in Jeremiah 1:5 concerning you that make you a person of importance and someone that really matters.

"I knew you before I formed you in the womb; I set
you apart for me before you were born; I appointed
you to be a prophet to the nations" (Jer. 1:5).

You were not an accident and you were not created for the negative, bad, wrong, and ugly things that have happened to you. Not only so, but also you are not someone that God knew before you were formed in your mother's womb, and He wanted you exclusively for Himself, so He set you apart before you were born. He then appointed you to be someone important, and He appointed you to be someone who matters. He also appointed you to just "be"! You can just "be" the person God has created you to be. Satan doesn't want you to just "be" because your ability to "be" he knows is powered by the image of God that you were and you are created in (Gen. 1:27).

So Jeremiah 1:5 makes you an important person and someone that matters, and that is something you should never forget. It doesn't matter what flaws, weaknesses, inadequacies, inabilities, insecurities, and failures, and it doesn't matter how many times you have made mistakes and you have fallen; you were and you still are someone God created to "be," someone that matters, and someone that is important. It doesn't matter what you think and how you feel when it comes to yourself, and it doesn't matter how you see yourself; you are still important and you still matter.

With that being said, that is the reason why Satan wants to kill your self-image, steal your self-worth, destroy your self-esteem, and devour your self-confidence. And the way he will go about doing that is by administering a constant, continuous, and consistent beat down upon your mind with all its capabilities and abilities, which entailed assaulting, attacking, assassinating, and assigning.

- ❖ *Assaulting* your mind, frame of mind, state of mind, mental condition and conditioning, and mental state of being by way of bombarding them with fear, doubt, worry, stress, and unbelief.
- ❖ *Attacking* your thoughts, train of thought, thinking, and way of thinking by bombarding them with a barrage of negative flashbacks and memories from your past and by way of keeping

alive unanswered questions and unsolved mysteries about yourself from your past alive.

❖ *Assassinating* your mind-set and mentality with fears about your future and the fear of your past becoming your future.

❖ *Assigning* and attaching a survivor-survival mode to your mind with all its capabilities and abilities.

All the assaults, attacks, and assassinating would end up being a vicious cycle that would eventually bring about a breakdown in your mind with all its capabilities and abilities (mental, thoughts, etc.), and none would have the power and authority and ability to function and flow and operate as they should.

CHAPTER THREE

Survivor's Mind and Mentals

ANYTIME A PERSON has suffered through and had to endure a traumatic childhood, teen, or an adult circumstance, situation, confrontation, matter, or moment to any degree, what they are left with are traumatic, terrorizing, tormenting, and torturing, memories and flashbacks that seemingly have the power and the authority to show up in their mind at will. The same applies when a daughter that grows up to be a woman and she did or didn't get what she needed, wanted, desired, and deserved and should have gotten out of her father-daughter relationship; she is left growing up with a traumatic void and emptiness that she at the time cannot and will not be able to see at the time when she is trying to recover, remove and replace, and respond and not react.

But one day, what she is missing, missed out on, or never had a chance to receive will show up and terrorize, torment, trouble, and traumatize her without her even knowing it; to the point where she will begin to make haphazard, irresponsible, damaging, destructive, dangerous, and self-destructive relationship, self-esteem, self-image, self-worth, self-confidence, life, and world, and opinions of men, choices, and decisions that will end up leaving her destitute and distracted and having a distorted view of life, love, living, marriage, ministry, money, happiness, hurt, pain, brokenness, and herself. She will also have a distorted view of what it means to accomplish, achieve, acquire, and accumulate; what it means to win, overcome, and have and exercise faith, hope, belief, and confidence; and what it means to be prosperous, productive, and successful.

Not only are some parts or all of what is supposed to go into making her who she was and is to be are damaged and distorted, but she is also disconnected, and she will end up with destitute feelings, emotions, and desires, which lead to her making self-destructive choices and decisions. Whenever a person has destitute feelings, emotions, desires, and thoughts, they are also having desires, dreams, visions, self-image, self-esteem, self-worth, and self-confidence, feelings and emotions that are without the basic necessities that are needed to give life. The most important part of who she is and what she needs to sustain and maintain a healthy, whole, satisfying, fulfilling, rewarding, and refreshing relationship, self-esteem, self-image, self-worth, self-confidence, life and world, and opinions she does not have, or she has (1) just enough of or (2) not enough of but she never has (3) more than enough of.

Having "just enough of" is not good because you will, at some place, point, and time, run out of what you need, and you will end up with and in a destitute mind, frame of mind, state of mind, mental condition and conditioning, and state of being. Whatever part of you that is destitute is also devoid of something. Having a destitute mind, frame of mind, mental condition and conditioning, state of mind, and mental state of being not only means all are lacking something needed or desirable, but they all will eventually end up being devoid of what is needed to lead them into helping you make relationship choices and decisions that help create, build, establish, and shape your relationship self-esteem, self-image, self-worth, self-confidence, life and world, and opinions. If any part of your relationship self-esteem, self-image, self-worth, self-confidence, and your relationship opinions are devoid of something, they are entirely lacking or free from what is needed to make them whole and healthy. If and when your relationship mind, relationship frame of mind, relationship condition and conditioning, relationship state of mind, and mental relationship state of being are devoid, what happens is all are entirely lacking or free from what is needed for a person to make the right relationship choices and decisions. The choices and decisions will help them sustain and maintain that relationship and help shape their and your relationship self-esteem, self-image, self-worth, self-confidence, and your relationship opinions.

Destitute and devoid

When your relationship capabilities and abilities are destitute and devoid, what happens is you will be left in desperate straits, and out of that and because of that, the only thing that can and will be produced, prepared, and presented is relationship dysfunction. You were deprived of a father-daughter relationship, and because of that, you were deprived of the vital and necessary relationship self-esteem, self-image, self-worth, self-confidence, and opinions that come out of a father-daughter relationship. Once you were deprived, you ended up in a destitute relationship state and condition, and that put in motion and put into effect different kinds and types of a relationship devoid. And those and that devoid opened your mind, frame of mind, mental condition and conditioning, and state of mind to relationship dysfunctions.

It all started the day and the moment when you were traumatically tormented, tortured, terrorized, and traumatized because of a bad, wrong, negative, and ugly unseen, unknown, undetected, unbelievable, and unplanned relationship matter and moment that you didn't see coming that has become an unforgettable memory. And because of the unforgettable, your mind and your frame of mind, state of mind, and mental state of being are left struggling and straining and trying to survive what happened or didn't happen to you and with you. The healthy and whole relationship part and parts of you that are supposed to be instantly and automatically, constantly, continuously, and consistently prosperous, productive, and successful end up being stranded, and that will draw, drive, pull, push, persuade, force, seduce, entice, entangle, entrap you into "relationship striving" or into having to exert much effort or energy and endeavor in a relationship.

When your mind, frame of mind, mental condition and conditioning, state of mind, and mental state of being are forced into being a slave to "relationship striving," all are being yoked, in a stronghold to, and in bondage to struggling or fighting forcefully to find and stay in a relationship and to contend with being in a relationship. There are some important enhancing female-to-male relationship qualities, characteristics, and features and self-esteem, self-image, self-worth, self-confidence, and opinions that you did not get as a result of not having a strong, safe, sound, solid, stable, and secure father-daughter relationship. Without them, you are not able to wholeheartedly embrace and reap the benefits that come with being in a healthy and whole relationship.

Something traumatic, tragic, and troubling happened to you, and you found yourself hurt and hindered and held up and not able to move forward, and your feelings and your emotions ended up being tormented, tortured, terrorized, and traumatized. That is when your mind and your mental capabilities and abilities were forced into action. They were forced into performing a protective and preventive survivor-survival recovery functioning and flowing action. And that is when your mind and your frame of mind, mental conditioning, state of mind, and mental state of being basically made an urgent and desperate call to your survivor-survival urges, tendencies, inclinations, intuitions, impulses, impulsiveness, and instincts demanding they immediate and quickly "do something" and demanding that they release your indwelling "lying dormant" protective and preventive tactical survivor-survival acts, actions, and deeds, and they did so.

You had no control over what was happening, and your mind, frame of mind, state of mind, mental condition and conditioning, and mental state of being forced your reactions and your reactionary responses into some survivor-survival soothing and satisfying survivor-survival protective and preventive self-performance, self-willed, and self-effort motives and motivations. You were not actively involved in what was happening to you. Whatever it is that you do not have a strong, solid, sound, stable, and secure foundation for and you do not have the right image, ideas, insights, ingenuity, inspirations, information, and instructions for, Satan will send and use fear as the weapon to challenge, confront, conquer, and change your mind and mental capabilities and abilities into something that can and will easily end up being seized, overpowered, overtaken, overthrown, and taken control, taken down, and taken over.

You mind, frame of mind, mental condition and conditioning, state of mind, and mental state of being were forced into a survivor-survival alerted action because of the unbelievable tragic and troubling trauma that you found yourself faced with that terrorized, tormented, tortured, and traumatized you. Fear gripped and seized your mind, mental capabilities and abilities, as well as your feelings and emotions and your desires and fear, and then overpowered, overtook, overthrew, and then took control of and took down and took over your mind and mental capabilities and abilities, right, power, and authority to find and function and flow on, in and out of faith. This is how you ended up in and with a survivor-survival mind, frame of mind, state of mind, mental condition and conditioning, and end up being in a survivor-survival mental state of being.

All the tragic and troubling traumatic circumstances, situations, confrontations, matters, and moments that tortured, terrorized, tormented, and traumatized your faith, feelings, and emotions gave place to your mind and mental capabilities and abilities being assaulted, attacked, and assassinated, and that triggered your mind and your mental capabilities and abilities being driven into survivor-survival functioning and flowing.

The dominance of your mind

You were scared and afraid because of what was happening to you and what you were going through, and there was something lacking and missing within you; and because of what you couldn't, wouldn't, and didn't get out of a father-daughter relationship, Satan used fear to trick, trigger, and trap your mind, frame of mind, mental condition, state of mind, and mental state of being over into a *state* and *condition* where you would constantly, continuously, and consistently function as a person who copes well with difficulties in the life and a person who survives and remains alive after an event in which others have died. And you would from that place and point flow over into a constant, continuous, and consistent mind, frame of mind, state of mind, mental condition, and mental state of being where you would be bombarded with images of you continuing to live or exist, typically in spite of an accident, ordeal, or difficult circumstances.

THE SURVIVORS MODE ⌁51⌁

And your mind and mental capabilities and abilities would also end up being constantly, continuously, and consistently bombarded with receiving inspirations, ingenuity, insights, information, and instructions on how to continue to live or exist, typically in spite of an accident, ordeal, or difficult circumstances even when there were none. You would be locked into that fearful mind and mental state and condition. Fear would trick your feelings into reacting in that state and condition and then trap you emotionally into reactionary responses out of that same state and condition and then trigger your mind and mental capabilities and abilities into agreeing with your tricked feelings and trapped emotions.

Everything that your mind, frame of mind, state of mind, and mental state of being processes will end up being filtered through what you were tutored, trained, and taught to do when you were a child and you didn't have a good, right, and positive father-daughter relationship and other relationship experiences and encounters, and that is to survive, be a survivor, and never leave out of an object or practice that has continued to exist from an earlier time that has kept you.

CHAPTER FOUR

The Seduction of Your Mind

PICTURE THIS, IN your beginning, the Genesis of who you were, are, and will become, be, and end up being came into existence, God was there, and He said, "Let there be you," and in that moment, your mom and your dad met, got together, and created you, and in that same momentous moment, you, everything that would be needed to help you be who you needed and should be and the life God had for you were conceived and created. There was no void, emptiness, and there was nothing missing and lacking, and everything that it would take for you to be the person God created you to be; and everything it would take for you to accomplish, achieve, acquire, accumulate, conquer, win, and overcome was conceived in that same momentous moment when "God said" let there be you.

Heaven and earth and the host of angels in heaven applauded your conception and creation, except for Satan, the devil. He was mad and angry and unhappy, and when "God said" let us create "you," His image Satan knew He would not be able to contain or stop you because you would have the very "life and breath" of God living, dwelling, and abiding within you. Not your mother's nor your dad's life and breath but God's. And with that life and breath of God being on the inside, you will manifest the same power and authority that was and is in God also being inside of you. There was nothing lacking in the creation of you, and that is when Satan knew he had to do something to stop you from recognizing and realizing what God has placed within you and stop you from recognizing and realizing not just "who" you are but "whose" you are.

Satan knew that one day you would do what David did and you would open up your heart, mind, spirit, and mouth and you would forever praise Him, God, your creator, because you would recognize and realize you were and you are fearfully and wonderfully made by God (Ps. 139:14). Satan knew that you one day would yearn after God with all your being and you would one day totally yield, submit, and surrender to Him and His purpose, plan, and perfect will for your life; and he really got mad and angry, would despise your conception and creation, and would rally all the demon spirits that were under his control and command and tell them to send everything and everyone that they had control over and would have control over and assign them with the command to kill, steal, and destroy you and your life, hopes, dreams, desires, visions, passions, and passionate pursuits, and most important of all, kill, steal, and destroy your destiny.

Assigned to your Genesis

Their assignment was to find a way and find ways, cause, create the atmosphere for, and contribute to ways and methods they could and would use to seize, overpower, overtake, overthrow, take control of, take over, and take down everything God said you can have, do, be and every place you can go as your inheritance. They were told to block your blessings or to get you or someone else, preferably someone that is close to you to block your blessings, hinder, hold up, and hurt you. A hit was placed upon your life long before you would have a life to live, and Satan and all his foul, wicked despotisms, the powers, the master spirits who are the world rulers of this present darkness, and the spirit forces of wickedness in the heavenly supernatural sphere (Eph. 6:12) would spend all their days and time working hard to "set you up for failure" and to make sure you spent your days and your life flawed, falling and feeling like a failure.

You never knew any of this, and that was Satan's game plan, his master deception. Their assignment was to be constant, continuous, and consistent in assaulting, attacking, and assassinating your Genesis and to assault, attack, and assassinate any attempts you would make at studying God's truth, His written word, the Bible, mediating on it day and night, obeying to the best of your human ability everything that is written within it. And most important of all, they were assigned the mission of making sure you do not prosper and you do not succeed in anything that you do (Josh. 1:8). They were told to help make sure you had flaws and failures and you would fall, and when those things came about, they were to expose them and exploit them, bringing hurt, pain, brokenness, shame, and embarrassment into your life and upon you.

They were also told to make sure you abandon faith and never remember the Lord your God, and assault, attack, and assassinate any efforts you would make to find, discover, and get linked to, connected to, tied to the truth, reality, knowledge, and understanding that long before you were conceived, birthed, and born, God in your Genesis had already given you the ability to produce wealth (Deut. 8:18). They were instructed to launch an all-out assault, attack, assassination hit on any efforts and attempts you would make to get yoked to, bound and limited to, in bondage to, and in a stronghold to confirming His covenant that He, God, made with you long before you even knew it and knew a covenant was made on your behalf.

They were told to use anything, everything, and everyone and to use and utilize every negative, bad, wrong, and ugly circumstance, situation, confrontation, matter, memory, moment, feeling, emotion, and desire that you would have against you so that you never discover, accept, adopt, adapt to apply, think, feel and believe, function and flow in and out of, and follow and make your truth and your reality these words, "Despite all things that happen to you past, present and future, you are more than a conqueror and you have an overwhelming victory and it is yours because your Genesis came through Christ, who loved you" (Rom. 8:37). There was so much God spoke, declared, decreed, poured into you, created you in and created within you, and invested in you long before you were conceived, birthed, and born that you didn't know anything about until *now,* but Satan and all his demonic spirits knew. And so a systematic and strategic hit assignment was placed upon your life long before you stepped into your life, the one you now have and you are and have been living in and out of.

And so there you were lying in the safety and the security of your mother's womb, innocent, no cares, no concerns, and no worries, and

God was there watching you in your innocence just being what you were supposed to be. And just like any proud parent, He was so happy that you were His that He *called you by name* and He said, "I will go before you and I will be with you, I will never leave you nor forsake you. Do not be afraid of what will happen and take place in your past, present nor your future; do not be discouraged. I will go before you" (Deut. 31:8). He would then, like any loving, caring, concerned, and compassionate parent, hold you and in Him holding you long before you needed to be held; in that holding you were protection and prevention and divine intervention and everything else you would need but never knew you would need and want.

After holding you, *Jesus wept* for you and He then prayed for you and His prayer was "Your faith fail not" no matter what flaws you have, no matter how often you fall, and no matter how Satan tries to suggest to your feelings that you are a failure and no matter how he tries to influence your emotions and you emotionally into thinking, feeling, and believing you are a failure. He prayed for you while you were still in your mother's womb (Luke 22:32). As He was there with you watching you grow, develop, and mature into your innocence. He loved you so much and He never wanted you to think, believe, and feel like you were lost and you did not have an identity. He never wanted you to get infected with peer pressure, but He wanted you to "put pressure on your peers."

So He validated you and told you who you were and who you are when He said, "You are not like and you will not be like anyone and everyone else, for you are a chosen person. You are a royal priest, a holy nation, my very own possession." And He then said, "As a result, you will have what it takes to show others the goodness of God to your family, friends, enemies and strangers, for I have called you out of the darkness into his wonderful light" (1 Pet. 2:9). He spoke this over you and into you because He knew Satan would never stop or give up on sending and using and utilizing everything and everyone he could to assault, attack, and assassinate what would be needed to shape your self-esteem, your self-worth, your self-image, your self-confidence, your world, your confidence, and your opinions of men. He knew you would one day need to have the right approach to your life and to life itself so that you would have the right criteria for you to build off in your own life, even if you end up choosing a different view of the world.

He saw your innocence, and like any heartfelt and sincere protective parent and father, first man in your life, He wanted to protect you and your innocence and make sure you did not wander around in your life and in life living aimlessly, living from pillow to post, a slave to an addiction of any kind, destitute, distracted, detoured, delayed, and denied the right to have a "destiny" and denied the right to live your life to the fullest until it overflow; so He looked into your innocence and He *called you by your name* and He said, "I know the plans I have for you, my plans are to prosper you and not to harm you, my plans are to give you hope and a future. I will make sure I give you an expected end to all of your faith praying" (Jer. 29:11).

After spending "quality" time with you in your Genesis and while you were in your mother's womb, He then looked at you, and with and out of all the love, care, concern, and compassion that a father and a "first man in your life" could have, He was "behooved" to make sure everything that was and is in your Genesis and everything that He had spoken over you and into you and your destiny would be sealed and you would hit your appointed destiny target. And there would be nothing said or done, past, present, or future, that would be able to stop, hinder, hold up, dismantle, derail, deny, and disconnect you from fulfilling what He spoke over you while He was spending quality time with you in your "Genesis and in your creation."

It "behooved" Him to seal what He spoke, declared, and decreed and what He said when it came to you, your life, and your destiny. He decided the only way to do that would be to suffer and die and rise from the dead on the third day and to defeat everything that Satan would send anyone to say and do to you that would disappoint, discourage, and defeat you and deny you the right to have your God-given inheritance. For Jesus to be "behooved" because of you and for your sake meant He felt it is His duty or responsibility to do what was needed and necessary so you would not be forever, distracted, detoured, detained, defeated, delayed, and denied to have and see the fulfillment of the plans He had for you and the things that He spoke into your Genesis. What He did for you was appropriate and suitable enough to satisfy what was needed to seal the plans He has for you and to manifest the plans He has for you, keeping them safe and away from everything Satan would do to assault, attack, and assassinate you and them.

And from the day Jesus died on the cross for you and shed His blood for you, your life, and the fulfillment of the plans He had and still has for you, Satan knew he had to set his sights on the seduction of your mind. He knew he couldn't touch and take what was sealed in and through the blood of Jesus, so he had to use and utilize something and someone that will get you of your own free will, yield, submit, and surrender the plans, purposes, passions, promises, and destiny and the power to be resurrected from defeats and destruction that Jesus paid the price for.

Satan can't take something from you, and he can't "make" you say or do anything that you don't want to say or do; he can suggest and then influence you, but the ultimate "giving in and giving up" is in your control. Satan knows that, so his way of killing, stealing, destroying, assaulting, attacking, and assassinating everything that God spoke into your Genesis and into your creation comes through the seduction of your mind. To have your mind, frame of mind, state of mind, and mental condition and conditioning, and state of being seduced by Satan is to have them *enticed* and attracted powerfully to a belief or into a course of action that is inadvisable or foolhardy.

The seduction of your mind, frame of mind, state of mind, mental condition and conditioning, and state of being involves the act or action of attempting to suggest and influence and attract your mind, frame of mind, state of mind, mental condition and conditioning, and state of being into a satanic suggested and influenced hurtful, painful, and harmful belief or into a satanic suggested and influenced course of action that is distracting, dangerous, deadly, damaging, and destructive. He goes about the seduction of your mind and mental capabilities and abilities by attempting to get your mind and your mental capabilities and abilities to "entertain" and then open up to what he is suggesting to you and what he is trying to influence you into thinking, feeling and believing, accepting, adopting, adapting to, and applying.

Caught, captive, and captivated

For fear to be prosperous, productive, and successful in, at, and with the seduction of your mind and your mental capabilities and abilities, Satan will send fear to torture, torment, terrorize, and traumatize your feelings and emotions to the point where you start making choices and decisions that are and end up being traumatic, tragic, and they end up being full of trouble, and bring about and put in motion unseen, unwanted, undetected, unbelievable, unforeseen, and unforgettable tests, trials, temptations, and tribulations that you were unaware of that were waiting on you. As this is happening and is taking place, your mind ends up being "captivated" and "caught" in what is taking place, and your mental capabilities and abilities end up being held "captive" to the place and point of being "caught up" in what is taking place, leading to neither can shake loose from and get away from what is going on.

For the seduction of your mind and mental capabilities and abilities to actually work, there has to be something, an inadvisable and foolhardy act, action, deed, choice, decision, belief, or a course of action that is so powerful that it can and will and do powerfully attract your mind and your mental capabilities and abilities to the point and place where they are *caught* like an animal that is trapped in a trap and/or they get stuck on what took place, how, when, where, and why what happened took place, showed up, and occurred.

And once caught, your mind and mental capabilities and abilities have to be powerfully drawn, driven, pulled, pushed, persuaded, tricked into being distracted and detained long enough to get "caught up" in the inadvisable and foolhardy, and this will take place when the person's mind keeps reviving, remembering, and replaying the inadvisable and foolhardy circumstance, situation, confrontation, matter, moment, and memory they were powerfully enticed, entangled, and entrapped into being attracted to and into. Anything that is unplanned, unwanted, and undetected that you are unaware of that happens or shows up that becomes and ends up being so unbelievable and so unimaginable that it is unforgettable will be what will end up being so powerfully attractive that it can and will attract the focus and the attention of your mind.

When that happens, your frame of mind, state of mind, mental conditions and conditioning, and mental state of being will then end up being enticed, entangled, and entrapped into a state of being caught and then into a condition of being caught up, captivated, and finally a captive to that same unplanned, unwanted, and undetected inadvisable and foolhardy choice and decision, act, action deed, way of handling something that you were unaware of that would happen and did happen and showed up; that was so unbelievable and so unimaginable and so unforgettable and so powerfully attractive that like a magnet, your frame of mind, state of mind, mental condition and conditioning, and state of being were powerfully drawn to and have a magnetic attraction to the inadvisable and foolhardy that took place.

The seducing and the seduction of your mind and your frame of mind, state of mind, mental condition and conditioning, and mental state of being also involves and has to do with all being so overwhelmingly captivated that they are powerfully attracted into easily being caught, and that will in turn produce, prepare, and present them being a captive that is powerfully attracted to being caught up in what turned out to be an inadvisable and foolhardy argument, theory, reasoning, proud and lofty thing, feeling, emotion, desire, belief, conduct, conversation, communication, behavior, and behavior pattern. Once the seduction of your mind is successful, Satan sends fear to "shock" your mind, and then that same fear "stuns" your frame of mind, state of mind, mental condition and conditioning, and mental state of being, and all will end up being "stuck" and they struggle, strain, and can't and won't be able to overpower, overtake, and overcome.

Your mind and your mental capabilities and abilities can't and won't have the power they will need to seize, take down, take control of, and take over what has captivated and caught them and has them distracted and detained and detoured and delayed and has them held captive and caught up in the inadvisable and the foolhardy that has enticed, entangled, and entrapped them. Fear kills, steals, and destroys

ANTHONY MCMARYION

your mind and frame of mind, state of mind, mental condition and conditioning, and mental state of being power and authority. Once your mind is seduced into a satanic and demonic suggestion and influence, it is then sucked into a "sinking sand" state and condition. Satan uses fear to "paralyze" and stifle your mind long enough so it can be seduced, tricked, trapped, yoked, in bondage to, in a stronghold to, bound and limited to, and a slave to being led into making damaging, dangerous, destructive, destitute, self-destructive and haphazard, inadvisable, and foolhardy choices and decisions.

And the next thing that automatically and immediately and suddenly happens is your seduced mind will open the door for, put into motion, and put into effect you functioning and flowing in and out of and living in and out of and following the processes, procedures, and principles that are coming out of a distorted, distracted, detained, detoured, dismantled, derailed, delayed, denied, destitute, and disconnected state of mind, frame of mind, mental condition and conditioning, and mental state of being.

Satan is the master of mind and mental capability and ability seductions, seducing, delusions, deceptions and unveiling, unfolding, and unraveling mind games. When he has masterfully completed the seduction of your mind, what he has done is use fear techniques and tactics as a way to win over, attract, and entice, and to complete the leading or drawing away of the element of that enables you to be aware of the world and your experiences, to think, and to feel; the faculty of your consciousness and thought away from principles, faith or an allegiance to faith principles, processes, and procedures. Your intellect and memory, the way in which you are identified with your intellectual faculties, your ability to pay attention, and your will or determination to achieve something have been attracted or led away from their proper functional and flowing behavior or thinking.

CHAPTER FIVE

Survivor's Thoughts and Thinking

ONCE FEAR HAS a person who has been in and through a traumatic, tragic, tormenting, torturing, troubling, and terrorizing circumstance, situation, confrontation, matter, and moment all the way over into a survivor's mind, frame of mind, mental condition and conditioning, state of mind, and a survivor-survival mental state of being; and is in place and it is up and running and it is fully operational and the persons survivor-survival mind and mental capabilities and abilities are dominating, manipulating, and controlling what kind and type of images, ideas, insights, inspirations, information, and instructions, the next thing that happens is the person will automatically get connected, linked, and tied to having survivor-survival thoughts, train of thoughts, thinking, and way of thinking.

- Survivor thoughts are an idea or opinion produced by thinking or occurring suddenly in the mind that the person uses and utilizes that help a person remain alive or in existence and help them carry on despite hardships or trauma and persevere and remain functional.
- Survival thoughts are ideas or opinions produced by thinking or occurring suddenly in the mind that the person uses and utilizes to help the person stay and remain in a constant, continuous, and consistent state or fact of continuing to live or exist, typically in spite of an accident, ordeal, or difficult circumstances.
- Survivor thinking involves the process of using one's mind, thought, or rational judgment to consider or reason about remaining alive after an event in which others have died.

- Survival thinking involves the process of using one's mind, thought, or rational judgment as the way to consider or reason continuing to live or exist, typically in spite of an accident, ordeal, or difficult circumstances.

Fear wants to make sure your thoughts, train of thought, thinking, and way of thinking are also tormented, terrorized, tortured, and traumatized to the point that you become or continue to be a person of two minds, hesitating, dubious, irresolute, unstable, unreliable, and uncertain about everything that you think, feel, decide, and believe. When you are, fear can keep you a slave to, yoked to, in a stronghold to, bound and limited to, and in bondage to survivor-survival thoughts, train of thought, thinking, and way of thinking.

Satanic fear will begin to use and utilize every negative, bad, wrong, and ugly self-esteem, self-image, self-worth, self-confidence, and opinions that were never properly shaped as a result of you having a right relationship with your father, with your faith, and with yourself as the way to (1) take down, take control, and take over and then seize; and (2) overpower, overtake, and overthrow your thoughts, train of thought, thinking, and way of thinking.

From the first moment, everything that you did not have to help influence and shape in the right way the type and kind of self-esteem, self-worth, self-image, self-confidence, and opinions of men and relationships, Satan had set his sights on exposing and exploiting the relationship deficiencies that you had. The moment when he gained control of your mind and mental capabilities and abilities by way of your feelings and emotions and desires having been tormented, tortured, terrorized, and traumatized, he was at that moment able to gain access to your thoughts, train of thought, thinking, and way of thinking. Not only was that the plan and goal, but in doing so, Satan would be able to easily dominate, manipulate, control, and dictate to and dictate through your thoughts, train of thought, thinking, and way of thinking your approach to life, love, living, faith, hope, belief, confidence, winning, overcoming, relationships, etc.

The ultimate plan Satan had for your thoughts, train of thought, thinking, and way of thinking long before you came into this life was to make sure they never would become, be, and end up being strong, stable, safe, secure, and solid in being faith functional but fear functional. With your thoughts, train of thought, thinking, and way of thinking entangled and entrapped into a fearful survivor-survival vicious cycle, there would not be enough focus and creativity available to help in the shaping of your self-esteem, self-worth, self-will, self-confidence, life, and world. Satan wanted to make sure everything and everyone who could and would serve as a good and positive example for you to build off in your own life was removed.

Every time you allow your thoughts, train of thought, thinking, and way of thinking to get to the point and place where they are consistently, constantly, and continuously seduced, deceived, enticed, entangled, and entrapped into a survivor-survival processes and procedures, you cannot and will not be able to move forward, and being scared and afraid will continue to reign and rule over you and your choices and decisions. Fear is throwing everything that has been bad, wrong, negative, and ugly that has happened to you at your thoughts, train of thought, thinking, and way of thinking. Satan wants fear to be your survivor-survival food, and Satan wants fear to be what your thoughts, train of thought, thinking, and way of thinking feed off and function and flow in and out of.

Satan wants to make sure there is not enough faith in your thoughts, train of thought, thinking, and way of thinking to help fight off fear, being scared, being afraid, OCD, PTSD, and everything else that torture, traumatize, and torment you. Your thoughts, train of thought, thinking, and way of thinking are the playground or the construction site for your creativity and your creative imagination, and if it is being used for survivor-survival's sake, it cannot and will not be able to produce, prepare, and present faith-based strong creative processes, procedures, and principles. When you were a little girl, you lived in and out of your thoughts and thinking, and your dreams, hopes, and desires were able to grow, develop, and mature in your thoughts and thinking. Your self-worth, self-confidence, self-esteem, and self-image were conceived, birthed, and born in your thoughts and thinking as well as your faith, hope, belief, and confidence.

When either your thoughts and thinking and everything that it housed when you were a little girl was shaken or taken or weakened or tampered with because of something that was trying, tiring, troubling, tragic, or traumatic happening to you, the door was opened for your train of thought and your way of thinking to be terrorized, tormented, and traumatized. And with that happening, you were, for the first time, driven, drawn, pulled, pushed, persuaded, and forced into survivor-survival thoughts and thinking. From that day forward, you would be a slave to survivor-survival train of thought and survivor-survival way of thinking.

> Survivor-survival *way of thinking* involves the act or practice of one that thinks; their thought and their way of reasoning that leads to producing, preparing, and presenting a final judgment that helps a person remain alive after an event in which others have died and leads to a person being able to a cope well with difficulties in his or her life. That same act or practice of one that thinks; their thought and their way of reasoning that leads to a final judgment is what they are led to think, feel, and believe will ensure they can and will keep them in the state or fact of continuing to live or exist, typically in spite of any present or future accident, ordeal, or difficult circumstances.

> Survivor-survival *train of thought* involves the way in which someone reaches a conclusion; a line of reasoning that they think, feel, believe, and is confident that helps and has helped them to be a person who survives, especially someone who remains alive after an event in which others have died. And when they think, feel, and believe this way, they believe that same way in which they reached a conclusion; a line of reasoning will keep them in the state or fact of continuing to live or exist, typically in spite of any type and kind of accident, ordeal, or difficult circumstances.

THE SURVIVORS MODE

My point is everything from your past or present that is now or has been traumatic and troubling and tragic that has traumatized, tortured, and tormented your feelings, emotions, has affected your mind, frame of mind, mental condition and conditioning, state of mind, and state of being, and it has also affected your thoughts, train of thought, thinking, and way of thinking.

Past becomes your future

The same thoughts, train of thought, thinking, and way of thinking you had when you went to sleep an innocent child in peace and woke up one day an adult with PTSD and you were finally able to recognize and realize that something was going wrong and something went wrong. The same thoughts, train of thought, thinking, and way of thinking you had when you were a child and you first sensed, felt, thought, and saw you would not get or have a father's love, have father-daughter dates, and have a clean, healthy, pure father-daughter relationship, and you had to, in your innocent mind, find a thought and a thinking that would help justify and make the reason(s) why you wouldn't get the father-daughter attention you saw your friends get from their fathers right. And the reasons that you came up with would become your "get me through" train of thought and way of thinking whenever something uncomfortable, unreal, unbelievable, and unforgettable was, did, and would be happening to you.

The same thoughts and thinking you had and held on to every time you woke up in your "child nightmare," shaking, shivering, sweating, crying, and hurting, oh, the pain! And daddy wasn't there, and mommy seemingly didn't care, and over and over it happened to you. Sometimes at a different place at a different time, a different person, maybe the same place and the same person, but "it happened" and it kept happening, and you were afraid to tell anyone; maybe you couldn't tell anyone; maybe you didn't know how to tell anyone. After all, who would listen to a little girl who is a dreamer, who really didn't feel pretty, who wasn't like the other girls, her siblings, and didn't feel like she was good enough?

How could you tell anyone, and would you? Who would listen to you? What if something bad happened to the people you loved and cared for if you told anyone? The same thought and thinking you had that kept you protecting the "family secrets" and your "secret," you know, the one that made you feel bad about yourself, feel nasty and unclean, and feel unwanted, and somehow and in some way you found a thought and a thinking that could, would, and did help you make it through all the things that had happened to you. That is the same train of thought and way of thinking your new friend "fear" wants you to keep and hold on to and make your survivor-survival thought, train of thought, thinking, and way of thinking today, tomorrow, the rest of your life, and forever!

You just wanted to be loved and feel loved, needed, and wanted, and to feel like you mattered and you were important. You just wanted to have innocent little thoughts, train of thought, thinking, and way of thinking other little girls your age had and should have. You just wanted to be touched and held in the way a father who really loved and protected his daughter and their father/daddy-daughter relationship should touch and hold his daughter. After all, you were supposed to be a daddy's girl, you know, daddy's little girl, and he was supposed to be there to protect you and he was supposed to be there to protect and shape your innocent little thoughts, train of thought, thinking, and way of thinking. You, out of childlike expectancy and out of childlike anticipation, thought, felt, and believed he would be there for you and with you, and he would protect your self-image, self-esteem, self-worth, and self-confidence, and he would protect your innocent and undefiled opinions.

And now you are a grow woman and you have come to the harsh reality and realization that what was supposed to be used to help "shape" who you are and what you are has been and always was "shattered," and since that day, that moment, and to this very day, your life and your world has been colored with "shame" and not with hope. Yes, and now you are a grown woman and you are still tied to, connected to, linked to, bound and limited to, yoked to, in a stronghold to, in bondage to, a slave to, and locked into your same old childhood thoughts, train of thought, thinking, and way of thinking. And in some ways, in most ways, you are and you still think, feel, believe, and even at times know you are still a child, an innocent little girl, a "wannabe" daddy's girl, a "should have been" daddy's little girl still making grown-up choices and decisions while you are still caught and caught up in your little girls world and in your little girl's times.

Your thoughts, train of thought, thinking, and way of thinking are not longer innocent, and they are and have been violated just like you are, have been. Why didn't they hear your silent screams that sounded so loud, and why didn't they, he, hear you calling them, and why didn't they come to your rescue, come help you when you showed them what a parent is automatically and instinctively supposed to see and know when it comes to their children, when it comes to a father knowing his daughter?

Family secrets, father-daughter secrets, my life and my world secrets, relationship secrets, self-esteem secrets, self-worth secrets, self-image secrets, self-confidence secrets, and opinion secrets all are locked in your thoughts and thinking, all are protected and prevented from being exposed, revealed, made known, and exploited because of your train of thought and way of thinking. Good or bad, happy or sad, right or wrong, positive or negative, and ugly or pretty thoughts and thinking sheltered and covered by your train of thought and way of thinking.

That's what you did, that's what you have done, that's what you knew to do and know to do to help you survive, make sure you constantly, continuously, and consistently become, be, and end up being a survivor and ensure you remain in a state or fact of continuing to live or exist, typically in spite of a childhood, teen, or a adult accident, ordeal, or difficult circumstance, situation, confrontation, matter, moment, and memory. Satan and fear want you to stay in that past thought, train of thought, thinking, and way of thinking so that it can become your present and future thought, train of thought, thinking, and way of thinking. Satan is and has been using fear as the method to force you to remember everything; faith has the power to release your thoughts, train of thought, thinking, and way of thinking from.

Your thoughts, train of thought, thinking, and way of thinking are recording every moment, every footstep coming down the hall, every door that closes or slams, and every choice and decision you ever made and your reason(s) for making them. Your thoughts, train of thought, thinking, and way of thinking are recalling, remembering, restoring, reviving, reliving, and recording broken promises, every threatening word, every touch, every feeling, every emotion, and every tear. He was . . . and you were . . . and that was . . . and then there was that . . . ! Trying to clean your thoughts, trying to purge your train of thought, trying to heal your thinking, and trying to make whole your way of thinking and still having a hole in your soul that will not heal. Walking away with the thoughts, waking up and thinking, and dealing with a tutored, trained, and taught train of thought and trying to disconnect a learned way of thinking.

Thoughts, train of thought, thinking, and way of thinking that are different on some days and yet the same on most days. Your past becoming your future and your present becoming your past, but your present never moving forward past your "past" and into the future. Recalled, remembered, restored, revived, relived, and prerecorded past, "what you have been through" thoughts, train of thought, thinking, and way of thinking; that is the place and point where Satan wants you to remain locked into and rely on.

The most important thing to remember is survivor-survival thoughts, train of thought, thinking, and way of thinking are fear-driven and motivated thoughts, train of thought, thinking, and a way of thinking that you open up your mind to entertaining; and in doing so, you are allowing and giving place to your feelings, emotions, nerves, reactions, response and reactionary responses being easily enticed, entangled, and entrapped, held captive, yoked to, bound and limited to, in a stronghold to, in bondage to, and a slave to being terrorized, tormented, and tortured by fearful, scared, and afraid. After this has happened, they will end up being thoughts, train of thought, thinking, and way of thinking you will use to help you survive and become, be, and end up being a survivor.

THE SURVIVORS MODE

It would end up being out of those same terrorized, tormented, tortured, and traumatized fearful, scared, and afraid thoughts, train of thought, thinking, and way of thinking you will draw, base, and source all final life, love, living and relationship choices, decisions, logic, and solutions out of.

CHAPTER SIX

Survivor Mind-Set and Mentality

THE MASTER DECEPTION, master delusion, master illusion, and master seduction of your mind has been put in motion and put in effect, and the devil is using fear to play mind games with you, and your mind is playing tricks on you. The next move Satan makes is to begin building and establishing and strengthening you in a survivor-survival attitude and mood so that you will being to think, feel, and believe you are, you will, and you should always be and stay in a state of survival even when there is nothing that you are going through; and you still need to be ready to survive, and therefore you need to stay in and be in a "ready to be a survivor" condition even when there is nothing and no one that is actually and physically terrorizing, tormenting, troubling, and traumatizing you.

After you constantly, continuously, and consistently begin functioning and flowing in and out of a survivor-survival attitude and mood, you will begin to get comfortable with being in it, and you will begin to become complacent, contented, and in a comfort zone with a survivor-survival attitude and mood. That is when Satan eases in and moves you over into a survivor-survival mind-set, and then he will use fear to help grow, develop, and mature you in a survivor-survival mentality. You will not see any of this happening to you; nor will he let you get to the place where you will be able to recognize and realize what is happening to you. His way of blocking, hindering, and distorting your focus away from what he is doing is by using and utilizing fear tactics as its diversionary wiles, trickery, scheme, device, deception, delusion, and illusion so that you end up being so distracted that you cannot and will not be able to clearly focus. He will then detour you onto the path where you will have a head-on collision with a survivor mind-set.

He has used fear to help seize and grip your mind and your faith, and he has used fear as a way to overpower, overtake, and overthrow your frame of mind, state of mind, mental condition and conditioning, and state of being. He has also used fear as the way to gain access to taking down, taking control of, taking over, and taking out your right and sound thoughts, train of thought, thinking, and way of thinking. What he has left you with are survivor-survival senses and survivor-survival perceptions that are not accurate, and they are survivor-survival feelings and emotions, driven and motivated. And what you have been set up for is a survivor mind-set and a survivor mentality.

Survivor mind-set

A person who is in a survivor-survival *mind-set* is someone who is linked to, connected to, and tied to an established set of attitudes they hold and demonstrate and deliver so that they can continue to be a person who can and will cope well with difficulties in their life and remain alive after an event in which others have died; all of which are derived from an object or practice that has continued to exist from an earlier time. Their attitude or their settled way of thinking or feeling about someone, something, their past and, what they have been through is typically one that is reflected in their behavior.

So, with that being said, when you want to see or get a clear picture or image of a person who is in a survivor-survival mind-set, look for someone who demonstrates a truculent or uncooperative conduct, behavior, and behavior patterns in a resentful or antagonistic manner. They are always on the edge, and they always have to take the lead and be in control. They are not willing to yield, submit, or surrender or allow themselves to be led; nor will they let their guards down even if what is presented before them and is being offered to them is good, positive, right, and beautiful. No matter what, a person who is in a survivor mind-set is always quick to demonstrate and deliver an expression of favor or disfavor toward a person, place, thing, matter, moment, memory, circumstance, situation, confrontation, conversation, communication, or event.

The reason is they still are being led to think, believe, and feel they are in an atmosphere and in an environment or in a position where they could be or will be faced with something that they need to be ready to be a survivor from. And they still think, believe, and feel they have to always be ready to demonstrate and deliver survival abilities and techniques. A person who has a survivor mind-set is also someone who also has a negative or hostile state of mind and mental position that can also be visualized in the way a person arranges the parts of a body or figure.

You can hear someone who is in a survivor-survival mind-set through the type of defensive, protective, and preventive conversations and communications he or she holds. The fear of being tormented, terrorized, troubled, and traumatized or being in a traumatic tragedy of some kind again is what is keeping you in a survivor mind-set. Everything that is said or done and everyone who approaches you and wants to get to know you, fear has you visualizing them as a threat of some kind and to some degree to you.

What's my point?

There are two points I need to and have to make for you to clearly understand how Satan uses and utilizes fear as a way to deliver his master deception of your mind-set so you will, without procrastinating, hesitating, and questioning, accept, adopt, adapt to, and apply a survivor mind-set and a survival mind-set quickly and immediately. Here are my points.

Point 1: Fear has drawn, driven, pulled, pushed, persuaded, tricked, seduced, deceived, and forced you into being settled into an established set of attitudes that manifests itself in becoming your established way of thinking or feeling about someone or something; that is being reflected in and through your truculent or uncooperative behavior and through your resentful or antagonistic manner. This kind and type of mind-set that you are demonstrating and you are deceived into thinking, feeling,

THE SURVIVORS MODE

and believing you always have to be ready to deliver out of and from is an object or practice that has continued to exist from an earlier time (from your past); that you still think, feel, and believe allows you to continue to live or exist, typically in spite of any kind and type of past, present, or future accident, ordeal, or difficult circumstances (survival) mind-set.

Point 2: You also have been drawn, driven, pulled, pushed, persuaded, tricked, seduced, deceived, and forced into a fixed mental attitude or disposition or an inclination or a habit that has already predetermined your responses and interpretations of any and all circumstances, situations, confrontations, matters, moments, and memories that *"seem, appear, look like, and feel like"* ones you have experienced and encountered before in your past; and you are "fearfully" influenced into thinking, feeling, and believing you have *no choice* but to be ready to cope well with what looks like and feels like and could be a difficult event in your life so you can survive and remain alive after others have died from such.

Survivor mentality

After you have been successfully linked to, connected to, and tied to a survivor mind-set and a survival mind-set, Satan then uses fear to force you over into a survivor mentality and into a survival mentality or into a survivor-survival mentality. Please understand that everything Satan is doing when it comes to the seduction of your mind is to seduce your mind, mental capabilities and abilities, thoughts, train of thought, thinking, and way of thinking away from faith, truth, and reality and from freedom and victory. And once he has done so, he will begin to lock in what he has done, making it hard, and for some harder, because Satan has launched a barrage of decoy distractions and deceptions.

Those decoy distractions and deceptions are sent for the purpose of gaining and getting your attention long enough to disconnect your focus so you will not see the truth concerning what has happened to you and what keeps happening to you. Satan wants to keep you being an active and willing participant in what keeps happening to you. Satan does not want you to engage in a "faith fight," but he wants you to stay involved in a "fear factor" when you are so spiritually, mentally, and emotionally incapacitated, dead, dry, and destitute that your feelings are "numb" and you are just going through the motions of being emotionless and lifeless. That is *not* God's perfect will for you and for your life. In fact, Jesus came to give you "life," and He came to also give you "life more abundantly" (John 10:10). You are supposed to living a prosperous, productive, successful, and abundant life in all or in at least some part or parts of your life; and if you are not, I can guarantee you are not in the right mind-set for things to change.

If you are in the wrong mind-set, then you will end up in the wrong mentality; and if you have the wrong mentality, it is because you are in the wrong mind-set about things. And if you are still in a survivor mind-set, a survival mind-set, and a survivor-survival mind-set, fear will forcefully transition you over into a survivor mentality and survival mentality that end up producing, preparing, and presenting you in a survivor-survival mentality. A person who is in a survivor-survival mentality is someone who is yoked, bound and limited to and because of, in bondage to, in a stronghold to, and is a slave to the characteristic attitude of their mind or way of thinking.

And they are deceptively led to think, feel, and believe the characteristic attitude of their mind or way of thinking they are entangled and entrapped in can and will help them cope well with the difficulties in their life so they can survive and remain alive after just in case an event in which others have died shows up again. Not only that, but they are also are being seduced into believing that by being in the characteristic attitude of mind or way of thinking they have settled in, they are able to be and remain constant, continuous, and consistent in the state or fact of continuing to live or exist, in spite of a past, present, or future accident, ordeal, or difficult circumstance.

A person who is in a survivor *mentality* is someone who actually believes he or she has been a person who survives and has remained alive after an event that has happened to him or her and he or she has suffered through in which others have died because of a natural or established process by which something takes place or is brought about (a mind-set) that they have used before and still utilize. What they don't know is Satan has used fear to draw, drive, pull, push, persuade, trick, trap, entice, entangle, entrap, force, and seduce them into that characteristic attitude of the of their mind and way of thinking through fearful suggestions and fearful influences. And whatever reactions and reactionary responses they demonstrate and deliver come out of and come about as a result of the mentality they have, especially if they think, feel, or believe they "might be" or could be faced with a circumstance, situation, confrontation, matter, moment, or memory, something said, done, or handled in a specific way or manner that "resembles" something they have seen and had experienced and encountered before that terrorized, tormented, tortured, and/or traumatized them.

Please keep in mind that those like yourself who are fearfully survivor-survival driven and motivated conduct themselves in the way they do because they are used to being in a troubling, terroristic, tormenting, torturing, and traumatizing environment and atmosphere that has been traumatic or tragic. So for them to be in and have a survivor mentality and be in and have a survival mentality is normal for them, and they use it as their tactical defensive mechanism or their tactical defense that is a natural or established process by which everything that has to do with them takes place or is brought about what they think, feel, and believe will allow and help keep them alive.

They also believe that by them being in a survivor-survival natural or established process by which everything that has to do with them takes place or is brought about, they will always become, be, and end up being someone who can and will have what it takes to cope well with difficulties in their life. With every mind-set you have, there will always be some kind of mentality that will mirror it or accompany it.

When you meet or know someone or you are a person who is in a *survival mentality,* you or that person is someone who demonstrates and even tells you he or she has an object or practice that has continued to exist from an earlier time that has grown, developed, and matured into the characteristic attitude of his or her mind or way of thinking. And their acts, actions, deeds, choices and decisions, behavior, conduct, and behavior patterns are used and utilized to help support and maintain their characteristic attitude of mind or way of thinking no matter what the consequences and collateral damage are and will end up being. They will sacrifice anything and anyone, even some part of or all parts of themselves and their dreams, hopes, desires, feelings, and emotions for the sake of protecting the mentality they have and preventing their mentality from being challenged, confronted, conquered, and changed.

The other way you know you have met people who, like yourself, are in a survival mentality is when you first meet them and they act like they are "hoarders" because they are so fearful and they never abandon functioning and flowing in and out of the state or fact of continuing to live or exist, typically in spite of, because of a traumatic, tragic, tormenting, torturing, terrorizing, or troubling accident, ordeal, or difficult circumstances that happened in their past that they are scared and afraid they will have to repeat.

Survivor-survival hoarder's mentality

And because they are constant, continual, and consistent in living in and out of and functioning in and out of the state or fact of continuing to live or exist, typically in spite of, because of a past or present or possible future traumatic, tragic, tormenting, torturing, terrorizing, or troubling accidents, ordeals, or difficult circumstances that have become the capacity for their intelligent thought.

When people have become survivor-survival "hoarders" or they have a survivor-survival "hoarder's" mentality that was conceived, birthed, and born in them when they were faced with traumatic, tragic, tormenting, torturing, terrorizing, or troubling matters, moments and memories, challenges, and changes, they ended up becoming someone who has a persistent difficulty and discarding or parting with "past" possessions because of a perceived need to save them. The reason is they are and have been tricked, seduced, enticed, entangled, and entrapped into holding on to something they used and utilized in their past that they feel they will need or might need or could use or should use in their present or future.

Not recognizing and realizing and understanding that what is used and utilized for something that you needed in that "moment" and at that "time" was made and given for that moment and time only, and it wasn't something or a solution that was meant to be used and utilized for everything and anything that "might" show up in your day or to be used and utilized for the rest of your life. The only thing that we can use at any time for anything and everything and it is never outdated or given for a specific moment or time are "faith solutions." There are "in the moment or at that moment" solutions that are given that apply only to what you are faced with "in that moment and at that moment" only.

Survivor-survival hoarders hold on to everything that is said or done, be that good or bad, right or wrong, happy or sad, and they stack them up in their mind, mental capabilities and abilities, thoughts, train of thought, thinking, and way of thinking, allowing fear to power them into becoming and being their survivor-survival mind-set and finally their survivor-survival mentality.

Satan wants you to always function, flow, and follow in and out of a survivor-survival "hoarder's" mentality, which means he wants to and he will use fear tactics and techniques as a way to draw, drive, pull, push, persuade, trick, entice, force, and seduce you into and lock you into a particular way of thinking or lock you into the characteristic attitude of mind (mentality) that brings about an instinctive lusting after and craving for, desiring, needing, and wanting what you have a persistent difficulty discarding or parting with "past possessions."

That can be things such as past thoughts, feelings, choices and decisions, ways of saying, doing, and handling things, and emotions, etc., that you still possess and hold on to because of a perceived need to save them (hoarder); for the sake of and for the sole purpose of ensuring you can and will still use and utilize them so you can continue to live or exist, typically in spite of, because of any and all past, present, or future traumatic, tragic, tormenting, torturing, terrorizing, or troubling accident, ordeal, or difficult circumstances (survival); and you will constantly, continuously, and consistently end up being someone who can and will survive and remain alive just in case a past circumstance, situation, confrontation, or event shows up in your present or future in which others have died (survivor).

Satan wants to make sure you are and will always continue to be a survivor-survival addicted person who has a survivor-survival hoarding mentality, and that survivor-survival hoarding mentality continues to be a fear-driven and motivated disorder that keeps you experiencing distress at the thought of out of "faith" getting rid of the past relationship items and past traumatic, tragic, tormenting, torturing, troubling, or terroristic experiences, encounters, methods, motives, motivations, memories, and moments. He wants to also make sure you keep an excessive fearful-driven hunger and desire for an accumulation of past and old survivor and survival characteristic attitude of mind or way of thinking (mentality), regardless of actual value that Satan can expose and exploit, use and utilize.

Manifested mentality

A survivor and a survival mentality is made manifest or it is clearly seen and revealed in the way people conduct themselves, in and through their behavior and behavior patterns, and in and through the choices and decisions they made. Their conversations and way of communication will also give you a hint to them being in a survivor and survival mentality. They are not open to receiving anything that can replace their old beliefs and belief system because Satan keeps suggesting that they need the past and the old to help them stay and be aware of the present and the new that "resembles," looks like, feels like, and even begins to unveil itself, unfold itself, and seemingly appear to unravel itself just like something from their past.

When you have this kind and type of survivor and survival mentality, Satan will constantly, continuously, and consistently draw, drive, push, pull, persuade, trick, entice, force, suggest to you, and influence you into what "resembles" reactions and reactionary responses that are survivor and survival triggered. Everything that has happened to you and is happening to you right now that keeps and has kept you in a survivor-survival mentality has been a chain-reaction-triggered

THE SURVIVORS MODE

event. Satan has you trapped in a survivor mentality and in a survival mentality, and that was his plan the first moment he seized, taken over, taken control over, took down, and then overpowered, overtook, and overthrew your minds and mental capabilities and abilities, power to retain and faith processes, procedures, and principles when needed and necessary.

Satan knows and knew how to and when to and where to initiate and implement using and utilizing fear tactics and fear techniques and fear tricks and traps as a way to maneuver you over into survivor and survival thoughts, train of thought, thinking, and way of thinking. The moment your thoughts, train of thought, thinking, and way of thinking were successfully masterfully maneuvered over into a survivor-survival state and condition, then his next move was to go after and pursue after your mind-set and mentality. Let me say it once again, you never saw any of this happening and occurring because Satan was using fear tactics, fear techniques, fear tricks and traps, fear deceptions, and fear delusions as a way to keep you distracted, detoured long enough so that he could detain and hold hostage your attention span and your focus.

He was not going to let you see what he was doing to you, what was happening to you, and let you see, know, or understand the place and point where he was forcing you to; he would not let you have a glimpse of or perceive the state and condition he was forcing you into. He had you busy being enticed, entangled, and entrapped in fear-driven and motivated survivor and survival fights.

He had a well-orchestrated, well-organized, and well-carried-out strategic plan, and the only thing left was to get your mind-set and mentality yoked to, bound and limited to, in a stronghold to, in bondage to, and a slave to survivor and survival arguments, theories, strategies, concepts, precepts, and reasoning that would appear to be "past" proud and lofty. He would use and utilize those same fear tactics, techniques, tricks, traps, wiles, trickeries, schemes, devices, deceptions, and delusions as a way to open you up to his fear-driven and motivated suggestions and influences.

And then he would seduce you into making hurried and unplanned and unprepared for choices and decisions because he has locked your mind-set and your mentality into an "always be ready" to demonstrate and deliver reactionary and reactionary response "urgency" releases that are derived from and "resemble" something that you have seen and been through and has happened to your perception and perspective. No proof of what is happening, what you "think" or feel is trying to happen or is trying to take place would be needed. You would then be forever be constantly, continuously, and consistently demonstrating and delivering what "resembles reactions and reactionary response releases."

Fear-driven mentality

Are you ready for what I'm about to tell you? Here it is. The only way Satan can get you into and keep you in a survivor mentality, survival mentality, and a survivor-survival mentality happens the moment when Satan has used a fear of what has happened to you and a fear of what can or might happen to you again as a way to get you over into a fearful mind-set. Once you are into a fearful mind-set, he will then put that same fear into your mentality. To do so, he has to influence you into "willingly," of your own free will, "let" or allow and give fear the freedom to dominate, manipulate, and control your mentality and then allow fear to dictate to your mentality.

The next move is to get you to "willingly" let and give fear the power, authority, and access to being in the driving force in your mentality by way of you letting fear be in the driver's seat of your mentality. To let that happen is a very dangerous, destructive, damaging, and costly move, choice, and decision. What will end up happening is fear will begin to treat your mentality just like it is a vehicle that it is driving. Fear will get you to run through life and relationship and choice and decision yield, approach with extreme caution, and stop at warning signs by applying fearful pressure to your mentality.

Just like a person who is driving a vehicle who runs past those same kinds of signs by putting pressure on the gas pedal and ending up in oncoming traffic, that is the same thing that happens when fear is in the driver's seat of your mentality; it is the driving force within your mentality. You will end up running directly into oncoming hazardous, damaging, destructive, dangerous, and deadly self-esteem, self-worth, self-image, self-confidence, and opinion of men traffic, where your self-esteem, self-worth, self-image, self-confidence, and opinion of men are bound to hit an unexpected, undetected, unseen, undeniable something, a bad, wrong, negative, and ugly circumstance(s), situation(s), confrontation(s), matter, or memory that ends up being so unforgettable because it caught you "off guard"; that it will end causing you and your self-esteem, self-worth, self-image, self-confidence, and opinion of men to struggle and strain to survive through trying to overcome the hit.

That unforeseen, unexpected, and nonanticipated hit will cause, create the atmosphere for, or contribute to you crashing, and you will end up being a relationship, self-esteem, self-worth, self-image, self-confidence, and an opinion "wreck." Satan is going to send and use and utilize every fear tactic, technique, trick, deception, delusion, illusion, etc., it can as a way to step on and apply pressure to the "gas pedal" in your mentality as long as he has control over it. Once in the driver's seat of your mentality, he will also have access to being in the "driver's seat" of your reflexes, reactions, responses, and reactionary responses.

This is how he can keep you linked to and into, connected to and into, tied to and into, and then you will be yoked to, bound and limited to, in a stronghold to, in bondage to, and a slave to a survivor mentality and a survival mentality, and that is how he is able to keep you fearfully scared and afraid to let go of your past and let go of what you were deceptively led to think, feel, and believe was past "savior and/or saving" conduct, conversations, communications, behavior, and behavior patterns. It all happens when fear is driving your mentality and fear is the motivator and the motivation for you mentality.

My conclusion to this matter

Just the thought of and the appearance of something that you have been through will trigger your survivor mentality, survival mentality, and survivor-survival mentality. PTSD, OCD, depression, self-esteem, self-worth, self-image, self-confidence, and opinion of men issue struggles and straining, migraines, phobias, addictions, sicknesses, infirmities, diseases, infections, afflictions, etc., and everything else Satan wants to plague, cripple, handicap, hinder, block, stifle, and stop you from moving forward with, he can easily do because he and his demon spirit called fear have gained control over your mind, mental capabilities and abilities, thoughts, train of thought, thinking, and way of thinking and, finally, your mind-set and mentality.

He can then dominate, manipulate, control, and dictate to every part of you and everything that goes into the making of you, who and what you are, and who and what you are wanting and trying to be, become, and end up being. He can also have access to dominating, manipulating, controlling, and dictating to your every expression, choices, and decisions, how you function, flow, and who and what you follow. He can at will easily bombard and beat up your feelings, emotions, desires, hopes, dreams, faith, self-esteem, self-worth, self-image, self-confidence, and opinion of men, etc., at will and build them in the way he wants to. My point is, when and as long as he has total control over your mind-set and mentality, he has total access to you. And when he has that, what you will end up becoming and end up being is his "puppet," and he will be the puppet master.

After his dominance and control methods are complete by way of using fear tactics, techniques, etc., fear will leave you two images of yourself, or it will leave you with two different character, personality, integrity, intellect, and conduct traits that you will grow, develop, and mature in, and they are the following:

1. A person in the state and condition where you can and will be someone copes well with difficulties in your life by using and utilizing an object or practice that has continued to exist from an earlier time that eventually seizes and consumes the capacity for your intelligent thought; thus causing and contributing to you having a survivor mentality, survival mentality, and being in a survivor-survival mentality.

2. A person who copes well with difficulties in their life by using and utilizing an object or practice that has continued to exist from an earlier time that is solely based on and sourced out

of a collection or supply of tainted and twisted, terrorizing, tormenting, terrorizing, troubling, traumatic, or tragic memories, instructions, images, insights, ideas, or information that you keep to yourself for future use that seizes and consumes the capacity for your intelligent thought; thus a survivor-survival "hoarder's" mentality.

Because your mind, frame of mind, state of mind, mental condition and conditioning, and mental state of being have been seized by fear and taken control by and taken over with and taken down by what is traumatic, troubling, and tragic, and your thoughts, train of thought, thinking, and way thinking have been overpowered, overtaken, and overthrew by what terrorizes, torments, tortures, and traumatizes.

The final effect is your life, love, living, and relationship information, instructions, and *conclusions* will end up being subjected to quickly, instantly, and automatically drawn and resourced out of a mind-set and mentality that is linked to, connected to, tied to being yoked to, in a stronghold to, bound and limited to, in bondage to, and a slave to what is traumatic, troubling, tragic, terrorizing, tormenting, and torturing.

CHAPTER SEVEN

Survivor Mode

F EAR HAS FINALLY gripped, taken control of, taken down, and taken over your mind, frame of mind, state of mind, mental condition and conditioning, and mental state of being. And fear has also seized, overpowered, overtaken, and overthrew your thoughts, train of thought, thinking, and way of thinking. In doing so, fear has gained access to your mind-set and your mentality, and both are constantly, continuously, and consistently being dominated, manipulated, controlled by deceptive and deceiving fear tactics, wiles, trickeries, schemes, strategies, devices, theories, arguments, reasoning, and logic. Both are also having fear-driven and motivated suggestive and influencing images, ideas, inspirations, insights, ingenuity, instructions, and information dictated into them by fear, which allows and keeps fear in the driver's seat of your mind-set and mentality.

With this being done successfully, the final thing Satan will do is to use and utilize fear in a way and in a manner that it can and will have enough strength, power, and authority to complete the final dominance of how your mind, mental capabilities and abilities, thoughts, train of thought, thinking, way of thinking, and mind-set and mentality will function and flow. Repetitious fear information processing will be used to draw, drive, pull, push, persuade, and force you over into a survivor mode and a survival mode, and then fear processes, procedures, and principles will be used to help grow, develop, and mature you in a survivor-survival mode.

All the fear processing, fear processes, fear procedures, and fear principles that are and were used and utilized by fear that you were enticed into, entangled in, and entrapped in were and they still are created, prepared, and presented each time you are and you were tricked and deceived into being in a tragic and traumatic state; and you were trapped into being in a troubling, tormenting, torturing, terrorizing, and traumatized condition. And each time you were a slave to thinking, believing, and feeling you were faced with and you were in a tragic, traumatic, troubling, tormenting, torturing, and terrorizing circumstance, situation, confrontation, and moment when you really weren't, but you, out of being scared and afraid, fearfully reacted and responded as if you were; that also is the moment and the times when fear processing and processors, fear practices, fear processes, fear procedures, and fear principles were grown, developed, and matured.

Those same repeated fear processing and processors, fear processes, fear procedures, fear principles, and fear practices, along with the dominance of your mind, mental capabilities and abilities, thoughts, train of thought, thinking, way of thinking, and with fear being in the driver's seat of your mind-set and mentality, and your hoarder's mentality, all of them would end up overwhelmingly linked to, connected to, and tied to a survivor-survival state and condition. Once that has taken place, that would be what's needed to draw, drive, pull, push, persuade, force, entangle, and entrap you into a survivor mode, survival mode, and survivor-survival mode. What exactly is a survivor mode and a survival mode, and how do they work together to be a powerful force that can transition you over into a survivor-survival mode?

> A *survivor* mode can be described as a way or manner in which something that a person is conducting themselves, doing things, and handling matters occurs or is experienced, expressed, or done that helps them survive and remain alive after an event in which others have died.

> A *survival mode* can be described as the way or manner in which something that has happened to a person has occurred or occurs or has been and is experienced, has been or is expressed, or has been and is done that forces a person to stay in a constant, continuous, and consistent state or fact of continuing to live or exist, typically in spite of an accident, ordeal, or difficult

circumstance that can be or could be or is traumatic, troubling, tormenting, torturing, and tragic.

When those two powerful modes join forces with the help of fear, the final results will end up you being transitioned over into a person who copes well with difficulties in your life because of an object or practice that you have used and utilized that has continued to exist from an earlier time that you have made the way or manner in which everything that challenges you occurs or is experienced, expressed, or done.

For you to survive and become, be, and end up being and remain a person who copes well with difficulties in your life and can remain alive after an event in which others have died, you have held on to a past and old object or practice that has continued to exist from an earlier time. And that past and old object or practice you keep remembering, reliving, restoring, reviving, and releasing has become your immediate and automatic manner, way, method, system, approach, technique, procedure, process, and practice you use when every time "fear" drives and draws you into thinking, feeling, believing, sensing, and perceiving something that "is," feels like, or "resembles" what could be and would be traumatic, tragic, tormenting, torturing, and terrorizing.

Let me paint the picture

"A way or manner in which something occurs
or is experienced, expressed, or done."

Life was supposed to be so simple and so easy; after all, you were just a little girl with big hopes, dreams, and desires. Your world was simple and easy, and the things that had to do with you were also simple and easy. Everything you had said and done and the choices and the decisions you made came out of your innocence. There was no people pressure, and there was no peer pressure; there was only you doing your best to find your place, find your way, and trying to find the place where you fit in. And like most little girls, you had your best friend and her name was "diary," and everything you thought and felt, wished for, prayed for, and was willing to wait for she knew because you took the time out of your day and life to let her know.

You knew that your secrets were safe with her; after all, she had been your best friend since "forever." The other people who were your friends understood and accepted "diary" as your best friend because they, too, had a best friend whose name was "diary." Everyday life for you was different from most of your friends on some days yet the same as theirs on most days. Sure, there were some unusual things that would take place but nothing that really caused you to be alarmed or scared and afraid. Family time was the best time, and you have a lot of fond memories of the way things were and the way things used to be. One thing you knew, and that was you were loved and cared for by your parents and family, because they took the time to tell you and show you. Sometimes, it looked like and felt like and you even thought things were not fair when it came to you, but for the most part, things were good and life for you was good. After all, you had a roof over your head and food to eat, clothes to wear, and you felt safe, stable, secure, and protected. Life and living as a little girl and in your home was so simple and so easy because you had people who really loved you and they helped made it simple and easy for you.

I know you remember "when"! Just go back to the way it was for just a moment. Sometimes, it was hard growing up alone even though there people all around you, in your life, in your day, and in your world; and yet still the aloneness and the occasional loneliness would try to show up. For the most part, you were happy and you had fun and you did your best to fit in. One thing was for sure: you had every opportunity to just "be." Everybody just knew how to just let you "be," and those were the most memorable days. And what about those summer times when school was out and you looked forward to feeling free and being free? And then there were those family reunions and those holiday gatherings at grandma's where the house would be filled with the aroma of your favorite foods.

What about the laughter that would fill the house and there would be people coming by and bringing food and gifts and you would have so many people to talk to and play with and hang out with? It was so easy doing those things. You never really knew what you did or didn't have because of the people that you still hold dear to your heart who held you close to them and they kept you encouraged and moving forward and kept you focused so you couldn't, wouldn't, and really didn't see what you did or didn't have and what you needed and wanted. Could we go back to the way it was?

A time of innocence and love

Things in your childhood may or may not have been the way we wanted it to be, and there were things that happened that you really didn't care for, but at least you had hope for a better day. That was so important back then—that you had "hope." You could get into your own world and wish upon a star and dream the dreams of the impossible dreamer. You could believe that life would take you afar as you wished upon that shining star you would see in the night and in your heart and dreams. You could at least "see" what it was that you could be and your love and life vision wasn't impaired and you had a heart song. And you believed in believing, had confidence in "being confident," and had faith in your "faith, all because it was instilled into your innocence.

You could trust in truth and you had a good concept and a good understanding when it came to what was real and what was reality, and that was because your world was so simple and your days were so easy. It was your innocence that made everything that you thought, felt, believed, hoped for, prayed for, anticipated, and expected simple and easy. Your love and your ability to give love and receive love were simple, easy, and innocent, and your heart was innocently open, innocently simple, and innocently easy. Somehow, you knew your happiness was waiting for you out in that big old world somewhere.

Out of your innocence, you could search your heart and find what it was you were looking for, and you could search for whatever it was you thought, felt, and believed belonged to you in. Back then, your mind was fresh and clear, and it wasn't cloudy with the complexities of the life you now live. You lived in a child's world, and out of your childlike innocence, you thought, felt, believed, and knew the people in your life respected your innocence and supported you with their love. Out of your innocence, you felt like you could actually walk among the stars at night and, at any given moment, you could take flight and go to that secret place where you would meet time and step into what you felt would be your eternity.

But it ain't like that anymore

And it happened, the unseen, the unexpected, the undetected, the unheard of, the unthinkable, the unbelievable, and the unforgettable, and your innocence is no longer "innocent" and your love is no longer an innocent love. No matter how hard you try, you just can't and won't be able to go back to the way it was. Some days you have a hard time remembering, reviving, restoring, and reliving those days and times when your life was so simple, when you could easily arrive at your did or your didn't and your would and you wouldn't. The reason, according to you, is "life" happened, and every time life happens, you end up at a place in your thoughts, train of thought, thinking, and way of thinking called "but it ain't like that anymore."

Every time you end up in that place and at that point, it turns out to be a destitute and desolate place and point. Most of the time, you still struggle and strain when you try to remember when life was so easy and you had people in your childhood, in your life, and in your world who said what they meant; you knew they were either for it and you or against. And the people that have been in your life and are still in your life are people that you weren't and you still are not sure what they meant and where they stood and stand. Your life suddenly and immediately, without any advanced warning, turned into a "but it ain't like that anymore" life.

When we could clearly see the way

They never prepared you for the days when you would not be able to clearly see the way I mean, see your way. The first man in your life, your father, and not your first "time" man was supposed to be the one to make sure you were prepared for the moment when the wrong men would try to come into your life, and he was supposed to make sure you knew how to recognize them and what to do so they would not take something from you that you now need. He was also supposed to prepare you for the good men that would come into your life, and when he showed up, you would realize it and you could and would be able to receive what he would give you that would remove and take away any possibility of you one day "needing" something that would be in your today that's "missing."

Because you can't clearly see your way now, for you to decide and determine whether it is up to you to choose whether to win or lose is cloudy and cluttered with circumstances and complications and complexities that are most of the time clearly complicated. What I'm talking about are those times when it was up to you to see and to know what it was you were to be and you wanted to be, but all that got lost in the times and the moments when you found yourself trapped in struggling, straining, and trying to survive. Somehow, while you were growing into your childhood, developing in your teenhood, and maturing in your adulthood, you got caught up in the mix of complexity, and the moment when you did it happened, he happened and they happened.

You find yourself crying out and asking God in your own way and with your own words, "How did I end up getting captivated by complicated, complex complexities and allowed myself to get caught up in them?" Your mind, your mental capabilities and abilities, thoughts, train of thought, thinking, and way of thinking, and, yes, your mind-set and mentality all captivated and caught up in the mix of complicated, complex complexities that are often consuming. It all happens now so much so that you cry and beg for the opportunity to remember when life was so simple.

THE SURVIVORS MODE

The "I remember whens"

It all has happened, and you struggle, strain, and still can't find the way and the path that leads back to your "I remember whens." The only thing you can do now is find your way into the "I can still remember" the moment, the year, the month, the day, the hour, the minute, the second when it happened, and how it happened. You, still being naïve and innocent, was seduced and then enticed and then entangled and finally entrapped and then removed and replaced, and that is the only "I remember when" you have, and it still has a hold on you. That revisited memory and that relived moment has its own "way or manner in which they occur and is experienced, expressed, or done," and when it does, you end up feeling like you are and your were a "victim" of it more so than you would feel like you were a victim to what happened to you.

You were there and it happened and it happened to you, and what you were left with and what you still have to do and maybe what you often think, feel, and believe is you will, for the rest of your life, have to always have a way or a method to use that can quickly, immediately, and suddenly link, connect, and tie you over into a survivor of the "way or manner in which those revisited and relived occurs or is experienced, expressed, or done." You don't want to remember how to revisit and relive because every time you find yourself doing so, your "I remember whens" get further and further away from helping you find your way back home. That home is the place where your truth and your innocence are housed and they both prevail, and when you are able to come home, you will finally be able to walk into that moment when your parent or parents were your light and through them you saw what was right.

You will find your way back home to the things they had said and done and tutored, trained, and taught you that were so full of truth they had to power and the potential to protect your innocence. And now, years later, and circumstances, situations and confrontations later, while you are in your hurt, in your pain, and in your brokenness and faced with what you are fighting with, a path sometimes opens up and it leads to something that your parent or parents said that was right. And just for a moment, that moment, the one you are now in, you can clearly and finally understand now how through them, you not only saw what was right but also saw the light.

I ain't like that anymore

What do you remember? What can you remember? Maybe going to sleep in a child's world and waking up in an adult's world and one moment making an innocent little girl's choices and decisions and then forced into making adults; not really getting a chance to change but being faced with a whole lot of changes. One moment feeling safe, stable, and secure and then not, and being the one who had to take care of everyone else even though you didn't want to, and what about you not having your own life and being able to live your own life as a result? And let's not talk about those unplanned and unwanted sacrifices you had to make, the private ones, personal ones, and even the public ones for the sake of others because of others and the ones made just so you could survive. The night after and the day after and the moment after feeling abandoned, rejected, insignificant, unimportant, and a lot of other bad, wrong, negative, hurtful, and harsh feelings. And what about being so emotionally driven and drained until you feel emotionally destitute and deserted and finally emotionally broken?

You know, it's really funny what you can and you can't, you won't and will, do and don't remember, and what remembers you. No matter how hard you try to get away from remembering, what you try not to remember keeps finding you and "remembering" what you don't want to remember. How can we turn off what "remembering" always remembers? How do you get away from something that you remember to get away from, run away from, and hide from when it keeps pursuing you, catching up with you, and pressuring you into remembering again and again and all over again? What do you do when your remembering is trapped into being a trigger and what is restored, revived, relived, and what is released is triggered?

And how about waking up and not knowing your mind, mental capabilities and abilities, thoughts, train of thought, thinking, and way of thinking are trapped into a mind-set and mentality trigger and not knowing that all it takes for there to be an "I ain't like that anymore" triggered reaction and reactionary response explosion and eruption is for "remembering" to catch up with and to connect with and to your attitude, mood, and mode? You were once a cool, calm, and collected person, and everything that has challenged you have changed you into that "I ain't like that anymore" person that you have become and you can be and you end up being. It's the violence and the being violated and the abuse and being abandoned, and it is the brokenness, loneliness, and the emptiness that send an invitation to your "remembering" enticing and seducing it to remember.

But I ain't like that anymore

The funny thing about remembering, reviving, restoring, and reliving is you can't and won't be able to release and you end up repeating the same memories and moments and even matters that your "remembering" just refuse and reject and resist letting go of. "But I ain't like that anymore"; that's what *you* say, but is that what your "remembering" says? Do you really know what's locked deep down on the inside of your "remembering," and do you really know what is lying dormant in your "remembering"? And why is it that you can't seem to let go of the very things and moments and memories and matters that your "remembering" and your power to remember and your power of thought seem to hold on to and won't let you let go of?

I know and I heard you, and I hear you when you say, "But I ain't like that anymore." OK, all right, I hear what you are saying, but is your "remembering" recording what you are saying; and if so, when will your remembering deliver and demonstrate the right "remembering" response? Could it be that your "but I ain't like that anymore" is linked to, connected to, and tied to "a way or manner in which it occurs or is experienced, expressed, or done" of its own? And could it be that your "remembering" is yoked to, bound and limited to, in bondage to, in a stronghold to, and a slave to "a way or manner in which it unfolds and occurs or is experienced, expressed, or done" and you just don't know it? And just maybe when you say you have "moved on" past what happened to you and what you have been through has its very own "way or manner in which it unveils, unfolds, and occurs or is experienced, expressed, or done" (mode) that instantly, automatically, suddenly, and quickly, without you even recognizing, realizing, and knowing it, draws, drives, pulls, pushes, persuades, forces, entangles, and entraps you over into a "remembered" trigger. You call this occurrence when you are talking to someone "something that they said or something that alarmed you."

The truth is there is something that is trapped in your "I have moved on past what I have been through and what happened to me and I'm not that person anymore" that has its own hidden "trigger," and all it takes are certain specific words, messages, images, ideas, inspirations, insights, ingenuity, information, instructions, and creative processes and procedures, etc., spoken, received, or demonstrated in a certain and specific manner or way that quickly and immediately put into motion and put into effect; a fearful tainted and distorted "way or manner in which they occur or are experienced, expressed, or done" (mode).

It has nothing to do with what the person had said, done, or demonstrated, or how they went about doing so; it has to do with your still "residue" touched and tainted with fear "triggered remembering" doing the receiving and the processing and then delivering a fearful interpretation and understanding of it all. Every time those vicious cycle "a way or manner in which something remembered occurs or is experienced, expressed, or done" (mode) manifests itself, you will not be able to remember when life was so easy.

Do you remember?

Do you remember when little boys grew into men and little girls like yourself grew up into women? That was not something we questioned or wrestled with. And do you remember growing up feeling you were different and not knowing why and not having anyone in your life that could help you understand why you were different? Everyday life and living for you who was just a little girl brought about some self-esteem, self-image, self-worth, and self-confidence struggling and straining. And you lived your life in fear being tormented, tortured, and traumatized by feelings that you didn't understand. When that wasn't happening, you were being constantly, continuously, and consistently terrorized by the thought that something was wrong with you.

For a little girl, those were confusing, traumatic, and tragic thoughts, feelings, and emotions to have, and the moments you had with those confusing feelings and the memories you had of how they drove you into an emotional quiet storm made and led you into being an emotional wreck. Satan was in hot pursuit of you during those times, and by you having those fearful feelings that were fear driven and motivated, Satan would expose and exploit and use against you. He then played and preyed on your self-doubt, self-rejection, identity questions and crisis, and confused feelings and mixed-up emotions, and he would then "set you up for failure."

You were conceived, birthed, and born into this world the way God wanted you to be, and there were no mistakes, and you were not a mistake because you didn't have the right relationship with the first man in your life, your father, or it was twisted and tainted, or he forced you into the image of what he wanted you to be and become and end up being. Fear seized and took advantage of those moments and times, and he took advantage of how you felt when he was doing that to you, and fear took advantage of you wanting to be accepted for who you were and be loved and needed and wanted, and he tricked, seduced and enticed you into challenging your creation. And you know what happened next . . . right?

You were either pushed too far or you were not pushed at all, or you were pushed in the right way to the right point and in the right direction that you should have, and you were either protected or left in harm's way. It really doesn't matter which happened; Satan used fear as a way to take advantage of the moment, and not only did fear expose and exploit what was happening on the inside of you but he also exposed what your were lacking and missing and what you were needing, wanting, craving, and lusting after, which was pure, innocent, unconditional, and untainted love to someone who had the wrong spirit upon them.

And Satan used those people. . . you know who they were, and they got you to open up to them, trust them, and when up of your "own free will" opened up to that person, they said what you wanted to hear or what you believed, thought, and felt you wanted and needed to hear. After doing so, it was easy for fear to trick your feelings and then trap your emotions and take advantage of you and them. What Satan and fear was using to confuse you, feelings, etc., the people who said they loved you and was supposed to protect you should have tutored, trained, and taught you how to challenge, confront, conquer, and change.

Because they didn't take the time to do that and no one took the time to talk to you, listen to you, hear you, and help you and no one took the time to explain what was happening with you to, fear stepped in and exploited what wasn't explained. Can you remember when you knew where you belonged, and do you remember when it was "childlike" clear what was right and what was wrong? Life for you ain't like that anymore because your life has become so fearfully advanced in ways you that you never would have imagined. And you sit in your aloneness and you see out of your loneliness and you speak out of your emptiness and you sense things out of what you have been through. The worst part is you still feel lonely and alone even when you are in a room full of people.

Need a simple yes or no

Complicated complexities and complicated conversations and communications now keep you sometimes emotionless and expressionless. Sometimes, you feel so numb that for you to "survive" in a relationship and feel again when you are in a relationship, you just need a simple yes or no from that person because of your childhood complexities. They show up on their own, and they overpower, overtake, and overthrow everything that can help you think, feel, and believe and know you are relationship sound, stable, safe, and secure. Back then, it was so easy for you to give a simple yes or no, but now that you ain't the same and what happened to you wasn't innocent, you now have insecurities that keep you in a should-I-stay-or-should-I-go "way or manner in which should I go or should I stay occurs or is experienced, expressed, or done" (mode).

Sometimes you wish you had a second chance, and if God would give you that second chance, you would go back to that life-changing and childhood-changing choice and decision crossroad that you, not by choice, came to but because of circumstances, situations, confrontations, challenges, and changes that you got caught up in; and once you were back at that childhood to adulthood changing moment, I know you would take the time to see what was bad and what was good. You would not have allowed you innocence to be taken and taken advantage of, and you would not have allowed your trusting heart and your trusting ways to be taken for granted.

You would have prevented the people who said they would protect you from doing so, and you also would have spent more time hanging out with your yea and your nay and befriending them and following them and you would have never said, thought, and felt like you "might" and you never would have said "maybe." And there would have been no compromising childhood complexities dominating, manipulating, and controlling and taking over, taking control of, and taking down your adulthood growth, development, and maturity.

Now, you are here and you are no longer where it all went down and where you went down, and what you are scared and afraid of the most and what you are fearful of is that you still will not be able to say yea or nay, and once again you would find yourself back at that same old familiar place called "I remember when"! Everything that happened to you had its own "a way or manner in which something occurs or is experienced, expressed, or done," and you had to find a way to survive and be a survivor of those moments and times.

CHAPTER EIGHT

The Survivor-Survival Journey

Led into the survivor-survival mode

IT'S OVER AND it happened to you, and what you were forced to deal with, go through, and suffer through was something that was bad, wrong, negative, and ugly, and it left you with a lot of discouragement, frustration, disappointment, hurt, pain, and brokenness and a lot of other thoughts and feelings that you never would have imagined you would ever think or feel. It was all unexpected, unbelievable, and unforgettable, and it was so traumatic and tragic and troubling that it has left you with terrorizing, tormenting, torturing, and traumatizing feelings and emotions. And without you knowing it and without you being able to recognize it and realize what is happening to you, fear has quickly and easily drawn, driven, pulled, pushed, persuaded, forced, and trapped into a survivor mode.

Fear never gave you an opportunity to figure out and analyze what was happening to you, and you were not given an opportunity to fight back. What you never knew was fear had been pursuing after you just like you were a wanted fugitive. For the rest of your life, fear would make sure you were and you would always be constantly, continuously, and consistently in a mind-set, mentality, and mode where you would overwhelmingly feel, think, and believe you would have to make some kind of relationship compromise just so that you could and would be able to be a "surviving-survivor" in a love, life, living, and relationship.

Every time fear could and would be able seduce, entice, draw, and drive you to a place and point where it "seemed like and looked like" and it even felt like you would come to the edge of love, living, life, and relationship thoughts, train of thought, thinking, and way of thinking and fear gave the deceptive illusion that you were looking at the end of them, it was all done to make sure you couldn't and wouldn't see the path to a new beginning for all of them. Fear would then pull, push, and persuade you into the attitude and mood where you felt you had to brace yourself for the struggling and straining and the falling and failing process that being fearful, scared, and afraid had you deceptively sensing and perceiving.

And in doing so, you would keep allowing yourself to be forced into a survival mode. You would then begin to function and flow out of that mode, and you would begin to align yourself up with and follow the survival mode patterns, patterns of behavior, conduct, thinking, way of thinking, thoughts, and train of thought. Fear will then pressure you into using and utilizing and speaking out of and from a survival mode conversation and communication dialogue. That kind and type of constant, continuous, and consistent dialogue will eventually produce, prepare, and present a survival mode mind-set, and you will end up getting all the way over into a survivor-survival mind-set and survivor-survival mode.

Survivor and survival mode feelings, emotions, and desires will show up and dictate to, dominate, manipulate, and control your reactions, responses, and reactionary responses. You will begin to process any and all life, love, living, and relationship matters, issues, and problems out of a survival mode state of mind, frame of mind, mental state of being, survival mode mental condition, and survival mode mentality. My point in telling you all this is any and every love, life, living, relationship, and self-insecurities and instabilities you have came about because

- you didn't have a father-daughter relationship;
- you didn't have the right kind of father-daughter relationship, and it wasn't good, right, or positive;
- you had a relationship, but it was too extreme to the point where you expected a man to be just like and a carbon copy of your father and the way he handled you and things that had to do with you, which means you were "spoiled" and you were used to getting what you wanted;

- what you were faced with and had to go through was something traumatic, troubling, or tragic; or
- you were terrorized, tormented, tortured, or traumatized.

It doesn't matter which one(s); either way, fear had a field day with your insecurities and instabilities, and fear would expose and exploit them and take advantage of you being scared and being afraid and force you into an overwhelming sudden and quick protective and preventive survivor-survival mode.

Fear has been dominating, manipulating, and controlling your character, conduct, personality, integrity, and intellect and dictating all kinds fearful information and instructions into your thoughts, train of thought, thinking, and way of thinking, making it hard for you to decide and determine and make decisions. Fear will keep forcing you into coming face-to-face with circumstances, situations, confrontations, challenges, and changes that would bring about you being led into you being enticed, seduced, tricked, trapped, entangled, and entrapped in a survival mode. Satan wants to keep you trapped, entangled, and entrapped into struggling and straining and falling and failing, and he wants to keep you in a survivor-survival mode.

Growing, developing, and maturing in the mode

Here's what you need to know when it comes to where fear of what has happened to you in the past and you being scared and afraid that what you have been through and what has happened to you happening again has finally driven you. Every time you are pulled, pushed, persuaded, driven, drawn, and forced into a survivor-survival mode, the *first place* you will find yourself is in the attitude, mood, mind-set, mentality, and in the state or condition where the only way you can and will allow yourself to live or dwell or abide and "be"; and the only place, state, condition, and process you can and will allow yourself to function and flow in and out is of that of a person who can cope well and survive, especially remaining alive after a traumatic, tragic, troubling, terrorizing, tormenting, and torturing difficulties or events

THE SURVIVORS MODE

in your life in which others have died. This is your *growth* process into the state or condition or how you grew into it.

The *second place* you will find yourself is in a state or fact of continuing to live or just exist, typically in spite of any past, present, or future "what seems like, looks like, and feels like" is or could and would become and be and end up being a possible traumatic, troubling, tragic, or terrorizing, tormenting, or torturing accident, ordeal, or difficult circumstances, situations, confrontations, or matters of the heart. That state or fact of continuing to live or just exist that you are in and how you will go about doing so came out of an object or practice that has continued to exist from an earlier time or from the initial moment and time when you first experienced and encountered something that was unexpectedly and unforgettably traumatic, troubling, tragic, or terrorizing, tormenting, or torturing. This is how you *developed* into the "I have to continue to live or exist" state or condition you are in and how you developed into the procedure, which makes it easy for you to get over into the "I have to survive and remain alive," which, in all actuality and reality, is a "just in case" state, condition, and procedure.

That *third* place you will find yourself is in the state and condition where you cannot and will not have the power and the authority you need to reject, resist, refuse, rebuke, and refute being in a (1) "cope well and remain alive," (2) "object or practice of continuing to live or just exist," and (3) "just in case" state and condition. And the fear of it all happening again and you being so scared and afraid that you once again will end up in that same old past place, state, and condition again has driven and locked you into a place where all three states and conditions would overwhelm you and overwhelming becomes a normal way or manner in which your acts, actions, deeds, the way you handle things, along with your behavior, conduct, and behavior patterns occur and would be experienced, expressed, or done. This is how you *matured* into the state and condition you are in.

Fear seized and gripped and exposed and exploited your already existent past fearful thoughts, feelings, and emotions and has used them or is still using them to scare you into being afraid that the same way and the same manner in which everything in your life that has been or once was or still is traumatic, tragic, troubling, terrorizing, tormenting, and torturing that was experienced, expressed, or done; it will happen to you again. And fear has forcefully scared you into thinking, believing, feeling, and even being afraid you will once again be hindered and hurt, in pain, brokenness, filled with frustration, disappointment, and discouragement, etc.

The *final* place you will find yourself in will be linked to, connected to, tied to, yoked to, bound and limited to, in bondage to, a slave to, and in a fully grown, developed, and matured survivor-survival mind-set, mentality, and mode, state, and condition stronghold.

The journey

Once fear has you locked into a survivor-survival mode, you will become someone who is fearfully led to think, feel, and believe you are still in harm's way and you are still in the harmful atmosphere and environment, circumstance, situation, and confrontation, and the place you were once in, even when you are not and you may even be years away from what you went through. When you are still in a survivor-survival mode, fear will keep you in a mind-set and in a mentality where you feel the need to

- ➤ analyze everything and everyone and analyze everything that is said or done or handled,
- ➤ be in a "I need to plan and be prepared just in case . . ." mind-set,
- ➤ be in a "I need to know what's going to happen and what to expect" before you allow yourself to open up and get and be involved,
- ➤ dictate what happens, and
- ➤ have some sense of control and be in control.

Fear will suggest you not to trust anyone, and fear wants to influence you into an "I need to know and I need to see what's happening to me and what they are saying or praying over me" mentality. For Satan to keep dominating, manipulating, controlling, and deceiving you, he will

THE SURVIVORS MODE   103

led you to what he wants you to be delivered from, and he will sacrifice some of its imps sprits to make you think, feel, and believe you got something that you really didn't get and/or you go something that you didn't get the totality of.

A fear-driven survival mode says don't yield, submit, and surrender to the Holy Spirit and don't let yourself be "slain" in the spirit because you need to see what's being said and done to you. Fear is able to drive, push, pull, and force you out of totally yielding, submitting, and surrendering to the power of God so that you will receive the fullness of God's delivering, cleansing, purging, healing, and made-whole power, bringing about you being "slain" in the spirit.

Fear is able to do so by getting your fearful feelings and fear-filled thoughts, train of thought, thinking, and way of thinking to reference and bring back to your remembrance a time when you were lying on the floor, bed, etc., and you were rendered badly hurt, in a unconscious state and condition, or in a coma at the hands of your abuser, and your abuser has done some other terrible things to you while you were in that state and condition. You were not able to see what was being done to you while you were at the mercy of your abuser, and you were not able to defend yourself. Afterward, you vowed and promised yourself you will never allow or let yourself get caught in that vulnerable state and condition, and you will not allow yourself to show any weakness and vulnerability.

Not only does fear not want you to totally yield, submit, and surrender to the Holy spirit of God but fear also does not want you to walk by faith. Because you are locked into a survivor mind-set, mentality, and mode, you will always be led and locked into thinking, feeling, and believing you will still need the same security blanket of some kind or type you had and held on to, a crutch of some kind for you to lean on (excuses, explanations, etc.), the same something you had used before or the same place or person you ran to when you were going through that helped you to get through and make it through what you were going through. Whatever it was that you used and utilized and wherever that place was that you ran to, you still have a sentimental attachment to that something or someone or place.

Being fearful, scared, and afraid keeps your survival urges, tendencies, inclinations, intuitions, impulses, impulsiveness, and instincts on high alert so you can "handle things," and fear basically keeps those survival urges, tendencies, inclinations, intuitions, impulses, and instincts speaking to you and saying, "You know what to do. You have been here before. Just do it." When you are in a survivor-survival mode, everything is based on what "appears and seems to be like, looks like, and feels like," etc., even though, in all actuality, what is being seen or perceived is not as it seems. And out of that fearful deceptive sight and perception, your survivor-survival urges, tendencies, inclinations, intuitions, impulses, impulsiveness, and instincts will say to your survivor-survival reactions, responses, and reactionary responses, "No delay, ignore the yield sign and the stop signs, and handle it," because it might turn out to be . . . "Better safe than sorry."

Fear will keep bringing to your remembrance references from something that was bad, wrong, negative, ugly, etc., that was from your past and pull them into your present for the purpose of you using what has been remembered and referenced as the solution to a present-day matter, moment, memory, etc. What has been referenced and remembered has absolutely nothing to do with the circumstances surrounding the present, and fear is using it as a fear tactic and as a weapon formed against you having confidence in faith and you trusting and totally relying on faith.

Fear voice disguised as confidence

Your survival thoughts, train of thought, thinking, and way of thinking will keep you locked into analyzing things that are said, done, or handled first; and then you will get into creating, building, establishing, causing, creating the atmosphere for and contributing to there being a "backup plan" just in case you are not in control, you lose control, and things are not going the way you want them to; all of which are derived from your need to survive. Your deceived fear-driven survival thoughts, train of thought, thinking, and way of thinking will keep you locked into the mental state of being, mind-set, and mentality

THE SURVIVORS MODE   105

where they will not allow you to get to the point and place when there is an argument or disagreement you will need and want them to go away.

Instead, fear will draw, drive, pull, push, persuade, and force you into a false sense of confidence, and when that happens, you will be locked into a "don't let it go, prove your point, you have facts and you have proof, and no matter what the repercussion and consequences are, you can and will make it through them just like you did before" mind-set and mentality. Being in a survivor mind-set, mentality, and mode and being in a survival mind-set, mentality, and mode will also keep you in a "you can make it through whatever they say and do to you because you are strong and you never show weakness; don't let them break you even though you are being and will end up being battered, bruised, and beaten" mind-set and mentality.

While you are in your survivor mode and your survival mode, you will hear fear disguising its voice as the voice of confidence saying, "You don't have to leave and you shouldn't have to leave. You didn't do anything wrong. That person needs to leave, so you just stay and wait it out/them out. You ain't no punk! Don't let him/them intimidate you and get away with badgering and bullying you. You can handle it. You made it this far through what they had said and done to you, and you will continue to make it through. Don't give up and don't give in." The other thing fear will do when it gives you a false sense of confidence or when fear disguises its voice as the voice of confidence, it will speak to your survival urges, and they will nudge, push, force, seduce, or trick you into feeling and thinking you need to tell him/them what they "need to do and should do" even if they do not like it.

And when you do your survivor and survival thoughts, train of thought, thinking, and way of thinking, your survivor and survival mind-set, mentality, and mode will deceive you by "pretending they can protect you" and they will have you believing and thinking you will make it through their bad, wrong, and negative response, reaction, or reactionary responses. You will sense and even hear fear disguise its suggesting and influencing into a voice of confidence when you hear, "It won't be the first time and the last time they demonstrated their disagreement with what you had to say, and you made it through their retribution and retaliation." When fear disguises itself as confidence, it will get you to the point and place where you are so scared and afraid that it can seduce and entice you into saying and doing things and handling matters in a way that ends up putting you in harm's way. Satan can portray what it suggests to you and what it tries to influence you into doing as a "voice of reason," and the logic that is used and utilized will be based on what you have already survived through at the hands of your abuser.

Survival conversations and communications

Just imagine for a moment your survival mode having a voice and what it would be doing is having conversations and communications with your survival urges, tendencies, inclinations, intuitions, impulses, impulsiveness, and instincts. And whatever it is that your survival mode instructs your fear-tortured, tormented, terrorized, troubled, and traumatized survival urges, tendencies, intuitions, inclinations, impulses, and instincts to do, to react to, and to deliver a reactionary response to, that is what they will do. Here are some of the conversations and communications that would be sent:

Your survival mode sends messages, information, and instructions to and into your mind-set, mentality, and mental state of being, suggesting and influencing them into getting you to block out, hear what you want to hear, or totally ignore what the person you are talking to is saying, and then seizing the conversation that you are having with someone, your abuser. It is then being suggested that you be influence into interrupting the conversation by you using "and, or, but, and maybe" when your abuser or a person is talking to you.

The reason for doing so is for the purpose of you being able to be in control of the conversation and being in control of what is being said, done, and handled; and so you can stay in control and you will know where the person you are talking to is going with what they are saying or where they are trying to go in what they are saying and doing and in how they are handling things.

THE SURVIVORS MODE

That same survival mode will also send sensory messages, information, and instructions into your mind-set, mentality, and mental state of being that is so fearfully overwhelming that you get the sudden and immediate urged tendency, urged inclination, urged intuition, urged impulse, and urged instinct to react and overpower, overtake and overthrow the conversation, and then takeover, take control of that same overpowered, overtaken, and overthrown conversation, and lead it along with any other type of communication. Your fear disguised as "confidence" says to you in doing so, you will not be caught off guard and you will not be "hit" with something that you didn't see coming; because that is exactly what has happened to you in the past.

The first time and the last time you were in a conversation, you were just trying to say what you had to say and you were just trying to prove your point and you didn't see him hitting, beating, and abusing you all because you said something, had done something, or handled something that the person you were talking to didn't like or want to hear. Your survival mode, mind-set, mentality, and survival instincts are talking to you, and they are saying, "Don't get caught off guard, unaware, unprepared, and don't get caught slipping again."

Your survival mind, frame of mind, mental condition and conditioning, and state of mind, if they had a voice, would say, "You have to make it through this. Find a way, lie, cheat, steal, deceive, trick, seduce, go along with, entice, entangle, and entrap. 'Play' and never become, be, and end up being a 'prey.'" They would say, "Don't pray because prayer and faith are weak and will place, position, and draw, drive, pull, push, persuade, and force you into harm's way, and you will become the 'prey' when you pray."

A survival mind, frame of mind, mental condition and conditioning, and mental state of being, if they were still talking, would say, "You don't have time to wait, so go on and be anxious. Don't be still. Make your move. Don't be patient, don't try to persevere, and don't be at peace." Every time you take heed to and you obey the urged suggestions and the urged influences of your survival mind, frame of mind, mental condition, state of mind, and mental state of being, it will first instill in you and then build and establish within you a "be anxious, don't trust, don't believe, don't hope, don't have faith, don't show you have faith, don't rely on faith, and don't show confidence in faith" frame of mind, mental condition/conditioning, state of mind, and mental state of being.

When your survival mind is engaged, it releases and puts in motion and puts into effect a "you don't have time and you are out of time" frame of mind, mental condition, state of mind, and mental state of being long before "time" itself becomes, is, and ends up being a variable or a factor. Your survival mind, if it had a voice to speak, would suggest and influence you into telling a person what they should and need to do or tell them they need to "do something."

My conclusion to this matter

The final points I want to make when it comes to you being entangled and entrapped in a survivor-survival mind and in a survivor-survival mind, frame of mind, mental condition, state of mind, and mental state of being are the following:

The survival mind that you are in because of PTSD and OCD; because of fear, being molested, raped, abused, rejected, not having the right father-daughter relationship, not having one at all, etc.; and because of something traumatic, troubling, tragic, terrorizing, torturing, and tormenting happening to you; if it had a voice, it would keep suggesting, influencing, and telling your frame of mind, mental condition/conditioning, state of mind, and mental state of being to be on and stay on high alert.

If your survival mind had a voice, it would tell your traumatic, troubled, tragic, terrorized, tormented, and tortured thoughts, train of thought, thinking, and way of thinking to keep seeking *closure* (the need for details and reasons) why you were violated and abused and to reject *resolve* (the need to bring an end to) without knowing the details and the reasons. It is important that you know that your survival mind, survival frame of mind, survival state of being, and survival mental state of being need to have and will crave for closure (answers, cause, reason, and understanding of) even if it means keeping you in harm's way.

THE SURVIVORS MODE

Being locked into a survival mode is simply being in a safety zone and in a safety mode where you give and invest just enough to get an instant, known, and easily recognizable something in return. You are only able to make safe investments into something or into someone that involve very little, minimum to no risk at all. You are only able to "give to get" what you need and want nothing less and nothing more and you don't allow yourself and your mind, mind-set, thoughts, train of thought, thinking, way of thinking, your mental capabilities and abilities, your mentality, and your heart to entertain, reaching for and expecting and believing and hoping and having faith, etc., that is beyond your safety survival zone.

When you are in a survivor mode, at the end of each day, the goal is to walk away from your day still alive, still existing, and still in a "what seems like and feels like" is an emotional, intimate, mental, and physical safe, stable, strong, and secure place. Please remember Satan is the master of deception and the master of illusions. And he will always use fear tactics and techniques as a way of drawing, driving, pulling, pushing, persuading, tricking, trapping, seducing, enticing, entangling, and entrapping you into his survivor web of deception, his survival web of deception, and his "you appear to be out of your survivor-survival mode" illusion. An illusion is a deceptive appearance or impression and it is a false idea or belief.

Here it is

It has been years since you were in that abusive and violent atmosphere and environment and you "appear" to be all right and you believe that you have been healed from what you went through and had been through. And you want to think, feel, and believe that since you have not been in that traumatic, troubling, tragic, terrorizing, tormenting, and torturing moment in years, you can move forward. After all, you went to a secular world healer, and they administered a secular world healing and everyone says you look good and you even feel good. You are led to believe that the scars, wounds, and bruises you had that came from what you had been through have been healed.

It's years later, and one day, something was innocently said and/ or done that suddenly and immediately triggered what you called an "alarm." Something that was said or done alarmed you, and it triggered a flashback memory and flashback moment of a matter that you thought and felt you had gotten past and you had finally gotten over. All of a sudden, you found yourself quickly, suddenly, and immediately drawn, driven, pulled, pushed, and forced back into that survivor-survival mode you thought you would never be in again in your life.

Why did this happen? Satan had you locked into a survivor-survival mode illusion and you didn't even know it. Exactly what is a survivor-survival mode illusion? How did you get into a deceptive and deceiving survivor-survival mode illusion? It was and is an attitude, mood, thought, train of thought, thinking, way of thinking, mind-set, and mentality fear led you into and left you in; and once you were left in it, Satan tricked and deceived you into thinking, feeling, and believing you are all right. When in all reality and in actuality, you were not all right. Satan had used fear tricks, tactics, and techniques as the way to deceive and trick and trap your thoughts, feelings, and emotions, and your mind and mental capabilities and abilities, and trick and deceive you into the following way of thinking:

A. You can think, feel, and believe you are no longer in a survivor-survival mode, mind-set, and mentality because you are years past what was traumatic, troubling, and tragic that happened to you that constantly, continuously, and consistently terrorized, tormented, tortured, and traumatized you, and you are in a relationship and love that is nothing like the one that you were in, and you have received a secular world surface healing you are and you look good and feel good, which means you have become ____

B. Satan wants to make sure you are likely to wrongly think, feel, believe, perceive, and interpret by your senses that you are someone who has survived and has remained alive after the traumatic, tragic, troubling, terrorizing, torturing, and tormenting event(s) you were faced with in which others have died; and as a result, you can continue to live or exist, typically in spite of any past, present, or future traumatic, tragic, troubling, terrorizing, tormenting, and torturing accidents, ordeals, or difficult circumstances no matter what kind of way or manner in which they occur or are experienced, expressed, or done because of your deceptive appearance or impression and image.

C. Satan will keep assaulting and attacking you with the fear of you reliving what you have been through until you accept, adopt, adapt to, and apply the false idea or belief about yourself, which is you are a person who coped well with the difficulties from your past and in your life because of an object or practice that has continued to exist from an earlier time in your life when you were faced with circumstances, situations, confrontations, matters, moments, and even memories that were traumatic, troubling, tragic, terrorizing, tormenting, and torturing.

D. The practice you held on to you also made it the way or manner in which everything and anything that is negative, bad, or wrong that happens to you in your present or in your future occurs or is experienced, expressed, or done or is processed when it comes to you; that false deceptive false idea and belief about yourself is based on a deceptive appearance or impression that is given.

You may have let go or have tried to let go of, or you are still trying to let go of everything from your past that has terrorized, tormented, tortured, and traumatized you, but fear won't let them let go of you. The reason Satan can constantly, continuously, and consistently keep your journeying into your past at will and keep you having unexpected, undetected, unbelievable, and unforgettable flashbacks from what happened to you is he was able to deceive you into thinking, believing, and feeling like you have overcome your past.

He did so by making sure that when you look back over it, all what you will end up seeing is likely to be wrongly perceived or interpreted by your senses; so much so that what you would see when you looked at yourself would end up bringing about a deceptive appearance or impression of yourself along with a false idea and belief concerning where you actually are in reference to where you once was and in reference to what you have been through.

CHAPTER NINE

The Next Chapter in Your Journey

NOW THAT YOU know how you ended up journeying into a survivor-survival mind, mental capabilities, and abilities; survivor-survival thoughts, train of thought, thinking, way of thinking; survivor-survival mind-set, mentality; and, finally, the survivor-survival mode, I want to give you a visual image of what that looked like and looks like to someone who wants to be in your life. Keep in mind something that I have already shared with you, and that was the first man in your life, your father or someone who fathered you, prepared you for the wrong man that would come into your life. He tutored, trained, and taught you the things you needed to know about that wrong person, their conversations, what they would be thinking, what they would want from you, and, finally, what you should do to protect yourself.

If you didn't have a father or the father you had did not father you in the right way and the wrong things happened to you, what has happened is you were left in harm's way because you did not have the man-and-woman relationship wisdom, knowledge, and understanding you needed for your journey into your "first man other than your father" relationship. If you had a father and you felt he was too strict on you, you were rebellious and you rebelled for whatever reasons, etc.

Maybe you had a good healthy father-daughter relationship and you got into a relationship with someone and you held him to "unrealistic" expectations. Those expectations you placed upon him were not realistically attainable and achievable because not every man can and will be like your father. It took your father years to get to where he could give you all the things you had and do for you in the way he did. To expect that out of someone who is still trying to find their way or someone who is trying to get where they can provide for you like they want to is something you shouldn't and never should have done. What you ended up doing was setting him up for "failure" and you set your relationship up for failure.

It took your father years to get to the "provider" level and to the "father image" you grew up seeing and knowing. He didn't get there overnight, and you should have taken the time to ask him what you should look for in a man, what you should expect out of a man, and, more important, what you should do if you meet a man that you really want to be with but he can't give you the lifestyle and the things he, your father, gave you. Your father should have taken the time to tutor, teach, and train you how to have a healthy, prosperous, productive, and successful relationship with God and then yourself and then with someone of the opposite sex.

The first man in your life who set the bar that high should have explained to you that a sound, solid, safe, secure, stable, healthy, and good relationship with a man is not based on or built on "what he can do for you"; nor is it based on and built upon that man being able to do for you like your father did. What happens when you do not have the "second man" knowledge that you need to have (the first man knowledge being that of your father)?

"My people are destroyed from lack of knowledge. Because you have rejected knowledge, I also reject you as my priests; because you have ignored the law of your God, I also will ignore your children" (Hosea 4:6).

When the first man in your life (your father) did not give you the right, healthy information and instructions you needed for the "second man in your life" (your first man, nonfather relationship), not only have you set him up for failure and you have set your relationship with him up for failure, but also you will end up being destroyed because of your lack of "the second man in your life" knowledge. Satan knew you didn't have your "second man in your life" knowledge or you didn't have the "full-of-living powered second man in your life" knowledge, and he took advantage of what you didn't know about right second man-to-woman relationship.

Without that knowledge of you having that "second man in your life" knowledge, you were cheated out of some valuable and priceless man-to-woman relationship instructions and information. All the bad, wrong, and negative things that happened to you when you were just an innocent little girl, Satan, along with all the "second man in your life" information and instructions you needed but never received, took advantage of it all, and he is and has been using both to keep setting you up for failure. Your first journey after leaving your childhood and your teenhood would find you entering into adulthood and entering into an unplanned and an unprepared for womanhood. Whatever it was you did or didn't get in your childhood and in a father-daughter relationship or the lack of one thereof; and whatever it was that maybe you got an excessive "spoiling" overload of would be what you would leave childhood and teenhood seeking after in a relationship with a second man.

He was being set up

Somehow, you found a way to make peace with what did or didn't happen in your childhood and in your teenhood, and you even found a way to accept what happened to you and accept what transpired because you had a father-daughter relationship or there was a lack of one. And now you are a grown woman, and the innocence of your mind, mental capabilities and abilities, thoughts, train of thought, thinking, and way of thinking is gone, and your "I remember whens" are far and few. The innocent mind-set and innocent mentality that you once had have dwindled away, and life has happened, and for you, life goes on and it has been going on.

Daddy wasn't there to show you that he cared. You were left with different people and even family members and in harm's way and you were just an innocent prey. Over and over, you would pray that God would help you and take the pain away and someone would not take advantage of you and not hurt you and not take something from you because you really didn't have anything that you felt was of much value left for yourself because of what you were forced to go through and endure. There was so much you grew up lacking, needing, and/or wanting and missing, and if that wasn't and would not have been the case, you would have the right-shaped self-image, self-worth, self-respect, self-esteem, and self-confidence.

If you would have had the right "second man in your life" information and instructions, you would have walked away with the right opinions of men. If your dad or you had a dad who would have taken the time to instruct you on how to approach life, love, living, and relationships, you would have had something to build off in your own life, and it never would have mattered if you chose a different view of the world. Not only did you walk away from your childhood with a lack of the "second man in your life" information, but you also rejected and/or ignored some instructions that you were given that could have and would have helped you avoid what you had to endure.

One day when you didn't expect it, he showed up in your life and he was the second man in your life or he was the man you just knew, without any doubt, was the right man that was supposed to be in your life, you know, the one God sent. You looked good and you sounded good, and things were going good for a while, and for the first time in your life, you felt good about yourself and you felt good about the relationship and the love you both had for each other and shared. He was nothing like the person you ended up being victimized by and abused by, and he was saying and doing all the things you always needed and wanted a man to.

But there were times when you struggled and strained to believe and even accept that you had someone in your life that loved you for you and accepted you for who you were/are. Sometimes, you didn't think and feel like you deserved to have someone like him in your life, and from time to time, you ask yourself, *What did I do to deserve this kind of man?* And then there are those days you, out of a survivor-survival tendency, inclination, intuition, impulse, and instinct, you find yourself emotionless and waiting for something to go wrong. Not because you really want something to go wrong but you find yourself in that way of thinking and in that mind-set because something has always gone wrong in your men relationships.

THE SURVIVORS MODE

And what went wrong has always been unexpected, undetected, unbelievable, unforgettable, and out of that place you sometimes find yourself on the edge, snappy, easily agitated and aggravated, nervous, and you even have found yourself expecting and anticipating something going wrong. So much so that you begin to analyze and read more into any insignificant and minute discussions and conversations that you and the person who is in your life are holding. Without you even knowing it, you sometimes find yourself waiting for and preparing for what you are used to happening when you express how you feel about something that you and he do not agree on; not because he is that way and it has happened before but it all came out what you had to survive through before you met the one you are with.

And then there are those moments when you find yourself waiting for him to reject you, tell you he is leaving you, put you down, and say things to you that make you feel like you are not good enough for him. He has never said or done anything to get you into those kind of thoughts and train of thought; it all just shows up on its own when you least expect it. And sometimes, every now and then, you find yourself feeling scared and afraid and even feeling lonely and all alone when there is no reason to. You know he loves you. He shows you and tells you all the time, and he does everything that he can do to make you feel safe, stable, and secure. But there are those moments when your insecurities show up, and they always bring with them your inadequacies and your inabilities.

But it's been a long time since all the bad, wrong, and negative has happened to you, and yet one day it happened—no, *you* happened! It was a normal, simple, and easy conversation that quickly turned into a misunderstanding and then a breakdown in communication. And what you thought he was going to say and do, that came out of what you were used to being said and done when a situation like that happened; it looked like he was coming toward you just like he did, you know the one from your past. Fear and being scared and afraid suddenly and immediately gripped and seized your nerves even though you were not faced with any kind of imminent hurt, harm, and danger. And before you knew it, your survivor-survival thoughts, train of thought, thinking, and way of thinking suddenly, immediately, and quickly kicked in.

Your survivor-survival thoughts, thinking, and way of thinking began to transmit urgent survivor-survival impulses through the power of your thought, train of thought, and power of your thinking and your way of thinking into your sense organs, and from your sense organs into your nerve centers. And the power of those transmitted survivor-survival sense sensation impulses that were sent into your nerve center put in motion and put into effect survivor-survival feelings, emotions, and desires that brought about survivor-survival reactions and reactionary responses.

What he ran into

He didn't see any of what was happening on the inside of you. He didn't know that in that moment, while he was trying to reason with you and reach out to you as he has always been successful at doing that brought about the right resolve for him and gave you the right closure you needed, your physical survivor-survival senses were transmitting what was perceived by those same senses as "what looks like, feels like, could be, or might be" something bad, wrong, and negative that had happened to you once before.

He didn't know that your survivor-survival urges, tendencies, inclinations, intuitions, impulses, and instincts were in control, and as he was still trying to reason with you, reach out to you, hold a conversation with you, and communicate with you, your survivor-survival urges, tendencies, inclinations, intuitions, impulses, and instincts were transmitting powerful survivor-survival sensations into your mind-set and mentality. And that is when he ran into your survivor-survival mode along with its tactics, techniques, traps, and triggers.

When he ran into your *trap,* what he ran into was what you never had for you to sustain and maintain a healthy, whole, prosperous, productive, and successful relationship with him. He never knew that when he met you and got involved with you, you didn't have the "second man in your life" or the "right man in your life" information, instructions, wisdom, knowledge, understanding, and experience; in fact, he didn't know you never had it. The only "man in your life" wisdom, knowledge, understanding, experience, instructions, and information you had came from you being terrorized, tormented, tortured, and traumatized in a traumatic, troubling, and tragic way and manner.

He ran into your trap, and when he did so, what he also ran into were all the right things that never received to shape self-esteem, world, self-image, self-worth, self-respect, self-confidence, and confidence on and opinions of men. What he didn't know was you never had that "first man in your life" role model to show you the way to approach life that you could use as an example for you to build off in your life. He never knew he would one day run into the childhood, teenhood voids and emptiness that you brought into your womanhood. The trap he ran into when he came into your life and tried to be the man you never had before that you always needed, wanted, and prayed for was your survivor-survival mind, mental capabilities and abilities; survivor-survival thoughts, train of thought, thinking, and way of thinking; your survivor-survival urges, tendencies, inclinations, intuitions, impulses, and instincts; survivor-survival feelings, emotions, desires, reactions, responses, and reactionary responses; and your survivor-survival mindset, mentality, and mode.

The moment when he ran into your trigger(s), what he ran into was something that would, without him knowing it or being able to see it, recognize, and even realize it, innocently say or do or handle in a way that would set off a memory tape or flashback transporting her back to the traumatic, troubling, tragic, terrorizing, tormenting, and torturing event of her original trauma. They were just talking and laughing and having a good time, and he in that "moment" demonstrated a specific harmless act, action, deed, conversation, conduct, behavior, or behavior pattern that he didn't know was her trigger. In fact, he never knew she had triggers because she never told him she did when they first met and since they have been in a relationship.

Triggers are very personal; different things trigger different people. The day and the moment when he ran into what would trigger something within her was the day and the moment when they were talking and they weren't really connecting and communicating as they always had, and then there was that day when he noticed she had begun to avoid specific circumstances, confrontations, challenges, changes, matters, moments, memories, events, things, and situations that needed and had to challenge, confront, conquer, and change. When he attempted to get her to help him do so, it would rouse and evoke a specific reactionary and reactionary response activity and energy within her that triggered a flashback.

As she was reacting to the flashback she was having, he was stunned, shocked, and he didn't know what he could say or do to stop the acts, actions, activity, and deeds she was demonstrating, and he didn't know what was going on with her and why all of a sudden her whole demeanor and the tone of her voice suddenly, immediately, quickly, and drastically changed from being cool, calm, and collected to being hostile and filled with anger. He was caught by what was happening, and as she kept going off on him, he eventually got caught up in it all. And before he knew it and before he could leave the room, he ran into a triggered emotional intensity that he had not ever seen her demonstrate and deliver.

It left him hurt and at a loss for words, and when he tried to love you and out of his love, care, concern, and out of the compassionate heart he had for you, comfort you and try to get you to calm down and try to help you calm down, there was no doing so. In fact, it seemed like things were getting worse and he was seeing rage and anger coming out of you he had never seen before and did not know was in you. What he didn't know was that what he was seeing and hearing was a reaction and a reactionary response that was similar to that at the time of the trauma that she had once experienced and had to find a way to survive through. He never knew you had triggers, and he never knew your triggers are activated through one or more of the five senses: sight, sound, touch, smell, and taste.

He had no idea that the senses identified as being the most common to trigger you are sight and sound, followed by touch and smell, and taste close behind. What he never knew was a combination of the senses is identified as well, especially in situations that strongly resemble the original trauma. Although triggers are varied and diverse, there are often common themes. He knew he loved you and he wanted you to be happy, but he ran into something that he never knew would trigger what he was seeing and hearing you say and do. The only thing he knew to do was to walk away feeling lost and confused.

CHAPTER TEN

The Survivor Mode Danger Zone

HE RAN INTO your trap and he ran into what would suddenly, quickly, and immediately trigger you without any conversation and communication and explanation rushing to retreat in your survivor-survival mode. The only thing Satan did was use your fears and you being scared and afraid that what happened to you and what you went through in your past would one day become your present or your future; or what you are faced with in your present would end up being your future.

He used them and he used and utilized your fears and you being scared and afraid as a way to bait him into your trap and into your triggers. Satan preyed on your fears and you being scared and being afraid, and he played fear mind games with you that gave the deceptive and deceiving illusion that you were, you would be, and you are in some kind of danger by allowing him to get to know you and get close to you. Satan also preyed on your fearful, scared, and afraid feelings, emotions, and thoughts to the point where he had you thinking, feeling, and believing you were still in some kind of harm's way when something he innocently or unintentionally said or done that was really different by it looked like the same something you had seen before triggered a traumatic, troubling, tragic, terrorizing, tormenting, and torturing past and old flashback.

And when you, in a negative way, reacted and then you began to demonstrate and deliver triggered survivor-survival reactionary responses, that was the day and the moment when the bait that was needed to draw, drive, pull, push, persuade, trick, entice, and force him into your trap and triggers was set. Any type and kind of fearful and being scared and afraid trespassing thoughts, train of thought, thinking, and way of thinking can trigger a survivor-survival mind-set, mentality, mental state of being, and mode. And that triggered survivor-survival mind-set, mentality, mental state of being, and mode can and will, at some place, point, and time, when you least expect, trigger a delusional, deceptive, deceiving, seductive, and enticing "into your trap" baited coerced conduct, conversations, communications, and understanding.

Once you arrive at that final place and point I just described, Satan will then use fear and you being scared and afraid to force you into a coerced attitude and mood that will also serve as the bait that is needed. That triggered and trapping "from your past" and old traumatic, troubling, tragic, terrorizing, torturing, and tormenting bait that fear forces your thoughts, train of thought, thinking, and way of thinking to formulate, articulate, and analyze is tainted, and it will then produce and prepare a deceptive, deceiving, delusional, and distorted perception of things said and done and handled that are honest, pure, and right.

My point with all this is everything from your past that was violating, abusive, traumatic, troubling, tragic, terrorizing, tormenting, and torturing that you swept under the carpet, pretended didn't happen, tried to overlook, ignored, worked hard to get past and get over, went to a secular world healer for, received a secular world healing from, and whatever methods and methodology that you have and still do use and utilize was nothing more than a surface help and healing, and the only thing that and everything else you say and do that you think is and has been helping you can and will only do one thing, and that is "clean up your appearance" or make you look good and attractive to the other men who came into your life after the person who terrorized, tormented, tortured, and traumatized you left you shattered into a million pieces.

If you have not been (1) delivered, (2) cleansed, (3) purged, and then (4) healed, and, finally, (5) made whole in that order, which can only come through you having a personal one-on-one encounter with the delivering power of Jesus, what anyone who have come and will come into your life after your first or last violator and abuser is gone will run into eventually "residue" triggers and "residue" traps and "residue" traumatic, tragic, troubling, terrorizing, tormenting, and torturing triggers and traps.

So many times when I have been led to pray for someone that they be delivered, cleansed, purged, healed, and made whole from something they thought they had been healed from, they will say they thought they had been healed from their past or they thought they had gotten past and over it. The person who really wants to be in your life is basically "set up for failure," and so is your relationship with him because of "lying dormant-lying in wait" residue triggers and residue traps that once triggered and they are put in motion and put into effect, the only place where your mind, mental capabilities and abilities, thoughts, train of thought, thinking, way of thinking and your mind-set, and mentality will end up at is in a dangerous, damaging, destructive, and relationship-destructive survivor-survival mode.

This is what you should know

There is a danger with being in a survivor-survival mode, and that danger is you will begin to build and put up walls. Those walls you build and put up are designed to protect you and keep you out of and away from making present or future commitment investments in someone because you are still scared, afraid, and fearful that what happened to you in your past and old traumatic, troubling, tragic, terrorizing, tormenting, and torturing relationship will happen again. That way of thinking sounds good and right, but what you should know and you have to know is those same walls you build and put up to keep out the past bad and wrong and negative are the same walls that will keep out the good, the right, and the positive, and, more important of all, true more than a conquering faith will be hindered, blocked, and kept out.

And in doing so, you will begin to grow, develop, and mature into a carnal-minded person and grow, develop, and mature in making carnal-minded relationship agreements, relationship commitments, and relationship investments, and also have carnal-minded hopes and expectations. The carnal mind is the mind of the flesh. It means walking according to reasoning that is dominated, manipulated, and controlled by what your traumatic, troubled, tragic, terrorized, tormented, and tortured feelings and emotions and desires are telling you or leading

THE SURVIVORS MODE

and forcing you to say and do. Your feelings and emotions and even your desires are not reliable guides; nor are your urges, tendencies, inclinations, intuitions, impulsiveness, and instincts because they often contradict what the Word of God says. You should never trust or follow any of them because they will keep you yoked to, bound and limited to, in a stronghold to, in bondage to, and a slave to a survivor mode, a survival mode, a survivor-survival mode, and a survivor-survival protective mode.

Anytime you put up your survivor-survival walls, you cannot and will not be spiritually empowered and spiritually mature, but you will be a babe in Christ and your level of understanding will be the same. Your only motive and motivation will be to remain in existence, carry on, cope with, manage to pull through, remain strong, outlive, outlast, and pull through and live through (be a survivor). This will open up the door for you to be driven by carnal or fleshly intents, intentions, aspirations, thoughts, feelings, emotions, and desires. Your human will and your human carnal mind will consistently, constantly, and continually be influenced, enticed, entangled, and entrapped in emotionalism and in emotion-driven and motivated survivor protective reasoning, analyzing, logic, outbursts, and displays.

Out of a survivor mode will come survival tactics, arguments, theories, reasoning, and every proud and lofty survival and survivor principle, process, and procedure that sets itself up against the true knowledge of how to have a prosperous, productive, and successful life, love, living, home, family, marriage, and relationship(s) that accomplish, achieve, acquire, and accumulate all the right things.

Every time and anytime you allow yourself to be driven and forced into initiating and implementing constant, continuous, and consistent survivor-survival mode processes, procedures, principles, processing, analyzing, articulating, comprehending, assumptions, accusations, conclusions, etc., you will continue to end up with a restricted self-esteem, self-worth, self-image, and self-confidence, and you will constantly end up with a restricted, bound, and limited opinion of men, and you will consistently keep processing marital and relationship information through your carnal or fleshly mind and intellect. A survivor-survival mode cannot and will not allow you to get linked to, connected to, and tied to a spiritual overcomer's mind-set, mentality, mental state of being, and mode.

A mind that has been detained and distorted by any type and kind of traumatic, tragic, troubling, terrorizing, torturing, and tormenting fearful thoughts and thinking cannot and will not have the power and the authority it needs or the ability to lead every past, present, or future traumatic, tragic, troubling, terrorizing, torturing, and tormenting "remain in existence, carry on, cope with, manage to pull through, remain strong, outlive, outlast, and pull through and live through" train of thought and way of thinking and purpose away captive into the obedience of Christ. You cannot and will not be able to successfully stand up against all the "remain in existence, carry on, cope with, manage to pull through, remain strong, outlive, outlast, and pull through and live through and just make it through" strategies and deceits.

Survivor-survival walls

Those same walls that you think, feel, and believe are survivor-survival "protective walls" will eventually end up being or end up turning into "preventive walls." Everything good that God has for you and everything good that could possibly happen in a relationship will not be permitted to flow into your life because of the survivor-survival walls you keep putting up. Those same walls that you put up to keep out the bad are also the same walls that keep out the good and keep out your deliverance, cleansing, purging, and healing, and they will keep you from being made whole again. You shouldn't want any walls because they can and they will restrict you and place boundaries and limitations upon you. Let me break down the definition of survivor-survival walls for you, and it is defined as

a thought, train of thought, thinking, way of thinking, attitude, mood, mind-set, mentality, or mode that is used and utilized and is perceived as a protective or restrictive barrier or acts as a barrier or defense that a person gets into and uses and utilizes to help him or her cope well with the traumatic, tragic, troubling, terrorizing, tormenting, and torturing difficulties in his or her life so he or she can survive and remain alive after a event that has been traumatic, tragic, troubling, terrorizing, torturing, and tormenting in which others have died; that ends up being the state or fact and the practice that a person has allowed to continue to exist from an earlier time so he or she can continue to live or exist, typically in spite of an accident, ordeal, or difficult circumstance that could turn out to be traumatic, tragic, troubling, terrorizing, tormenting, and torturing.

The danger zone you will, at some place, point, and time, get into by allowing fear to draw, drive, pull, push, persuade, deceive, trick, force, and get you into using and utilizing survivor-survival walls is you will end up protecting a deceptive, deceiving, and illusion-driven *perception* of things. And when that happens, you will begin to accept, adopt, adapt to, and apply a way of regarding, understanding, or interpreting what has been traumatic, tragic, troubling, terrorizing, tormenting, and torturing that is deadly, self-destructive, dangerous, damaging, and destructive in a way that it disconnects you from faith-facts, faith-truths, faith-logic, and faith-reason and reasoning that will release you from any and every traumatic, tragic, troubling, terrorizing, tormenting, and torturing trigger and trap.

The second thing that will happen is you will also constantly, continuously, and consistently get a deceptive, deceiving, and tainted mental impression of what has been traumatic, tragic, troubling, terrorizing, tormenting, and torturing for you in a way that you will not be allowed to get into your journey, manage your journey, and then know when to get out of the journey. What you have been through is not something you should continue to go through, and what has happened to you should not be something that you should always think, feel, and believe is always going to happen to you.

Victim or a survivor

It is that kind and type of deceptive, deceiving, and tainted thoughts, train of thought, thinking, and way of thinking that initiates, puts in motion, puts into effect, and implements the placing of protective and restrictive mental capability and ability, mind-set, and mentality barriers that act as a defense. One of the most damaging things that happens when you are in a survivor mode and when you allow yourself to function and flow from behind survivor protective barriers, restrictive barrier that acts as a defense and a survival protective and restrictive barrier that acts as a defense is you will continue to be a victim masquerading as a survivor. I can tell you that is a really dangerous and self-destructive place to be.

When you are a victim masquerading as a survivor, what you have basically done is self-"willed" yourself past everything in your life that has brought you to the place where you have been shattered and shamed and tormented, tortured, terrorized, and traumatized. You may even be years away from and past what happened to you, and it looks like you are doing just fine. In fact, you know the survivor script and you know the survivor song and you know the survivor sayings and you even have mastered the survivor acts, actions, deeds, conversations, communications, conduct, behavior, and behavior patterns. When people listen to you, they hear your survivor testimony, but what they don't know is you used self-healing techniques and/or you used the instructions and information a secular world healer gave you to help you portray someone that you really are not.

And you know how to put on a survivor self-performance, survivor self-will, and survivor self-effort show, and when you do so, the victim or the victimized part of you that you have never been delivered, cleansed, purged, healed from so you could be made whole is hidden from sight behind your survivor wall. You don't want anyone to see that you are still struggling and straining because you have not surrendered being a victim and you have not surrendered being a survivor and you have not yielded, submitted, and surrendered to being an overcomer and more than a conqueror.

You still have not accepted the fact that your feelings and your emotions are not your friends and you should not listen to or obey what fear that is the force behind them is suggesting and influencing you to use them (your feelings and your emotions) into declaring, decreeing, and demonstrating. Fear is the force and the spirit that is powering your feelings and emotions, and every time you give a fearful feeling and a fearful emotion expression and demonstration, you are instantly and automatically driven into a survivor self-performance show and survivor self-will acts, actions, and deeds and driven into survivor self-efforts.

The only way people will know you are in a dangerous survivor-survival mode and you are hiding behind your survivor-survival walls is they accidentally or incidentally rub up against that victim part of you that you do your best to keep guarded and protected and hidden behind your survivor protective barriers that act as a defense. My point is God never created or intended for you to be a victim and it is not His perfect will for you to be a victim masquerading as a survivor. The only type and kind of person you can and will ever become, be, and end up being if you stay in that mind-set, keep that mentality and attitude, and continue to function and flow in and out of that mode is a "victim who is surviving" or a surviving victim.

Why be complacent, contented, and in a comfort zone and make compromises with that when you can become, be, and end up being a victor, who is a person who defeats an enemy or opponent in a battle, game, or other competition instead of being a victim? Fear has driven you into the mind-set, mentality, and mode of being a victim who is masquerading as a survivor, and it is your survivor-survival walls that protect that mind-set, mentality, and mode.

Some days, you still think and feel and believe and act just like you are a victim and you make victim choices and decisions. A victim is described as a person who has been harmed, injured, or killed as a result of a crime, accident, or other event or action, and long after the initial act, he or she is still terrorized, tormented, tortured, and traumatized by that initial event. And then there are those days when you think, feel, believe, and act just like you are a survivor. A survivor is someone who has survived and copes well with the traumatic, tragic, troubling, terrorizing, torturing, and tormenting difficulties in his or her life and had become a person who remained alive after an event in which others have died. A survivor is the deceptive and deceiving perception that Satan keeps forcing you into delivering and demonstrating. The choice is yours; you can continue to be a victim or a survivor, or you can be an overcomer of both and forever be a conqueror.

CHAPTER ELEVEN

Unmasking the Masquerade

WHEN YOU MEET someone who is a victim masquerading as a survivor, the kind and type of person you encounter is a person who has been harmed, injured, or killed as a result of a crime, accident, or other event or action, and long after the initial act, he or she is still terrorized, tormented, tortured, and traumatized by that initial event, who puts on a false show or pretense and pretends to be someone who has survived and copes well with the terrorizing, torturing, tormenting, and traumatizing difficulties in his or her life and has remained alive after a traumatic, tragic, or troubling event in which others have died.

The person who innocently got involved with you had no idea you were in a survivor mode danger zone, and he had no idea you had a survivor-survival wall. He didn't have a clue that you were a victim masquerading as a survivor. He didn't know you were still tormented, tortured, terrorized, and traumatized by what harmed, injured, or killed as a result of a crime, accident, or incident that you were involved in. He didn't know you were putting on a false show for him and you got involved with him under a false pretense. You never told him that you were not really someone who has survived and is coping well with the terrorizing, torturing, tormenting, and traumatizing difficulties in life and has remained alive after a traumatic, tragic, or troubling event in which others have died.

He never knew that you were someone who was linked to, connected to, and tied to an acquired (learned) personality trait in which you tend to regard yourself as a *victim* of the negative actions of others, and to think, speak, and act as if that were the case even in the absence of clear evidence. You never told him that you had a false reason and a false explanation that you used and will continue to use to hide your real purpose. He never knew he was being drawn into an act or appearance that you gave that looked real but it was false. He was taken in by your claim of having the particular qualities, abilities, etc., that he needed in a companion.

And as your relationship with him was being unveiled, it all looked good and felt good and right. It seemed like you had finally found and gotten into the relationship that you had been looking for; and it would be one that you really felt, thought, believed, and even knew would help you get to where you have always been trying to get to when it comes to your self-esteem, self-determination, self-image, self-worth, self-confidence, self-respect, and what would shape your world and shape your opinion of men. You were so excited, and you sensed and perceived your approach to life would change for the better and you would finally get the right view of life, love, living, relationships, the world, and her world.

As your relationship began to unfold, revealing the contents and the ingredients of what you both shared, it looked like and it felt like you had finally found the relationship that you had been waiting a long time for. And for a while, everything seemed to be going just great. Life for you was good, and for the first time in your life, you were finally getting the things out of the relationship that you always wanted and needed, and there were even some things that you got out of the other person that you never asked for or thought of. What that did was really make you feel really good about yourself and about your life. But for some reason, all of it seemed to be too good to be true, and from time to time, you found yourself feeling a little scared and afraid that what you were experiencing and getting was just temporary. On those days and in those moments, you would find yourself preparing for something to go wrong.

And then there were those days and moments when you had said or done something that wasn't right, good, and positive, or you handled a matter in the same way that made things harder between you and the person you were in a relationship with. He didn't know it all came out of you being scared, afraid, and fearful and it came out of you not

THE SURVIVORS MODE 133

knowing how to accept, adopt, adapt to, and receive what you had never received out of any relationship you had ever been in. What he didn't know was there were days when you struggled to believe you were receiving all the right love, affection, and attention you never had before and he was someone who was actually listening to you, hearing you, and he gave you a voice and he valued your thoughts, feelings, emotions, and thoughts.

All of it was just too good to be true, and you began to think and feel and believe you really didn't deserve someone just like him and you really didn't deserve to feel the way you felt. Every now and then, you would find yourself feeling a little shaky, unsure, anxious, worried, hesitating, dubious, irresolute, and halt between two opinions. Fear would seize and grip the very core of your being, and fear would seize, overpower, overtake, and overthrow your faith, and when those things happened, you would end up being so scared and so afraid that you were going to lose what you had/have and/or things would end up like they always had for you, which was traumatic, tragic, and troubling.

And then there was that fear that you would end up being just like you were in the last relationship you were in, you know, the one that delivered you into the hands of you experiencing and encountering intrusive memories, avoidance, negative changes in your thinking and in your moods, and changes in your emotional reactions. It wasn't anything that he had said or done that triggered you feeling the way you would feel without him even knowing it. He didn't know that there were days and moments when things were going so good and there were times when you were lying safe and secure in his arms and feeling the love, care, concern, and compassion he had for you that you would drift off into recurrent, unwanted, distressing memories of the traumatic, tragic, troubling, terrorizing, tormenting, and torturing events that you went through.

You would, while being in the safety of his arms, be triggered into reliving the traumatic event as if it were happening again, flashbacks, and there would be those upsetting dreams about the traumatic event that he had no knowledge of was occurring while you were with him. Sometime when he would touch you in a certain way and say something, while he was doing so, you would start having severe emotional distress and physical reactions to those "something" moments because they reminded you of the terrorizing, tormenting, torturing, and traumatic events you went through in the past.

And then there were those times when you knew the only thing he wanted was for you to be happy and be healed and whole and he wanted to help you get past what you had been through; but when he would try to communicate you with and he tried to get you to open up and share because he wanted to listen to and hear you, he never knew in those moments your survivor-survival walls would come up and you would immediately and quickly try to avoid thinking or talking about the traumatic event.

He never knew why there were times, sometimes, a few times when there were certain places he wanted to take you to but you didn't want to go with him; and the reason was your survivor-survival walls and mode would keep you avoiding "what looked like would be" places, activities, or people that would remind you of the terrorizing, torturing, tormenting, and traumatizing trauma, tragedy, and troubles you had found a way to get past.

You would never forget those "what was supposed to be" wonderful and awesome times when he would be loving you just the way you always wanted and needed to be loved, and something in those moments and times would trigger you having negative feelings about yourself, and you with those feelings would come an inability to experience positive emotions. And when that would happen, you would begin to feel entangled and entrapped in being so emotionally numb that you would begin to demonstrate a lack of interest in the intimate activities you once enjoyed. You would be just going through the motions of loving and being loved when all along you are and you were emotionally detached and disconnected from the moment.

Every time you were linked to, connected to, tied to, and locked into your dangerous survivor-survival mode, your survivor-survival walls would automatically, immediately, and suddenly come up, and you would begin not only having negative feelings about yourself but also having negative feelings about other people often, and that would

THE SURVIVORS MODE
135

draw and drive you into demonstrating a lack of interest in the activities you once enjoyed. No matter how hard he tried to assure you that you and he would be together "until death do you part" and he wanted to be with no one else but you, you would still feel hopelessness about your future with him. He never knew you had a difficulty maintaining close relationships.

He never knew the reason why you had a hard time talking about what you went through was sometimes because of you having memory problems, including you not being able to remember important aspects of the terrorizing, torturing, tormenting, and traumatizing event. You really wanted to talk to him about your traumatic, tragic, and troubled past, but fear had you scared and afraid you would lose him and you would be all alone. And when there was a breakdown in communication between you and the other person, it was always because of your irritability and you demonstrating angry outbursts or you demonstrating an aggressive behavior. Those kinds of demonstrations would come about because it "sounded like" he was trying to reject you and push you away just like the other person did.

You had decided and determined within yourself in those moments that you would beat him to the punch because you knew the speech and you had heard it before and had learned from past experience to always be on guard for danger and for rejection. You had no proof that he was trying to reject, resist, and refuse you, but fear had suggested and influenced you into anticipating and expecting and even waiting for the day when he would say, "We need to talk" or "I need to talk to you." Fear had already analyzed and articulated what he wanted to say to you long before you actually heard what he wanted to talk about, and fear forced you into your survivor-survival mode, mind-set, and mentality.

When it came for you and he to have the conversation that he said he wanted to have with you, he never knew that while he was trying to communicate with you so that you both would have a good understanding, your survivor-survival walls had gone up and your survivor-survival attitude and mood was initiated, showed up, and was put into motion and put into effect. And you would then begin to follow the "fear of being rejected and pushed away" script fear had prepared, produced for you, and presented to you after the first time and after those other times when you experienced being rejected and treated just like you were insignificant, you didn't matter, and you weren't important.

You really loved him and you really loved, needed, and wanted to share in a long-lasting relationship with him and you knew he didn't understand the conduct, conversations, communication, behavior, and behavior patterns you often displayed and demonstrated. And that was because you really didn't know how to tell him you were a victim masquerading as a survivor, and you being in that state and condition was because you had to endure some severe trauma or a life-threatening event and/or you felt like your life or the lives of others were in danger, or you thought, felt, and believed that you had no control over what was happening in a circumstance, situation, confrontation, and matter.

And for those reasons, you are often unstable and unreliable and uncertain about everything you think, feel, and decide when he needs you to help him make critically important choices and decisions that involves others and involves your relationship with him. Fear tells you in those times to "avoid," assume, accuse, and then accept, adopt, adapt to, and apply the assumptions fear has enticed, entangled, and entrapped your thoughts, train of thought, thinking, and way of thinking into processing. He had no way of even knowing your survivor-survival feelings and emotions were in control, and he was talking to them and not your logical reasoning, and they were listening to him as he was trying to communicate with you so that you and he would connect and have the right understanding.

He didn't have a clue that you were still a victim masquerading as a survivor and you were still being terrorized, tormented, tortured, and traumatized. And you sometimes didn't feel good about your life and about yourself no matter what he said or did to encourage and motivate you, and you really didn't feel like you mattered and you were important. He didn't know that behind those survivor-survival walls and behind that survivor-survival mode was someone who had a shattered and broken self-esteem, self-determination, self-image, self-worth, self-confidence, self-respect, and self-will, and there was someone who also had a shattered and broken opinion of men.

Every now and then, he would hear you say things about yourself that were demeaning and derogatory that he really didn't like or understand; and that was because, from time to time, you felt an overwhelming guilt and shame because of your past, and when you feel that way, you feel the urge and you have an overwhelming tendency, inclination, intuition, impulse, and instinct to yield, submit, and surrender to self-destructive behavior.

It didn't matter to you if that self-destructive behavior is or was drinking excessively, driving fast in a vehicle, or some other dangerous act, action, or deed; the spirit of suicide kept telling you no one would miss you and you can end your pain if you just end your life. There were those times when he was sharing his heart and his deepest, innermost feelings with you, and you were physically there and you heard what he was sharing and saying, but you had a problem hearing what he was saying and understanding what he was requesting and requiring of you. That was because of you having trouble concentrating on what he was saying, and later on when what he was sharing with you manifested, you were not able to deliver the right response, and that brought about some fearful feelings.

Those fearful feelings would cause you to have trouble sleeping because the fear you had was that something traumatic, tragic, and troubling was going to happen to you as it did in past times and in past relationships when you didn't respond as the person wanted and demanded you to. He didn't know that you were so scared and so afraid that when he started to walk toward you, he easily startled you and frightened you, and what he saw you demonstrate were survivor-survival reactions and reactionary responses.

And when you did so, he was stunned, shocked, and at a loss for words. He didn't understand what was happening with you, and he was walking toward you with the intent of trying to calm you down and comfort you and communicate with you. Fear wouldn't let you see his coming toward you was out of pure and innocent intentions and he meant you no harm.

My point is as long as you say in a victim masquerading as a survivor mode and you continue to have, function, and flow in and out of that mind-set and mentality, you will continue to have revisited and relived stress reactions as a result of that traumatic event you went through; your emotions and behavior will continue to change in ways that are upsetting to you, and your life will constantly, continuously, and constantly end up being disrupted, making it hard to continue with your daily activities. You will continue to find it hard just to get through your day.

Invisible ceiling

If you continue to function and flow out of a survivor-survival mode and out of a victim masquerading as a survivor, you will continue to end up in a self-destructive danger zone. The vicious cycle that will constantly, continuously, and consistently come out of you doing so is you will never be able to (1) look at your life and (2) look at the choices and decisions you have made and clearly see them through the right lenses. The lens you will see them through will continue to be a survivor-survival lens, and the view you get of them will also be that of a survivor-survival view. Fear will not allow you to take a look at your life and look at the choices and decisions you have made and see them from the right perspective.

You will end up being yoked, in bondage to, in a stronghold to, a slave to, and bound and limited to seeing the both of them through a fear-driven and motivated survivor-survival selfishness, survivor-survival self-righteousness, survivor-survival self-centeredness, and survivor-survival self-justification. For everything that you, out of a victim masquerading as a survivor and out of you being in a survivor-survival mode, attempt to remove, it will end up being replaced with something that is from both of the same modes. As long as you, out of a victim masquerading as survivor mind-set, mentality, and mode and out of a survivor-survival mode, keep saying you don't need a man, your desire for a man will eventually be *removed* and it will be *replaced* with a desire for someone of the same sex as yourself.

THE SURVIVORS MODE
139

Remember, you can have what you say and your words have power and they form your world. Another effect that being in a survivor-survival mode and being in a victim masquerading as a survivor mind-set, mentality, and mode have is you will never know your life and know who you are, and you will constantly, continuously, and consistently question yourself, and you will continue to ask yourself, *Am I enough for him?* That type and kind of feelings of inadequacy, inability, and insecurity shows up because you are still not only a victim masquerading as a survivor but also a surviving "survivor victim" and you are in a survivor victim mode.

A *survivor victim* is a person who is and has been able to remain alive, remain in existence, remain functional and usable, and carry on and cope well despite the terrorizing, tormenting, torturing, and traumatizing hardships, difficulties, events, and trauma in their lives in which others have died and in spite of being a person harmed, injured, or could have been killed as a result of a traumatic, tragic, and troubling crime, accident, or other event or action.

The final thing that you should know is as long as you are a victim masquerading as a survivor mind-set and mentality and you continue to remain in a survivor-survival mode, you won't have what the other person will need when they need it. You can't give someone something that you don't have yourself. If you continue to bring a victim masquerading as a survivor mind-set, mentality, and mode into a new relationship, you will always have a need for survivor-survival tactics; and you will continue to cause, create the atmosphere for, and contribute to that relationship being stagnant and then stifled, and you will continue to be the reason why there will be an invisible relationship ceiling hovering over that relationship. This is the portrait of someone who is a victim masquerading as a survivor.

Deceptive survivor-survival tactics

Because Satan knows you are a victim masquerading as a survivor and he knows you have been hurt, wounded, downtrodden, terrorized, tormented, tortured, and traumatized, he will make sure you sense, feel, and see the need for and the need to have a survivor-survival mind, frame of mind, state of mind, mental condition, and a mental state of being; and you sense and see the need to be in a survivor-survival mind-set, mentality, and mode, and you also sense and see the need for utilizing and exercising survivor-survival protective preventive tactics.

When Satan has you locked into using and utilizing deceptive and deceiving survivor-survival protective and preventive tactics, what he has done is deceived you into using and utilizing a fear and selfish, self-centered, self-righteous, and self-justified driven and motivated *action or strategy carefully planned to achieve a specific end* that he has tainted and distorted and has tricked and deceived you into thinking, feeling, and believing can and will protect you and prevent something that you have already been through that was traumatic, troubling, and tragic from happening all over again; thus, allowing you to continue to be a survivor and allowing you to continue to "exist" just like you did in times past.

When Satan has tried to suggest and influence you into using and utilizing survivor-survival protective and preventive tactics that he has devised, the first thing you need to know is those tactics are fear driven and motivated. The second thing you have to know is Satan has used fear as a way to draw, drive, pull, push, persuade, and force you into being enticed, entangled, and entrapped into thinking, feeling, and believing your "get even with" and get back at the person who has caused, created the atmosphere for, and contributed to you being constantly, continuously, and consistently tricked into being trapped in what has terrorized, tormented, troubled, tortured, and traumatized motives and motivation is just you protecting yourself from having those same things happening to you all over again and you are preventing yourself from going through what you had to get through to survive and so that you could be a survivor.

So when fear deceives you into looking at something through the "look like" lens and fear forces you into accepting what "feel like" is the same thing you had been through before (but it really isn't), fear then wants you to suddenly, quickly, and immediately, out of being nervous, scared, and afraid, react and then run quickly to demonstrate and deliver wrong, bad, and negative reactionary responses. My point is your

THE SURVIVORS MODE ~141~

"get even with and get back at" motives and motivation and tactics is not you protecting yourself and it is not you preventing yourself from going through what you have been through before from happening again.

In all actuality and in all truthfulness and reality, any and all survivor-survival protective and preventive tactics, methods, motives, and motivation that you use is nothing more than mere revenge-filled and vengeful desire-filled urges, tendencies, inclinations, intuitions, impulsive, and instinctive ways used and utilized for the purpose and intent of "getting even" with the person who has terrorized, tormented, tortured, and traumatized you through their bad, wrong, and negative behavior, conduct, acts, actions and deeds, choices, and decisions.

Fear that keeps terrorizing, tormenting, torturing, and traumatizing you has helped make sure you are also still holding on to those same revenge-filled and vengeful desire-filled urges, tendencies, inclinations, intuitions, impulses, and instincts "just in case" something is said or done or handled that "looks like and feels like" it is going to be a flashback of what you have been through; you can justify using your hidden and held-on-to survivor-survival protective and preventive tactics.

What happens when you have that kind and type of thoughts, feelings, emotions, and desires is Satan sneaks in and seizes the moment you are caught up in and then seizes those "what appear to be" protective and preventive feelings, emotions, desires, thoughts, motives, and motivation and use them to seduce, trick, trap, entice, entangle, and entrap you into thinking and believing and feeling you are not having "get even with and get back at" the person who "looks like" he is going to do what has been done to you "again" thoughts; but you are having "just in case" protective and preventive survivor-survival thoughts, train of thought, thinking, and way of thinking.

And every survivor, survival, protective, and preventive tactic you use is pure and innocently devised, used, and utilized. The other thing that happens when you are in a survivor-survival protective and preventive mode is you will be kept "emotionally" blind and "emotionally" bound so you will not see the truth and be released from being "emotionless" or emotionally numb. In closing, I have some questions I want to ask you, and I ask you to be honest in your answering them. Which one of the following would best describe the mind, mind-set, mentality, and mode you have or you are still in? Are you someone who is (1) fighting to die, (2) fighting to survive, or (3) fighting to live?

Mollie and Rose: the journey to survival

CHAPTER TWELVE

Mollie: Surviving the Journey

MY BODY HURTS in places it shouldn't. My heart hurts in ways it shouldn't. My mind is shattered into a million pieces. I cry all the time. The laughter is gone. If I smile, it is rare. I am depressed, and that is a dark place to be. Depression has a friend whose name is fear. Fear has a minion whose name is PTSD. Depression has two lovers, and they are suicide and PTSD. All of them have a mutual kindred connection. They worked together in a joint effort to take me out—yep, little ole me from the backwoods country town of Blakely, Georgia. Why did everyone and everything in my life want to kill me? Why? Why me?

Time after time

One thing you must understand is a person suffering with PTSD will, in time, realize it's about to happen if they are awake. What we don't know is that it's a *hallucination*; for every intent and purpose, what we are hallucinating feels as if it is truly happening in real time. If we are asleep when it happens, it's a real nightmare that we actually feel as if we are interacting and alive in. When these episodes come on, we truthfully are not able to stop it, control it, and control whom we hurt or how we hurt them. However, those who suffer this special brand of mental torture will usually take special precautions to protect those we love as best we can. I walk into my bedroom, and suddenly everything around me changes. I grab for my bed in hopes that I can at least sit down before the nightmare/hallucination begins again. Thankfully, no one is around me this time. He is standing over me with his contorted body.

His nostrils are like a bull snorting smoke. He shuffles his feet across the floor like he is revving up to run at top speed. I am shaking, screaming, curling up in a bundle trying to protect myself from what is to come. He is coming at full speed toward me and swings my cane over me again. I feel myself screaming and hitting at him. Drawing back his fist, he goes for another shot at my head but misses me by an inch. The breeze blows through my hair from the movement. I can hear his taunts and his name-calling. I can feel the cut going into my flesh again, and I grab my chest trying to breathe; metal and flesh meet. I reach for my cane to swing back, but I miss and it lands on the floor. He goes for my throat, laughing at me, but somehow, I manage to kick him off me. I wake up shaking, sweating, crying, gasping for air, clenching my chest and my throat while screaming, "Dear God, help me!" I scream and throw myself on the bed in a pool of tears.

Why was this happening to me? What was going on inside me? What was this? PTSD feeds off fear. With each episode I wanted desperately to end my life. I wanted to end the misery and end the tremors in my hands and end the pains in my stomach. The sweat falling off me knows it's about to start all over again. Nothing helped. He was gone, but the fear he instilled still gripped me. It still rules my life. Anxiety attacks filled my days and managed my nights. I installed three locks on my bedroom door, and I took the glass panes out of my windows and put in fiberglass-type window panes. I was afraid I would throw something and break the glass or one of my kids would walk in and get hurt. To protect others, I had to push them away. But I needed them just as badly. The pain inside of me grew each day. The shattered love I once had for someone lay in a coffin made of fear in some grotesque contorted reality. Scientists say there is a possibility of alternate realities; if this is true, then those who suffer PTSD have a private wormhole to them on such a consistent basis as to cause a rupture in space and time itself. How did I get to this point? What drove me to madness? Was it all him?

HOW I GOT THERE

I grew up without my father in my life. My mother divorced him by the time I was one. He was and still is an alcoholic. The running joke among us siblings is that he is embalming himself while living. Back in those days, divorce was taboo. A woman raising children by herself was a disgrace to the family. Many times I was called a bastard child, and I wasn't. I don't blame either parent, and I forgave him the day I met him. I didn't even know what he looked like until a few years ago when I met him for the first time at my sister's funeral (whom I had just found a few months earlier). I realize some people make not having a mother or father in their lives an excuse for bad behavior. I want to shed some light on this subject. It also will make a person become self-destructive, make horrible choices, and try to gain in adulthood what they didn't have as a child. The majority of the reason I was with this man I married was my father was not in my life, and I longed for a man, any man, to give me love.

Men, if you have children you don't see, take it from me . . . you're doing that child a disservice and you have no clue of the harm you are causing. Yes, I had my grandfather, uncles, cousins, preachers, music directors, and male friends in my life, but there is something about the connection between a father and daughter that cannot be replicated by any other connection. Daughters need their fathers to love them and show them how men should treat them. Without a father saying "I love you" to his daughter on a regular basis, she will grow up lacking vital relationship knowledge. If that father is a bad influence, then it's understandable he wouldn't be in her life. But if he is a good man and truly wants that time, then, ladies, let him see his daughter. She needs him more than you ever thought you did. Get past your selfishness and let them build a relationship together.

Men, step up and love your daughters. Take care of them, speak positives into their lives, pray over them, and encourage them to reach for their goals. I didn't have any of this, and it is one reason I made the horrible choices and mistakes that I did. I paid that price. Moms, I know we do all we can do for our kids. Forgive and let the fathers bond with their kids. I grew up bullied, picked on, tormented, treated as an outcast. They talked about me, and I was ridiculed, shamed, unloved, unwanted, and undesired. I had a fairy-tale dream that a man would one day sweep me off my feet, love me, we would have children, and I would be like my grandmother—stay home tend to the house, the kids, prepare the home for winter, store food for the year, and have my church activities. I sort of had it but at a high price. I was allowed to be a stay-at-home mom but only because he couldn't see the sense in my working just to pay child care. If it saved him money, he was for it. Now, back to my story!

Fighting to survive

By the time I was in the fourth grade, I was attacked by meningitis. My mom took me to a different doctor because our usual one was out of town on vacation. He said it was strep throat and sent me home with antibiotics. I had a high fever and a sore throat. The fever didn't break, and that night, my mother ran me back to the hospital. There I had a seizure. She ran screaming into the halls for help. They loaded me onto the ambulance and told my grandfather not to try to keep up because he wouldn't be able to. My mom said she saw the ambulance at the light make a left and never saw it again. They took me to Flowers Hospital in Dothan, Alabama, where a doctor only looked at me and said it's meningitis. A spinal tap later confirmed it, but, thankfully, he already had me on the medication. I was in such bad shape. I started having seizures and then a loss of consciousness and even a coma at one point. The doctors told my mom to call the funeral home and make arrangements because I was going to die. They had me hooked to every wire I think they could find. I had wires coming out of my head and an IV in my arm. I was in a coma (104 fever will do that), and I was enjoying playing with the angels and talking to Jesus. I could see what was happening in the hospital room too. I heard what the doctors said, and I asked God about it.

God told me, "You will recover from this. Have your mom call Brother Ansley to pray for you. I will hear his prayer and heal you."

When I woke up, I told her to go call him and I told her what God had said to me. I remember pulling out those wires from my hair. My mom said they did CAT scans and tests on my brain. Brother Ansley came and prayed for me, and I was healed instantly of the fever. The fever damaged my memory and hearing and left me weak. I didn't go to school for a long time. A teacher would come every day after school to help me stay up on my work. When I did return, I was on medications for seizures. I hated that medication. It changed me from a sweet girl to a weirdo. My grades dropped, too, and how I learned things changed. I had trouble memorizing anything. I had to relearn multiplication, and to a degree, I had to learn to read again. I caught myself reading backward a lot, and also telling time backward was easier.

There were a few positives, and they were I could speed read, sight read music for the piano, and sing soprano. But still I couldn't hear the pitches well enough to tell you which notes I was hearing. I couldn't play the piano by hearing, and I was odd. The doctors were surprised at my progress, and in a year, I was being weaned from the seizure medications. Oh, and the wires had pulled my hair out; my beautiful blond hair was gone. What grew back was brown, and I didn't like that at all.

A girl in my choir class at school asked me one time why I didn't like her. And it was true I couldn't stand this girl. She asked me in front of the whole class. So I was honest. Because when we were in elementary school, she would fight me on the playground and push me into the fence all the time. The teachers did nothing. (Hello, teachers, stop talking to other teachers, pay attention to the students, and stop the bullying). One day, I finally got her back good and tore into her, and she didn't like getting tossed into the fence.

I beat her up really badly, which, of course, the teachers all saw, and they took me to the principal's office while she was smiling at me. He called my mom, who had to drive all the way from Alabama to the school. She lit my hind parts up with her shoe in front of everyone, and she didn't even wait to hear my side. So, yes, I hated this girl who got by with what she had done to me. Once I told her why I didn't like her, she looked at me and said, "Mollie, I am truly sorry. I don't remember doing that, but I am so sorry. Please forgive me." I did, and we became friends. Not best friends but friends. She died not too long ago of a broken heart. I am glad we mended our fence (our differences). The boys picked on me, and I was the butt of many of the jokes. Try living as a teen girl and the boys don't ask you out. Wouldn't you feel ugly? I did. I never had a boyfriend at my high school. Each boyfriend I had was a distance one. I longed for what the other girls had. They got to wear the boy's letterman jacket and class ring.

They got to go to parties when I couldn't leave the house without a chaperone being my mom. They were given cars for their sixteenth birthdays, while all I got was a dinner at the local fish house. They were beautiful and they dated jocks. They were asked to homecoming dances every year, and when I went, no one would dance with me. Try going to the prom with your best friend's brother.

Me and my mom

My mom, she worked all the time, so, basically, it was my grandparents raising me. Back then, I couldn't understand what was wrong with her. We would clean the room (we shared a room) and she wouldn't take out the bagged-up garbage. She said my grandfather would yell at her for putting it in the trash can. That may be half true because he was known to go through the trash on occasions. I think what he was yelling about was how much came out of the room. She would throw her clothes on the floor and walk all over them. I saw her put on dirty clothes and wear them again to work. Granted her job was nasty, but, geez, at least she could wash them sometimes. Everywhere else in the house would be spotless (my grandmother and I did that) except for that bedroom she and I shared. She didn't want to throw things away.

Now, neither did my grandparents, and you see that a lot from those who survived the Depression. But they had their stuff organized and put away neatly. Not my mom; she just threw all her things around the room, and wherever they landed, that's where they would stay and be. I hated it when she would wash my clothes. I just couldn't figure out how in the world could and would she wash my stuff and it smelled worse coming out than going in? I had to go to school in that stinky stuff, which only added to the abuse and loneliness. I later found out she washed my clothes with her work clothes. That's why they stunk.

She worked in the peanut mill, and that was nasty dusty work. Plus, she would let the clothes sit wet in the washer for days, and instead of washing them again, she would put them in the dryer. Once I found out what she was doing, I had to take over the laundry along with everything else in the house. I thank God my grandfather would hire me some help once a month. It would take a whole weekend to get caught up. There is only so much a teen can get done in a week with school and everything. I would come home and fix supper and precook breakfast.

I taught Papa how to warm up the breakfast and the lunch. My mom would come in late, and so she was never a help with chores or cooking. We had to turn the breaker box off so my grandmother wouldn't try and cook. I am sorry I ate many things growing up, but I draw the line at rocks and grass. I had to go straight home after school so I could take care of the house, watch my grandmother (who was in first stages of Alzheimer at the time), cook dinner, practice, and try to focus on my ballet/tap dance lessons, voice lessons, and piano lessons. I knew my childhood was over when my grandfather raised his hand to hit me because I had not done the things my grandmother usually did. No one had sat me down and told me I had to be the adult. And so in high school, while everyone else was growing and maturing into beautiful young men and women, I was at home being what I felt like, which was a slave. I didn't mind the cooking and baking (although I don't think you need bread at every meal despite my papa thinking and preaching otherwise) because those were outlets for me.

Because of my activities, I stayed a nice size 10; but when your dance teacher says lose weight so you will fit in a costume, guess what? You get a complex and you think you're fat even though you're not. Plus, I was a vegan, so meat and I rarely crossed paths. I thought I was ugly because the same lady told me I couldn't audition at Disney World because I wasn't pretty enough like the other girls. Should that have mattered

THE SURVIVORS MODE

considering the talent I had? It did to her. I was crushed. I auditioned for the Sound *of Music* in high school. I practiced and I knew the songs backward and forward. I sang my heart out and I wasn't chosen. Why? I wasn't a senior. It broke my heart. I loved theater. I wanted to be on Broadway one day. I wanted to perform in *Cats* or *The Phantom of the Opera.* My dreams were shattered.

There was this one guy and he was from Alabama, and he and I met in Atlanta, and we fell in love in a whirlwind of three days, and on day four, he asked me to marry him. I said, "Yes, but let's wait until we are eighteen." He agreed. I did love him and he came to visit me a couple of times and we talked on the phone a lot. It could have lasted, I think, but I broke it off. He cussed a bit too much for me. Considering what I had . . . .oh, well, bad choices. He was an excellent drummer, so I am sure he probably went on to play for some wonderful rock band somewhere. I did like his mom and I liked how he treated her.

Watching me

I had a boyfriend after him who loved his bulldog more than me. But the real reason things didn't work out was simply he loved his mama and she controlled him. His father was such a sweet man. There was one other guy before the guy from Alabama. He lived in Florida, and I met him when I was down there on a mission trip. We went to a flower garden, and I remember someone took pictures of us together by the rose bushes. Nice guy, and I loved his red hair, but we just grew apart. Long before any of this took place, me meeting those guys, I was in college where the boy with the red hair and I met. I was asleep one night and I woke up with a feeling like someone was watching me. There in the corner of the room where I was there was a grim reaper. Yeah, people make light of him in cartoons, but, ladies and gentlemen, that one is real.

I saw him with my own two eyes standing in the corner watching me. I slid as far under the covers as I possibly could in hopes he would go away. There is nothing you or I can do that will make the grim reaper leave. I did the only thing I could think of, and I prayed and I poked my head out, and he was still there. He was just standing in the corner with his black robe on and he raised his scathe ready to take my soul. I cried out and said, "Jesus, help me, please." When I peeked back out, he was gone. A few months passed, and I befriended a man who actually was a preacher, but the word out was he dabbled in the voodoo. Now, I don't know if that was true and I really didn't care about that. All I know is this: when everyone else was ready to put me in the asylum, he explained to me the meaning of the things I was seeing.

I was seeing the moon smile and hearing bushes talking. I even heard a dog ask a question, and I was dreaming every night, and I had visions as I walked through my days. Try to study with all that going on inside your very being each day. One day, I was at my boyfriend's house, and he was on one of his rants with his family. I was sitting on the porch, and the preacher was next to me. He looked at me and asked me what I saw. I said, "I see a chariot of fire coming down from heaven and a rider whose face is like death." He stopped everyone and said, "She has seen the chariot of fire. This must end now." Everyone stopped. They went inside, and I sat on the porch. He told me that God had blessed me with special gifts so I could see the spirit realm and the natural realm at the same time. In time, I would learn to understand what I would see and hear. After that, things calmed a bit and I was able to function again and finish school, and I even went in the army. I still see and hear things from behind the veil, and to be honest, I miss it being to the degree it was then. Oh, and that chariot I saw that day left without a passenger. I have seen it many times since, sometimes with a rider and sometimes without.

Remember, Jesus defeated death, hell, and the grave. Only Jesus can save you in those moments. If you think death is not a real being, then please allow me to introduce you to hell. I don't mean a living hell on earth; I mean the big *hell,* the place. What I am about to tell you is a real account of what happened to me. Remember, God placed in me the gift to see what others normally cannot.

THE SURVIVORS MODE

Drawn and driven into the darkness

My then husband and I were asleep in the living room on the floor, and I woke up being pulled. I rolled over to see these imp creatures pulling me into a hole. I began to kick and scream and try to grab anything to stop them from pulling me. For little creatures, they sure do pack a punch. As they pulled me down into a hole, it got darker and darker and then the walls began to move, so I stopped grabbing at them. They were slick, too, with yucky stuff. At the end of the tunnel, they let me go, and there I hit the ground with a thud. I quickly looked around me and I saw fire like water everywhere . . . it was the main light source. There were tunnels that led off in different directions.

There were cave-like areas with bars in front of them. I hid behind a wall and watched what was going on. Demons of different sizes came out and would torment the ones behind the bars and keep going. The screaming was constant like music is constant here in our day-to-day life. It smelled of burning flesh, and it would expand as needed. Then Satan came out and, knowing I was there, began to call me out. First off, folks, Satan does not look like that cartoon version with the pointy tail, pointy ears, pointy nose, and red. He has organ pipes coming out of his back, and he is beautiful, not ugly. So throw your cartoon thoughts out the door. I tried to sneak over to another area, and it was worse than where I started. I saw people whose flesh was being eaten off them by these worms, and then it would start all over again.

The people I heard screaming were in pain and agony, and they cried day and night for eternity, but hell would be their home because of their unforgiven sins. They were also continually tormented. I heard him, Satan, coming for me, so I ran into another entrance. That was chilling because I saw men and women who had preached for years but they had led God's sheep astray. They were in these pools of sorts being tormented day and night, and they were crying out to Jesus and asking Him to get them out of there. The film would play on the walls over and over again of Jesus saying to them, "Depart from me I know you not." I was finally captured and pulled to the area where Satan sat on his throne. I could see earth and how he had demons everywhere tormenting people as they would go about their day-to-day living. He said to me, "I will kill you and take a special pleasure in doing so." He flung his hand in the air and I hit a wall.

Folks, the walls were made up of people, and the slimy substance was, well, you get the picture. I screamed, "Jesus!" As soon as I said that, the demons went running. Satan smiled and said, "He won't come and get you. He doesn't love you." And he just started laughing at me. I screamed, "Jesus!" A hand reached down and grabbed me and pulled me back up, and there I was back on the floor of the living room. I had scratch marks on me and I reeked of smoke. I cried and thanked my Jesus for saving me. It was a long time before I could sleep without a night-light again. Don't be deceived; Satan is real, and so is hell.

Note: Satan does not need a reason to destroy you and me. The reason that he was after me was not that I had done anything wrong to him but that he knew what I would eventually do for the kingdom of God. That alone made me a target. My husband and I were not long married, and he was attending a really good university. He was majoring in music and was actually a really good pianist. I was visiting one time, and his piano professor was nice at first. Then suddenly, he turned crazy on us. He began yelling at him, and at one point, he stopped yelling. I looked at my then boyfriend and said, "Come on, we got to get out of here." I left, and he, my then boyfriend, who eventually would become my husband, stayed in that room. The professor locked that door, and as he yelled, the music began to play. Whatever he did to him in that room, he was never the same again.

He would have flashbacks and would constantly talk about it over and over and over again. He would call the man and accuse the man of putting homosexuality in him. Looking back, something did happen and something did transfer. I watched a normal man become a monster before my eyes, and there was nothing I could do. In the bedroom, he wanted me to fulfill some acts for him. Let's just say I was grossed out and it wasn't happening. I truly had no idea what to do. I just knew in my heart it was wrong. Was I wrong for not fulfilling those things? Some would say so, but I say each person has to decide what he or she believes and then stand by those beliefs. The woman he would eventually leave me for did those things for him, and I am fine with that. If she can handle such things, then go for it. I am just thankful my nightmare is over.

My mother had been sick with cancer for a while. The first round she did fine and seemed to recover from it. The second one took her. I hate cancer. You see it as a disease and I see it as a demonic being destroying lives. Cancer took her money, her life, her hope. When you lose hope or a desire to live, then death has you. I was asleep at home and she was in the hospital. I was married, and my son was a little over a year old. I was awakened in the middle of the night by Jesus. He sat on my bed, smiled at me, and hugged me. Then Jesus put me back to sleep. Jesus awakened me again and did the same thing, and, finally, once more He would do the same thing. I knew then my mother was going to pass and God was giving me my comfort so I could make decisions. I woke to the phone ringing, and it was indeed the hospital. I got there as quickly as I could, and as I was leaving, I was grabbing family numbers as I went out the door.

Letting go

Once there, the doctor explained to me that clots had formed in her lungs and they were having trouble stabilizing her, and her heart was in A-fib, and fluid was backing up inside her lungs and around her heart. At first, I told him to do what he could to save her and then transfer her to Dothan, Alabama. He agreed with me and went back to her room to continue. I sat in that cold, drab waiting room praying. I was alone. Then a friend of hers from church came, and she had the nurses move me to the private waiting area. She went about making calls for me. I sat there stunned. I couldn't cry at that moment. As I was sitting there still shocked and stunned, in walked some angels.

One knelt at my feet and stayed there with me through everything. I wasn't alone any longer. This friend of my mom came back in, and not even knowing or seeing, she sat in the only spot really available. The codes were being called on the loud speaker, and I knew when they said it was for her room again that it was time to make the hard choice.

Sure enough, the doctor came running in and explained how her status had taken a turn for the worse. I looked at him and I said, "Let her go."

She wouldn't want all this. No hooking her up to machines to breathe for her. No cutting her open to get the heart going or stabilized. I said it again, "Let her go." The doctor said, "Are you sure because when she has the next one, we won't do anything and she will die?" I said, "Yes, let her go." That was the hardest decision I have ever had to make in my life. She would have been a vegetable, and her quality of life would have diminished. I couldn't do this to her. Her friend held me as I finally began to cry, and she even agreed it was the right thing to do.

The doctor allowed me to go in and see her. I stood at the foot of her bed and told her how sorry I was for all the things I had done wrong. I told her how much I loved her and that I was going to miss her so much. I explained that I had to let her go so she would finally have peace. Her hand flinched and I held it and she squeezed mine. I knew I had made the right decision. I left the room because I didn't want to be in there when she passed. She wasn't alone, though, when she left this world. I went to call her favorite cousin, and I told her my mother had gone to see Jesus. We cried on the phone together, and she got to me as fast as she could.

Before I left the hospital, I signed the paperwork for her eyes to be donated so others could see. I would like to think someone somewhere has my mom's eyes and she can still see me. I watched as the mortician rolled my mom out of the hospital. It was a small town, and even the mortician was sad. He had watched my mother grow up, and now she was gone. I left the hospital because I needed to go home for a few moments. A few ladies from the church showed up to help me get the house ready for all the people. The ministry of helps is broad, but don't ever look down on anyone who serves God this way. If it wasn't for those ladies, I could not have received guests or dealt with any of what I did. They even held my hand at the funeral home. She passed on a Saturday and we buried her on a Monday, which happened to be Martin Luther King Jr. holiday.

THE SURVIVORS MODE

Stabbed in my heart

One beautiful sunny day when I was married, my then husband and I were riding down the road. He was fussy as usual, and I was praying as usual. A voice spoke to me so clearly and said, "Whatever you do, don't let your husband take the job at P&G. If he does, then he will cheat on you and you will end up divorced." That was it. I literally pushed myself as far back into the seat as possible. He said, "What's wrong with you?" I told him what I heard. He said nothing. Years went by and he worked for Cooper Tire, and then one day, he said, "I have put in for a job at P&G and I am leaving Cooper Tire if they hire me." My mind went back to that sunny day and I began to cry. I begged him not to take the job. I offered him anything he wanted. He gave me a stone look, and I knew he didn't hear anything I said.

A couple of months later, he was working at P&G, and my life, as I knew it, would change forever. He came home one day and told me about a woman he had met. I heard a voice say, "He will sleep with her and leave you for her." I didn't say anything to him. But guess what? He came home one day, packed his things, and left me and the kids. I dreamed that he would stab me in the heart and my heart would break in two. And that, ladies and gentlemen, is exactly what happened in what you read above.

I wish I had known back then what I know now. I think we all have those moments. My life, my heart, all of me . . . shattered into a million little pieces. I wasn't perfect, but my life was forever changed. For the longest time, I hated myself. I hated feeling like I had been so dumb because I let those things happen. I hated not being woman enough for him. I hated the fact I gave him the best years of my life and it was all for nothing. It hurts to know that in all I endured, I can never regain my youth and vitality again, and it's all because of my selfish decisions and poor choice making. I still cry sometimes. Not because of anything he did but because of what I lost. I lost my innocence, and I lost money, inheritance, cars, homes, land, family, and friends.

Divorced and alone

And so there I was, divorced, a single mom with four kids I had to raise on my own. I had to get myself together because they needed me. If it had not been for God and my kids, I would not be here. My kids kept me grounded in hope and love, and God saved me physically, spiritually, mentally, and in every way possible. God kept me through it all. I will never forget I was at the mall with a friend shopping and I saw a man who looked similar to my ex-husband. I couldn't breathe. I couldn't walk. I couldn't talk. When I did manage to finally speak, my friend handed me her inhaler, which helped me to finally breathe easier. Anxiety attacks are triggered by a deep-rooted fear even if it's a fear of heights, a fear of car accidents, or a fear of dying. To me, granted, I never had one before that day, anxiety attacks are worse than an asthma attack.

Anxiety attacks cause a physical problem with you first because what happened to you were physical things that the person had done to you, and to see someone who has the same physical features as the person who hurt you brings about the physical effects. The physical part of you produces reactions that are generally not caused by fear. I can't tell you how many times someone else had to drive me where I needed to go because of anxiety. I can't tell you how many times my good friend would drag me out of stores and home because of anxiety. I couldn't drive without shaking and sweating. I couldn't go shopping by myself; I always had someone with me. I always scheduled everything I did so I would be home before dark. Everyone was an enemy. No one could be trusted. Everyone talked about me. No one loved me. Everyone used me.

I had to walk with a cane because all the beatings had damaged my sciatic nerve. It was so painful to move let alone enjoy walking in the woods. It hurt to sit. It hurt to stand. It hurt to lie down. It hurt to turn my head. My feet felt like every bone was broken and like I was walking on thumbtacks. The cane helped me keep my balance because being slammed against walls and cars tends to cause concussions, and that, in turn, affected my balance. I was hooked on painkillers because of all the pain I was in and did what I had to for the fix. I had a prescription, and it was my only friend.

It was time to end the pain and suffering. Who would miss a woman who couldn't keep her marriage together? I was repeating what my mother had went through, and I was raising my kids by myself in a divorced home. I felt guilty, remorse, ashamed, and I felt like I was dead. Oxycodone was good to me. We had a lot of good sleep together. One day, I decided I wanted to go to eternal sleep, and I decided to take my good friend with me. I won't forget that day. It was my last time ever taking those pills and my last time at attempted suicide. I had written my will, written my note, kissed my babies with my tears, and locked myself in my room. I began to take the pills. My phone rang. It was a text. A text so moving it changed the course of my life. The text read

You're signed, sealed, and delivered. I love you.

God has a way, doesn't he? I ran into the bathroom and forced myself to throw up the pills. Then I curled up on the bathroom floor and cried until I fell asleep. I woke up feeling like a huge weight was lifted from me. I got flat on the floor and prayed, "God, remove this from me, please. I can't live like this any longer." I stayed there until I knew I was heard. Things changed that day for me. I gave my life back to God, and I haven't looked back. I had been brought up in the church, and I knew better, but I hadn't done better. I went to church in tears from pain. I hadn't touched the oxycodone in weeks. My body was in withdrawals. My mind was reeling from the PTSD and anxiety attacks. I sat through the service crying through a box of tissues the ushers were kind enough to give me. I kept saying, "God, let it end soon. I need to go home and stretch out."

"Please, God, heal me . . . How can I draw close to you with this pain?" At the end of the service, I stood up crying and wiping my tears. A hand pressed into my back exactly where the main pain point was, and I felt my vertebrae snap back up into place. I felt the pressure release off the sciatic nerve, and the pain left me. Folks, to this day, I don't have that painful issue. I was healed that night in a moment by God. The cane made its way to a donation center for another person to use. My feet felt young again, and I was soon walking all over the place. I lost two hundred pounds in the course of six months. PTSD never bothered me again. All those things that once held me back were now gone. But the residual dirt of their time with me remained. But with God's help and unfailing grace, I was able to overcome them.

Being honest

I want to be honest about myself and what I brought to the relationship. I believe we all need to give that account here on earth, so when we get to heaven, it is already dealt with. I wanted a boyfriend. I wanted someone to love and give attention to. I wanted someone to love me back. I also wanted to leave home and not go back. I wanted a family, and, yes, I had a dream to be a stay-at-home mom like my grandmother. I didn't mind working, don't get me wrong, I just wanted to be there for my kids and not pass them off on to others so they could raise them. For me, I was just giddy, and it wasn't long before a guy asked me out.

And for once, I could say yes and not worry about my mom and grandparents interfering. I wasn't asked out by many boys growing up. And I had the ugly duckling self-esteem issues going on. So I brought low self-esteem, a need to escape by any means necessary, feeling of neglect, one attempt at suicide under my belt, insecurity, and the fear of being an old lonely maid like my great-aunt. Also, all the warning signs were there concerning the guy I married, but since he was the only guy giving me attention, I stuck it out. I made excuses for his behavior, and I lied to cover up the pain inside. I gave what I thought was all of me to him.

Let me put it this way—I thought I gave him all of me, and that was because, in reality, we can truly only give all of ourselves up to God. A friend of mine from college tried to warn me. I can't speak for men on this one, but, ladies, if your man is disrespectful to his mama, then run away from him and don't look back. If he can't take the time to write his name on a Mother's Day card and send it to her, then run. How a man treats his mother is the first sign indicating how he will treat you. I won't go into every encounter I had, but I do, however, want to give

THE SURVIVORS MODE

you a heads-up bird's-eye view into what I lived with and lived through. I want to share with you a detailed account of something that happened. We weren't married at the time. But it had been a while since we had time alone. I was so happy to see him. We were at his mom's house.

She was gone to work. He asked me to go for a walk with him, and I happily went along. We walked down from her house about a mile, and then we went into this field. It was barren and looked like an area that had been dug out. I was just walking along looking at the surroundings, and it was dark out. Then, out of nowhere and for no reason, he hit me in the back of the head, and down I went to my knees. He kicked me around and picked me up and threw me like I was a sack of flour. Then he took off his belt and began to beat me with it, and when that end of the belt wore out, he turned the buckle part on me. I was screaming for help, but either no one heard me or no one cared. Then he started kicking me, and after he did all that to me, he still forced me to get up and walk back to his mom's home.

Once we got back to his mother's house, he slapped me around and stripped my clothes off me. He smiled as he had me turn around for him and show him my wounds. With blood coming out of my wounds, he demanded sex from me. He was ready for action and demanded oral sex first. Then when he had enough of that, he got on top of me and ignored my screams of pain. The movements rubbed along the wounds and made them larger, and it felt like hot fire going through my whole body. He didn't care that my head was banging into the headpost. Nor did he care I was crying. I begged him to stop many times, but he couldn't hear me. Then he shoved me off the bed, and he lay down and demanded I be on top. When I refused, he grabbed me and pulled me on top of him. He smiled at my bruises and said, "I did that" . . . like it was a painting. All while I was on top of him, he was hurting me. I prayed for the nightmare to end. When he finally got a release, he still wouldn't let me go. Finally, by God's grace and mercy, he went to sleep. I went to the bathroom to try and nurse my wounds. I looked like a fresh hell warmed over. I remember looking in the mirror and not recognizing who I was.

He came in and got a cloth and helped me clean up all while I cried. He said he was sorry and didn't know what came over him. I felt like I had been raped, like my soul was ripped out of me, like my heart had died a long painful, demoralizing death. And in a way, I did die that day. I was no longer a child. I was no longer innocent. I wasn't even really a woman. I was a shadow of a woman, and it would be many years before I would love or laugh again. To make matters worse, he woke up and came in where I was and took the washcloth and tried to clean up my back for me. I didn't want him to touch me. I just wanted to go home. To go to my bed and curl up with my teddy bear and be a child again. He begged me to forgive him. I just wanted to sleep. I wanted to bathe him off me. I wanted new skin. I wanted a reset button.

Same old thing

That happened in 1992. There were many other times to come of those episodes. Sometimes, I was thrown against walls with my breath knocked out of me. Sometimes, I had my head slammed into doors and walls. But each time, he demanded sex afterward and sometimes before and after. It was never for me to gain any enjoyment from it, and, of course, that was because he was selfish. If he was here as I'm sharing this with you or if he was to read this book, he will claim that what I have shared is not true, but it is. I remember being married, and we didn't have any children at the time. He went into a jealous rage because I had gone to see my mother and we spent time together.

He beat me with his belt and then with the buckle; both did their job real well. He threw me against the wall and kicked me until the air left my lungs. He took the broom handle and beat me across the back with it until I couldn't scream any longer. When I could finally get to my feet and he took a break to drink his Kool-Aid, and when he did, I ran into my bedroom, I locked the door, and I fell down on the floor with my face on the carpet, and I prayed. I cried and I prayed, and then I cried and prayed some more.

The house was totally calm and quiet. I drifted to sleep. I woke to him knocking on the door. I refused to open it. I heard him pick up the keys and the front door slam shut. I still wouldn't move. I heard the car crank up and leave. I still wouldn't move. Later, I heard him come back and flip on the TV. I crawled into the bed and slept. I never unlocked that door. I woke up the next morning and slowly opened the door to find he had fallen asleep in the living room. I went to the bathroom and cleaned myself up. And before I knew it, there he was behind me. He grabbed me by the neck and told me to never lock him out again. He then let me go and went on about his day like nothing ever happened. He even told me I was silly to act that way. It wasn't until we were divorced that he told me he heard voices in his head.

Left in harm's way

Now, why didn't I call the cops? Like I said, no one came to help me the first time. Nor any time after that. Neighbors would hear me yelling, and not one time did anyone call a cop; nor would they come to help me out. I did call the cops a few times, but he always convinced them I was the problem, not him, and that he was just doing his husband duty and setting his wife his property straight. Finally, he did stop the physical abuse. I guess he finally tired out, but he never stopped the mental, emotional, or spiritual abuse. I wasn't allowed to go to church because that would take me from him. And he couldn't trust the men in the church to not look at me. I wasn't allowed a have a Bible. I wasn't allowed to visit or to call my friends. When I did make a friend, he would find a way to befriend them and then turn them against me.

He had the neighbors around me watching every move I made, and they watched who came in and out of the house while he was gone, and they reported to him. He brainwashed them. One lady always knew when I was leaving the house, and she would be outside to watch me come out get in the car and leave, and then she would go back in. She would sit on her porch and talk on the phone about me to him in front of me. Oh, did I mention he had moved out on me and the kids and was living with another woman? He could do as he pleased because he made all the money, which was funny because when I made the money and kept the bills paid, he still did as he pleased.

ANTHONY MCMARYION

He was a really good-looking guy, and he wanted what he wanted, when he wanted it. I cooked for him all the time, in addition to cooking for the kids. When he was at work, I stayed in the house and tended the house. My job was the kids and the house. His was the money. He ran up credit card bills in his name and mine. I didn't want all those cards, but he thought that made him a big shot. A wallet full of debt!

When he was gone, I would pull out my hidden Bible and read, and I would watch the television evangelist. I was allowed to take care of the kids, cook, and clean. I did my best to make him happy, but it wasn't enough. The only reason he allowed the kids to go to church was the van picked them up and he had me to himself for a couple of hours. I would ask the kids when he wasn't around what they learned. It helped me. I look back now, and I realize I went into that relationship with my blinders on. I went into it with expectations and hopes and dreams, and what ended up happening was we clashed. His dreams were not the same as mine. He wanted to chase a dollar. I wanted to chase God. I wanted to raise a family. I wanted to be a stay-at-home mom. I sacrificed love for what I thought and felt was an opportunity to chase after my dream that never came to pass. He never one time sat me down before we married and told me what he expected out of me and what he wanted out of the marriage or anything.

He did not communicate with me what his desires were at all. He would say all the time, "I told you this," and I would look at him because he only thought he had. He told all his work buddies that we never consummated our wedding night, which was an outright lie. Finally, one day, I had enough of the lies and the beating me upside the head, and I took him for a moment-by-moment encounter of our wedding day. He finally realized the truth and stopped that nonsense. You cannot go into any relationship with preconceived ideas that are not of God. Get rid of your baggage before remarrying anyone. It's not fair to the person you want to start your life all over with, and it's not fair to the children. You should never bring the old husband/wife into the new life. Our last few days together were the best and worst for me. He had been on the road for a very long time.

THE SURVIVORS MODE   165

He hardly called me, and when he did, it was to yell at, cuss at, belittle me, and basically remind me he was the man and I was the slave. He finally showed up on the door step one night late. I let him in because I didn't want him to wake the kids. We got into the bedroom, and I thought, well, I can sleep, but he had other plans. Ms. Nosey, the neighbor next door, had told him I had a man coming over regular to the house, which was true. What she didn't tell him was this guy was helping me repair things around the house, and I had receipts to back up everything he was doing. I even reminded him that he gave me permission to get the work done.

So he calmed down long enough to eat. The next day, I had a meeting at church. Mind you, he stayed gone months at a time, so I began going to church. I was a music leader and a Sunday schoolteacher in Albany. We had sort of a singles group thing, and I went. He said he would watch the kids for me. So I went, and the guy who helped me with the repairs was there. When we finished, we were outside, and he helped me to my car. Then he kissed me. No lie. And I won't lie either; I returned that kiss. He was gentle and kind to me, and he knew what I was going through and dealing with. That put me on cloud 9,000. So I get home, and I thought everything was fine. Let me add here; never ever let others know what is going on in your relationships.

The devil will use it against you and present you with a wolf in sheep's clothing solution. He said, "Let's go for a walk." And I went with him. He told me he saw the guy kiss me and demanded to know who he was, phone number, address, and everything. I told him that wasn't going to happen. I felt if he wanted to know so badly, he should get Ms. Nosey to tell him or his girlfriend. He shoved me, and he told me to get to the house. I made the kids go to bed, and I went into the bedroom. He lit into me like the Fourth of July was on Donkey Kong. No, he didn't hit me physically, but he got me in every other way. Mind you, I had not slept with the guy who kissed me. It was just what he saw, a freaking kiss.

But he could have his girlfriend, and mind you, she was just the recent one on a long list of others. I sometimes wonder if he wanted to be in polygamy. Finally, I had enough. I stood up and looked him dead in his eyes, and I screamed, "In the name of Jesus, by the blood of Jesus, I command this mountain to be removed from my sight and never bother me again." He closed his mouth, went to bed, and fell asleep. I could not sleep because I knew he wouldn't let it go. The next morning, I got the kids up and out the door for school. When I came back in the house, I walked into a sight that was a scene from the best horror flick around. The person I saw standing there in the house waiting for me was not a man; he was pure beast. His whole body was blown out, and he snorted out smoke from his nostrils.

I ran into the bedroom and tried to lock the door. He, my husband, busted it open and threw me onto the bed. He grabbed my walking cane (yeah, did I mention I had to walk with a cane?) and swung at my head. I saw an angel grab the cane and throw it against the wall away from me. He grabbed my dog tags (from when I was in the army) and used them to cut my chest. I didn't realize I was bleeding until later. He pulled back his fist to punch me, and I covered up my head with my arms to try and protect myself from what was to come. When no punch landed, I looked up. He was standing there with his fist pulled back, but an angel was holding his fist. He couldn't move, and I got up and ran to the bathroom and locked all the locks. I called my best friend and said, "Code red."

She called the cops. They were slow coming. The house was quiet, and I took a shower as fast as I could, and I got dressed. I got to the door, and he stopped me. He said, "I don't know what you think you're about to do, but I advise you not to do it." Then he held his finger to his head and did the motion like a gun being shot off. I told him I was going to have coffee with my friend and then to get the kids from school. Then I would be home. Slow cops. I made it to her place. She cleaned my wounds and bandaged them. We went and got the kids. She called the police again, and this time, they flew to her house. I lived in the country, so we were optional. But she lived in the city, and cops flew to my aid. They came and took my statement and took pictures. They left to go get him, and I heard the Holy Spirit say, "Get in her house now."

I ran inside and sat on the sofa crying. He, my husband, pulled up, and I was shaking so badly I thought my skin would come off. My

THE SURVIVORS MODE

friend wasn't about to let him near me or the kids. She called the cops again, and she then told him he was trespassing. He yelled he wanted his kids. She said, "No, you don't." Eventually, the cops pulled up, and they took him to the side, and they talked to him. He tried to tell them I was the blame. The cop who showed up was a woman, and she wasn't buying his story. They arrested him and carted him off to jail. He stayed there the whole weekend. I was so scared that he would hunt me down and kill me. God stepped in and said . . . "He won't hurt you ever again."

My story for His glory

Praise God I am living to tell this story. But while I am telling you my story, I also need to shed light on what I said and did that was wrong. I wasn't perfect. While he was gone for months on end, I got hooked on painkillers (remember I walked with a cane), I drank, and, yes, I admit it, I slept around with some guys that were unsavory. Painkillers are not cheap on the black market. When you are hurting and need the fix, you do what you got to do to get what you are addicted to. What got me about his reaction to that kiss was he knew I was sleeping around and he didn't get upset over that. He would make me act out the stuff I did with the guys I slept with so he could see it. But he sure got mad over a kiss. Know why? I believe it was because he saw a man with feelings for me, and he knew his grip was gone on me. The others were just flings, and he knew it.

I admit my faults so you can see I have no problem telling on myself. I was selective, and there were five of them. I look back now and shudder. I also want to note here that I didn't have an affair until the last year of our marriage; that doesn't make what I did right. Meanwhile, he had many women and even brought them into our home, and he left our babies alone to visit them, and he gave them gifts (he never even gave me a wedding ring or a balloon). He took the kids to see them, and he threw what they did in my face, lied to me, watched porn, enjoyed many strippers, and went to motels with them.

Want to know how I got straight? I went to a Pentecostal church high and drunk. I went for the wrong reason. But God! There were two ladies, who are still very dear to my heart, who met me and gave me real smiles and real hugs. They asked me to sit with them. Folks, if you think your actions don't mean something to visitors, you're wrong. Whether a person returns love is not on the pastor, and it has no implications on his sermon; it is on you and how you receive that person. I needed a tissue. Walls started breaking. The pastor preached a fire-filled sermon, and I went to the altar. When he grabbed me, the anointing left him and literally went inside me and knocked me down and knocked the desire for pills, loose sex, and booze out of me. I woke up wrapped in a drape of sorts, and some ladies came and helped me up. I never drank excessive again after that. I haven't touched drugs that aren't prescribed for me again since.

I haven't slept around in so long; I think I have forgotten how. Not saying I don't think some guys are good looking and that God broke the mold with a few. But I don't want to sleep with them. I had to learn to tame the flesh because when that drive gets turned on, it's hard to turn off. I learned there is a difference between the lust of the flesh desire and the love bond shared between husband and wife. I hope to one day know that true bond. Still, I came out of that marriage angry. I felt like I had given him my best and he cared less. So I asked myself, did I really give him my best? Honestly speaking, no, not all the time. And I alone am accountable for that before God. He is accountable before God for his actions. Did I forgive him? Yes. It was hard. I hated him for making me into a person I didn't recognize or like. But the truth is I did it to me. Not the horror part but the staying part.

Why do battered women stay?

I can say we stay because we love and we love hard. We stay because of fear, and we stay because we think and feel have no one to turn to. We stay because we are truthfully and simply *lost souls*. Now, I realize men are abused too. I cannot speak on why men stay in abusive relationships, but I imagine it is a similar reason. Some of those who know me and know I was in the military would ask, "How come you couldn't beat him? You were military trained." Yes, I was trained for combat, and I was in combat, but I was not trained to deal with demons. Demons working through someone will beat you to a pulp quick, fast, and in a hurry. No military force on earth can defeat them.

Only the blood of Jesus can. It is the only line they cannot cross, will not cross, and are scared to cross. I had to still deal with PTSD, and it was literally the stuff like nightmares coming alive and walking around in my house. I thought I was going to lose my mind. Really, I did. If you know someone who has PTSD, do not write them off. They need your help. Show them *love* all the time.

Can you see what not having a father did to me? I made a lot of poor choices and decisions. I looked for love in the wrong places. I took that hurt and void into my marriage, and, of course, my then husband had no clue how to handle that. No more than I had a clue how to handle his rages that came out of nowhere. Life is funny, though. Wounds heal, hearts mend, lives get put back together, and in the end, God gets the glory, not us. The Bible talks about how weeping will come, but joy comes in the morning. It's true. It took me fifteen years to get here, but Praise God I am. God has blessed me to become Minister Mollie Catherine Blount. I am somebody in the body of Christ, and Satan was wrong . . . God does love me, you, and everyone. My joy in the morning has come. Praise God Almighty!

About Minister Mollie Blount

Minister Mollie Blount has overcome many obstacles to become a licensed minister with the state of Georgia. She has an associate's degree in music from Andrew College and an associate's degree in biblical studies from Victory/Grace Bible College, and she is a certified PCA with the state of Georgia. She has worked in mental health and recently works with the elderly in rehabilitation. Her unique life experiences have given her a birds'-eye view into the mind of those who suffer from post-traumatic stress syndrome, or PTSD. She met author prophet Anthony McMaryion over two years ago, and God used him to help her get totally and completely delivered, cleansed, purged, healed, and made whole from all of what she was still suffering from. Author prophet McMaryion was and still is her spiritual mentor and spiritual father, and he was the one responsible for making sure she was licensed for ministry. She is a staff leader for Lodebar Ministries Inc., which is a nonprofit community service ministry. Mollie has a heart for those who are in need, for those who suffer from PTSD, and she has a heart for abused men and women. Mollie was born in Columbus, Georgia, but was raised in Blakely, Georgia, and now she resides in Albany, Georgia.

CHAPTER THIRTEEN

Rose: The Journey of a Survivor

HOW DID SHE get to this place? It is dark. It is deep. It is lonely. Every day is the same. Every day is a struggle. She looks around, and there is no way out. For years and years, she has been trying to find a way out, fighting hard against the thoughts in her head that tell her, "You are so stupid and ugly. Whatever you have to say is ridiculous and not worth listening to, so just *shut up!* Who would ever want to be with you?" There is no one who can help her. Her last hope is the doctor, and all she heard him say was "You are on the highest medication. There is nothing more I can do for you."

She went to see him, the doctor, because she could not stop crying, and now . . . she could not stop crying. She went to see him because she wanted him to get her out of her hellhole. She came out with no hope. The doctor referred her to someone else, a counselor, to talk to. He told her it is a special center where only clients who have been referred by a doctor can go. It may take up to six weeks to get in. Six weeks! She did not have six weeks. She may not even be here tomorrow. She is stuck. She is stuck in this deep, dark, miserable place that she cannot get out of. Oh, wait. Yes. There is a way out. It is the only way.

She tells herself, *No one will miss you. Well, they might for a short while, but they will get over it and continue with their lives. You are just a burden on them. They will be better off without you.* She is standing in the middle of the road, about to cross to the local shop. What stopped her from stepping out in front of the huge truck that was approaching? The truck that would have taken her from this deep, dark place she was in. It was the hand of Jesus. The hand of Jesus has been on her life from the day she was born and before. In June 2013, He pulled her from the depths of darkness, which only He could do, and from that day forward, her life was no longer hers . . . .it belonged completely to Jesus. In reality, her life was never her own. It always belonged to God.

As she looks back, she can see the hand of Jesus on her life, every moment, of every day. He was with her in the trials, the torment, and the tribulations. One day, in His good and perfect way, He would use everything He allowed her to go through; He would use it for good. Romans 8:28 says, "And we know that in all things God works for the good of those who love him, who have been called according to his purpose." God has a plan for her life. (Jer. 29:11, "'For I know the plans I have for you,' declares the LORD, 'plans to prosper you and not to harm you, plans to give you hope and a future.'")

On that day in June 2013, the healing power of Jesus removed the blanket of darkness. The same power that raised Jesus from the dead removed the dark blanket from her life, and she was able to see God's beauty all around her. He set her feet upon a rock, high on a mountain. She could see the valley below where she had spent most of her life. She knew how dark and cold it was down there. She had been deeper than the valley. She had been in that deep, dark hole that descends below the valley. From this day forward, she began to blossom in all areas of her life. The tightly closed bud began to open up into a beautiful, sweet, fragrant flower. She praised and worshiped Jesus with a deep passion, with a deep desire to know Him, with an exhilarated excitement that "He did not save her to sit, He saved her to serve."

She would give the rest of her life to go wherever the Lord would lead her. She has a passion to see Jesus at work through her, to set broken lives free from the bondages of darkness. She is not immune from the attacks of Satan, but she has the victory through the Name of Jesus— Jesus, who defeated Satan over two thousand years ago when, on that third day, He rose from the grave. And that same power is available to each of us when we accept Him as our Lord and Savior, acknowledge that He is the Son of the one and only Living God, and ask Him into our life.

I pray my testimony will encourage you to not give up hope. I pray you will have ears to hear God speak to you, in your own unique situation, because you are special, and you are His treasure.

THE SURVIVORS MODE

Journey 1

In the Beginning

On that beautiful autumn day in March 1961, Rose was born into the very special family of a dairy farmer and his wife. She already had two older sisters, and in twenty-one months, her younger sister would be born. She was strategically placed in her family. She was beautifully and wonderfully made with a bit of this and a bit of that, from her parents' genes, her grandparents' genes, and from as far back as was needed, to make her the precious and unique little girl she was. She was loved and cared for, nurtured and protected, from the influences of the world, for she lived on a farm. Life passed by, and as she grew up, she did all the things that were expected of her.

She played sport, she went to Sunday school, and she aimed to please her parents. She was never a part of the "cool group" at school; nor was she gifted in the "physical beauty department." Rose was not academically gifted, and so she left school early to work in a job that had been arranged for her. It was assumed that, one day, she would marry and have children, and her job would then be "housewife." Rose never saw her parents argue, and so she thought a marriage "just happened." A man and a woman come together and live happily ever after. For Rose, a man and a girl came together. She was only sixteen, and he was five years older.

She was not yet an adult and was easily enticed into the world of adulthood. Rose already had the words etched in her brain, "You are so stupid and ugly," and now she added some more. "He loves you. You are not going to find anyone else who loves you," and so she took what she thought would never come along again; after all, marriage "just happens." Rose soon realized that the voice she once had was slowly being squashed. Her voiced was being squashed deep inside her by someone who was physically and mentally stronger than she had ever known anyone to be. Rose thought that maybe if they had a baby together, everything would be as it should be. Should be! That word "should" has a lot to answer for. Rose knew what her life should look like. If she had a magic wand and could wave it, just once, like the Fairy Godmother did in Cinderella, her life would be full of laughter, love, harmony, and happiness.

Isn't that what all little girls want as they grow up? Rose did not require fame or fortune, riches or prestige. She required the simple things that are free—you know, the things that fill her heart. Well, Rose became a housewife, and a mum! A young mum! She now had the responsibility of a human life on her hands, and she now had to rely on her husband for financial support. Her independence was taken away. She was now dependant on someone else to provide for her and had someone dependent on her for all their provisions. Rose went through the motions of the day. She had no love for the man in her life, and it became increasingly more difficult to be intimate with him. Rose realized that marriage did not "just happen"; it had to be worked at by two parties.

She did what she thought she had to do, and that was let him have sex with her so "his needs" were met. She would roll over and cry when the deed was done. There was no romance, no intimacy, and no love. Rose would spend most of the day preoccupied with wondering if he would want sex that night, an act she came to loathe. If she avoided it that day, she spent the next day with those same thoughts consuming her mind. If she only did what was expected of her, she could at least have the next day free from those thoughts. But then again, the more she gave, the more he wanted. And the experience was becoming more degrading and repulsive the more she was infringed upon. She had to get out.

Rose had two boys by now, and she packed them up in the car and headed to the hills, to mum. This was a safe place to go but not a place she could stay, and so it was agreed she would move back into the home and he, her husband, and father of their children would move out. He moved out and into the arms of many different women—women he would parade in front of Rose when he brought the children back home after spending some fun time with them. He was then free of responsibility, free to go socialize with more women who were willing to give him what he required.

THE SURVIVORS MODE

Months passed by, and Rose decided to try again at their marriage. They sold their two-story house with a swimming pool and moved to a little cottage in the country. The little cottage was set apart on its own, with the fire station on one side and a church enfolding the back and other side boundary. Rose was willing to give their marriage a fresh start.

The Hand of Jesus: Psalm 139:13–16, "For you created my inmost being; you knit me together in my mother's womb. I praise you because I am fearfully and wonderfully made; your works are wonderful, I know that full well. My frame was not hidden from you when I was made in the secret place, where I was woven together in the depths of the earth. Your eyes saw my unformed body, all the days ordered for me were written in your book before one of them came to be." Before Rose was even a "twinkle in the eye" of her mum and dad, God had thought about her. He knew the two people He would bring together to bring her forth into the world.

He knew where she would be placed in the family. He knew which genes He would use to create her. He was so proud of what He had made, and He loved her with an endless, unconditional love. God knew what was going to happen before it even happened (verse 16, "All the days ordained for me were written in your book before one of them came to be."). God placed Rose right at the doorstep of a church. The gate of their backyard opened into the church yard. There were no houses either side, just church.

My encouragement to you: You are not a mistake. You have been fearfully and wonderfully made by the one and only Living God who created the earth and everything in it. He also created you! God does not force Himself into our lives; He has given us all a free will to accept Him or reject Him. You cannot sit on the fence. It is either one or the other. If you haven't accepted Him, then you have rejected Him. If He forced Himself into our lives, He would be a "controlling God." He is not a God of rules and regulations; He is a God of love (John 3:16, "For God so loved the world that he gave his one and only Son, that whoever believes in him shall not perish but have eternal life").

When you accept Him into your life, He begins to reveal Himself to you, and the more time you spend with Him, reading His Word (the Bible) and talking to Him (praying), you will learn more about Him and He will reveal more of Himself to you, and you will want to live life His way because His way is the best way for us. It doesn't mean that everything bad will go away immediately, but you can know that "God knows what you are going through" and He has an antidote for everything you are going through in His Life Book (the Bible). Can you see the hand of Jesus on Rose's life? He has placed her right next to a building where people who know Him go to praise Him and learn more about Him. People who are more mature in their relationship with God, who will deposit words of wisdom into her life, give her encouragement along her journey and water the seed that was planted in Sunday school. God knows you. Do you know God?

Journey 2

Turbulent Marriages

Rose started to attend church, as did her husband. They renewed their wedding vows before God and the church congregation. Both were water baptized as a public declaration that "it's no longer I that live, but Christ lives in me!" All seemed well for a while until the same problems emerged, and Rose once again became a spectator in her own marriage, and her marriage was deteriorating, a relationship that was unhappy and unhealthy. Rose's husband even discussed with the pastor his reasoning of wanting to indulge the services of prostitutes to satisfy his sexual desires and how this could help the relationship. Rose was right back in the same place she had been years before. She could not do what was expected of her, and the attempt to keep her marriage together had failed again.

Her husband moved out. Unbeknown to Rose, this action would infuriate and unleash a whole tribe of demon-infested gremlins who would attack her like an army of feral critters wherever and whenever they could. Her husband's family banded together in force against her. They had no shame in spitting words of hateful revenge at her. They had no shame in spitting on the ground in front of her. They had no shame in manifesting lies against her. They fed on hate, and their hate grew to insurmountable proportions that were intentionally and precisely fired directly at Rose. Rose knew she was partly responsible for the marriage breakdown; however, she felt like she was being led to an open arena, surrounded by the firing squad. She felt vulnerable and ill-equipped for the onslaught.

The battle was taken to the family law courts. In the courtrooms, the character and true nature of the family could not be contained, and the judge ruled that Rose have custody of the children. The attacks toward Rose continued. She did all she could to make it look as if she was coping to the outside world, but she was becoming weaker and weaker as they set about to destroy her. Rose was unaware that someone was watching her, someone who wanted to get to know her on a more personal level. Rose thought her knight in shining armor had come along. He was bigger and stronger than her attackers. He protected her from them; he was the shield that stood between her and them when they fired their ammunition that they had been away preparing for the next attack.

Rose was ignorant to the obvious fact that the knight in shining armor was an alcoholic and a gambler, and he had connections with unsavory people of society. Rose soon found herself in a web, the web of fatal attraction. She did try to get out of the web, but her "spider" would keep pulling the web tighter and then inflict force upon her. People from the church tried to untangle her from the web, but the "spider" had intimidating powers over her. She was trapped. Had God heard her desperate prayer?

Did He know of her desperate longing as she would lie prostrate on the floor, crying out to Him, "Lord, You said You would not put me through any more than I could handle. Well, I cannot handle any more! Please! Get me out of this!" Rose could only see that there was one way out. She walked her two boys to school on that day, for it would be the very last time. She walked the long way back to her home, sat on her bed with the box full of tablets next to her, and pondered what she would write in her letter to each of her boys. The phone rang. It was a friend who, unbeknown to Rose, had been threatened by the "spider" to "stay away from her."

Rose kept the conversation short. Soon after hanging up the phone, there was a knock at the door. The ambulance was parked out in front of her home, and the male ambulance officer told Rose he had a phone call from a concerned friend who told them they needed to come see if everything was OK. Rose was taken away in the ambulance to spend time in the nearby hospital. Visitors were restricted to family and selected friends. The man in her life was prohibited from visiting the hospital; however, on release, no support system was set up for Rose, and he strategically pulled her back into his web. He promised he would change; that being married would give him a reason to change. He started going to church, and they married.

THE SURVIVORS MODE
179

Things did not change. He insisted they have a child together, as this would give him the responsibility to change. Rose knew from past experience not to use a child as a solution to a problem, and she was not prepared to bring a child into this relationship. Rose kept taking birth control contraception secretly. How did he know? How did he find out? It is one little tablet that takes only one second to swallow, and yet he found them. Rose paid the consequences for that deceit. She could only pray to God that He would keep her from bringing a child into the diabolical relationship.

A beautiful son was born, and Rose loved him with all her heart, as she did her other two boys. Rose knows that God does not make mistakes, and all of Rose's children are a huge blessing to her life. Her husband did not change. The abuse continued; verbal (emotional), financial, social, sexual, and physical abuse.

The Hand of Jesus: Even though Rose could not see it, the hand of Jesus was on her life all the time. Rose was not attending church before she moved to the little country town where her only neighbor was church. Rose was not aware at the time that the praise and worship songs she was singing with so much honesty and yearning in her heart, on a Sunday and through the week at home, were actually scriptures (God's Word) being prayed to Him in song. In Rose's defense, the pastor stood up for the fidelity of marriage, backed by scriptures that state, "Put to death, therefore, whatever belongs to your earthly nature: sexual immorality, impurity, lust, evil desires and greed, which is idolatry" (Col. 3:5) and Romans 8:5–6, "Those who live according to the flesh have their minds set on what the flesh desires; but those who live in accordance with the Spirit have their minds set on what the Spirit desires."

The mind governed by the flesh is death, but the mind governed by the Spirit is life and peace. Even though Rose was to go through more difficult times, God's promise in Joshua 1:5 ("No one will be able to stand against you all the days of your life. As I was with Moses, so I will be with you; I will never leave you nor forsake you") was evident through the obedience of Rose's friend, who had a strong impulse to just call at that particular time. Of all the people God could have prompted, He prompted the person He knew would follow through, no matter how bizarre it seemed. One hour later, and the outcome could have been a whole lot different. Can you see the hand of Jesus on your life?

My encouragement to you: You may think that God does not care about your situation, or He is just being an onlooker, not willing to get involved. I can tell you He is involved. He made you, you are His child, and He cares about you. In the book of Matthew 10:29–31, Jesus says, "Are not two sparrows sold for a penny? Yet not one of them will fall to the ground outside your Father's care. And even the very hairs of your head are all numbered. So don't be afraid; you are worth more than many sparrows." He loves you. You are important to Him. I challenge you to stop and think about a situation in the past. I mean, stop and think. Have you got one? Now, looking back at the situation, can you recognize particular happenings or maybe a specific individual who came across your path who said something that was relevant or applicable to what you were going through? Because you were "in it." you were too consumed with all the events going on around you that you were oblivious to see or hear the hand of Jesus on your life.

I also encourage you to be the one that God uses. Rose's friend did not know what Rose was intending to do, yet she acted promptly on her "intuition." She was obedient to God's prompting. Do not be discouraged if you think, "Oh no, I should have said something," which you think may have changed a situation. God is bigger than any situation. He is almighty; He is all knowing; He is omniscient (having complete or unlimited knowledge, awareness, and understanding, and perceiving all things). If it wasn't you who said or did what He wanted, He would use someone else. Our God is an amazing God!

THE SURVIVORS MODE

Journey 3

Trapped in Abuse

Rose's husband insisted they move from the small country town they lived in, and he arranged a rental property through a contact of his. Rose did not want to move from the home that was hers, but she was too afraid to oppose, and so she prayed, "Lord, if I have to move from here, I want to be where I see the sun set every night." Rose imagined a house not too far away from where she lived, in the country, on top of a hill, facing the west, and seeing the beauty and love of God in the sunset every night. This would be better than the previous place he wanted to move to, in outback Australia where they live underground because it is so hot. When they went to visit the outback township, the mirror in Rose's car fell off because the heat melted the glue that was keeping it where it was meant to be! Rose found a moment of boldness when she absolutely refused to move to that place!

They moved to a three-story townhouse in the city that was in need of many repairs, but that did not matter to Rose because the house was on the Esplanade overlooking the ocean. No one could build in front or obstruct the view of the spectacular sunsets . . . every night. The sunsets were absolutely spectacular; however, Rose felt isolated. Her husband indulged in the array and abundance of hotels in the city environment, feeding his alcohol addiction and gambling addiction. Rose suffered at the hands of verbal abuse, financial abuse, social abuse, sexual abuse, and physical abuse. There were days she would have to check the washing machine to see if there was any money that may have inadvertently been left in the pocket of his clothes just so she could buy some milk for her children. It was a good day when she found some.

Maybe only five cents, but it all adds up. He had access to what once used to be Rose's bank account, and so there was never any money in it. Rose did whatever she could to not make him angry. When his anger escalated toward her, Rose would hide behind bushes outside of the house in the public gardens for hours until she knew he had calmed down, leaving the children inside with him because he had not yet hurt them. One night, she slept in the car with her three-month-old son, too scared to return to the house (her other children were on access visit with their dad). Rose did whatever she could to keep safe, and each day was like "living on egg shells" because she never knew what to expect.

One day, a pamphlet was left in the letter box that caught Rose's attention. The local community center was advertising free, confidential, one-on-one counseling sessions for women in abusive relationships. Rose contacted the center and, for the first time in her life, was able to confide in someone who listened and understood what she was going through on a daily basis. Rose felt comfortable with the counselor because she was patient and did not tell Rose what she had to do; instead, she educated Rose on abuse, rape within marriage, isolating the victim, power, and control of the abuser, the abuse cycle, the "honeymoon period," and gave life skills that would one day come into effect when she had to flee. That day came when he brutally kicked into Rose while she lay on the floor playing with their eighteen-month son. He finished with saying, "Your kids will be next." Rose knew she had to flee. When he left the house the next day, Rose left with bare minimum essentials for herself and her children and headed for the hills, to Mum and Dad . . . again. Rose would never go back and live with him no matter how often he threatened to kill her.

The Hand of Jesus: Rose's prayer was answered in an almighty way. It was not how she thought it would be; it was better. If Rose had traveled to outback Australia at a different time of the year, it may not have been as hot as the day they traveled, and Rose could have been looking out over the vast dry and sandy desert instead of the cool, refreshing ocean.

God says in Isaiah 45:2–3, "I will go before you and will level the mountains; I will break down gates of bronze and cut through bars of iron. I will give you hidden treasures, riches stored in secret places, so that you may know that I am the LORD, the God of Israel, who summons you by name." Rose was immensely blessed in her turmoil and reminded of the hand of Jesus on her life every moment of the day as she looked out over the beautiful ocean and experienced incredible sunsets every night. From the top level of the townhouse, Rose could see the sunrise. In Psalm 139:9–10, the psalmist David knows full well,

"If I rise on the wings of the dawn, if I settle on the far side of the sea, even there your hand will guide me, your right hand will hold me fast."

Rose never saw a pamphlet come in the letter box again like the one that came in that desperate, lonely hour. Jesus had His hand on Rose's life. The song "Through It All" by Selah written by Andre Crouch and the Disciples depicts exactly what Rose was going through. I encourage you to watch the music video.

My encouragement to you: God created us to be relational, to reflect His image and live our life as Jesus did. Abuse within relationships destroys the loving relationship God desires us to have. Are you in an abusive relationship? It is not up to me to tell you to "get out." I won't do that. That has to be your decision. It is your life. However, I want you to know that you are special. You are precious. You are God's child. He sent His one and only Son to die on a cross just so that He could redeem the relationship with you that was destroyed in the Garden of Eden. God loves you. You are His purchased possession, which makes you worthy of being treated with utmost respect and love. God never intended for you to be treated in any way less than this.

And so I can *and will passionately urge you* to consider other options. I am not telling you to "get out." If your relationship can be salvaged— that is, your partner is aware and willing to work on issues, then I urge you to seek professional help, someone qualified in the area, someone you can trust, and someone who will give you "homework" for both of you to work on. If you can relate to Rose's situation, my encouragement to you is to seek the right help on your own as I did. Your self-esteem and self-worth have been knocked around and battered to the point that you are unable to make wise decisions. You are unable to see "a way out." Maybe you are unsure what abuse looks like in a relationship. Let me just take some time and briefly outline some of the behaviors that demonstrate abuse.

- Physical violence includes physically hurting a person, forcing a person to engage in nonconsensual sexual practices and damaging objects, buildings, or family pets.

- Emotional violence consists of verbal threats, put-downs, and intimidation, which erode a person's self-esteem.
- Social abuse controls a person by isolating them from family and friends, humiliating them in public, constantly checking up on them, and wanting to know every detail of their day.
- Financial abuse includes controlling finances, keeping money from a person so they are financially dependent upon the other, and demanding accountability of money spent.
- Spiritual abuse involves degrading a person's spirituality and selectively using scripture out of context to validate behavior.
- Sexual abuse includes forcing or coercing a woman to perform sexual acts against her will, physically attacking the sexual parts of her body, demanding sex, rape, bondage, using objects, and treating her as a sexual object.

Sexual abuse can be put in the category of physical violence. I personally put sexual abuse in a category all of its own.

Abuse facts

From my personal experience, I learned a very hard lesson, and that is abuse has an extremely negative impact upon a relationship and can ultimately destroy the relationship God intended for us to have. Abuse also has an extremely negative impact upon the victim. Being a target for abuse, I also learned of some staggering statistics as I was on my journey into being an abuse survivor, and what I learned from my personal experience were the following:

A. Intimate partner violence is the most common type of violence against women, affecting 30 percent of women worldwide. Violence against women is a serious problem, and in Australia, where I lived over twelve months, on the average, one woman is killed every week as a result of intimate partner violence.
B. A woman is most likely to be killed by her male partner in her home.

C. Domestic and family violence is the principle cause of homelessness for women and their children.

D. Intimate partner violence is the leading contributor to death, disability, and ill-health in Australian women aged fifteen to forty-four. One in three women has experienced physical and/or sexual violence perpetrated by someone known to them.

E. One in four children is exposed to domestic violence, which is a recognized form of child abuse.

F. The cost of violence against women in the Australian economy is estimated to rise to $15.6 billion per annum.

G. One in five women experience harassment within the workplace, and one in five women over eighteen has been stalked during her lifetime.

H. In the first fifteen weeks of 2015, thirty-one women had been killed in domestic violence situations in Australia. That's two women every week killed by violence by someone within their family circle.

The most significant *information* the counselor gave Rose was educating her on the "abuse cycle." I encourage you to educate yourself on this if you do not know about it. Learn to recognize the cycle in your own relationship. The most significant *advice* the counselor gave Rose was to have an "emergency bag" packed and ready to leave in a hurry.

Pack in the bag: a change of clothes for yourself and child/children, toiletries (toothpaste, toothbrush, and deodorant, whatever you think you may need), money, and bank account numbers (so you can put a stop to bank accounts that have your name on them; it may very quickly go into overdraft). You will be unable to think what you need if and when that time comes to flee. At the time, Rose was not thinking of leaving, and she thought the counselor was overreacting. However, that day came, and Rose was so very grateful for the advice. So hide your emergency bag. Hide it in a place where he will not find it because when you are in a desperate situation, nothing else matters except getting out with your life and your children's lives. Rose was challenged with her biblical beliefs that instruct the woman to be submissive to the husband

(Eph. 5). Rose's husband took these few words and demanded the day after they married that he was now the head of the home and she had to do what he said; however, he did not read the rest of the verses (spiritual abuse) that state, "Husbands, love your wives, just as Christ loved the church and gave himself up for her to make her holy, cleansing her by the washing with water through the word, and to present her to himself as a radiant church, without stain or wrinkle or any other blemish, but holy and blameless. In this way, husbands ought to love their wives as their own bodies. He who loves his wife loves himself." How easy would it be to submit to a husband who did all this! This is God's original plan for relationships. He did not create relationships to be abusive.

Journey 4

Faith to Change

It wasn't until Rose was a single parent that she noticed families . . . in the shopping center, at church, at the beach, on placards and billboards, on the television; families everywhere. Advertisements always portrayed "happy families" that consisted of "mum, dad, and two children." This cut hard to the core of Rose's heart. She was no longer a family, and she had failed her children the right to a "normal" happy family life.

The landlord of the three-story townhouse insisted Rose be the tenant, and she moved back into the house that was way too big for her. To help pay the rent, Rose mowed the lawns and cleaned the toilets of the nursing home that her landlord owned and managed. Rose had attended several churches in the area until she found one that she liked. When the townhouse was put on the market to be sold, Rose needed to find other accommodation. An elder of the church offered Rose a rental unit he owned that was becoming available just at that time. Rose gratefully moved into the unit, which was diagonally across the road from the church. She no longer had to mow lawns to supplement the rent of the townhouse and was able to apply for a cleaning job at a hotel . . . cleaning up after alcoholics.

THE SURVIVORS MODE

Rose had been financially destitute from her previous marriage; however, with the help and generosity of her parents, she was able to put a deposit on a house that would become her home. Rose did not see the filth in the bathroom or the smoke-stained walls, the dirty windows, and stained ceilings, or the white ants that had taken residence in one of the rooms. When Rose walked into the home, she could only see what it could become with a little bit of tender loving care. Rose's brother-in-law went into the fierce bidding battle for the home as Rose anxiously was waiting at his side. The bids were rising fast. Rose had a limit on what she could go to, and it was obvious from the speed of the bidding that it was going to be out of her reach. Rose's brother-in-law quickly consulted with her, asking if she could go $1,000 more. The bid was in . . . and then . . . quiet. No more bids. It was as if the mouths of all the other bidders were shut.

The bids were advancing so fast, and then it just stopped . . . on Rose's bid. The familiar words . . . "Going once! . . . Going twice!" rang out over the crowd of people. The auctioneer was pointing toward Rose and her brother-in-law as he lifted and then lowered his outstretched arm after each statement . . . "Sold!" It was an unbelievable moment! Rose owned a home again! A mass of people from the church Rose was attending, along with family, came and cleaned, painted, scrubbed, and rejuvenated the neglected house into a warm, welcoming home. The white ants were eradicated, and Rose took residence in her "new" home.

It was 2003 (Rose was forty-two years of age) when she noticed the vision in her left eye was deteriorating. Rose was diagnosed with a genetically inherited eye disease inappropriately called Best's disease. It is *not* the best disease, and Rose faced the prognosis of slowly losing her sight as the rods and cones behind each eye progressively deteriorated. Rose was told, "There is nothing that can be done for you. There is no cure." Rose always had perfect vision in both of her eyes, and so it was devastating for her to know there was nothing that could be done to prevent facing the inevitable . . . slowly becoming blind. A group of people from church began to meet weekly and pray for her; however, it was one night in 2004 while attending a small church "home group" that a simple prayer was prayed, and Rose knew she had been touched by the power of Jesus. When Rose checked the vision in her left eye, there was significant improvement in its vision. Rose had experienced the healing power of Jesus!

The same power that raised Jesus from the dead miraculously repaired what no human genius, with all their scientific expertise and medical equipment, could do. Rose had experienced partial healing in her left eye. A miracle! It was not complete healing, but Rose knew it was enough to sustain her when the other eye's vision would start to be visually evident. Rose diligently worked at her cleaning job, getting up in the early hours of the morning so she would finish before the required time. Delinquent men were also out in these early hours of the morning, prowling the streets for a crime to commit. On several occasions, Rose unintentionally stumbled across the offenders in the act of a crime. Rose had never been so scared in her life. She had no idea what they were capable of doing if they saw her. Her knees physically began to shake as she kept herself protected and shielded from the offenders and called the police for help. It was time for a career change.

The Hand of Jesus: Jesus continues to noticeably have His hand upon Rose's life. The unit Rose moved into became available just at the time Rose needed to be out of the townhouse. If Rose had chosen another church to attend, she would not have been aware of the unit's availability. Once again, her awaiting home was within view of the church she attended. Neither Rose nor her brother-in-law had any control over the purchase price of the house that became Rose's home. Many people could argue different reasons why the other bidders had stopped, but Rose was told many times after the purchase that she got the home very cheap. Rose had a limit, and God had the power—the power to stop the bidding when it did. God had the power to shut the mouths of lions when the king ordered Daniel to be thrown in the lion's den (Dan. 6:16–22), and we know "Jesus Christ is the same yesterday and today and forever" (Heb. 13:8).

Rose had attended many prayer meetings for the healing of her eyes with more-mature Christians in the church. They came with their knowledge and faith, diligently praying and believing for a miracle; however, the healing did not come through the striving and good works of these diligent people; it was within a small group setting, through the simple prayer of a "doubting Thomas" that Jesus performed His miracle. Who is a "doubting Thomas"? Someone who doubts what he cannot see. Thomas was one of Jesus's disciples who needed to see for himself the wounds in Jesus's hands after He rose from the dead. Jesus told him to also place his hand in His side. It was only then that Thomas believed (John 20:24–27). The healing of Rose's eye was twofold, threefold, fourfold, ten-thousandfold! It increased the faith of Rose; it increased the faith of the "doubting Thomas"; it increased the faith of the church; and it must surely plant a seed of faith in those who do not believe, like the eye specialist, family and friends, all those people whom Rose undoubtedly shares the moment her eyes were healed.

This is a stark reminder that it is "not by might nor by power, but by my Spirit, says the LORD Almighty" (Zachariah 4:6). There is absolutely no doubt that Rose's left eye was healed by the healing power of Jesus, and He gets *all* the Glory! Many times, the hand of Jesus on Rose's life needed to be blatantly obvious, as Rose is someone who does not like change; she likes security. It took Rose to be so scared when she came face-to-face with criminals in the act that she was encouraged to consider a career change. For Rose, faith needed to be implemented. "Now faith is confidence in what we hope for and assurance about what we do not see" (Heb. 11:1); however, "faith, by itself, if it is not accompanied by action, is dead" (James 2:17). Rose needed to step out of her comfort zone and leave the cleaning job, in faith, before she even knew what her next employment option was.

My encouragement to you: Just as the hand of Jesus was always on Rose's life, His hand is also on your life. We are all on a journey, a spiritual journey. The road is long, and there will be good times, and there will also be obstacles along the way. Some are so big that you will not be able to see the road ahead. Some will be smaller in height but stretch out far in front of you. These obstacles are in your path to teach you and strengthen you, even though at the time, you cannot appreciate the value of them. You can either travel this road alone or you can acknowledge Jesus as your companion. He will sometimes go ahead of you; sometimes, He will be walking beside you; other times,

He will be walking behind you; and there will be times when He will be carrying you.

I encourage you to stop for a moment and take a look at your journey and see where Jesus was through it all; the times He went ahead of you and made the path clear; the times He walked right beside you and was your comforter and friend; the times He walked behind you and was your encourager to keep you moving forward; and those times when He carried you through the pain and torment of a storm. Jesus knows how to get you to your destination point because He already knows what and where it is. He is the Alpha and the Omega (Rev. 22:13). He is the beginning and the end. He knows your beginning and your end, and so wouldn't it make sense to trust in Him to know how to get you to your destination? Proverbs 3:5–6 tells us to "trust in the LORD with all your heart and lean not on your own understanding; in all your ways submit to him, and he will make your paths straight."

God has a plan for each of our lives, and He will use everything we go through for good (Rom. 8:28) even though Satan intends for it to hurt us. So thank Him for the people He has put in your path; they are there to teach you something valuable. They are there for a reason, and they are there for a season. Just as seasons pass, so do some people pass through our lives. And when those winter storms come upon your life with rain, lightning, and thunder and you feel like you are being tossed about in a small boat out in the wide ocean, with waves crashing down over you, just know that as with any storm of nature, it will end. You can see the dark clouds rolling in over the ocean, about to dump a whole lot of rain on you, but they will pass; they do not go on forever.

There is always an end to a storm. So thank God for the good times and thank Him for the bad times you go through because it is testing and strengthening your faith, which, in turn, produces perseverance (James 1:3), which is a character needed on any journey. He knows the plans He has for you, "plans to prosper you and not to harm you, plan's to give you hope and a future" (Jer. 29:11). You can know that God is with you in all circumstances. So thank Him . . . *in all circumstances* (1 Thess. 5:18).

Journey 5

Damaged and Depressed

Rose's home became a hub of activity each day as it was overflowing with the enjoyment and laughter of little children who were dropped off by their parent/s to the family day care business Rose had started in her home. Her home was set out perfectly for the child care center to meet the needs of little ones. Rose's home also became a safe place for women and their children to stay when they needed to escape for a short period from an abusive relationship.

Rose had divorced her husband, but she continued to suffer verbal abuse from him as he found ways and made excuses to be in contact with her, often just turning up on her doorstep uninvited and unannounced. He still had power to influence and degrade a very fragile Rose, who had been bombarded repeatedly with his malicious, vicious, offensive, degrading assault of words that were now embedded in her brain. When he was not in contact physically, the words he had deposited in Rose's brain would rise up like soldiers and repeatedly fire the deadly ammunition over and over and over again, which consistently attacked Rose's self-esteem. The cruel, critical, nasty, negative words were the first thoughts that Rose would access, no matter how hard she tried not to.

They were always there at the forefront of her thinking, and they had the ability to roll over and over in her mind, like a snowball rolling down a hill, gathering momentum, picking up other negative thoughts along the way, pulling them in, and sticking them onto the rolling boulder. The boulder continued to build in size, like a huge, massive tumor in Rose's brain. The massive tumor of thoughts took over and controlled Rose's life. Life through Rose's eyes was gray. It was a struggle every day to get out of bed. It was demanding to just get through the day. It was a lonely, dark place to be.

After years had passed by, Rose was physically exhausted from the demands of the family day care business. It was time to close the business, and Rose once again became unemployed. Job prospects were limited as the vision in her right eye was deteriorating and her age was increasing. Rose was encouraged by an employment agency to study in a specific profession so she would then have qualifications to support job opportunities. Study! Rose? Study! She had never done that in her life! However, while attending a Christian conference, the words of an international motivational speaker rang in her head . . . "What would you do if you knew you could not fail?" Well, Rose had a dependable, reliable friend who would remind her of these words and encouraged Rose to "investigate" the possibility of a counseling course at a Christian college. Rose went to the interview, and before she knew it, she was accepted and enrolled in the course that very day!

Rose likened the experience to being on a water slide. If you have never been on a water slide, let Rose tell you of her experience of only ever being on one, once in her lifetime (she will never go on one again!) She sat at the top of the slide. The water was flowing fast, down the long and windy half tunnel. Rose let go, and at that point, she had given up all sense of having any control again, until she got to the bottom. Rose was swished from one side of the slide to the other side as she zoomed around one bend after another, being swept up the side of the slide with the flow of water. Rose was sure she was going to be flung up over the side and land on the ground below.

In desperation, she tried to take back some control to slow down the increasing pace of being swept along the half tunnel. Rose put her hand out and grabbed the side of the slide, only to have her arm pulled half way out of its socket! She relented. She had to! She surrendered. There was no other way. She gave in. It was all she could do until she got to the end of it. And then . . . she was thrown into the pool of water at the bottom, and she began plummeting down, down, down, wondering when the downward plunge would stop and she would start to come up for air. It seemed to take forever! Well, this was the exact feeling Rose had when she went for the "interview" to study an associate's degree in counseling. Before she knew it, Rose was enrolled to start in three days' time. How could that have happened?

Rose's friend was a "lifeline" in this time of desperation. She kept Rose from drowning on many occasions. She taught Rose how to write

THE SURVIVORS MODE

an assignment and sat with Rose on the floor of the Christian bookstore, looking up words Rose never even knew existed in the human language. She would sit with Rose in her study area and persuade Rose's fingers to type the words onto the Word document—words that were supposed to be in Rose's head. But the words would not come. There was a blockage. That little army of soldiers blocked all points of entry and fired their ammunition . . . "You have got to be joking! That is not right. You can't say that! That just sounds so stupid!"

Rose's fingers did not move, and her friend squeezed and squeezed and squeezed, like you squeeze the tube of toothpaste to get that last little bit out. Well, Rose and her friend could not even get the *first* little bit out! Rose spent many hours . . . in tears, over her assignments. But she persisted, and when her first assignment came back with an impressive grade on it (a "pass"), Rose began to knock those soldiers down like fireflies, one at a time.

The Hand of Jesus: The Twenty-Third Psalm is a well-known psalm. The amplified Bible expresses it this way: "The LORD is my Shepherd (to feed, guide, and shield me), I shall not lack. He makes me lie down in (fresh, tender) green pastures; He leads me beside the still and restful waters (Rev 7:17). He refreshes and restores my life (myself); He leads me in the paths of righteousness (uprightness and right standing with Him—not for my earning it, but) for His name's sake. Yes, though I walk through the (deep, sunless) valley of the shadow of death, I will fear or dread no evil, for You are with me; Your rod (to protect) and Your staff (to guide), they comfort me. You prepare a table before me in the presence of my enemies. You anoint my head with oil; my (brimming) cup runs over. Surely or only goodness, mercy, and unfailing love shall follow me all the days of my life, and through the length of my days the house of the Lord (and His presence) shall be my dwelling place."

This psalm articulates how Jesus is with us all the time. Jesus had walked before Rose and knew which home would be perfect for her to work a family day care business from, and one of the mums would become the lifeline Rose would need in the next part of her journey, just up the road a bit, which Rose could not yet see. Jesus carried Rose through the times of abuse from her ex-husband. "I will fear or dread no evil, for You are with me" (verse 4). The police provided protection during the times of assault, and her friend provided positive, uplifting encouragement on a daily basis. Jesus had prepared the way for Rose to study at the university level, and He stood behind her and watched as the process swept Rose into the place He wanted her to be. Jesus walked right beside Rose through the support and encouragement of her reliable friend, as Rose labored through the workload and expectations of the university.

My encouragement to you: What would *you* do if you knew you could not fail? I am asking you this sincerely, what would you do? I know it is difficult to even dare think about it when you have had your dreams shattered over and over again; however, this is our time to stop and *dare to think.* Let me pray for you . . . Heavenly Father, Lord, I thank You for this dear, precious child of Yours. Lord, I pray that at this very moment, You will strip away all negative thoughts, all doubts, Lord, and all unworthiness. Lord, let this child of Yours know how precious and special they are to You. Let them know, Lord, that You are right there with them and You will not let them fall. I thank You, Lord, for the people You have already placed on the path of their journey. I thank You for the plans You have for this precious child of Yours, and I thank You, Lord, that You are greater than he who is in this world. I praise You and thank You, in Jesus's precious name.

Let me tell you that the opinion of other people does not matter because they don't have to know what you are thinking; it is just you and me, and I am not going to know anyway. Oh, hang on, there is someone else . . . Jesus is listening! But just let me encourage you . . . He already knows what it is anyway! He has put that thought in your head, and He already has the path set out, and the right people on that path will come into play right at the precise moment. You cannot and will not fail! I would like to share this letter with you. It was for one of my assignments at the university. I woke up in the early hours of the night, opened my laptop, and my fingers typed the words that came into my head (yes, a miracle!). The assignment required me to do something for someone.

This left options wide open, but when these words came to me, I knew they were not my words; they are from God. I knew the lovely lady I was to share them with, but I also knew they were meant for me . . . and they are meant for you as well. This is a letter from God . . . to you. Read it slowly and allow the words to settle in your heart, or have someone read it out loud to you.

"I want you to know just how much I love you. I have known you before the foundations of the earth. I created you and chose you to be my child. You are so special to me. I watch your every move, I know your every thought, and I have saved all the tears you have cried.

Accept my love

I left the comfort and purity of my home and became just like you. I was ridiculed, put to shame and suffered a cruel death, just to have a relationship with you. There is nothing you can do to make me love you. I love you now, as I have always loved you. I see you through the eyes of my Son, Jesus Christ. You are just as I have always wanted you to be. You are perfect.

Accept my love.

I have chosen you, to live my life through. Your body is my temple. You are holy, because I live in you. You do not have to become pure and holy for me to love you, I love you just as you are. I have so many wonderful blessings I want to share with you now. You are my child.

Accept my love.

You are feeling lost and lonely, and yet I am right here waiting for you. You do not have to prove to me, in any way, that you are worthy of my love. Jesus did that. Come to me so I can hold you in my arms and love you like no one else can love you. I will love you from the inside out.

Accept my love.

I did not create you to live a life of misery. I created you to live a life with me. I want to share in everything you do. Look around and see all the things I have given you to enjoy. Take time to enjoy them and delight in the things you already have. I have so much more I want to give you.

Accept my love.

I am not hard to find. You do not have to search for me. I am right here. I am just waiting for you . . . to accept my love."

Do you know Jesus as your personal Savior? He is waiting for you to accept His love. All you need to do is ask Him into your life . . . "Lord, I accept You as my Lord and Savior." Acknowledge that Jesus is the Son of the one and only living God, who died on a cross and rose from the dead. Ask Him to forgive you for doing life on your own and tell Him you want Him as Lord and Savior of your life. It is that simple. Jesus says, "Ask and it will be given to you; seek and you will find; knock and the door will be opened to you" (Matt. 7:7).

If you have prayed and asked Jesus into your life, I encourage you to find a church that will support you in your journey. A little bit of advice from me to you . . . do not look at the people when choosing a church. They are people just like you and me, broken and in need of a Savior. Look for Jesus. Are they teaching you about the love and grace of God? Love and grace . . . not rules and regulations. If the love of Jesus is being preached from the pulpit, you will see evidence of Him in the people attending. Find a church that suits your needs. Ask God to lead you to one, just as He has done for Rose. Talk to Him daily. He is your friend.

Journey 6

Abuse, Depression, and PTSD

Rose was able to get an assignment handed up on time, but it still took her many long hours in a day that turned into weeks before she had learned what she needed to learn to answer the assignment question. The end of the time frame had come for the associate's degree, and Rose was encouraged to continue on to obtain the bachelor's degree. Reluctantly, Rose continued, which took her into four years of study! If she had known that she was going to be at a university for four years in the beginning, she would never have signed the application papers, but facing the challenge in stages was the best Rose could do. The subject content was very informative, challenging, and changing. Rose felt like she was in one big counseling session as she personally applied the information to her own life.

There were three major happenings that occurred during Rose's time at the university that unveiled a hidden reality and unveiled a heart-wrenching truth to Rose. The first one was when Rose was sitting in a sexual abuse lecture and the lecturer was talking about the Stockholm syndrome. She explained how, in 1973 in Sweden, Stockholm, three women and one man were held hostage by two gun-wielding men for five days. The hostages became emotionally bonded to their captors during this time of torment and abuse, defending them to the public on their release. The lecturer then started to give an in-depth, detailed account of how this can happen in an abusive relationship.

As she explained a fabricated scenario, Rose's heart began to increase rapidly, and it sounded like the lecturer was talking in slow motion. The words were clear, precise, and all so real to Rose. Rose wanted her to stop! Why was she talking so slowly? Why was she going on and on and on about every intricate detail! Rose could not take it anymore and had to get out of that room! She tried to leave discreetly, but soon after exiting the room, the lecturer's assistant followed to check on her. After explaining what happened, and in tears, Rose was encouraged to access counseling from within the university, as this was not a "normal" reaction to what was being shared. The second occurrence was during the Working with Mental Health subject, which Rose found to be very interesting.

As Rose was studying the symptoms of depression from the assigned textbook *Abnormal Psychology*, she was enlightened to another form of depression called dysthymia, which incorporates the same symptoms as depression but in a more mild intensity and over a longer period. This was Rose's reality, and she could trace it back for thirty years! At another time, Rose was reading about "impulse control disorders," which include pyromania (the urge to light fires), kleptomania (the urge to steal even if not needed), and trichotillomania (pronounced "trick-a-tilla-mania").

Rose had never heard of this one, but, whoa . . . wait up . . . this is what she does . . . compulsively pull her hair out. She has done it for years. She pictures going to the hairdresser and the hairdresser noticing the little stubs of hair growing back on top of her head. Rose was unaware she was doing it, and she could not explain the reason for what the hairdresser thought was breakage. As Rose read on, it tells her that this impulsive disorder is most often associated with post-traumatic stress disorder. Seriously? That can't be possible. Doesn't that only happen to men who have fought in wars? Rose had a lot to take in. In a weird way, it gave her comfort to know there was a name that she could now put to her messed-up life.

The third occurrence was during a counseling session Rose was required to attend. The bachelor of social science in counseling required the student to attend counseling sessions that were conducted by students who had already graduated from the bachelor's Degree and had progressed to a higher level of study. The counseling sessions were intended for the impending counselor to experience what it feels like to be a client. During these sessions, Rose was confronted with talking about her past and confronted about the abuse she had been victim to. At the conclusion of one of the sessions, the counselor and Rose concurrently named the types of abuse Rose had suffered at the hands of her partners—physical, verbal, social, financial; however, neither could think of the fifth one. The counselor included neglect as a form of abuse, but that was not it. Minutes passed by . . . why could she not recall that last one? It finally came to Rose . . . sexual abuse.

The counselor got up from her seat telling Rose, "That is your spider"; that is where the source of abuse began. She explained that it is like a spider's web; all the other forms of abuse have been concealing the spider. She walked over to the whiteboard and drew a spider's web. In the middle, she drew a big black spider, picked up the red marker, and drew a red stripe down its back and said, "Sexual abuse is your spider." It was the end of the session, and Rose walked out of the counseling room with that thought in her mind, mystified at the origin of the spider.

That night, Rose had a vivid dream. Very clearly, Rose heard the words "1961, ask Mum" as she was asleep in her bed. That was it. Nothing else, just "1961, ask Mum." Rose remembered it very clearly in the morning, and she was puzzled. She thought, *I was born in 1961. I was a baby.* Rose asked her mum if she had ever been left alone with someone when she was a baby. The only time Rose was left with someone else was when her younger sister was born and she was left with family . . . and yes, she was a baby. What happened? Rose will never know; she was a baby, and Rose did not need to know what happened. Just knowing that something may have happened that has contributed to Rose making the choices she has made was good enough for Rose. There was a reason why she had made the choices she had made.

The Hand of Jesus: Rose was studying at a Christian university, and as we know, the hand of Jesus had made the way for her to be there. It was in this caring and supportive environment that Rose's mental health conditions were revealed to her in the gentlest of ways possible. The lecturers at this university knew their students by name, and they made time to support and care for each one in their personal journeys and challenges. God says in His Word, "For I am the LORD your God who takes hold of your right hand and says to you, Do not fear; I will help you" (Isa. 41:13). It was impossible for Rose to know that something happened to her when she was just a baby; however, God knows . . . everything. Psalm 139:1–6 affirms, "You have searched me, LORD, and you know me. You know when I sit and when I rise; you perceive my thoughts from afar.

You discern my going out and my lying down; you are familiar with all my ways. Before a word is on my tongue you, LORD, know it completely. You hem me in behind and before, and you lay your hand upon me. Such knowledge is too wonderful for me, too lofty for me to attain." This information would become vital in Rose's healing.

My encouragement to you: I am not suggesting you go searching for a reason why you are as you are or why things have turned out the way they have. Yes, there will be a reason, but it is not a reason to blame and it is not an excuse. It is not an excuse to stay the way you are. Use the reason to empower you to take the step out of your past and step into a new and better way of living. We all have a past that is tainted in some way, and those who have tainted it have a past that is tainted as well, and it goes back and back and back through the generations. We all experience things differently because we are different from the person next to us or in the same family as us. We are made uniquely and we have been nurtured uniquely, so do not compare yourself to anybody else. You are you, and no one can *understand* you except your Creator . . . God.

And so I urge you to *strive* (endeavor, exert, try hard) in moving forward and not being content with where you are. Be *pro*active and not *re*active. Research what depression is; what major depressive disorder is; what dysthymia is; learned helplessness, etc. And I implore with all my heart, if you know of someone who compulsively pulls their hair out, do not discount it or try to get them to stop without dealing with the underlying reason. Rose had counseling on this specific area and was challenged to look at the situation surrounding the behavior, her thoughts, and her emotions. This is purely and simply cognitive behavior therapy as a therapeutic model to alleviate the behavior and emotions attached to it. Cognitive behavior therapy looks at your thoughts, which affect your emotions, which affect your behavior. So change your thoughts, and your emotions and behavior will also change! Easier said than done, but the brain is amazing, and it can be done!

It can be challenging because your train of thought has already made connections within the brain that will require repeated effort to change and make new pathways. If you can imagine for just a moment a piece of wood you are holding in your hand and it has a narrow grove in it from the top to the bottom. Drop a "thought" (a small ball bearing) into the groove, and it follows the already made path for it. Now, try to change that path and make the ball bearing (your thought) move off the path it is on and make a new path. This is a comparison to the challenge we have to change our thoughts when we have "trained" them in a certain way. CBT will work if you experience anxiety, panic, fear, anger, or depression. The Bible tells us, "Whatever is true, whatever is noble, whatever is right, whatever is pure, whatever is lovely, whatever is admirable—if anything is excellent or praiseworthy—think about such things (Phil. 4:8).

This will make new pathways! Rose's faith in Jesus Christ, *believing* what is written is His Word and *applying* it to her life, has had the power to change her thoughts. 2 Corinthians 5:17 states, "Therefore, if anyone is in Christ, the new creation has come. The old has gone, the new is here!" Rose speaks this out when negative thoughts come to attack her. She no longer lives in the past. It happened to her, but it is gone! Rose discovered that trauma, anxiety, and fear were linked to the impulse disorder trichotillomania. If you do know of someone whom you believe may have this disorder, I suggest you give them something to put in their hands to "work with." What works with Rose is blue tack or rubber bands, something that can be molded, moved, and stretched in her fingers.

What are you challenging? You cannot change what you do not acknowledge, and so I pray, you will have ears to hear God speak to you in your own unique situation, because you are special, and you matter to Him and to a lot of people in your life.

Journey 7

Online Dating

Rose's life was lonely. She had been on her own for twelve years. She was not interested in socializing (just another disorder to add to her list of mental health issues). Where was Rose going to meet company from the opposite sex in a safe and secure environment? What better place than in her own home, on the Internet? This would be ideal because she could look at what was out there without having to actually meet anyone, and at the click of a button . . . they are gone. Rose knew she could never be with a white man again, and to ensure no one would pressure her to meet them, she would look overseas; after all, Rose just wanted to talk before ever allowing herself to trust a man again.

Rose tried different websites, and it very soon became incredibly obviously that there were a lot of men, white, black, pink, or purple. It didn't matter what color they were; they were looking for the one thing Rose was not looking for! Rose considered the experience as a bit like window shopping—you just walk right past something that does not catch your attention, and then when you happen to see something that has caught your eye, well, you go into the store, pick it up, look at it, hold it up against you, try it on, and put it right back on the rack if it doesn't fit.

Rose put a lot of items back on the shelf, and sometimes very quickly, like they were a hot potato in her hand. Rose knew what qualities she was looking for in a man and in a relationship. She soon became very savvy at discerning the language used, as she was not on these websites to disclose how much money she earned or had in her bank account. When asked, Rose would cry poor, and she would never hear from them again. Rose protected her heart and her finances, as both had been through the wringer.

It was a Christian website that Rose felt comfortable and safe on. It seemed that it was highly monitored, and there were times when someone had made contact with Rose one day and they were gone the next, deleted by security staff. Rose got to chatting with a man, and after six months, he invited her to visit . . . New York. Rose had never been outside Australia, never had a passport, and was going to go to New York . . . on her own! With the encouragement and support of her middle son, Rose booked her flight. She booked her motel accommodation, made a list of all the sights she wanted to see in New York, and was oblivious to the international airports she would need to navigate around by herself. She was just excited that there would be someone in New York who would show her the sights. Rose boarded the plane in Adelaide, which took her to Melbourne.

The man she sat next to was going to LA, which is where Rose was going, so she asked if she could follow him around, as she had no idea where the international terminal was. She even followed him to the duty free store while he purchased what he wanted. Rose took her seat on the huge jumbo jet set for Los Angeles, and a man and a woman sat either side of her. They were husband and wife, and Rose felt like she had come between them, which she had, but they assured Rose that one liked the window seat and the other liked the aisle. They were on their way to New York! Rose asked them if she could follow them around the LA airport, as she had never traveled overseas before and she had no idea where to go.

They told Rose it was a quick transfer and so they would need to hurry once they landed. Rose landed at the John F. Kennedy International Airport and collected her luggage, scanning the crowd for the man whom she assumed would pick her up from the airport. Rose waited and waited and waited. He did not come. Rose caught a taxi to her motel room and waited and waited and waited. He brought her food at a late hour, after he had finished his shift at work, but left soon after arriving. Rose saw him twice, two hours maximum, and then she did not hear from him and could not contact him again.

Rose was calling his phone from a public phone booth when she turned around to look at the shop she had stopped in front of. In big white letters painted over the entire window were the words "And we know that in all things God works together for the good of those who love Him. Romans 8:28." Rose stared at it and knew it was time to move from Brooklyn to Manhattan.

Rose spent the rest of her holiday exploring New York by herself, and it was amazing! When she returned to Adelaide, the normality of life hit Rose, and the symptoms of depression intensified. Rose went to the doctor and was prescribed medication. Years passed, and Rose decided to look closer to home for male company/friendship. She had been chatting with someone online, via text, and by phone when Rose decided it was time to meet this person. The mutual meeting place got changed to his home town, and then the public meeting place was tactically maneuvered to his home. Rose initially refused until she was promised that she "was safe as long as God is my witness." Rose told the man straight out that she was not interested in him, and it seemed like he seemed accepted what she had said, but he did not want her to leave.

Rose's youngest son called her phone and asked when she would be home. This was Rose's opportunity to get out of there. She got up to leave . . . and he got up and went to the door . . . and locked it. Seeing the key turn in the door triggered something within Rose, and she froze. She was trapped. Rose was too afraid to speak up to protect herself . . . in fear of the response. Rose was living with post-traumatic stress disorder, and she was yet to learn and recognize a trigger; however, Rose *was* triggered the very moment that man locked the door. Rose had protected herself for so many years and then walked right into a trap. She cried all the way home. She had been halfway around the world and was safe, yet in her own home state, she was raped. Rose's doctor was sympathetic toward her, keeping check on her depression and conducting regular blood checks on sexually transmitted diseases for eighteen months, to which all came back negative.

The Hand of Jesus: Rose was amazed how God made His presence felt through the people He placed right next to her on the journey to New York. A coincidence? Not at all, for it says in Joshua 1:9, "Have I not commanded you? Be strong and courageous. Do not be afraid; do not be discouraged; for the LORD your God will be with you wherever you go." This was a time in Rose's life where she stepped out of her comfort zone and really *experienced* the presence of God with her. The Bible scripture on the window of the shop that Rose had walked to, with her suitcase in hand, was big and bold in front of her, filling the whole window.

When Rose read it . . . "And we know that in all things God works together for good" . . . she knew she needed to move on from Brooklyn to Manhattan. Before leaving her home in Adelaide, Rose's neighbor had told her to have a plan B in place just in case things did not turn out as she expected, and so Rose had already researched accommodation in Manhattan, which came in very useful in this situation. God had used so many people and spoke through so many people at this particular time of Rose's life. It was also a time for Rose to really know the presence of God herself.

As she stood on the Brooklyn Bridge looking out over Manhattan, the Empire State Building in the distance, it was a moment she will never forget; realizing she was on the other side of the world, all by herself; so far from family and friends . . . she felt the presence of God with her. God used this moment to let her know that He will never leave her or forsake her. It says in Joshua 1:5, "No one will be able to stand against you all the days of your life. As I was with Moses, so I will be with you; I will never leave you nor forsake you."

My encouragement to you: The Internet may have felt like a safe place for Rose with her mental health issues, but it can be a very dangerous place to be and requires you to be vigilant, on your guard, alert, cautious, and careful. Satan is prowling around, waiting for any opportunity to pounce, so he can steal and kill and destroy (John 10:10) anything that potentially belongs to God . . . and that is *you*. So be on guard. Initially, Rose was so proud of herself when she did what she thought was the right thing to do; she agreed to meet in a public place; she told the guy straight out that she was not interested in him, but Rose's kindness and naivety *and her weakness* were taken advantage of by someone who manipulated her words, the situation, and her trust.

Yes, she did the wrong thing and paid dearly for it. Where was God in all this? Well, He has given us a free will to make choices. Rose was praying to God in the first situation, but she did not include God in the second one. Rose was living her Christian life as best she knew, but she still had a lot to learn, especially about Satan, who is out to destroy God's plan. Let me give you a very condensed version of the characteristics of Satan, and then we will compare them to Jesus. I will leave it up to you to take it further, because the best way to learn is to research for yourself, and it is the best way to know God for yourself.

Satan: Satan was an angel created by God before the creation of man, in the heavenly realms. He was perfect in beauty, full of wisdom, and every precious stone adorned him (Ezek. 28:12–13). He was anointed as a guardian cherub (verse 14) and was blameless, until wickedness was found in him (verse 15), and he rebelled against God (verse 16). God cast him out of heaven, to earth (verse 17). Satan had beauty, wisdom, and perfection, yet he wanted more and pride attributed to his fall (Isa. 14:12–16). Satan wanted more power and wanted to be above God. He despises God and His plans and wants people to follow and worship him. In John 10:10, Jesus tells us that "the thief comes *only* to steal and kill and destroy" (I have added the emphasis). He tempted Jesus while in the wilderness for forty days (Luke 4), he twists scripture to suit himself (verse 3, 9), and when the devil had finished all this tempting, he left him until an opportune time (verse 13).

Satan is prowling the earth and prowling my/your life for an opportune time to enter. He has been twisting scripture to fit his own purpose since the beginning of time, in the Garden of Eden when he tempted Eve to eat the forbidden fruit (Gen. 3). But Satan has limited power. We see in the book of Job (1:12), God allowed Satan to test Job's faithfulness to God but commanded Satan "on the man himself do not lay a finger." Satan may have power, but God has power and authority.

Jesus: Jesus is the Son of God who also resided in heaven before God sent Him to earth to redeem (buy back, purchase, reclaim, restore) the sinful relationship that was a result of Adam and Eve eating the forbidden fruit the serpent (Satan) tricked Eve into taking a bite from. The beautiful, perfect, sinless relationship God had created man for was now full of sin. Satan was out to destroy what God had created . . . man to have relationship with Him, and he continues that to this very day. The only way we can have a relationship with God now is through Jesus. The death and resurrection of Jesus redeemed the relationship between man and God. John 3:16 explains this for us . . . "For God so loved the world that he gave his one and only Son, that whoever believes in him shall not perish but have eternal life." Jesus is the only way to a relationship with God and everlasting life. Jesus tells us, "The thief comes only to steal and kill and destroy." He then says, "I have come that they may have life, and have it to the full" (John 10:10). The amplified Bible says, "I came that they may have and enjoy life, and have it in abundance (to the full, till it overflows)."

During His time on earth, Jesus healed the sick and cast out demons. It is written in the book of Luke (9:1) that He gave the twelve disciples "power and authority to drive out all demons and to cure diseases." He then sent out seventy-two others, two by two, to do the same. "The seventy-two returned with joy and said, 'Lord, even the demons submit to us in your name.' He replied, 'I saw Satan fall like lightning from heaven. I have given you authority to trample on snakes and scorpions and to overcome all the power of the enemy'" (Luke 10:17–19). Anyone who believes and accepts Jesus as their Lord and Savior has inherited power and authority over the devil.

Resisting the devil: James (4:7) tells us, "Submit yourselves, then, to God. Resist the devil, and he will flee from you." Simple! Let's break this down . . .

Submit to God: God defeated Satan. He "raised Christ from the dead and seated him at his right hand in the heavenly realms" (Eph. 1:20). He already has the victory! It is a spiritual battle. Ephesians 6:12 tells us, "For our struggle is not against flesh and blood, but against the rulers, against the authorities, against the powers of this dark world and against the spiritual forces of evil in the heavenly realms." If someone has done wrong against us, we can know that Satan has waited for an opportune time to enter. If we are not living a peaceful life, we can know that Satan has entered. We have allowed him to enter. We are told to "be alert and of sober mind. Your enemy the devil prowls around like a roaring lion looking for someone to devour" (1 Pet. 5:8).

Resist the devil: Jesus said, "Get behind me, Satan! You are a stumbling-block to me, you do not have in mind the concerns of God, but merely human concerns" (Matt. 16:23). When we have accepted Jesus as our Lord and Savior, we inherit that same power and authority to say, "Get behind me, Satan!" Paul says in Ephesians 1:18–20, "I pray that the eyes of your heart may be enlightened in order that you may know the hope to which he has called you, the riches of his glorious inheritance in his holy people, and his incomparably great power for us who believe. That power is the same as the mighty strength he exerted when he raised Christ from the dead and seated him at his right hand in the heavenly realms."

And he will flee: By knowing and speaking out scripture (God's Word), the devil will flee. Jesus said, "Away from me Satan! For it is written: 'Worship the Lord your God, and serve him only'" (Matt. 4:10). There is power in the name of Jesus, for "God exalted him to the highest place and gave him the name that is above every name, that at the name of Jesus every knee should bow, in heaven and on earth and under the earth" (Phil. 2:9–10). The devil will flee at the sound of His name. And don't do it passively; get angry with him (the devil), be assertive, for he is not your friend! In these two situations, Rose sought God in one and not in the other.

It is so sad that we are so quick to blame God when bad things happen to us, but in fact, the blame belongs to Satan. It is God who wants good for us, and Satan is out to destroy that. Rose came out of that situation with her life, shattered as it may be. We learn from our mistakes, and this was a costly one. There are many good stories that come from online dating; it is not all bad. My encouragement to you is . . . be careful . . . heed the precautions that are often set out on these websites, and if it happens too fast, get out.

Journey 8

Guilt to Forgiveness

Depression had a grip on Rose, and its grasp was becoming tighter, and triggers were becoming more regular and lasting longer. Rose had no idea when they would strike their harsh blow and deliver their debilitating effect on her body. Rose's youngest son was the only child living at home with her at this point in her life. He lived through the days of depression with her, bringing her a box of tissues when she could not stop crying, rubbing her back and telling her, "It will be OK, Mum." He knew when she was triggered, and he knew he had to just walk away because he didn't want to make it worse. It was only after an episode had ended that Rose could go to her son and tell him it was not his fault. It could be days before she would be able to explain to him what she was beginning to understand and what was happening in her body. It would only have to be a few words or a tone of voice or a certain behavior that would trigger her, and Rose would freeze, like a statue. Fear flooded her body and all functioning shut down.

Rose would be able to see the look in her son's eyes as he realized that he had done or said something . . . something . . . but what was it he had done? Rose could see that he did not intentionally want to hurt his mum, but he also learned that he had to walk away from her and wait until the process had taken its course and he would have his mum back once again. He would call his brother for support, and Rose's middle son would call his mum regularly to keep check on her. He got to know when she was not good, and he would just leave work and go straight to her anytime of the day. Rose's mental health conditions were affecting her children more and more; those who were closest to her.

On Mother's Day 2012, Rose was asked by the pastor of the church she was attending to share with the congregation a single mother's perspective of Mother's Day. Rose was reluctant, but he insisted that he wanted her to be one of the mums he had asked to share. Rose called him and said it might not be a good idea because, as Rose wrote down, "What my life is like as a single mum, it was not going to be like a pretty bunch of flowers being presented to the people there." He was still insistent that Rose share. Well, it was one of the hardest things Rose had to do. After the other two mums shared their experience as a mum, Rose took the microphone . . . and took a deep breath. Her hand was visibly shaking, and the paper she was holding was visibly shaking as well. Another deep breath, and she started . . .

WHAT MY LIFE IS LIKE AS A SINGLE MUM

Guilt . . . guilt lingers like a disease and can strike at any particular moment, aiming directly at my heart . . . because . . . the choices I have made have had consequences on my children. Each child has endured different consequences:

My eldest son

- It tore him apart not to have his dad around.
- He was detested and tormented by my new partner.
- He attempted suicide at age twelve . . . the rope broke.
- He left home to live with his dad.
- I was not and could not be a mum to him.

My middle son

o He lived in the tension of an abusive second marriage.
o He was emotionally tormented by my new partner.
o Physical twitches and habits give me a glimpse of the internal torture my son was too scared to express.

Youngest son

- He would have no memory of his mum and dad ever living together.
- He was eighteen months old when I left the abusive marriage.
- My choice meant he had to endure weekends when he wanted to see his dad so much, but his dad was too drunk to have him.

What my choices meant

1. My choice has meant my boys . . . have never been in a normal, happy family.
2. My choice has meant my boys . . . have never seen how a husband should treat his wife.

3. My choice has meant my boys . . . have never had normal family outings . . . going to dinner "as a family," watching them play sport "as a family," having fun at the beach "as a family," going on holidays/camping "as a family."
4. My choice has meant my boys . . . have never had dad at home to ask the things boys ask their dads on the spur of the moment.
5. My choice has meant my boys . . . have not had their dad around to play the rough and tumble games.
6. My choice has meant my boys . . . have not had a good role model to learn their male responsibility in a relationship.

After fourteen years as a single mum, my heart still aches when I see a family (mum, dad, and kids) together in the shops, at church, or anywhere, and I realize I failed at providing this for my children. When I look back over my journey as a single mum, this is what I realized:

A. As a single mum . . . I have had to make all the decisions with bringing up my boys and within the home.
B. As a single mum . . . I have had to do the work of both the mum and dad. When the drain blocks, I have to clear it; when the tap drips, I change the washer; I mow the lawn and trim the edges; if I don't put the bins out, the bins won't get emptied.
C. As a single mum . . . I do not expect my boys to take the place of a dad.
D. As a single mum . . . I have tried to protect my children from the abuse I endured so they wouldn't see their dad as a bad person.
E. As a single mum . . . it hurts to know I have denied my children a "normal" family life.

Mother's Day is a day that magnifies my failure to provide my children with a happy, "normal" family.

Over the years, I am learning how to put God at the head of my home. I seek Him for strength; I seek Him for guidance, and I know He loves my boys even more than I do . . . and so . . . I know . . . I can trust God with their lives.

Psalm 139: "You have searched me, LORD, and you know me. You know when I sit and when I rise; you perceive my thoughts from afar. You discern my going out and my lying down; you are familiar with all my ways. Before a word is on my tongue you, LORD, know it completely. You hem me in behind and before, and you lay your hand upon me. Such knowledge is too wonderful for me, too lofty for me to attain. Where can I go from your Spirit? Where can I flee from your presence? If I go up to the heavens, you are there. If I rise on the wings of the dawn, if I settle on the far side of the sea, even there your hand will guide me your right hand will hold me fast. If I say, 'Surely the darkness will hide me and the light become night around me,' even the darkness will not be dark to you; the night will shine like the day, for darkness is as light to you. For you created my inmost being; you knit me together in my mother's womb.

"I praise you because I am fearfully and wonderfully made; your works are wonderful, I know that full well. My frame was not hidden from you when I was made in the secret place, when I was woven together in the depths of the earth. Your eyes saw my unformed body; all the days ordained for me were written in your book before one of them came to be. How precious to me are your thoughts, God! How vast is the sum of them! Were I to count them, they would outnumber the grains of sand—when I awake, I am still with you. If only you, God, would slay the wicked! Away from me, you who are bloodthirsty! They speak of you with evil intent; your adversaries misuse your name. Do I not hate those who hate you, LORD, and abhor those who are in rebellion against you? I have nothing but hatred for them; I count them my enemies. Search me, God, and know my heart; test me and know my anxious thoughts. See if there is any offensive way in me, and lead me in the way everlasting."

When I was asked to share, I squirmed and tried to run; however, no matter how far I ran, I could not hide from God. It has been through this time of reflection that God has revealed to me . . . it is time I forgive myself. I work well with pictures, visions, and analogies. God gave me a picture of what this looks like . . . I have been in a small dinghy, and guilt has been my anchor. It is time to forgive myself and cut the rope of the anchor . . . so my dinghy can move forward. Rose could almost sail the dinghy with the flood of tears she shed as she stood up in front of everyone and revealed the contents of her heart, and there were others shedding tears with her. It was during the time of preparing what she was going to share about her life as a single mum that God revealed to Rose she needs to forgive herself.

The Hand of Jesus: It was through the belief and persistence of Rose's pastor to share what Mother's Day is like for a single mum that it was revealed to Rose she was harboring a lot of guilt through the decisions she had made and how this affected her children. Guilt is an emotion that shows up when we know we are doing something that is against a moral standard. God will use guilt to convict us of what we are doing is wrong, and this requires us to change our ways; repent and turn away from wrongdoing. The devil will use guilt to condemn, judge, criticize, and keep reminding us what we have done and hold us in bondage to guilt. John 3:17–18 tells us, "For God did not send his Son into the world to condemn the world, but to save the world through him. Whoever believes in him is not condemned, but whoever does not believe stands condemned already because they have not believed in the name of God's one and only Son." Romans 8:1 tells us, "There is now no condemnation for those who are in Christ Jesus, because through Christ Jesus the law of the Spirit who gives life has set you free from the law of sin and death." As we have seen in John 10:10, Jesus tells us, "The thief comes only to steal and kill and destroy; I have come that they may have life, and have it to the full." God wanted to release Rose from condemnation, which was robbing her of life, and life to the full.

My encouragement to you: Have you done something so bad that you don't think you deserve to be forgiven? Are you punishing yourself just as Rose did? Has someone done something so bad to you that you "could not possibly forgive them"? I would like to share with you my experience with forgiveness. I say "with forgiveness" because unless you actively do something with it, it is powerless; but when you choose to activate it, it becomes powerful. Imagine being handcuffed to the person who has hurt you and you are being dragged around by that person wherever they go, yet in your hand, you have the key to the handcuffs! The key that will set you free! It is the key of forgiveness. Let's have a look at forgiveness and God, forgiveness and others, and forgiveness and me.

Forgiveness and God: God created humans to have relationship with Him; however, sin entered the world when Adam and Eve ate from the forbidden fruit. To redeem the relationship with man, God sent Jesus as the sacrifice that would once again allow us to have a personal relationship with Him (John 3:16). It is up to us, you and me, to accept this gift from Him. He offers it to each one of us. If you can imagine God saying to you, "I created you to have a relationship with Me, but because of the sin in your life, I can't . . . I have no sin in Me, and I cannot have sin around Me . . . so I sent My Son to bridge that gap, and He has taken on *all* the sin of the world so that when you believe in Him, your sin is forgiven . . . it is left at the cross . . . you are cleansed and pure . . . and I can now be in your presence and you can commune with Me. It is a gift I give to you." Continue to imagine God holding in His hands a gift for you. He extends His hands to you and says, "This is for you."

You stand there and look up at Him, and you look back down at the gift in His hands . . . all you have to do is accept it . . . it is free. It is the gift of forgiveness that will bring you back into right relationship with God . . . it is Jesus. Paul tells us in Romans 3:23–25, "For all have sinned and fall short of the glory of God, and all are justified freely by his grace through the redemption that came by Christ Jesus. God presented Christ as a sacrifice of atonement through the shedding of his blood—to be received by faith."

Forgiveness and others: As a Christian, it is required of us to forgive others. Jesus says, "For if you forgive other people when they sin against you, your heavenly Father will also forgive you. But if you do not forgive others their sins, your Father will not forgive your sins" (Matt. 6:14–15). As a non-Christian, it is a highly beneficial act that is healing and liberating. What is forgiveness? Does it mean I have to forget what someone has done to me as if it has never happened? No, not at all. In fact, forgiveness is not about the other person at all; it is about you. Choosing to forgive releases you from bondage to the other person.

THE SURVIVORS MODE

When someone has done or said the wrong thing to you, a whole lot of thoughts and emotions start to well up within you, and the more you feed them, the more they grow. But I wonder what the other person is doing? Probably getting on with their life and not even caring how you are affected.

Forgiving them for what they have done releases you from being tied to their wrongdoing and being drawn deeper into emotions that do not feel good and are not good for you. Emotions eat you up, while they are going about doing their every day thing, oblivious to how you are feeling, and not caring anyway! Let me share with you my very first real experience of the power of forgiveness, which happened to me in my early twenties. I was in a house looking for a mentally unstable woman who had gone missing. Other members of the household had wondered outside down the road and the beach calling out for her. It was late at night. I had stayed in the house in case she came back. I started to look for her in cupboards and wardrobes.

I opened up one wardrobe door, and there she was! As I opened the door, she lifted her arm. She had a knife in her hand. As I said, she was mentally unstable, and she thought I was her husband. In her unstable mind, she saw her husband standing in front of her, not me, and she was threatening to kill me. Her voice was unrecognizable, deep and angry, as she spoke. Someone came back, the police were called, and she was taken to the hospital, but I held on to "whoa, what about me" thoughts and feelings for years before someone from my church talked to me about forgiving her for what she had done. She had no idea that I was harboring these thoughts and feelings, so it wasn't affecting her, and the moment I spoke out loud, "I forgive her for what she did," I felt freedom from being tied to that incident that had happened years before. I still remember it, but it does not affect me. I have had to make a conscious decision to forgive my ex-husbands. At first, it was not easy, so I just went through the motions because I had already experienced the freedom of being released from the bondage of hurt and pain.

Is there someone you need to forgive? Are you holding on to hate or resentment against someone? I encourage you to take that step of saying out loud, "I forgive (say their name) for what they have done." At first, you may not mean it, but continue to say, "I forgive them," every time those thoughts come back to haunt you. One of the disciples asked Jesus, "Lord, how often should I forgive someone who sins against me? Seven times?" "No, not seven times," Jesus replied, "but seventy times seven!" (Matt. 18:21–22 NLT). In my early days as a Christian and living in an abusive relationship, I would often go to this verse and tell God that I have surely forgiven this person seventy times seven (that's 490 times if you haven't already worked it out!). But then, I discover it is seventy times seven for each sin! The essence of this verse is to forgive continually.

Forgiveness and me: How do I forgive myself? And why do I need to forgive myself? Well, Jesus came so that we might have life; to enjoy life; life in abundance (John 10:10). It is the devil who comes to destroy that. Guilt or shame is not from God; it is the devil robbing us from the fullness of life that God wants us to have. So why am I feeling like this? I know why God has sent Jesus. I have accepted Him into my life; however . . . I still want to punish myself! Why would God do this for me?! Look at what I have done! I just need to punish myself a little bit longer. This is Satan trying to trick and deceive you. God does not want us to punish ourselves; He gives the gift of forgiveness freely.

When you are thinking like this, you may have accepted what God has done for you in your head, but it now needs to make the connection in your heart, and this requires a 100 percent acceptance of what Jesus has done for you and thanking Him for taking all your sin. In the visual above, it is like you have your hands on the gift, but you have not yet taken it because the devil is whispering in your ear, "You really don't deserve to be forgiven." Satan is the father of lies (John 8:44), the deceiver (Rev. 12:9). Do not listen to him! Recognize it is the devil.

If God did not put the guilt there (something you need to repent of), then refuse to even think about it. It is a choice. We can choose what we think about. Philippians 4:8 tells us to think on what is pure and good and praiseworthy. Resist the devil, and he will flee. You will experience the forgiveness of God when you can fully accept His gift.

THE SURVIVORS MODE

Rose has been forgiven of her sin, and all guilt has been washed away. Rose now knows that her children are being offered the same gift, and it is up to them to accept it, and then God will take them through the healing that they need, just as He has with Rose.

Journey 9

Deepest Depression

Rose had reached the deep, dark depths of a cold and lonely pit that was closing in on her. Everything in her life appeared gray and lifeless. Life was a burden. It was difficult to get out of bed. It was difficult to think what needed to be done. It was difficult to go shopping and think what was needed to be bought. It was difficult to get through each day. There was no joy in her life. She purely existed. She could only think about getting through today. Today had enough problems of its own that needed to be accomplished. Thinking about tomorrow was too much to cope with. Her mind felt like a jumbled mess, and adding one more stress to it could be the one thought that would make her head burst. Rose held her head in her hands, holding it together. It felt like it was going to explode.

In June 2013, Rose took herself to the doctor because she could not stop crying. The waiting room was full of people. Rose scanned the entire waiting area and headed for the quietest corner. With sunglasses on, she looked out the window and continued to wipe the tears running down her face uncontrollably. Rose was called to the doctor's room. He asked, "What can I do for you?" With tears streaming down her face, Rose told him she could not stop crying . . . the medication is not working, and she needs it to be increased. The doctor looked at Rose's file on the computer screen and then turned to face her. He leaned back in his big office chair and folded his hands just under his chin as he visibly analyzed Rose and took a moment to think. Then he said, "You are on the highest medication. There is nothing more I can do for you." He suggested adding a mood stabilizer to the medication she was already taking but appeared to be at a loss as he looked at the emotional wreck in front of him. He then turned to his filing tray and pulled out a piece of paper, which he started to write on, explaining he was referring her to counseling at a specialist center where only clients who have been referred by a doctor can go. He gave Rose information about a website that will educate her on eating foods that will assist with depression.

THE SURVIVORS MODE

He told Rose she needed to exercise regularly to produce . . . something. Rose had switched off by now. The word "exercise" did that for her. Does he not understand that *everything* is a struggle? How could she possibly introduce exercise into her already dismal day?

Just thinking about it was adding to the depression and made Rose cry even more! Rose left the doctor's office worse than when she went in. She went in with hope that he could help her. She came out with no hope. Rose called the special counseling center to make an appointment. The earliest appointment they had was in six weeks. Six weeks! Rose did not have six weeks! She may not even be here tomorrow. She made the appointment anyway. Rose needed to go to the local shop to purchase a few necessities. As she crossed the road, she stood in the middle and waited for the traffic to subside. A huge truck came into her vision. Rose looked at it as it roared closer to her on the inside lane. For a moment, it was all Rose could see. "Go on! Step out in front of it. All your pain will be gone." Rose focused on the huge grid on the front of the truck. An image flashed in her mind of standing in front of the fast-approaching truck, standing there with her arms stretched out wide, the truck's horn blasting loud, and the impact. Her body plastered face-first against the huge grid.

Too late . . . the truck sped past with a gush of wind and a loud roar, like that of a mighty beast. Rose carried on as if nothing had happened, for these thoughts of how she was going to die were becoming more regular. Rose began to plan her funeral. She knew she would have it close to where her mum and dad lived because they were elderly and would not be able to travel too far. She knew what song she wanted to have played . . . and that was about it. Her pain would be forever gone.

Rose would do small regular shops for the things she needed; however, this particular day, she called into a grocery store that she did not normally shop at. Wandering the aisles aimlessly, Rose crossed paths with a friend whom she had not seen in a while. Both admitted they don't usually shop at the store, but it was a convenient stop to buy a few things they needed, as they were both on their way home. The exchange of conversation was short in both length and depth; however, the very next day, this friend was on Rose's doorstep after school drop-off because she had been worried about Rose and was concerned for her well-being. Over a cup of coffee, this dear friend listened to Rose's negative perspective on life. She leaned forward and placed her hand on Rose's hand . . . She looked compassionately into Rose's eyes and said in a calm, gentle voice . . . "I know who can help you."

The Hand of Jesus: I would hope by now that you would be able to say, "Yes, I can see the hand of Jesus on your life, Rose. He was with you in the depression . . . He was with you in the doctor's room . . . He was with you as you crossed the road . . . He orchestrated the chance meeting you had with your friend in the grocery store . . . He was with you all the time. And I can't wait to see where He is leading you to get the help you need." Why hasn't He stepped in before now? Well, God's ways are *always* perfect (Ps. 18:30).

My encouragement to you: Depression is a debilitating illness. There are chemical imbalances in the brain that prevent you from functioning in a healthy manner. Medication, diet, exercise, counseling, changing thought patterns, and supportive family and friends are all building-blocks that can have a positive influence in turning the deadly illness around. If you are in the same position as Rose and you have tried them all, then there is only one answer . . . Jesus. Yes. *There is* still hope. You need to stop that thought, that there is no hope. That is the devil deceiving you. Jesus is with you right now. Ask Him to take you on the path of restoration. Go back to chapter 5 if you need to and read what God is saying to you in the letter and set into motion the advice given after the letter, for "faith by itself, if it is not accompanied by action, is dead" (James 2:17).

THE SURVIVORS MODE

Journey 10

Healing

Rose made the phone call that very day. A few days later, Rose made the one-hour drive from her home to her friend's mum, who is one of the pastors of a Baptist church, for her first appointment. The one-hour sessions were precise and to the point. Rose already knew where the root of sexual abuse originated. The quiet, confident female pastor led with precision. Prayers were specific and uneventful, breaking the chains of generational curses (including the curse of Freemasonry), breaking the bondage of all previous sexual partners, forgiving those who had wronged and those who had failed to protect, and praying healing into the brokenness.

Rose knew from her knowledge of the Bible that "our struggle is not against flesh and blood, but against the rulers, against the authorities, against the powers of this dark world and against the spiritual forces of evil in the heavenly realms" (Eph. 6:12). The battle was between Jesus and Satan in the spiritual realm; it was quiet and calm in the physical realm. It was after the second session that Rose knew she was healed. How did she know? She just felt different from when she went in and she believed. As she left the church for the drive back home, she sang worship songs in her car, praising and thanking God for healing her! It was an amazing day!

Three days later, in the morning, when she was about to take her antidepressant medication, these words came into her head, very clearly . . . *See, you don't think you have really been healed! You are still taking your medication!* Rose was in a good mood, feeling happy and full of joy. At that very moment, Rose walked over to the bin with the box of medication in her hand and threw it, with determination, into the bin, saying out loud, "Yes! I have been healed!" Rose never took another antidepressant again! Yes, her body went into withdrawals, but she wasn't crying! If Rose ever missed a tablet in the past (usually if the script hadn't been filled), she would cry involuntarily until she was able to feed her brain the chemicals it needed to function rationally.

Rose broke out into sweats, but she continued to go about her day triumphantly, knowing full well that Jesus had healed her! He had done what no other person, doctor, psychologist, counselor, or medication could do! The same power that raised Jesus from the dead broke the chains of depression and set her free! Rose walked into the next prayer session with a bounce in her step and joy beaming from her smiling face. Her first words were "I've been healed! I don't have depression anymore!" It was obvious to those around her that Rose was different, the complete opposite of what she had been like. The female pastor rejoiced in the good news with Rose, and there was laughter and excitement for Rose all around.

When Rose explained that she was still getting the shakes and having hot sweats because of how she came off the medication, the pastor was surprised that she just stopped taking the medication. She told Rose it was not a good idea to go off them "cold turkey." Rose said she had no choice because Satan was trying to tell her that she was not healed, and she had to prove to him that she was! The pastor smiled. A quick, short prayer later . . . and the hot sweats were gone! Hallelujah! Jesus, the Master Physician! While He was at it, Rose thought she would ask for complete healing for her eyes as well! It seems *that* healing will be for another time. For now, she could see things differently out of her eyes! Life was in color!

The following Saturday, Rose went to watch her middle son play football as usual. Aussie Rules Football is a winter sport. Rose set up her chair just back from the boundary line. She had her coat and gloves on, a blanket over her legs, and an umbrella on standby to either stop the wind or the rain (or both). Rose settled herself in the fold-out chair and got her little pair of binoculars out because she could not see the players clearly without them. She put them to her eyes and began to search the field for her son, but her eyes caught sight of the beautiful scenery beyond the scramble of men on the football field. Trees that were all different shapes and shades of green! And, wow . . . look at that one! . . . It has a very long, straight trunk that goes all the way up and then just a little bit of bushy green at the very top! What an unusual tree! Rose

THE SURVIVORS MODE

could see houses nestled in the hills, with greenery all around them, and the clouds in the sky! Look at the different colors of the clouds!

Rose's eyes were opened to the beauty all around her . . . God's beautiful creation that had always been there, but the depression had kept her from seeing it. Amazing Grace, how sweet the sound, that saved a wretch like me! I once was lost, but now I am found; was blind, but now I see! Just before Rose was about to leave for her first appointment, she quickly checked the Christian online dating website to see if anyone had viewed her profile. Oooh, someone had sent her a "smile." Rose quickly looked at his profile . . . but she had somewhere to be right now, so she turned the computer off and left it for a few days because he might just disappear.

A few days later, and he was still there, which is always good. It means he has passed the website security staff and he has made it to first base. Rose paid the minimum membership time so she could have contact with him, and the rest . . . is another testimony! To God be the Glory! Rose could not contain her overwhelming joy that was emanating from her body. She felt like she had swallowed illuminating liquid that had seeped into every part of her being, and she was aglow like a neon light. And when people would ask, "How are you?" Rose's eyes would lighten up with pure joy . . . her whole body would tell the story of how Jesus pulled her from the deep depths of darkness and healed her from *all* the abuse, depression, post-traumatic stress disorder, and trichotillomania.

Rose could not understand why people did not have the same excitement and awe that she had. It didn't matter. She knew where she had come from, and she knew how she felt now, and no one could take that away from her! Rose was a tightly closed bud that was blossoming into a beautiful, sweet, fragrant flower. She praised and worshiped Jesus with a deep passion and a deep desire to know Him. She had an exhilarated excitement and knew "He did not save her to sit, He saved her to serve." She would give the rest of her life to go wherever the Lord would lead her. She has a passion to see Jesus at work through her, to set broken lives free from the bondages of darkness . . . just as He has done for her. Thank you, Jesus!

The Hand of Jesus: Jesus had brought Rose to her place of healing. He did what only God could do through the same power that raised Jesus from the dead. He healed her.

My encouragement to you: God sees what you have been through, and He knows where He wants you to be. His hand is on your life . . . He hears your cry . . . He hears your prayers. His answer may not be what you think it should be. His answer may just be . . . "yes," "no," or "not yet." He is Almighty God and He is all-knowing. Rose's healing took a fifty-two-year journey, but Jesus never left her side. He worked all things together for good, and He continues to do so. Whatever you are going through, whatever you need . . . take it to the Lord in prayer.

Karen Newman, a.k.a. Rose, has experienced the healing powers of Jesus Christ, who has delivered her and have set her free from the affects/trauma of verbal abuse, physical abuse, sexual abuse, financial abuse, social abuse, depression, being raped, post-traumatic stress disorder, low/no self-esteem, and suicide tendencies. Karen knows what it is like to have no hope. She met author prophet Anthony McMaryion over two years ago, and through his personal ministering to her as the Holy Spirit gave him a gift of a word of wisdom, a gift of a word of knowledge, and other spiritual gifts, he would be the instrument that God would use to help her get delivered, cleansed, purged, healed, and made whole from the residue bondages she was in. It is her desire to reach out to others who are trapped in the bondages of abuse, depression, and PTSD, and let them know there is still hope. Karen has lived her life in Adelaide, South Australia. In 2012, she graduated from Tabor Adelaide with a bachelor of social science in counseling, and since then, she has been working with children who have lived with abuse.

THE SURVIVORS MODE

CHAPTER FOURTEEN

Drifting into Darkness

MOLLIE AND ROSE went to sleep in a child's peace and woke up in an adult's PTSD. They both found themselves in a place neither one had any idea they would have ever had been in. From the time they grew up and had their first relationship dream, neither would have dreamed their relationship journey would take them into a world that they, in their wildest dream and imagination, never would have thought would have happened to either one of them. They would end up spending the days of their life fighting to survive and fighting to try and figure it all out. These are two different women who live on two different sides of the world experiencing basically the same things. How they experienced and encountered PTSD and the other things they had to face, deal with, and overcome may have showed up in their lives at different times, and what they had to go through may have been different, but the results were the same.

They both found themselves in a very dark place, and neither one knew how they got into that dark place. Both came face-to-face with their greatest fear, and that is "fear" itself and that fear that they experienced and encountered kept them drifting into darkness. This was no ordinary darkness; this was a darkness that housed and hid a foe called fear, and on many occasions, they, in their own way and in their own time, drifted off into their private and personal darkness and even public darkness. And at times, they just found themselves being drawn, driven, pulled, pushed, persuaded, seduced, enticed, tricked, and forced into those dark places. It would be there and in those times and on those occasions they would come face-to-face with a foe who wanted to be their friend.

Had that darkness been shadowing their lives from the day they were thought of, conceived, birthed, and born into this life? Was what happened to them waiting for them? What exactly was it that drew that darkness to them? Was it something that they said or done? Was it something that they had on that day? Was it something they handled the wrong way? Were they just two people who happened to be at the wrong place and at the wrong time who just met the wrong person? There are so many questions we could ask, and there would probably be so many different conclusions we could and would come to. The fact being that no matter who, what, when, where, and how, everything that was waiting for them had one mission and one assignment, and that was to kill, steal, destroy, assault, attack, and assassinate them and remove them from this life.

Anytime a person has been terrorized, traumatized, tortured, and tormented to any degree and for any period, he or she will, in the process, try to find a way to survive and make it through the ordeal. To survive is to continue to live or exist, especially in spite of danger or hardship. And when they were not trying to survive, they were being forced into that place called survival. To find yourself forced into engaging into survival is to find yourself engaged in the state or fact of continuing to live or exist, typically in spite of an accident, ordeal, or difficult circumstances. They were trying to and had to find a way to survive, and they were forced into finding survival techniques and tactics. In the end, the one who has been tutored, trained, and taught how to survive has also learned the art of adversity survival, and he or she ends up discovering how to become, be, and end up being a survivor.

Being a survivor becomes, is, and ends up being a traumatized, tortured, and tormented person's mission, goal, and purpose in life. A survivor is a person who survives, especially a person remaining alive after going through a traumatic, troubling, and tragic event in which others have died or had been severally distracted, detoured, damaged, dismantled, derailed, delayed, denied, and/or destroyed. Neither would have the opportunity to live their life and live the lifestyle that they had dreamed, hoped, and imagined they could and would have. They would be forced to just survive and "exist" and to, at the end of their day, be thankful for their meager existence. They went to sleep a child and woke up an adult, and they went to sleep innocent and woke up violated. Their hurt, pain, and brokenness would run deep into the core of their being, in a place where neither could have and would have known hurt, pain, and brokenness could live and exist.

When a person drifts into darkness and he or she is having experiences and close encounters and up close encounters and up close and personal experiences with darkness and what is hiding in the darkness, that person is coming face-to-face with and having face-offs with the unseen, the unimaginable, the unreal, the unbelievable, and the unforgettable. This is not something that the person planned for, was prepared and positioned for; nor was the person expecting or anticipating what they ran into. Fear is that driving force that's in the darkness that draws, pulls, pushes, persuades, tricks, and seduces you into a survivor-survival mode, mind-set, and mentality. Fear will also drive you deeper into a survivor-survival darkness.

For every person who drifts off into darkness where he or she will come face-to-face with fear, his or her fears, he or she has to find a way to survive and make it through those times. There is no prescription, and there is no perfect protective and preventive plan, and there is no specific way a person should act, behave, or conduct themselves or think or feel. Anything that catches a person off guard has found a way to seize, overpower, overtake, and overthrow their power of reason, and anything that is able to take down, take over, and take out a person's faith, hope, belief, and confidence has found a way to stifle that person's ability to be resilient and has also found a way to steal their ability to put up resistance. That is exactly what fear does, it suddenly and immediately jumps out at you, stifles you, freezes you, and takes away right reasons/reasoning, right resilience, and right resistance responses, and the person ends up like Mollie and Rose, reacting and demonstrating reactionary responses.

The gift of fear

Satan had a lot of gifts that he had waiting for Mollie and Rose, and the gifts he had for them he was freely offering it to them. Most of the gifts they received from Satan, he underhandedly assigned and attached it to them without them knowing it, or they came along with the gifts they did accept from him the moment when they were forced into a survivor mode. They didn't see him sneaking it into their lives, and they didn't even know they had received gifts from Satan. They were too busy doing what we all would be doing if we were faced with what they were faced with, and that is to find a way to hang on and survive. The abusers in their lives were Satan's gift givers, and he would use them as the way to get his gift into Mollie's and Rose's life. The question I must ask you before we begin on this journey is what gift(s) did you receive today, and what gifts and residue gifts from your past experiences are you still in possession of knowingly or unknowingly?

You see, there are only two gifts that you have received today, and they are (1) the gift of fear and (2) the gift of faith. One of these two gifts you will receive to start your day off and to take you through your day. Throughout your day, you will spend time running in and out of either one of them, and that is not good. For you to overpower fear, overtake fear, and overthrow fear, you are going to have to be constantly, continuously, and consistently receiving the gift of faith and be constant, continuous, and consistent in rejecting, resisting, refusing, and rebuking receiving Satan's gift of fear.

The Bible says God has not "given." Anything that is "given" is a gift that you don't have to earn or work for it or struggle and strain to get to have it or to obtain it; the only thing you have to do is "receive" it and it is yours. Satan can only suggest and influence you into receiving his gift called "fear." It's up to you to either reject it or receive it. Satan cannot force you to accept fear; you are a free moral agent, and you have a right to choose. Don't you continue to let Satan bully, badger, swindle, cheat, bamboozle, and rob you out of your right to "power of choice." Your power of choice is one of the most powerful and precious treasures that you have, and all day long, Satan is always at work trying to find ways to steal your power of choice, kill your right to use your power of choice, and get you to open up the door so he can steal your power of choice.

Before you got up this morning, there were some gifts that were already waiting on you, and which gifts did you take with you as you were going about your morning and getting ready to walk out of your door heading to your means of transportation? You, without you even knowing it, accepted and grabbed a hold of the gift of fear or the gift of faith, and you took it with you on your journey. Which gift you accepted as the gift of the day will show up when you are challenged, confronted, and when a negative circumstance, situation, confrontation, matter, or even a past and old memory immediately and suddenly shows up. One that you thought you had finally gotten past and had gotten over with. Just like every day there are brand-new mercies, there is a brand-new dispensation of faith or and new exemption from a rule or usual requirement of and for your "today" faith.

The faith you had for yesterday's fear fight may not be the faith you will need for each new day's fear fight, and that is because the fear tactics Satan uses are never unveiled the same way, and when his tactical fear unfold in and at the place and point you, "of your own free will," gave him access to, fear will begin to unravel your mental and emotional stability, security, and soundness. The results will always be the same.

See it as it really is

Let me show you fear through God's eyes and from His perspective, and let me get you ready for what you are about to do. If you can seize what I am about to share with you and accept it, adopt it, adapt to it, and apply it to your day-to-day living and apply to the tactics and techniques that fear uses to get you to the place and point where you are driven, motivated, dominated, manipulated, and controlled by it, then you will not only overpower, overtake, and overthrow fear but also overcome it. When God looks at you, He sees you doing and being able to do the following:

1. To overpower fear is to defeat or overcome it with superior strength. This can and will happen when you become so spiritually aggressive, and you become and be too spiritually intense for fear, and in your fight against fear, you end up overwhelming it and removing it from having the right to have easy and direct access, power, and the authority of your mind's mode, mind-set, and mentality.

2. To overtake fear is to catch up with it and pass it while traveling in the same direction with it, and when you do so, the next thing you do is (especially of misfortune) come suddenly or unexpectedly upon it (fear) and defeat it by disconnecting it from your mind, frame of mind, state of mind, mental condition, and mental state of being.

3. To overthrow fear is to remove it forcibly from power and from having power over your life, choices and decisions, thoughts, train of thought, thinking, and way of thinking. To overthrow fear is also to seize it, dominate it, and then destroy it and then demonstrate its removal from having power over your thoughts, train of thought, thinking, and way of thinking. When you defeat OCD, PTSD, depression, cancer, stress, high blood pressure, migraines, addictions, lust, envy, etc., all of which are wiles, trickeries, devices, deceptions, delusions and techniques fear uses to draw, drive, pull, push, persuade, trick, seduce, and force you into its grips, you are overwhelmingly demonstrating its demise and/or downfall.

Here is your place of power and authority, when you are doing the exact opposite of what fear has been and wants to continue to do to you, and that is to pursue you and torture and torment you, what's happening is you are flipping the script, and instead of you becoming and ending up being the pursued prey, you now become the one who is pursuing, overpowering, overtaking, and overthrowing. You become the hunter and not the hunted, and you become the one who is tormenting and torturing fear.

Demonstrating fear's defeat

Fear is defined or described as an unpleasant emotion caused by the belief that someone or something is dangerous, likely to cause pain, or a threat. When you are walking and living in and out of fear and you are functioning in and out of fear, you are in a mode, mind-set, and mentality where you are afraid of (someone or something) past, present, or future as likely to be dangerous, painful, or threatening that can and will hurt and harm you. That someone or something can be from your past, present, or even in your future. The way to demonstrate fear's defeat will require you to (a) be constant, continuous, and consistent in your aggressive (b) assault, attack, and assassination of fear. You cannot be playing games with fear, and you cannot be up and down in your warfare. Fear is not going to let up on you, and it is not going to take a lunch break or go on vacation; it is a very aggressive spirit, and it never sleeps or rests.

You are going to have to be the same way, and you are going to have to make sure your mode and your motive, mind-set, and mentality is to take fear with all its strategies out completely. Don't take any fear hostages, such as OCD, PTSD, depression, cancer, stress, high blood pressure, migraines, addictions, lust, envy, doubt, worry, unbelief, etc. Attack, assault, assassinate, and kill them all the moment when they show up. You have to be (c) aggressive and adamant in standing against fear and all its friends and family members. Fear *hates* you, and the mere thought of you being alive really irks fear, and it sparks a real bad and nasty hatred inside of itself for you. Fear wants to trick you and trap you into being scared of it when all along fear is afraid of you.

Did you get that? Let me say it again, "Fear is afraid of you!" Fear is afraid someone just like me is going to "awaken" the victory, power, and authority that God has given you over fear that is on the inside of you. So to that, I say, "Wake up!" You are a winner, and you always win the battle against fear. Wake up . . . wake up! You are not powerless; you are powerful. And you are not fear's prey; you are fear's playmate and you are fear's "greatest fear." It is afraid of you! Stop being pursued by fear, all kinds of fears, and become the pursuer and take back what fear has stolen from you. Be aggressive and adamant in not fighting with fear, but be aggressive and adamant in overpowering, overtaking, overthrowing, and overcoming fear.

When you overpower, overthrow, overtake, and then "overcome" fear, you have succeeded in dealing with an unpleasant emotion, problem, or difficulty that is caused by the belief that someone or something past, present, or future is dangerous, likely to cause pain, or is a threat. You are successful in succeeding in not being afraid of OCD, PTSD, depression, cancer, stress, high blood pressure, migraines, addictions, lust, envy, doubt, worry, unbelief, being raped or molested again, being battered, etc., as likely to happen again. Those past and old memories, thoughts, feelings, and everything else associated with, linked to, or connected to the someone or something that brought about that fear is seen as likely to not be dangerous, painful, or threatening anymore.

Just like you allowed an unpleasant emotion caused by the belief that someone or something is dangerous, likely to cause pain, or a threat to *punk* you, it's time for you to rise, receive the gift of faith that is always waiting for you to accept it, and take it with you and punk fear and overpower, overthrow, and overtake it with all its family members and friends, which are OCD, PTSD, depression, cancer, stress, high blood pressure, migraines, addictions, lust, envy, doubt, worry, unbelief, etc.; all of which are blocking spirits that are protecting fear, and they are preventing the root cause of what has been your fear from being exposed and revealed.

Once you are in a constant, continuous, and consistent mode, and you are in an assault, attack, and assassinate mind-set, and you are in and have an aggressive and adamant mentality, you are now ready to (d) challenge, confront, conquer, and change being afraid of someone or something as likely to be dangerous, painful, or threatening that can and will hurt and harm you (fear). You are out to permanently remove fear, get rid of it, and not replace it with a watered-down version of fear, which is "unbelief." The friends and family members of fear-driven and motivated "unbelief" are doubt, worry, and stress. Unbelief is a fear tactic, as with all its friends and family members.

THE SURVIVORS MODE

Fear-driven and motivated "unbelief" is described as being afraid that having and trusting in a religious belief or trusting in faith is something as likely to be dangerous, painful, or threatening that can and will hurt and harm you. Fear wants to make sure you are so afraid of having faith that you stay in a mode, mind-set, and mentality where you demonstrate a lack of religious belief or an absence of faith. The plan that Satan has for you and the gift he wants to give you every minute, every second, every hour, every day, every month, every year, and every decade is the gift of being afraid of the state or quality of not believing, incredulity or skepticism, especially in matters of doctrine or religious faith as likely to be dangerous, painful, or threatening that can and will hurt and harm you.

Is that the gift you want? If not, you have the God-given right, power, and authority to challenge, confront, and conquer that gift, and you have the right to resist, reject, refuse, and rebuke it. You have the God-given right, power, and authority through the shedding of Jesus's blood on Calvary; through Him going down and defeating death, hell, "fear," OCD, PTSD, depression, cancer, stress, high blood pressure, migraines, addictions, lust, envy, doubt, worry, unbelief, etc., and the grave on your behalf; you have the right, power, and authority to change your receiving mind, frame of mind, state of mind, mental condition and conditioning, and mental state of being. You have a right to receive what you want to receive and reject, resist, refuse, rebuke, and refute what you want to refute.

Suggest and influence

The devil can't make you accept and receive fear, OCD, PTSD, depression, cancer, stress, high blood pressure, migraines, addictions, lust, envy, doubt, worry, unbelief, etc. You have to want them and desire them on your own; he can only suggest and influence. Close that door by challenging, confronting, and conquering the fear-driven feelings, emotions, and the fear-driven urges, tendencies, inclinations, intuitions, impulsiveness, and instincts. Stop being a "punked victim" and stop letting the devil torment, torture, trick, and trap you into yielding, submitting, and surrendering. Your blood of Jesus sheds power and authority over any and all unpleasant emotions and feelings that are caused by the belief that someone or something is dangerous, likely to cause pain, or a threat is going to come upon you and hurt and harm you.

OCD, PTSD, depression, cancer, stress, high blood pressure, migraines, addictions, lust, envy, doubt, worry, unbelief, being raped, molested, battered, etc., anything that is negative, bad, and wrong or ugly are all driven and motivated by fear. Once again, I'm going to say, "Fear is not your friend." Stop protecting it and stop preventing it from being "cast out" of you and being removed and being replaced with the gift of faith. Satan can only *suggest* you receive an unpleasant emotion caused by the belief that someone or something is dangerous, likely to cause pain, or a threat is going to happen to you or come upon you. The only thing he can do is *influence* you into receiving an unpleasant emotion caused by the belief that someone or something is dangerous, likely to cause pain, or a threat is going to come upon you and hurt and harm you. His major deception and delusion is to suggest to you that receiving anything that is good, real, and right and receiving anything and anyone that is and will be (a) good to you and (b) good for you is something you should be afraid of and you should consider such as likely to be dangerous, painful, or threatening to you.

Satan wants to influence you into believing and accepting that having someone in your life that is good to you and good for you and having someone who can and will bring out the best in you is something, is a thought, train of thought, thinking, and a way of thinking that you should be afraid of and you should see and perceive as a thought, train of thought, thinking, and a way of thinking that is likely to be dangerous, painful, or threatening to you. Satan uses fear as his *reverse psychology* tactical weapon, and whatever it is that he is telling you, he knows the opposite is what God has purposed to happen in your life and in your day.

He knows that by constantly, continuously, and consistently tormenting and torturing you with fear-driven and motivated OCD, PTSD, depression, cancer, stress, high blood pressure, migraines,

THE SURVIVORS MODE   235

addictions, lust, envy, doubt, worry, unbelief, etc., he can keep you away from receiving any kind and type of good from coming into your life. Fear is a gift from Satan that you do not have to receive. And you have the right to challenge, confront, and conquer it and change the way it has affected and change the way it has affected you.

The gift(s) that God has given you is (1) the right, the power, and the authority to overpower, overtake, and overthrow fear, OCD, PTSD, depression, cancer, stress, high blood pressure, migraines, addictions, lust, envy, doubt, worry, unbelief, fear of being raped, molested, battered again, etc. He has given you (2) love and the ability to love yourself and to not be afraid to love yourself. He has given you the gift of love, to receive good and the right kind of love from others. You don't have to be afraid to give love and to receive love. He has given you the gift of (3) having a sound mind so you can make sound choices and decisions.

Fear wants to keep you procrastinating, hesitating, questioning, second-guessing, halting between two opinions, dubious, a person of two minds, irresolute, unstable, unreliable, uncertain about everything you think, feel, or decide. This is what happens when you allow and give fear the freedom to dominate, manipulate, and control your every move, choice or decision, thoughts, train of thought, thinking, and way of thinking. One of the most dangerous, damaging, and self-destructive things that you can let fear do to you is to let it get you into a comfort zone, place of contentment and complacency with it, and get you to make compromises with it as if it is something that deserves that kind of attention. Fear doesn't like you, and it wants to remove you and your children, your family, and your generations off the face of this earth.

Fear wants to dominate, manipulate, and control the power, love, and sound mind God has *already* given you. He wants you to be afraid to use the power God has given you over him and his fear tactics and maneuvers. He wants you to be afraid and fearful to use the power you have over him and over his tormenting and torturing fear. He wants you to be afraid or fearful of love and the power to love others even when they did not love you the right way and treated you the right way. He also wants you to be fearful when it comes to you loving God. God has given you the power to love Him and not be fearful that He is trying to rule over you like a mad dictator does and run your life and He is trying to get you to do something or say something that is going to bring hurt, harm and danger to you. God has given you His power so you can love, believe in love, receive love, accept love, adapt to love, and follow love.

That gift of love that God has given you will drive out anything said or done, past, present, or future, that can and will or have hindered, blocked, or delayed you having a sound mind. You don't have to be fearful of loving yourself, believing in yourself, and you don't have to be fearful when it comes to you loving again, living again, and winning again. God did not give you a spirit of timidity, of cowardice, of craving and cringing and fawning fear; those are not His gifts to you, and that is not what He wants you to receive as if it was from Him. He has given us the right and the power and the authority to have a calm *and* well-balanced mind *and* discipline *and* self-control. Who is your gift giver, God or Satan? Which gift have you received, fear or faith?

CHAPTER FIFTEEN

Traps, Triggers, and Trespassers

AS I STATED before, your feelings and your emotions are not your best friend. Every time you allow yourself to function and flow in and out of and you follow your survivor-survival feelings and emotions, they won't let you receive anything and anyone that could, can, and will be (a) good to you and (b) good for you and will (c) bring out the best in you and not bring out the worse. With that being said, let me expose you to and reveal and bring you into the function and flow of the fear survival traps, triggers, and trespassers that both Mollie and Rose had waiting for them. Let's first look into and at what wiles, schemes, trickeries, devices, deceptions, delusions, theories, arguments, reasoning, and seductions that were set for them and they walked into.

The traps

Mollie and Rose often found themselves being seduced, tricked, deceived, trapped, led, entangled, and entrapped in a lonely, dark, and cold place, and neither one of them knew there were being constantly, continuously, and consistently drawn into. Fear was always pursuing and chasing after them and setting traps for them. And each time fear had cornered them, it kept distracting them long enough for all its friends to show up in their life and in their day. Not only was this happening on a consistent basis but also what neither of them ever knew was fear had gained access and had gotten control and was in control of their mind, frame of mind, state of mind, and mental condition/conditioning, and it was doing all the shot calling, dominating, manipulating, and controlling.

Fear then would step up its game, and it would use all its twisted and sick friends, imps, and cohort spirits that would bring sin, sicknesses, diseases, and infirmities to launch and assault and attack and assassinate and keep their feelings, emotions, and desires distracted long enough so satanic and demonic fear could and would suggest to Mollie's and Rose's thoughts, train of thought, thinking, and way of thinking into overpowering, overtaking, and overthrowing logical reasoning and faith reasoning and they should take and make some kind and type of survival reaction acts, actions, deeds, and it also suggested to their mind, frame of mind, state of mind, mental condition, and conditioning that they had to "do something" and make some kind of move to protect and prevent Mollie, Rose, and yourself from falling, failing, losing, going down, and proving what their naysayers said about them was true.

Fear suggested to Mollie's and Rose's mind, frame of mind, mental condition/conditioning, and state of mind that they should not wait on God, be patient and long-suffering, persevere, exercise or trust faith or fight back, but some kind and type of survival action needs to be implemented and initiated. As fear was doing its distracting, it was also detaining their attention span and their focus; it was also detouring their mind, frame of mind, and state of mind away from faith, hope, belief, confidence, trust, and hope. Because of the multiplicity of things that was happening to the both of them at the same time, they could not focus and they did know how to; nor did they have time to stand, resist, reject, refuse, rebuke, and refute.

Once the suggesting, detaining, and detouring had been successful, and their mind, frame of mind, mental condition, and state of mind had taken the bait, and their feelings and emotions and desires were detained and detoured long enough for fear to get them connected to, linked to, tied to and became yoked to, in a stronghold to, in bondage to, bound and limited to, and because of and a slave to the suggestions fear had whispered; and their feelings, emotions, and desires had instantly and automatically reacted accordingly to what was suggested; fear would then suggest to and influence Mollie's and Rose's urges, tendencies, inclinations, intuitions, impulses, impulsiveness, and instincts to seize, take control, and take over and be and stay in control. Fear would then influence their urges, tendencies, inclinations, intuitions, impulses, impulsiveness, and instincts into taking action because they needed to take over and help Mollie and Rose survive through what they were going through.

Fear had influenced their urges, tendencies, inclinations, impulses, impulsiveness, and instincts into delivering and demonstrating some kind and type of survival reactionary responses. This whole process and procedure I just shared with you became and would be a continuous, constant, and consistent vicious cycle of fear-driven and motivated events, happenings, and occurrences. Each time a survival reaction and reactionary response was delivered and demonstrated, what I just described would one day become, be, and end up being a habitual and addictive way of life and way of behaving, behavior pattern, and conduct for the both of them.

Fear had tricked and trapped their feelings, emotions, desires, mind, frame of mind, mental condition, and state of mind, and it was detaining them and preparing to detour them away from faith and faith responses. Neither could, would, and did see and know what was happening and what was going on behind the scenes of their very lives. It was all well planned, prepared, positioned, and orchestrated by Satan and his demon spirit called fear. Mollie and Rose didn't intentionally or unintentionally say or do anything wrong that would draw, drive, pull, push, persuade, or force what was happening to them into their lives. It all was a satanic and demonic setup. The trap was set for them to fall into long before they were thought of by their parents, long before their parents got together, and long before they were conceived, birthed, and born into this world.

The only way fear could disconnect Mollie and Rose from faith of any kind, it had to trap their mind, frame of mind, mental condition and conditioning, and state of mind, their urges, tendencies, inclinations, intuitions, impulses, impulsiveness, and instincts, attention span, and focus long enough to suggest to them, influence them, distract them, detain them, and detour them onto the path of being connected to thinking, feeling, and believing they had to become, be, and end up being a survivor, and they had to learn survival techniques and tactics.

They couldn't and wouldn't and didn't see any of this coming, and, therefore, they could not, did not, and would not be able to prepare for the assault and attack and assassination of their faith; nor could they protect themselves and prevent what was and would be happening to them with the measure of faith God had given them (Rom. 12:3).

Fear mentor

They both met someone who tutored, trained, and taught them what fear is and how to be fearful and why they should be fearful; and when they had learned the fear lessons through being a victim of traumatizing, torturing, and tormenting fearful acts, actions and deeds, words, conversations, communications, conduct, behavior, and behavior patterns their fear tutor, trainer, and mentor was teaching through his bad, wrong, negative, and ugly choices and decisions they made and through the bad and wrong and ugly and negative ways things were handled; and through bad, ugly, wrong, and negative things that the person had said and done to them.

The only thing their fear tutor, trainer, and mentor could and would be able to tutor, train, and teach the both of them was what was on the inside of them and what they had been tutored, trained, and taught and had learned. That's not to say what they did to Mollie, Rose, and what your fear mentor is tutoring, teaching, and training you is right, because it isn't, and it never can or will be right. The person from whom you learned what fear is and how to fear and why you should fear was just the person Satan dominated, manipulated, controlled, and used to dictate into your life, fear.

It would also be the person Satan would use to be the source for trapping your mind, frame of mind, mental condition and conditioning, and state of mind; your urges, tendencies, inclinations, intuitions, impulses, impulsiveness, and instincts, your attention span, and your focus; long enough for fear to suggest to them, influence them, distract them, detain them, and detour them onto the path of being connected to bad, wrong, ugly, and negative reactionary thinking, feeling, and believing, acts, actions, and deeds. I'm sure the person whom Satan was using to mentor you in how to be fearful never thought, felt, expected, anticipated or believed he or she would be the one who was taught the same thing he or she was not teaching.

Once again, I want to say that doesn't make what they did to you right. What I want you to see and what I want you to know is whatever it is that is bad, wrong, ugly, and negative that comes through you, me, or someone else, all of what we know and give away is "learned behavior," which I can assure you is connected to and is sourced out of a family-inherited generational curse that was not dealt with in the way it needed to be and it got out of control. We inherit good and bad behavior, behavior patterns, conduct, conversations, communication, personality traits, as well as good and bad intellect and integrity qualities from our mother, father, or family's passed-on genes.

Repent, release, or repeat

When a person has been tutored, trained, taught, and has learned how to fear and how to become, be, and end up being fearful, the danger is that same person will end up becoming and being someone who (a) causes, (b) creates the atmosphere for, and (d) contributes to innocent others being traumatized, tortured, and tormented by fear at your hands or at the hands of someone else in that person's present or future. In other words, the fear victim ends up becoming and ends up being a fear victimizer.

The person has learned how to accept, adopt, and adapt to being fearful, being traumatized, being tormented, and being tortured. And he or she has gotten good at opening himself or herself up to being tormented, tortured, and traumatized by depression, hallucinations, mental torture, anxiety, alternate realities; being called and feeling like a bastard child; meningitis, sickness, seizures, nightmares, loss of consciousness, having fevers; being set up for comas, voodoo, the death spirit; accepting sciatic nerve disease, damaged memory, reading backward, anger, concussions, rejection, and low self-esteem.

The person also knows how to cause, create the atmosphere for, and contribute to him or her receiving a broken heart; being abused; being in a lonely mode, mind-set, and mentality; feeling false responsibility; having a complex; being open to sexual passivity, masturbation; feeling no self-worth; being addicted to prescription drugs, guilt, oxycodone; being remorseful, being ashamed, being entangled and entrapped in escapism, being neglected, being raped, being on painkillers; addicted to fear, addicted to self-condemnation, and not knowing how to receive self-forgiveness, accepting bests disease, word curses, suicide, sexual abuse, dysthymia, trichotillomania, and being addicted to accepting self-guilt.

What you have to know is whatever you have been through that is bad, wrong, ugly, and negative and that is sourced out of and from fear, you can become, be, and end up being addicted to it, and when that happens and occurs, your ability to resist, reject, refuse, rebuke, and refute becomes so low that it is ineffective and powerless. Whatever it is that is bad, wrong, negative, and ugly that you can unknowingly expect, anticipate, accept, adopt, adapt to, and apply, you can end up becoming addicted to without you even knowing it and without you even being aware that you are doing it and you are opening yourself up to it happening to you.

This is another way Satan strategizes using satanic and demonic fear as a way to trick and trap you and your mind, frame of mind, mental condition and conditioning, state of mind; your urges, tendencies, inclinations, intuitions, impulses, impulsiveness, and instincts; your attention span and focus long enough to suggest to them, influence them, distract them, detain them, and detour them. You become someone who expects and anticipates accepting, adopting, adapting to function, and flowing in and out of what your first and/or last fear mentor tutored, trained, and taught you. You can and will, without you even knowing it, start causing, creating the atmosphere for, and contributing to you and everyone you meet or close to how to open themselves up to applying fear, OCD, PTSD, etc., processes, procedures, and principles.

Whatever it is that your first or last or present fear mentor tutored, trained, and taught you about being fearful, scared, afraid, and how to survive and how to and when to be in a survivor-survival mode, mind-set, and mentality, and when and how to and why you should release

THE SURVIVORS MODE

survivor-survival tactics will continue to be a part of who you are, and you will continue to be addicted to it, accept it, adapt to it, apply it, restore it, remember it, and relive it. And you will continue to be caught in and caught up in the vicious cycle of it all and be a slave to it until the day you repent and release it. You are not going to just wake up one morning and fear, with all its friends, is gone out of your life.

Whatever it is that you have been through that you keep negatively reacting to and having reactionary responses to and negatively responding to that you do not and have not fully repented of and released, you will keep on repeating. The reason is there are still some remaining survivor, survival residue thoughts, feelings, emotions, desires, expressions, reactions, and reactionary responses lying dormant inside of you. What has to take place is you are going to have to get some deep-rooted core inner deliverance, cleansing, and purging so that you can be healed and made whole again. We will get to this later one in this book.

Triggers

Once fear has gained access to any part or parts of you and it has trapped the parts of you it needs to trap, the next thing that fear has to do is to trigger you into functioning and flowing in and out of an instant, automatic, sudden, immediate, constant, continual, and consistent survivor-survival mode, mind-set, mentality, and mental state of being, and trigger you into instantly, immediately, suddenly, constantly, continuously, and consistently flowing into following a survivor-survival tactical mind-set and mentality and having and being in a survivor-survival tactical mode and mental state of being.

A trigger is something that cause, create the atmosphere for, or contribute to an event or a negative, bad, wrong, or ugly circumstance, situation, confrontation, matter, memory, and moment to happen or exist. It can be something from your past or present that Satan knows you are still holding on to (residue) that you have not repented of, released, that you are still fearful of frightened of, scared of, and afraid of that keeps you in a state of mind and in a condition where you constantly, continuously, and consistently procrastinate, hesitate, second-guess, and you are reluctant to open up to, receive, engage in, or get involved with, accept, adapt to, and believe.

When you unknowingly or knowingly practice being in a vicious fear cycle, you will grow, develop, and mature into having and demonstrating a constant, continual, and consistent "trigger" mind-set and mentality, and from that, you will be led into being in a constant, continual, and consistent "trigger" mode, and you will be locked into a constant, continual, and consistent "trigger" mental state of being. When this happens, what you are basically doing is expecting and anticipating and setting your own self up for something fearful to happen to you showing up in your life and day. And with that comes you being in a survivor-survival "readiness" mode, mind-set, and mentality.

Whatever triggers you being in a survivor-survival mode, mind-set, mentality, and mental state of being will end up being locked into your mind-set and mentality, and it will end up being the mode you will always be in, and that will become the mental state of being that you will always function and flow and make choices and decisions in and out of. Your trigger can be a traumatic, troubling, and tragic thought, a feeling, an emotion, a belief, a desire; something that has been good, bad, ugly, negative, and even something or some part of you that is unfulfilled and you have not received personal satisfaction in. Anyone who is in a survivor-survival mode, mind-set, mentality, and mental state of being because of something bad, negative, wrong, ugly, and fearful that has happened to him or her is always ready to "release," and he or she is ready to "set off" and "fire" survivor and survival arguments, survivor and survivor theories, and survivor and survival reasoning.

They are in a survivor-survival mode, mind-set, mentality, and mental state of being, and they are instantly and automatically triggered into leading every faith thought and faith-based purpose away captive. Please understand fear is the spirit and the force that is behind the "releasing, setting off, and the firing and the leading away captive," and fear triggers what is to trigger survivor-survival behavior, conduct, behavior patterns, conversations, communication, understanding, character, personality, intellect, and integrity.

THE SURVIVORS MODE
~245~

Everything that happened to Mollie and Rose and everything they went through that was traumatic, troubling, and tragic that they had to deal with and had to make it through would be what would trigger them easily flowing over into a survivor-survival mode, mind-set, mentality, and mental state of being. At no time was releasing, firing, and setting off Mollie and Rose and your survivor-survival tactical mode, mind-set, mentality, and mental state of being carefully thought out, planned, and prepared for reaction and reactionary response; it would be one that was delivered and demonstrated on the spot and released, set off, and fired spontaneously, immediately, suddenly, without any advance warning.

Mollie and Rose made it through what they were faced with not knowing fear had taken control, not knowing fear had trapped their mind, frame of mind, mental condition and conditioning, state of mind; their urges, tendencies, inclinations, intuitions, impulses, impulsiveness, and instincts, as well as their attention span and focus long enough for fear to suggest to them, influence them, distract them, detain them, and detour them. After that, fear would move over into initiating, implementing, and inundating their mode, mind-set, mentality, and mental state of being with survivor-survival triggers. Neither one of them knew they had triggers locked, loaded, and imbedded in their mode, mind-set, mentality, and mental state of being.

The only way they would find out and discover they did was when something that resembled or "looked like" something they had been through and had to find a way to survive and make it through, or someone said or done something, or an act, action, deed, conversation, communication, a way and a manner something or someone was handled, certain and specific behavior, conduct, behavior pattern, image, insight, personality or integrity, trait, motion, movement, motivation, motive, choice and decision, etc., were demonstrated or delivered and heard or seen. That would trigger a specific and certain mainly negative, past, ugly, and wrong past or present fearful thought, feeling emotion, desire, etc., showing up.

In most cases, people who are in a survivor-survival mode, mind-set, mentality, and mental state of being would not notice or pay any attention to what triggered them getting over into a survivor-survival mode, mind-set, mentality, mental state of being where they would, without thinking and without feelings and emotions, fire off, set off, and release survivor-survival tactical protective and preventive messages, information, and instructions. In that moment when they are triggered, they have visualized a fear-filled survivor-survival image in their mind's imagination, and they have dismantled and derailed faith hearing and listening and obeying, and they are going about creating and constructing and building and establishing the survivor-survival tactical protective, preventive, defensive-offensive mode, mind-set, mentality, and mental state of being they are locked into a trance.

My point is reexperiencing the trauma symptoms. Intrusive memories that interrupt everyday life, flashbacks that cause, create the atmosphere for, and contribute to acts, and you acting or feeling like you're still in the middle of the event again, reoccurring nightmares about the trauma, intense distress or irritability when reminded of the event, physical reactions, like rapid breathing, sweating, or nausea, when remembering or being reminded of the trauma, increased distress as the anniversary of the event approaches, avoidance symptoms, feeling emotionally detached from others, experiencing hopelessness about the future ("No one will ever love me" or "I know I'm going to die young"), inability to remember important aspects of the traumatic event, arousal or anxiety symptoms, bouts of moodiness or anger, insomnia or difficulty staying asleep; a sense of being "on alert" or "on guard" (also called hypervigilance), developing a destructive addiction to alcohol, drugs, or even gambling, and suicidal thoughts or actions are all triggered by something. You take away what triggers them, and you can disconnect them and defeat them.

Fear traps something that has been troubling, torturing, tormenting, terrorizing, and traumatizing you in your mind, frame of mind, mental condition, state of mind, and mental state of being, and whatever it is that is or has been trapped acts and becomes, is, and ends up being and births triggered thoughts, triggered train of thought, triggered thinking, and triggered way of thinking. And once what is trapped is triggered, you automatically and instantly, suddenly, quickly, and

THE SURVIVORS MODE 247

immediately get over into a survivor-survival attitude, mood, mind-set, mentality, and mental state of being.

Once you are there, survivor-survival urges, tendencies, inclinations, intuitions, impulses, impulsiveness, and instincts are triggered, and they will begin to dominate, manipulate, control, and then trigger your survivor-survival feelings, survivor-survival emotions, survivor-survival desires, survivor-survival acts, actions, deeds, survivor-survival things and matters handled, and survivor-survival choices and decisions you will make.

The triggers and survivor-survival triggers hide, hibernate, live and reside and grow, develop, and mature while they are in your mind-set and mentality. They gain strength, power, and authority when they can dominate, manipulate, control, and dictate to and decide and determine the type and kind of mode you get into, which is reflected in and through the mood you get into, and they are reflected in and through the motives and motivation you have and demonstrate. The only way you will know a survivor-survival trigger has been triggered is the person becomes easily agitated, and they get over into an attitude that changes the positive, good, and right atmosphere that was around you and them.

Trespassers

Anything that traps you or any part of you and holds that part or those parts of you hostage and anything and everything that hides and then hibernates inside of you against your will and without you knowing it is a trespasser or a squatter spirit, and it is trespassing. When people are in a survivor mode, mind-set, mentality, and mental state of being, they are not focused on, nor are they aware of or paying attention to what is being introduced to them, what is waiting to seize, grip, and gain entrance and gain access and control over them, as well as what they are susceptible to. That's because they are distracted and they are trying to make it through what they are faced with.

Fear is that distraction, and it is busy suggesting to you that something bad, wrong, negative, and ugly is going to happen to you, and it influences you to protect yourself by any means necessary. And while you are busy reacting to what has been suggested and what you have been influenced to do, Satan is sneaking something else into what is already going on, another trespassing spirit, and you may not and will not even know it until sometime later. Trespassers are not going to send you a note, give you advance warning, or give you a warning sign notifying you that they are going to overrule, overpower, overtake, and overthrow some part(s) of you and they are going to break through and violate you in some kind of way.

A trespasser spirit is a spirit that enters some part of you unlawfully and without your permission. When that spirit gains access and begins to occupy and refuses to leave, it is called a squatter spirit. Anything that is a squatter spirit is a spirit that unlawfully occupies an uninhabited part or parts of you or an unused part of you. Whatever part or parts of you where there is not full-of-living powered active and alive truth that comes from God or where there is self-deception, self-delusion, easy enticing, entanglement, and entrapment, refusing, rejecting, resisting, rebuking, and refuting of truth and reality, brokenness, hurt, pain, frustration, discouragement, disappointment, compromises, complacency, contentment, comfort zones, etc., those places are or have uninhibited and unused places within them, and they are open to satanic and demonic suggestions and influencing, indwelling, and possessing. Trespassing spirits are "as" or they are like a roaring lion that prowls around like a roaring lion looking for someone to devour, indwell, possess, dominate, manipulate, control, seize, grip, overpower, overtake, overthrow, takeover, take down, and take out or remove from faith to fear (1 Pet. 5:7).

Once fear distracts you and your focus and then uses suggestive and influencing deceptions to deceive you and then detours you away from faith and then delays you long enough for its trespassing squatter friends to show up and gain entrance and access to the uninhibited and unoccupied and unused part or parts of you and then deny you the right, power, and authority to use your power of choice, fear then seduces, entices, tricks, and traps you into accepting, adopting, adapting to, and functioning and flowing in and out of a survivor-survival mode and following survivor-survival processes, principles, and procedures

THE SURVIVORS MODE

as part of your daily mind-set, mentality, and mental state of being, willingly our unwillingly, knowingly and unknowingly.

Some of those unlawful occupying trespassing squatter friends of fear are OCD, PTSD, depression, hallucinations, mental torture, anxiety, alternate realities, feeling like a bastard child, meningitis, sickness, seizures, nightmares, loss of consciousness, fevers; comas, voodoo, the death spirit, sciatic nerve disease, damaged memory, reading backward, anger, concussions, rejection, and low self-esteem; a broken heart, abuse, loneliness, false responsibility, having a complex, sexual passivity, masturbation, feeling no self-worth; addiction to prescription drugs, guilt, oxycodone, remorseful, being ashamed, being entangled and entrapped in escapism, being neglected, being raped, being on painkillers, addicted to fear, addicted to self-condemnation and not knowing how to receive self-forgiveness, accepting bests disease, word curses, suicide, sexual abuse, dysthymia, trichotillomania, and being addicted to accepting self-guilt, sickness, disease, and infirmities of any kind.

They all act as settlers with no legal title to the part of you they have occupied. Typically, they seize parts of you that you have not yielded, submitted, and surrendered totally and completely to the Holy Spirit. All of them act as master builders that help direct you into, connect you to, link you to, and tie you to and help you create, build, and establish you in a survivor-survival mode, mind-set, mentality, and mental state of being. All of them are fear's helpers, and their job and responsibility is to help you see the need for and to help you get in and be in a survivor-survival mode, mind-set, mentality, and mental state of being on a constant, consistent, and continual basis. None of what has happened to you was a coincidence or an accident; all of it was strategic and methodically carried out.

You have the right, the power, and the authority to evict, get rid of, and be free of being in survivor-survival mind, etc., and you have the right to be free of fear, along with all its trespassing and squatter spirits. You don't have to be trapped in a survivor-survival mode, and you don't have to let survivor-survival and fear triggers live, dwell, and abide in your frame of mind, mental condition, and state of mind, and you don't have to let those trespassing squatter spirits dominate, manipulate, and control your thoughts, train of thought, thinking, and way of thinking. And you don't have to continue to let them dictate to your mind-set, mentality, and mental state of being. You don't have to continue to be tormented, tortured, and traumatized by fear and its trespassing squatter spirits, friends, and imps.

CHAPTER SIXTEEN

Sense and Reason

Now, the mind of the flesh (which is sense and reason) without the Holy Spirit) is death (death that compromises all the miseries arising from sin, both here and hereafter). But the mind of the (Holy) spirit is life and (soul) peace (both now and forever).
—Romans 8:6 AMP

WHEN PEOPLE ARE drawn, pulled, pushed, persuaded, seduced, enticed, tricked, deceived, and they are forced into a survivor-survival mode, that mode has a supporting cast that acts as a survivor-survival mode support system. The support system for a person who is in a survivor-survival mode is made up of two entities: (1) sense and reason, and (2) appetites and impulses. They have something that they have to do for fear to keep having a hold and a grip on you and to keep faith away from you. Their assignment is to make sure you stay in a survivor-survival mode, mind-set, mentality, and mental state of being while you are going through and long after you have gotten past what you were going through.

Survive

Before I begin to break those two down, I have to tell you the moment when you are functioning and flowing in and out of a survivor-survival mind-set and you have the survivor-survival mentality and you dwell in a state of being where you instantly and automatically sense, feel, think, and believe you are and you have to become, be, and end up being a person who *survives:*

- continue to live or exist, especially in spite of the danger and hardship you endured;
- must remain alive, sustain oneself, pull through, get through, hold on/out, make it, and keep your body soul and mind together;
- continue to live or exist in spite of a bad, wrong, negative, and ugly accident, ordeal, circumstance, situation, confrontation, or matter you have been through;
- must remain alive after the death of a marriage and relationship;
- manage to keep going in difficult circumstances and times.

Survivor

Once you know how to survive while being in a survivor-survival mind-set, the next thing that happens while you are still functioning and flowing in and out of that survivor-survival mind-set, you then end up in a mentality where you begin to constantly, continuously, and consistently dwell in a state of being where you instantly and automatically start sensing, feeling, and believing and having the kind of thoughts, train of thought, thinking, and way of thinking that will ensure you end up being a *survivor,* which is someone who has to

- ➤ remain alive after an abusively dangerous, deadly, destructive, damaging circumstance, situation, confrontation, matter, or event in which others have died;
- ➤ be on guard, take no chances, react, have and deliver and demonstrate a reactionary response just in case, so you can and will make it through "what looks like and feels like" it is something that you have seen and been through before;
- ➤ be sure you are always the sole remainder or the sole remaining person of a group of people who have been through and have had the same or similar things said and done to them that you have and they didn't make it through it in the past, in the present, and in the future; and

THE SURVIVORS MODE

➤ be a person who copes well with the difficulties that have happened and occurred in your life.

Survival

✓ You know how to survive and you know how to be a survivor because you have a proven, demonstrated, tutored, trained, and taught survivor-survival mind, frame of mind, state of mind, mental condition and conditioning, mind-set, mentality, thoughts, train of thought, thinking, and way of thinking that have been exercised; and as you are still functioning and flowing in and out of a survivor-survival mind-set and you still have the survivor-survival mentality and you still are dwelling in a fearfully driven and motivated state of being, you have grown, developed, and matured in a *survival mode*, which means you know when to, know how to, and where to get into

✓ the state or fact of continuing to live or exist, typically in spite of an accident, ordeal, or difficult circumstances;

✓ a focus or a practice, process, and procedure that has continued to exist from an earlier time that had helped you make it through what you have already been through;

✓ the act or fact of living or continuing longer than another person or thing; and

✓ the continuation of life or existence.

To help make sure you do abandon thinking and feeling and sensing the need to survive and you continue be driven to be a survivor and you stay entangled and entrapped and connected to, liked to, tied to, yoked to, in a stronghold to, in bondage to, bound and limited by, and a slave to survival urges, tendencies, inclinations, intuitions, impulses, impulsiveness, and instincts; and to help make sure you are fully continuously, constantly, and consistently in a reactionary and a reactionary response survivor-survival mode, fear calls in its first survivor-survival duo to help assist with keeping your motives and motivation coming out of a survivor-survival tactical mind-set, mentality, and mental state of being; that duo is called sense and reason.

Setup for sense and reason

When you are or have been driven, drawn, pulled, pushed, persuaded, tricked, seduced, and enticed into trying to survive and be a survivor and you are locked into survival, because of the unexpected, unplanned, unknown, undetected, etc., things that you have been through or you are still going through that are or have been bad, wrong, negative, and ugly, you will end up functioning and flowing in and out of a survivor-survival mode. And once you land or arrive at that place and at that point, the first two supporters of a survivor-survival mode and the support system that are set in place for a survivor-survival mode are called sense and reason.

Everything that fear suggests to you and everything fear influences you into saying and doing, as well as your acts, actions, deeds, choices and decisions, how and what you think or feel, as well as your emotional makeup, how, when, where, and why you handle things, etc., everything that comes out of you derives and flows and is sourced from fear, and you are being set up for the spirit of sense and reason. Fear will make sure sense and reason have the freedom to show up or manifest itself in choice and decision-making part or parts of you and that can happen because you are in so much hurt, pain, and brokenness that you are no longer moving in the ways of the spirit but in the ways of the flesh.

Because of what you have been through and because of what you think and feel you "should do, need to do, and have to do" to make it through what has happened to you and knowing where you need to get to just to survive, your life is no longer governed by the standards and according to the dictates of the spirit but controlled by the flesh. Satanic and demonic fear has tricked you into bypassing your logical sound mind, frame of mind, mental condition, state of mind, and mental state of being; and it has suggested to your survivor and survival urges, tendencies, inclinations, intuitions, impulses, impulsiveness, and instincts that you need to "handle things and do something." And then that same satanic and demonic fear has and will influence you into having survivor and survival thoughts, train of thought, thinking, and way of thinking.

Once fear has gotten you into survival and survival thoughts, train of thought, thinking, and way of thinking, and it has stirred up your survivor and survival urges, tendencies, inclinations, intuitions, impulses, impulsiveness, and instincts, the next thing fear does is make sure you have survivor and survival feelings, emotions, and desires. Once you do, the next thing that fear does is entice, entangle, and entrap you into a survivor and survival mind-set and mentality. After that has taken place, the next move of satanic and demonic fear is to make sure your mind, frame of mind, mental condition, state of mind, and mental state of being are so focused on what has taken place that have you broken, beaten, and battered; then demonic and satanic fear, without you knowing it, seeing it, and feeling it, easily gets you connected, linked, tied, yoked, bound, and limited by and to, in bondage to, and a slave to a survivor stronghold and a survival stronghold and to a "need to survive" stronghold.

The final move that satanic and demonic fear make is to make sure what takes place is you will begin to see and be seized, overpowered, overtaken, overthrown, and consumed with survivor images and survival images. As this is happening, satanic and demonic fear will begin to infect you with, affect you with, and affect all of you with survivor and survival ideas, ingenuity, insights, instructions, and information that you will end up being constant, continuous, and consistent in functioning and flowing in and out of. You will then end up following survivor-driven and motivated processes, procedures, and principles and survival-driven and motivate processes, procedures, and principles; fear will then have the vital and necessary parts of you, and it will have you where it wants you, and what will quickly, suddenly, and immediately grow, develop, and mature is a survivor-survival mode.

Once satanic and demonic fear has done its job suggesting you need to "survive" and influencing you into thinking, feeling, and believing in "survival" and your need to be a "survivor," the supporters and the support system for you surviving, being a survivor, and you knowing how to get into survival quickly and effectively and for a survivor-survival mode show up without you even knowing it or inviting them to show up. The supporters for survivor-survival acts, actions, deeds, choices, and decisions, way of handling things, behavior, behavior patterns, conduct, conversation, communication, personality, integrity, intellect, etc., are known as sense and reason. The survivor-survival support system that fear will have you relying on, running to, and receiving from is manned up, and it is controlled by sense and reason.

Hello . . . we are sense and reason

Let me now take the time to introduce you to sense and reason and the vital role they will play in making sure you see and feel the need for being in a survivor-survival mind-set, mentality, mental state of being, and mode. They will begin by introducing you to and inundating you with survivor sense, survivor reason, survival sense, survival reason, and survivor-survival sense and reason. Let me introduce you to sense and reason by telling you something about them, and then I will tell you what they do. Both are a spirit, but for you to clearly see how and what Satan is using those two unclean spirits to do when you are in a survivor-survival mode, we are to look at them as if they have human features and characteristics.

Sense is described as a feeling that something is the case; a keen intuitive awareness of or sensitivity to the presence or importance of something and a reasonable or comprehensible rationale.

Reason is the power of the mind to think, understand, and form judgments by a process of logic; a cause, explanation, or justification for an action or event; good or obvious cause to do something; a premise of an argument in support of a belief, especially a minor premise when given after the conclusion; what is right, practical, or possible; common sense.

First mission: When they first show up, their job and their responsibility is to do damage assessment or to make sure all the right part or parts of you are distracted, damaged, destitute, destructive,

THE SURVIVORS MODE   ~257~

destroyed, detained, detoured, derailed, dismantled, deceived, delayed, denied, blocked, clogged up, hindered, held up, held hostage, etc.

Second mission: After the first mission has been completed, sense and reason will then make sure you and all the part or parts of you that are needed for you to have the "overwhelmed" and overwhelming need, want, and desire to survive and for survival; and the vital and necessary part or parts of you that are needed for you to be dominated, manipulated, and controlled by and with a survivor-survival attitude and mood(s), mind-set, mentality, feelings, emotions, desires, and instincts are in place and you are totally and completely leaning and depending on them and they can easily be accessed and dictated to.

Third mission: The next mission that sense and reason have is to make sure you feel no personal and private and public accountability and responsibility for what comes out of you, what you say and do, how you handle things, etc., because you are in a survivor-survival mode. You are to have no connections to your conscious and have no communication with your conscious. What this involves is sense and reason making sure you can and will resist, reject, refuse, rebuke, and refute faith arguments and you wholeheartedly embrace survivor-survival theories and survivor-survival reasoning and every proud and lofty survivor-survival thing that sets itself up against the true knowledge of faith. Sense and reason is to make sure you can and you will constantly, continuously, and consistently lead every faith thought and faith purpose away captive. They are to make sure faith accountability and faith responsibility do not reach your consciousness and your thoughts, train of thought, thinking, and way of thinking.

Fourth mission: Remember fear is the spirit that is controlling everything that happens when you are in a survivor-survival mode. For you to be completely over into a survivor-survival mode and have a survivor-survival mind-set and mentality, everything that you process is filtered through the need to survive, the desire to be a survivor, and the overwhelming drive for the necessity for survival and to be survivor-survival motivated. This will require the removal of your logic and the logical part of you. The logical part of you is the part of you that is characterized by or capable of clear, sound reasoning. Real reality reasoning is something that fear has to get you to look at and see in a twisted way.

Fear wants you to think, feel, and believe that you using real reality reasoning can and will be bad, wrong, negative, dangerous, damaging, and destructive to you and for you. So the assault and the attack would be to get your mind, frame of mind, mental condition, state of mind, and mental state of being to accept what is being suggested when it comes to real reality reasoning, adopt it, adapt to it, and follow what is being suggested. Fear wants to assassinate your ability to use logic or use reasoning conducted or assessed according to strict principles of validity. Fear wants to influence your mind and mental capabilities and abilities into receiving real reality reasoning as something that is harmful to you and for you; therefore, you should be scared of it and afraid of it, and you should react to it and then reject, resist, and refuse it.

Fifth mission: After everything has been checked and assigned its proper survivor-survival function, flow, process, and procedures, you will have to be influenced into demonstrating you are fully over into a survivor-survival mode, and this is done by you yielding, submitting, and surrendering fully to self-willed survivor-survival acts, actions, and deeds, self-performance survivor-survival acts, actions, and deeds, and self-effort survivor-survival acts, actions, and deeds. Your conduct, conversations, the way you communicate, and how you do so, and your behavior and behavior patterns should be and will be the place where you yielding, submitting, and surrendering to self-willed survivor-survival acts, actions, and deeds, self-performance survivor-survival acts, actions, and deeds, and self-effort survivor-survival acts, actions, and deeds can and will be recognized and seen.

Survivor-survival sense at work

Everything that I had been sharing with you in the above statements and topics, fear was, is, and had been behind the scenes of your life orchestrating and setting you up for survivor-survival sense and survivor-survival reason. Exactly what is survivor-survival sense?

- It is a feeling that people who has been abused, have OCD, PTSD, etc., get that something is the case that they immediately and suddenly without thinking act or have acted upon that they think, feel, and believe helped them end up being someone who survives, especially remaining alive after an event in which others have died; that becomes their instant and automatic acted-upon object, practice, state, or first line of thought that they make an established reactionary truth, reactionary reality, and fact of continuing to live or exist, typically in spite of an accident, ordeal, or difficult circumstances that have continued to exist from an earlier time.

And when people accept what is being felt, adopt what is being felt, adapt to what has been felt, attach a demonstrated reaction to what is being felt, and deliver a reactionary response to what is being felt, that delivered demonstration becomes the indication that they receive what is being felt. People are led to believe, think, and feel what they are feeling is harmfully real and it is right with or without proof and evidence and they need to protect themselves.

- It is an awareness or feeling that people get that lead them to think, feel, and believe they still and will always be in a harmful state and they have a sudden and immediate reactionary instinctive urgency to make sure they are someone who survives or remains alive after an event in which others have died, and they are driven by the thought they have to get to the state or fact of continuing to live or exist, typically in spite of an accident, ordeal, or difficult circumstances.

The awareness that people get is a self-awareness that derives from low self-esteem that can be based on a lot of bad, wrong, negative, and ugly thoughts, feelings, emotions, and desires they have about themselves that can lead them into thinking, feeling, and believing they are insignificant and inadequate and inferior in some kind of way to others, and they need to make it through the negative things that are said and done to them and make it through the negative way they feel about themselves.

- They are people who cope well with difficulties in their life in a way or manner, that what comes alive and what comes into being and what was put into motion and put into effect as a result of is an instant, automatic, constant, continuous, and consistent something to help them cope and make it through "practice" that continues to exist that came from an earlier time, which has transitioned people's mind-set, mentality, mental state, and mode of being into a keen intuitive awareness of or sensitivity to the presence or importance of themselves and of being a survivor and of survival.

A fear-driven and motivated surviving and survival thoughts, train of thought, thinking, and way of thinking have drawn, driven, pulled, pushed, persuaded, seduced, led, and forced the person into placing importance upon "self-survival" only, first and foremost, and making it the person's first priority, matter of importance, the center of attention, their focus, top priority, and their only mode. The person's value and emphasis is placed on "self-survival" reacting and reactionary responses and not upon responding the right way for all nonselfish right reasons. It is about "self-survival" no matter what the cost is.

- They are people who survive and remain alive after an event in which others have died and how they were able to do so would become, be, and end up being their method or practice that has continued to exist from an earlier time often manifested in and through them in what appears to be a sane realistic attitude to situations and problems.

People who are in this mind-set, frame of mind, and have this mentality basically have and demonstrate a different attitude, different approach, and different perception of and perspective on what actually is and what looks like something that they have seen before and have

THE SURVIVORS MODE · 261 ·

been through before. So when "similar" but not the same circumstances, situations, confrontations, matters, moments, and even memories show up, they quickly get over into functioning and flowing in and out of a survivor-survival process and procedures.

They are able to keep their composure, appear to be in a sane realistic attitude even though what they are sensing and are reacting to is not an actual or real occurrence or happening. They also have been tutored, trained, and taught, and they have also tutored, trained, and taught themselves to always be in a "ready" mode, mind-set, and mentality and to never take chances and to act and then react and, finally, overreact "just in case." That attitude they are in that seems sane to them is "you never know, it's better to be safe than sorry." And afterward, if they need to clear up and clean up their collateral damage as a result of doing what they will call is sound, "reasonable, and realistic reacting," they will do so. They have been tutored, trained, taught, and have learned what to do and how to handle what "appears to be" and "what is" because of what they have already been through.

- They are people who survive, especially remaining alive, after an event in which others have died, and the way they were able to survive, grow, develop, and mature into them being locked in on being focused on the state or fact of having to continue to live or exist, typically in spite of an accident, ordeal, or difficult circumstances as their constant, continuous, and consistent thoughts, train of thought, thinking, and a way of thinking that produce, prepare, and present a reasonable or comprehensible rationale surviving and survival mind-set, mentality, mental state of being, and mode.

People who are connected to, linked to, tied to, locked into being, bound and limited to, in bondage to, yoked and in a stronghold to, a slave to "reasonable or comprehensible rationale" surviving, survivor, and survival thinking and way of thinking are those who don't know how to do anything else because they have done so for so long, and they are easily targeted to be enticed by, entangled in, and entrapped into fair and sensible, fairly or moderately good, able to be understood, intelligible set of reasons or a logical basis for their course of action or a particular belief.

- They are people who survive, especially remaining alive after an event in which others have died, and how they were able to survive would become a practice that came from and has continued to exist from an earlier time, causing, creating the atmosphere for, and contributing to them being aware that something said or done or handled that resembles something from an earlier time can end up being the same case they were faced with without being able to define exactly how one knows.

People who are at this place and point are those who are dominated, manipulated, and controlled by being in an on-the-spot, sudden, and immediate ready reactionary response mode, mind-set, and mentality, and the survivor-survival choices and decisions they make come out of an urged instinct that derives from a past and old tendency, inclination, intuition, impulse, and impulsiveness. They deliver the sudden and immediate ready reactionary response without thinking about it, planning and preparing it, and being able to define exactly how they know when, where, why, and how to deliver what they deliver; they just do it.

- They are people who cope well with difficulties in their life because their frame of mind, state of mind, and mental state have been tutored, trained, and taught the art and fact of continuing to live or exist, typically in spite of an accident, ordeal, or difficult circumstances; and the way they have learned to cope has drawn, driven, and forced what they have learned into being a practice that has continued to exist from an earlier time. And how that person survives and how they remain alive after an event in which others have died has brought about a sane and realistic attitude to situations and problems.

THE SURVIVORS MODE

Survivor-survival sense is information and instructions given and implemented that are designed to make sure you are a person who has strong, solid, and stable survivor-survival wisdom, survivor-survival common sense, survivor-survival sagacity (having or showing an ability to understand difficult ideas and situations and to make good decisions), survivor-survival discernment, survivor-survival perception, survivor-survival wit, survivor-survival intelligence, survivor-survival cleverness, survivor-survival shrewdness, survivor-survival judgment, survivor-survival reason and reasoning, and survivor-survival logic that make you think and feel and believe and give you the sense (a feeling that something is the case) that you are safe and secure.

Survivor-survival reason revealed

Now that you have a clear understanding of what survivor-survival sense is, let us move forward into providing you with a clear understanding and insights into what it means to have survivor-survival reason or reasoning and why fear wants to make sure you are infected with it. When we are talking about survivor-survival reason at work, within you or a person, we are looking at and we are talking about

> ➢ a person who survives, especially someone who remains alive after an event in which others have died, that eventually becomes, is, and ends up being someone who is functioning and flowing in and out of the thought and the state or fact of continuing to live or exist, typically in spite of a past, present, or future unseen, unknown, unplanned, unwanted, unexpected, undetected, unbelievable, unforgettable, etc., accidents, ordeals, or difficult circumstances, and that thought, state, and fact bring about an instant and automatic readiness to bring about a cause, explanation, or justification for an impulsive and instinctive action or event;
>
> ➢ a person who copes well with difficulties in his or her life because of a focus or a past or present and a one day future

"make it make sense, make it thorough" practice that he or she, of his or her own free will, has allowed to continue to exist that came out of and from an earlier time that the person is led to think, feel, and believe is still a good or obvious cause to do something that is an urged tendency, inclination, intuition, impulse, and instinct;

➢ a person who survives, especially a person remaining alive after an event in which others have died, and because he or she was able to do so, he or she remained and allowed himself or herself to be yoked, bound and limited, in bondage to, in a stronghold to, and a slave to that same thought, feeling, and emotional desire and state or fact of making sure he or she continues to live or exist, typically in spite of an accident, ordeal, or difficult circumstances; by allowing the power of the mind to think, understand, and form judgments by a process of logic;

➢ a person who copes well with difficulties in his or her life because of a focus or a process, procedure, principle, and practice he or she had implemented and still implements that continues to exist from an earlier time when he or she was going through that the person still uses and utilizes as a process, procedure, and premise of an argument in support of a belief, especially a minor premise when given after the conclusion;

➢ a person who survives and remained alive after an event in which others have died and because of how he or she was able to survive, and what it took for him or her to remain alive, it keeps their thoughts, train of thought, thinking, and way of thinking constantly, continuously, and consistently connected to, linked to, and tied to the state or fact of continuing to having a strong-willed determination and desire for wanting and needing and having to live or exist, typically in spite of any accident, ordeal, or difficult circumstances; and that has brought and led the person into being in a mind-set where he or she allowed a life and living statement or fact to be produced, prepared, and presented that is due to and is based on what the person has previously encountered and experienced; that

THE SURVIVORS MODE

explains why something is the way it is with him or her, why the person does, thinks, or says something, or why that person behaves a certain way;

➤ a person is led to think, feel, and believe he or she can and will cope and he or she has coped well with the difficulties in life, and that has forced him or her into being drawn, driven, pulled, pushed, persuaded, seduced, tricked, trapped, enticed, entrapped, and entangled into being focused on being and staying in a state or fact of making sure he or she can and will continue to live or exist, typically in spite of any unforeseen upcoming accidents, ordeals, or difficult circumstances; and to keep coping, the person has decided and determined he or she has to be in a mode where he or she is open to realizing, recognizing, and receiving a fact, condition, or situation that makes it proper or appropriate for him or her to do something, feel something, etc.;

➤ a person who copes well with difficulties in life, and how he or she was able to do so has become the main focus, and that main focus has transitioned over into being a formula and a principle and practice that have continued to exist that came about from and because of an earlier time; and that he or she feels, thinks, and believes gives him or her the right to be free to have the mentality and be in the mentality where he or she can freely seize, take over, take down, take out, overpower, overthrow, overtake whenever he or she wants to, and he or she can demonstrate self-will, self-performance acts, actions, deeds, and get over into self-effort at any given time, and he or she can, at will, release the power of the mind to think and understand in a logical way.

When the spirit of fear-driven and motivated survivor-survival "reason" is in control and it is doing what it does, what it ends up doing is make sure faith of any kind and to any degree is bypassed, and you can only deceptively see, sense and feel, quickly recognize, and realize without procrastinating, hesitating, questioning and second-guessing, yearn for, and desire survivor and survival cause (grounds), basis, rationale, motive, motivation, purpose, point, aim, intention, objectives, and goals, which end up becoming and being your only focus and focal points.

Fear is the spirit that is working behind the scenes of your life, and it will use everything and everybody that it can to make sure you are and you keep receiving and having and being in a survivor-survival attitude, mood, mind-set, and mentality. Fear accomplishes and achieves this through making sure you have survivor-survival explanations, justifications, arguments, defensiveness, excuses, pretext, and vindication readily available when and after your survivor-survival urges, tendencies, inclinations, intuitions, impulses, impulsiveness, and instincts have seized, taken control, taken over, overpowered, and overtaken a conversation or communication or would-be conclusion to a circumstance, situation, matter, or moment without you getting any advanced warning. And as a result, you end up finding yourself driven, drawn, pulled, pushed, persuaded, seduced, enticed, tricked, and forced into a survivor-survival attitude, mood, mentality, mind-set, and mode.

Once fear has you yoked to, in a stronghold to, bound and limited to and because of, in bondage to, and a slave to being "survivor-survival needy" and to hungering and thirsting and craving for survivor-survival logic, reasoning, cognition, calculating, concluding, reckoning, thinking, judging, deducing, inferring, surmising, and informal figuring, that survivor-survival hungering, thirsting, and craving will lead to producing, preparing, and presenting a strong overwhelming secure connection to being linked to, tied to, and locked into strong, solid survivor-survival entanglements and entrapments. Because of that happening, occurring, and taking place, that will in turn open the door to and open you up to being constantly, continually, and consistently functioning and flowing in and out of survivor-survival reason, mind-sets, mentalities, modes, attitudes, and moods.

THE SURVIVORS MODE

The finished work of survivor-survival reason

In the end and after the finished work of survivor-survival fear, reason has accomplished and achieved its mission, goal, purpose, and plan, and the result is survivor-survival "fear" wants to make sure it can immediately, quickly, and suddenly get you over into constantly, continually, and consistently (a) lusting after, (b) leaning and depending upon, (c) running to, (d) hiding behind, (e) opening the doors for and (f) opening yourself up to and (g) opening yourself up for, and get you over into (h) protecting: survivor-survival motives, motivations, purposes, points, aims, intentions, objectives, goals, bases, explanations, justifications, arguments, defense, vindications, excuses, pretexts, rationales, causes (grounds); survivor-survival logic, reasoning, cognition, calculating, concluding, reckoning, thinking, judging, deducing, inferring, surmising, and informal figuring.

The other mission, goal, purpose, plan fear has for you being locked into a survivor-survival attitude, mood, mode, mind-set, mentality, thoughts, train of thought, thinking, and way of thinking is so you can, without thinking about it, without you being a person of two minds, hesitating, dubious, irresolute, unstable, unreliable, and uncertain about everything you think, feel, and decide and you are able to deliver a statement or fact that explains why something that has to do with you is the way it is, why you do, think, or say something the way you do, or why you behave in a certain way. And why, when a certain and specific fact, condition, or situation shows up in your mind and in your way of thinking, it makes it proper or appropriate to do something, feel something, etc., that others cannot and will not understand. Nothing will hinder or block the power of your mind to think and understand your reactionary-reactionary response survivor-survival acts, actions, and deeds in a logical way.

Fear wants to make sure you have a deep-rooted survivor-survival conviction and survivor-survival beliefs, and there is an overwhelmingly strong survivor-survival feeling living, abiding, and dwelling within you, and there is also a close connection between reason and emotion alive and active within you.

Keeping you connected

Survivor-it is a person who survives, especially a person remaining alive after an event in which others have died, and it is a person who copes well with difficulties in his or her life.

Survival-it is the state or fact of continuing to live or exist, typically in spite of an accident, ordeal, or difficult circumstances, and it is a focus or a practice that has continued to exist from an earlier time.

The mission, goal, and plan of sense is to get you to "see and feel" the need for being survivor-survival driven and motivated, and the mission, goal, and plan of reason is to get you over into overwhelmingly "sensing, thinking, feeling, and believing" to the point of even knowing you have a need for being survivor-survival driven and motivated and to keep you a slave to, in bondage to, bound and limited as a result of, and yoked and in a stronghold to having that need for being survivor-survival driven and motivated. As survivor-survival sense and survivor-survival reason are at work working against you and not working for you, their collective mission, goal, purpose, and plan is to make sure you constantly, continuously, and consistently have and be in the following:

1. survivor-survival urges, tendencies, inclinations, intuitions, impulses, impulsiveness, and instincts
2. survivor-survival mind-set and mentality
3. survivor-survival mode
4. survivor-survival mind, mental frame of mind, state of mind, mental condition and conditioning, and mental state of being
5. survivor-survival dreams, hopes, and desires
6. survivor-survival feelings and emotions
7. survivor-survival thoughts, train of thought, thinking, and way of thinking
8. survivor-survival acts, actions, deeds, choices, and decisions
9. survivor-survival ways (ways of saying, doing, and handling things), methods, motives, and motivation
10. survivor-survival drive, ambition, awareness, sensations, and sensibility

11. survivor-survival beliefs, confidence, character, conduct, conversations, and communication
12. survivor-survival personality, integrity, intellect, conduct, behavior, and behavior patterns
13. survivor-survival words, messages, images, ideas, ingenuity, insights, inspirations, information, and instructions
14. survivor-survival complacency, contentment, compromises, and comfort zones
15. survivor-survival place, point, processes, procedures, and principles
16. survivor-survival tutoring, training, and being taught
17. survivor-survival yokes, strongholds, bondages, boundaries, limitations, and slavery
18. survivor-survival links, ties, and connections
19. survivor-survival addictions, analyzing, assumptions, and accusations
20. survivor-survival enticing, entanglements, entrapments, enslavement, and entitlements
21. survivor-survival tests, trials, temptations, and tribulations
22. survivor-survival aggravation, agitation, and irritation
23. survivor-survival distractions, detours, discipline, deceptions, and delusions
24. survivor-survival procrastinating, hesitation, questioning, and second-guessing
25. survivor-survival engaging, experiences, and encounters
26. survivor-survival takedowns, takeovers, and takeouts
27. survivor-survival overpowering, overtaking, and overthrowing
28. survivor-survival constants, continuations, and consistencies
29. survivor-survival accepting, adopting, adapting to, and applications
30. survivor-survival yielding, submitting, surrendering, and fate
31. survivor-survival self-effort, self-will, and self-performance
32. survivor-survival frustrations, discouragements, and disappointments
33. survivor-survival preparation and positioning

34. survivor-survival dominance, manipulation, and control

35. survivor-survival life, lifestyle, and living

Sense's and reason's job is to get and keep you over into thinking, feeling, and believing it is your job and it is your responsibility to make room for, make excuses for, justify, explain, and protect being survivor-survival conscious, aware, alert, active, and alive.

Their job is to suggest to you that is important for you to get over into and stay over into and be heavily over into thinking, believing, feeling you are accountable and responsible for trying to "make sense of" your survivor-survival reactions and reactionary responses and unknowns. And their final job is to also influence you into getting over into what ends up being unbelievable, unforgettable, unexpected, and unplanned survivor-survival acts, actions, and deeds without taking any thought and without thinking.

This is what I want to say

The ultimate job of survivor-survival "sense" is to make sure your mind, frame of mind, state of mind, and mental state of being function in and out of "it makes sense" to be in a survivor-survival attitude, mood, mode, mind-set, and mentality. And the ultimate job of survivor-survival "reason" is to make sure everything that should, could, would, and can will and does happen to you, and everything that is said or done to you and how things are handled when it comes to you goes through, is processed through, and is analyzed through the "I have a reason for the reaction and reactionary response I am going to deliver" part of your mind, frame of mind, which in turn helps builds and establishes "a" or your survivor-survival state of mind, mental condition, and mental state of being. And when that happens, your mind, with all its mental capabilities and abilities, can and will begin to grow, develop, mature on, thrive on, and flow on, in, and out of "there is a reason why and for you having survivor-survival thoughts, train of thought, thinking, and way of thinking"; and "there is a reason" why it is important for you to quickly, immediately, and suddenly, constantly, continuously, and consistently formulate survivor-survival behavior, behavior patterns, and conduct.

The most important thing that you must know is it is dangerous, destructive, and damaging to get to the place and point where you are comfortable, complacent, contented, and in a comfort zone with "survivor-survival" feelings, emotions, and desires that you, without challenging and confronting and without trying to conquer and change, of your own free will give and allow "sense" to have access to your mind, frame of mind, state of mind, mental condition and conditioning, and mental state of being and to also allow that same "sense" the freedom to infect and influence your mind, state of mind, mental condition and conditioning, and mental state of being.

It is also deadly and self-destructive to get to the point and place where you are so relaxed and friendly with having "survivor-survival" urges, tendencies, inclinations, intuitions, impulses, impulsiveness, and instincts that you allow, let, and give "reason" the freedom to suggest, dominate, manipulate, control, and dictate to your thoughts, train of thought, thinking, and way of thinking without doing any resisting, rejecting, refusing, and refuting; the result is your thoughts, train of thought, thinking, and way of thinking will end up being yoked to, in a stronghold to, in bondage to, and a slave to "reason" words, messages, images, insights, ideas, inspirations, ingenuity, information, and instructions. Your ability to demonstrate and release faith, hope, trust, belief, and confidence is disconnected and is rendered powerless and useless.

And when both sense and reason can freely initiate, build, and establish their processes and procedures and do what they do on a constant, continuous, and consistent basis, what will end up happening is those same "sense and reason" processes and procedures can and will cause, create the atmosphere for, and contribute to the person's attitude, mood, mode, mind-set, mentality, and mental state of being destitute of faith and truth and reality. That will in turn open up the door for survivor-survival deceptions, delusions, and deceiving, and mode, mind-set, mentality, and mental state of being deceptions, delusions, and deceiving. Your mind's mode, mind-set, mentality, and mental state of being will also be tortured, tormented, terrorized, traumatized, and trapped with "what makes sense" or "that makes sense" and there is a reason for" thoughts, thinking, way of thinking, and logic.

Fear sense and fear reason objective

Fear has a vision and a plan and an objective for your life, and it is the opposite of what Jeremiah 29:11 declares. Fear's plan for you is to make sure you cannot, will not, and do not prosper, and you face disaster, you are harmed, and your hope and future are taken away from you, and to make sure you never see the expected end that you desire when and if you pray and have faith and believe. For the rest of your life, you are to think, feel, and believe it makes "sense" for you to be in a survivor-survival attitude and mood, and it makes "sense" that you be in, stay in, and have a survivor-survival mode, mind-set, and mentality. And you should have a "reason" and you should have every "reason" to be in a survivor-survival mode, and you have every "reason" to stay in and stay on high survivor-survival alert. That way of thinking should continue long after you are far away from what happened to you and what you went through. Fear also wants you to strongly think, feel, and believe you have a right to and you have a "reason" to forever be in a survivor-survival attitude, mood, mode, mind-set and mentality.

The plans fear has for you is to make sure you never abandon your survivor-survival attitude, mood, mode, mind-set, and mentality, and you continue to just exist and you never have a life, you never live, and you never get over into really living, and you are always denied the lifestyle you have been trying to get to and into, and you never have the love and relationship and the good, positive, and right feelings about yourself that you rightfully deserve.

For the rest of your life, fear wants to suggest to you and influence you into thinking, feeling, and believing it makes "sense" for you to hold on to the "reasons" why you are and you continue to function and flow in and out of a survivor-survival thoughts, train of thought, thinking, and way of thinking as your mode, mind-set, and mentality, and as your established mental state of being.

THE SURVIVORS MODE

For the rest of your life, what you are to constantly, continuously, and consistently think about, have thoughts of and dreams of, go through your day having thoughts of, and be thinking about and wake up thinking about is being a survivor and always having survival in the back of your mind and as your backup plan even when there is nothing you have to survive through. You are to spend the rest of your life being survivor-survival nervous and having survivor-survival nerves.

My conclusion to this matter

Mollie and Rose came out of what they had been through not knowing that fear had assigned and attached survivor-survival sense and reason to their mind, frame of mind, state of mind, and mental condition, and mental conditioning. They did not know fear was at work behind the scenes of their mind and mental capabilities and abilities working at distracting, detouring, derailing, dismantling, damaging, delaying, denying, disconnecting, and detaining their "sound" mind so they could not and would not be able to make safe, stable, secure, sound, and solid choices and decisions.

Fear would make sure the both of them would be so overwhelmingly emotionally distracted and impacted and destroyed that their feelings would be out of control. When a person is not emotionally safe, stable, strong, solid, and secure, he or she will end up being vulnerable and susceptible to any and every thing that is suggested and influenced. Satanic fear will make sure the person not aware of what is happening to him or her because fear has gripped him or her, and surviving and being a survivor and survival and being scared and afraid have his or her attention, and it becomes his or her focus and focal point. Once fear was able to get Mollie and Rose away from faith and it was able to get them to the point and place where they would be consumed with being a survivor and having and following survival instincts, fear would then have the both of them where it wanted them.

They would no longer have a mind of the spirit, but they would have a mind of the flesh or a mind that is focused on fleshly or carnal "sense and reason" urges, tendencies, inclinations, intuitions, impulses, impulsiveness, and instincts. When they stepped over into a mind of the flesh because of what they were going through, that is when fear-driven and motivated survivor-survival "sense and reason" was introduced to their mind and mental capabilities and abilities. Fear for years had been setting them up for survivor-survival sense and reason, and when they started to seek after something they did not get from the first man that was in their life, "their father/dad," the door was opened for them to be a target for survivor-survival deceptions and delusions and deceiving.

Both were just trying to fill their relationship voids, emptiness, and they were both trying to find and get healing for their relationship wounds that could and would come through a pure love, affection, and attention, which neither one of them was able to find. Fear had found a way to force them away from faith, and they ended up with a mind of the flesh, which is and consists of "sense and reason" without the Holy Spirit. Everything they ended up saying and doing so they could and would be able to survive had to and did make "sense" to them, and sense would make sure they had a "reason" or reasons for reacting the way they were and they had a "reason" for the type and kind of reactionary responses they would begin to function and flow in and out of without thinking about it.

They did not know that by them doing so, functioning and flowing in and out of survivor-survival "sense and reason" that is devoid of the Holy Spirit would bring about death. It would bring about death to their consciousness and their awareness and their ability to function and flow in and out of faith and their ability to flow faith freely of their own will. They would no longer have a mind of the spirit and a mind to follow spirit-led spiritual processes, procedures, and principles that would bring them the victory they would need over what they would come face-to-face with and end up going through. The death they ended up experiencing not because they wanted to do so would comprise and consist of all the miseries arising from being disconnected from their faith.

Once disconnected from their faith, they both would end up having their thoughts, train of thought, thinking, and way of thinking detained long enough for fear to begin tormenting, torturing, terrorizing,

THE SURVIVORS MODE

troubling, and traumatizing them. Mollie and Rose would end up with feelings and emotions and desires that would not lead to or bring them peace. If they still had a mind of the Holy Spirit or a mind that was still being driven and motivated by the Holy Spirit, both would have been connected, linked, and tied to the victorious words, messages, images, insights, inspirations, instructions, and information that would have given them life and soul peace. In the midst of what they were going through, their mind would have faith power and would be faith powered, and they would have been able to exercise and have authority over fear, being scared, and being afraid.

The fleshly or carnal survivor-survival flow

They were not able to get to that place and point because fear had made sure they were driven into a survivor-survival attitude, mood, mind-set, mentality, and mode because they were fearful and scared and afraid they were not going to survive and make it through what they were going through, and they were fearful, scared, and afraid they did not have the survival strength they would need so that they could overcome what they were faced with. They were not prepared for what happened to them, and when they found themselves caught up, entangled, and entrapped in a fight for their survival, the mind of the flesh or a mind that is dominated, manipulated, and controlled by fleshly or carnal survivor-survival urges, tendencies, intuitions, inclinations, impulses, impulsiveness, and instincts suddenly, instantly, and immediately kicked in and took over, bringing with it fleshly or carnal survivor-survival images, ideas, inspirations, insights, ingenuity, information, and instructions.

At the time and in the moment when they were faced with their own individual, personal, private, and public relationship abuse and they were doing their best to fight through the relationship adversities, challenges, and changes they were faced with, their mind at the time could and would only produce, prepare, and present two things, and they were and are

➤ *Carnal thoughts*-they are an idea or opinion produced by thinking or occurring suddenly in the mind that is not spiritual; merely human; temporal; worldly: relating to physical, especially sexual, needs and activities.

Because of the fight Mollie and Rose found themselves in, not by choice, their thoughts, train of thought, thinking, and way of thinking could and would only have the power to focus on and function and flow in and out of what was pertaining to or characterized by the flesh or the body, its passions and appetites involving acts of considering or remembering someone or something satanic, and demonic fear had found a way to draw, drive, pull, push, persuade, seduce, entice, trick, and force them away from their faith.

They would no longer be on the path for spiritual encounters. They would find themselves led off into a life that would be filled with endless and fruitless religious and wavering faith experiences. Their creativity, ability to be resilient, consciousness and the place within themselves where there should be a heightened sense of spiritual awareness would forever be bombarded with and distracted by thoughts, feelings, emotions, desires, and things pertaining to the flesh or is characterized by the flesh or the body, its passions and appetites that put in motion and put into effect (1) appetites their mind or attention craved and lust for; (2) acts of considering or remembering someone or something other than themselves; (3) an intention, hope, or idea of doing or receiving something that derives from a reactionary response; (4) the action or process of thinking, careful consideration, or attention that is reactionary driven and motivated; and (5) the formation of opinions, especially as a philosophy or system of ideas, or the opinions so formed, careful consideration, or attention that is to protect a person and prevent them from what seems like, looks like, and feels like is hurt, harm, or danger.

The most important thing to remember is all the above is carnal-driven and motivated, which means there is an instant, automatic, sudden, and immediate reaction and reactionary response act, action, and deed demonstrated and delivered without the person thinking before they act or react. Carnal thoughts have superseded spiritual thoughts.

> Carnal purposes-this entails a person who ends up heavily over into everything relating to physical, especially sexual, needs and activities and thinking occurring suddenly in the mind that is not spiritual; merely human; temporal; worldly that becomes the motive and motivating reason for which something is done or created or for which something exists.

The true thoughts, intentions, motives, and motivation for a person who has fear-driven sense and reason in the driver's seat of their choices and decisions and what drives and motivates them to say, do, and handle things the way they do shows up in their revealed purpose. When sense and reason are driving a person's mind, mental capabilities and abilities into a survivor's survival mode, mind-set, and mentality, their thoughts, train of thought, thinking, and way of thinking end up not only getting filled with carnal thoughts but getting filled with carnal purposes or carnal intentions and/or objectives.

You must remember fear is the dominating and manipulating force that is doing all the dictating to that person's urges, tendencies, inclinations, intuitions, impulses, impulsiveness, and instincts, and fear-driven and motivated sense and reason are in "control" of that person's thoughts, train of thought, thinking, and way of thinking, so their carnal thoughts and their carnal purposes have to make sense, and the reason for their carnal thoughts and carnal purposes also have to make sense and have a reason for their existence.

To have sense and reason in control of a person's carnal purposes is to empower that person's carnal purposes with the power to (1) persuade, push, and pull the person's sense of resolve or determination; and (2) persuade, push, and pull a particular requirement or consideration, typically one that is temporary or restricted in scope or extent. Whatever it is that you once was able to "purpose" in your heart to say and do and you would end up saying and going about doing changes because you have ended up in a survivor-survival attitude, mood, mode, mind-set, and mentality, and fear has seized and is dominating, manipulating, and controlling your thoughts, train of thought, thinking, and way of thinking.

Fear-driven sense and reason are dictating to every part of you that delivers and demonstrates reactions, reactionary responses, and responses of any kind and to any degree. Fear is in control of your thoughts and purposes, and that also gives fear control over how you view things, how you perceive matters, moments, memories, circumstances, situations, and confrontations, and your acts, actions, deeds, and how you handle things. Fear-filled sense and reason won't allow you to perceive and interpret anything out of your faith, and they will not allow you to find, function, flow, and follow faith thought and purposes.

Once fear had made your "purposes" a slave to survivor-survival sense and reason, what ends up happening or taking place is the reason(s) for which something that you do or has done or created or for which something exists in your mind had to make "survivor-survival sense," and your purpose and all of your purposes had to have a "survivor-survival reason." And what you have to have or what you end up having as your intentions or objectives have to be survivor-survival driven and motivated.

Here it is

What I'm trying to show you and get you to see is when and while you are and were in that fight to be a survivor and fight for survival, there were a lot of things happening to you at the same time behind the scenes of what you were going through. Having a mind and mental capabilities and abilities that are survivor-survival oriented, filled, driven, and motivated can only produce, prepare, and present thoughts, train of thought, thinking, and way of thinking that are fleshy and carnal and are overpowered and overtaken with carnal thoughts and carnal purposes. You can't get something spiritual out of something that is carnal, and you can't get something carnal out of something that is spiritual. The spiritual produces, prepares, and presents what is spiritual; and the carnal produces, prepares, and presents what is carnal.

Everything produces of its own kind. An apple seed cannot produce an orange. The moment when you are driven, pulled, and forced into a survivor-survival mind, frame of mind, state of mind, mental condition, and mental state of being, you will then end up being connected to functioning and flowing in and out of a survivor-survival attitude, mood, mode, mind-set, and mentality. Survivor-survival sense and reason instantly, immediately, automatically, suddenly step in and link and tie your thoughts, train of thought, thinking, and way of thinking to being bound and limited to, yoked to, in a stronghold to, bound to, and a slave to carnal thoughts and carnal purposes. The results is and will be you will end up overwhelmed, overpowered, and overtaken by survivor-survival emotions, feelings, and desires. Fear is not going to allow you to see all this, and everything within you will end up lusting and craving for survivor-survival sense and reason summations, accusations, and assumptions.

What is really important for you to know is by you having and holding on to carnal thoughts and carnal purposes and by you allowing the both of them to hold on to your mind with all their capabilities and abilities, what you are making choices and decisions out of, carnal thoughts and carnal purposes; both are hostile to God because they do not submit themselves to God's faith laws. And that is exactly what happens when you get over into a fearful survivor-survival attitude, mood, mode, mind-set, and mentality. Everything that pertains to God's faith laws, your mind, mental capabilities and abilities, mind-set, mentality, thoughts, train of thought, thinking, and way of thinking will begin to reject, resist, rebuke, refuse, and refute.

Your feelings, emotions, and desires will get in on the rejecting, resisting, refusing, rebuking, and refuting of God's faith laws. Fear will have you where it wants you and everything that it will take to keep you in a fear-driven survivor-survival attitude, mood, mode, mind-set, and mentality. OCD, PTSD, nervousness, migraines, etc., fear will send. As all this is happening to you, fear will make sure it all "makes sense" to you, and fear will make sure you have "a reason" for being in a survivor-survival attitude, mood, mode, mind-set, and mentality and you have a "reason" for demonstrating and delivering survivor-survival reactions and reactionary responses and responses at the moment when you are being abused and years after when you are far way from what happened to you. Long after you are past what happened to you, fear is still keeping your "faith" focus distracted, detoured, and detained long enough so you will continue to be denied receiving the fullness of God's faith Laws. Fear wants to keep you thinking, feeling, and believing you still have to and need to and should keep fighting to survive.

CHAPTER SEVENTEEN

Appetites and Impulses

*So then those who are living the life of the flesh catering
to the appetites and impulses of their carnal nature cannot
please or satisfy god or be acceptable to him.*
—*Romans 8:8*

THE SECOND SURVIVOR, survival, survivor-survival duo of destructions that shows up to help support you being in a survivor-survival attitude, mood, mind-set, mentality, and mental state of being is called survivor-survival appetites and survivor-survival impulses. When you have been tortured, tormented, traumatized, and terrorized to the point and place where you end up in a survivor-survival attitude, mood, mind-set, and mentality and you are in a survivor-survival mental state of being, not only are you being dominated, manipulated, and controlled by survivor-survival sense and reason and survivor-survival carnal thoughts and carnal purposes, but you are also being seduced, tricked and trapped, forced and enticed, and entangled and entrapped into living your life out of your flesh and carnality.

What that means is you will continue to live your life and be in relationships catering to the appetites and impulses of your survivor-survival carnal nature. Why? It's because fear has you thinking, feeling, and believing something is wrong with you, and fear has you living in and out of, functioning and flowing in and out of low self-esteem feelings and emotions. Fear also has you oversensitive to and constantly in touch with the voids, emptiness, loneliness, and aloneness that you brought out of your childhood and out of what you didn't get out the first man that was in your life, your father. Maybe what you did get from him wasn't enough to help validate and make you feel whole.

And maybe what you didn't get from him was what you needed to help build you up and help you believe in yourself and help build your self-confidence and self-esteem. The point is, your father, the first man in your life, was to be the first one to validate you, speak into your life, and tell you who you were and who you are. And when that didn't happen, it left you with an open "appetite," hunger, craving, or lust for something you never had that you should have been given. And with that appetite came an impulse, and you became a survivor-survival "appetite impulsive" person out of the carnal nature of course. In your mind, it made "sense" for you to try and get your father-daughter relationship voids, emptiness, loneliness, and aloneness fulfilled and satisfied, and you felt you had a "right" reason for doing so.

Survivor-survival self

Your survivor-survival appetite and impulsiveness grew, developed, and matured out of your survivor-survival sense and reason attitude, mood, mind-set, mentality, and mental state of being. Listening to and obeying and following the lead of survivor-survival sense and reason logic kept you over into survivor-survival carnal thoughts and survivor-survival carnal purposes, and you then ended up being a slave to survivor-survival self-performances, self-will, and self-efforts. The moment when you were opened up to those three and you engaged and indulged in survivor-survival self-performance, survivor-survival self-will, and survivor-survival effort acts, actions, and deeds, that is when you were opened up to survivor-survival appetites and survivor-survival impulses. Once again, fear and what you were going through and what you were trying to make it through would not let you see what was also happening to you behind the scenes of your life and what you were going through.

Whatever it was that you didn't get out of your father-daughter relationship, you had an appetite for, and you became an impulsive person when you saw someone offering what looked like and what felt like something that would fill that father-daughter void, emptiness, aloneness, and loneliness that you had since childhood. You were

THE SURVIVORS MODE · 283 ·

looking to and seeking and needing and wanting self-esteem and self-image validation, and when you didn't get it, you began to make relationship choices and decisions that came out of what you didn't get out of your father-daughter relationship. Whether he said and did just enough or not enough, it left you with a void and an emptiness appetite and impulse.

You didn't get or gain his influence, which was vital in helping shaping not only your self-esteem and your self-image but also your world and your confidence and opinions of men. When you didn't gain or get that, you were left with a feeling of not being good enough; emotions and feelings of inadequacy, inability, and insecurity showed up, and that is when fear stepped in and took over and made those feelings a survivor-survival appetite, attitude, mood, mode, mentality, and mind-set. And out of that came survivor-survival appetite reactions and reactionary responses and survivor-survival impulse reactions and reactionary responses. My point is the "self" and the dangerous, destructive, damaging, and self-destructive part(s) of you took over, which was and is driven by fear.

Every time fear assaulted, attacked, and assassinated your self-esteem, self-worth, and self-image, you found yourself in an attitude, mood, mind-set, and mentality where you felt driven to try and survive, and your way of survival became to try and "prove" that there was nothing missing in your ability to be a woman even though you did not get or have your father's influence so that you could and would have the right confidence and opinion of men and of yourself. You not being properly shaped by your father opened up the door for Satan and satanic fear to get into your life. And you not being properly shaped by your father's influence left you feeling like there was something missing in you and there was something wrong with you.

Feelings of being rejected opened the door for you to be survivor-survival emotionally driven and motivated. In your heart and mind, it made "sense" for you to go looking for what you needed to help properly "shape" your self-esteem, self-worth, and self-image; all of which are important ingredients when it comes to the proper growth, development, and maturity of a little girl, female, and woman. Everything bad, wrong, negative that you felt about yourself and everything that you did or didn't get out of your relationship with the first man in your life, your father, fear seized, took over, and took control over, and has used to take you down and take you out.

Instead of you having a spiritual appetite, you ended up with a carnal appetite; and instead of you ending up with good, right, and positive spiritual impulses, you ended up with carnal impulses. And with those came an overpowering and an overtaking of carnal feelings and carnal emotions. One satanic fear had you a slave to carnal appetites and carnal impulses that came out of what you did or get out of your father-daughter relationship. Bad and wrong relationship choices and decisions came about, and that is when fear slipped into your life. You came out of your childhood with something missing that you needed, and you also came out with an appetite for what you didn't get out of your father-daughter relationship. That is when fear drove, pulled, pushed, persuaded, seduced, tricked, trapped, enticed, and forced you over into making fearful impulsive relationship choices and decisions. That relationship appetite you have developed that came out of the father-daughter relationship you never had but wanted and desired, fear grabbed a hold on and used it to get you to make wrong and bad relationship impulsive choices and decisions.

It went down this way

Survivor sense and reason and survivor-survival carnal thoughts and carnal purposes all ganged upon your self-esteem, self-worth, and self-image through suggesting and influencing, and then they began to assault, attack, and assassinate them with "fear" weapons and tactics. Fear was masterfully working to seize, overpower, overtake, overthrow, take over, take down, and take out your self-respect. Fear suggested what you were feeling about yourself, and instead of you, out of faith, rejecting, resisting, rebuking, refusing, and refuting it, you just, for a moment, entertained what was suggested, and satanic fear seized the moment and grabbed a hold on bad and wrong feelings you had concerning yourself that came out of your father-daughter relationship and then stirred up your emotions over what you were feeling.

Once you became emotionally impacted, driven, and motivated over the way you were feeling about yourself, fear had you emotionally distracted long enough to detour you away from faith and faith choices and decisions. That is when fear influenced you into seeking after what you did or didn't get out of your father-daughter relationship, and when you did so, that is when your survivor-survival carnal appetites and carnal impulses came alive. Fear had all along been setting you up for a "faith failure" and for a survivor-survival attitude, mood, mind-set, mentality, and state of mind and being. Your self-esteem, self-worth, self-image, and self-respect had to be taken over, taken down, and taken out, and that came about as a result of you seeking to satisfy and fulfill your father-daughter voids and emptiness and nonshaping.

Fear suggested to you that it made "sense" for you to have the carnal appetites you had, and fear told and influenced you into thinking, feeling, and believing you had a "reason" to have the carnal appetites you had. And then fear told you it made "sense" that you would have the type of impulses you had and you had a "reason" for having them even though both kept you in harm's way. The moment when you realized and was able to recognize something was wrong and what was happening to you wasn't what you were wanting, it was too late; fear had a grip on your mind, frame of mind, state of mind, and mental state of being.

Everything that made you or would make you a reasonable, logical, and sound-minded relationship person was being terrorized, tormented, tortured, and traumatized, and out of it would come a survivor-survival attitude, mood, mode, mind-set, mentality, and state of mind, which drove you deeper into an canal appetite addiction and a carnal impulse addiction.

Let me finish what I started

Before I go further into revealing Satan's fear secret, I want to finish telling you what happened to you and how it all went down. Are you ready? Here we go. Out of innocence and out of what you thought, felt, and believed was for the right reason(s), you went looking for what you did or didn't get out of your father-daughter relationship. Satanic fear was watching you, and it was waiting for you, and it was waiting for the moment when you would go looking for what would satisfy and fulfill your relationship needs, wants, and desires. Fear was hiding and lurking in the shadows of your life and in the shadows of your choice and decision making.

You were innocent and you were making childlike innocent choices and decisions. Satanic fear set you up for failure; it would do so by waiting for the moment when it could seize, overpower, overtake, take control of, and take over those innocent childhood appetites you had. The moment came when fear was able to suggest and influence and navigate you, your thoughts, train of thought, thinking, and way of thinking, your urges, tendencies, inclinations, intuition, impulses, and instincts, and your thoughts, feeling, emotions, and desires into the path of a person, place, thing, circumstance, situation, confrontation, matters, choice, and decision you made that ended up terrorizing, tormenting, torturing, and traumatizing you.

You didn't know it was going to happen; you didn't see it happening to you because you were just following what you thought and felt was your age of innocence childlike feelings, emotions, and desires. You didn't expect, nor did you anticipate being tormented, tortured, terrorized, and traumatized, but it happened to you, and what you end up being left with are tormenting, terrorizing, torturing, and traumatizing thoughts, feelings, emotions, memories, and moments that you have to relive because they keep showing up on the highlight reel of your heart and mind and thoughts and feelings. After you were tormented, terrorized, tortured, and traumatized, you found yourself trying to find a way to survive and make it through what unexpectedly happened to you. Not only were you terrorized, tormented, tortured, and traumatized, but you were also left nervous and shaking, scared and afraid, and having flashbacks. What are supposed to be your normal thoughts, train of thought, thinking, and way of thinking would be seized, hindered, and held hostage long enough for those thoughts, train

THE SURVIVORS MODE 287

of thought, thinking, and way of thinking to be transitioned over into torturing, tormenting, terrorizing, and traumatizing dreams.

The unseen, unknown, undetected, unwanted, unbelievable, unbearable, unthinkable, unplanned, unimaginable, and unforgettable had come out of the shadows when you were unaware of what was going to happen and take place and seized, overpowered, overtaken, overthrew, taken control of, taken over, taken down, and taken out your childlike innocence, your childlike faith, hope, belief, trust, and confidence. And in the process, your self-esteem, self-worth, and self-image, how your world would be shaped, how you view the world, and your confidence and your opinion of men would be challenged, confronted, conquered, and changed. Day in and day out, you would find yourself curled up in a ball, screaming or shouting and shaking and trembling because of those unforgettable terrorizing, tormenting, torturing, and traumatizing thoughts, feelings, emotions, and memories. While you were in that state and in that condition, that is when satanic fear influenced your survivor-survival urges, tendencies, inclinations, intuitions, impulses, and instincts into kicking in, taking control, and taking over. Survivor-survival sense and reason then showed up to get into the driver's seat of you just wanting to survive, be a survivor, and you knowing about how to easily get over into survival. Fear sense and reason had driven away faith, sense, and reason, and that opened the door for carnal thoughts and carnal purposes to be your guiding light and your dominant force instead of faith.

Those carnal thoughts and carnal purposes would transition and then transform into survivor-survival carnal thoughts and survivor-survival carnal purposes. To finish you off and to make sure you are forever in a survivor-survival attitude, mood, mode, mind-set, mentality, and mental state of being, fear makes sure you are yoked to, bound and limited to, in a stronghold to, in bondage to, and a slave to appetites and impulses that, like the others, transition and transform into survivor-survival appetites and survivor-survival impulses. For the rest of your life, you are to live off, feed off, and function and flow in and out of survivor-survival sense and reason, survivor-survival carnal thoughts and carnal purposes, survivor-survival appetites, and survivor-survival impulses. This is satanic fear's plan for you and for your life.

The bottom line, the truth, and the reality is you were set up for what happened to you in the military and for what happened to you in marriage, ministry, and when it came to money and when it came to the "myself" matters, moments, and memories that left you terrorized, tormented, tortured, and traumatized. Satanic fear took advantage of your innocence, your father-daughter voids, emptiness, and he found a way to isolate you and get you away from faith, hope, trust, belief, confidence, truth, and reality. Once you were isolated, fear suggested to you that you were all alone, no one understands you, no one cares about you, you don't matter, you are not important, and no one likes or wants you.

Fear influenced you into bad, wrong, and negative thinking, feeling, and believing, and fear also influenced you into making choices and decisions out of low or no self-esteem, self-worth, self-image, and self-respect, and out of feeling lonely and out of believing you are all alone and all by yourself. It all started because you didn't get out of a relationship, and out of a choice and decision you made, something that you did or didn't get out of your father-daughter relationship or what you did get of that relationship or choice and decision you made was not only tormenting, terrorizing, torturing, and traumatizing but also twisted, troubling, and trifling. What you wake up to, go through your day with, and go to sleep with are distracted, detoured, detained, and disconnected, and, most of the time, distant thoughts, feelings, and emotions.

Your mind and mental capabilities and abilities, along with your thoughts, train of thought, thinking, way of thinking, mind-set, mentality, attitude, mood, and mind's mode are also distracted, detoured, detained, disconnected, and distant from self-truth and self-reality. Fear has managed to drive a big hole within you, and it has managed to distract, detour, disconnect, and distance you from faith. Not just normal plain faith but more than a conquering faith and winning and overcoming faith. In the end, you will spend the rest of your life being a slave to, functioning in and out of, and following survivor-survival

THE SURVIVORS MODE

self-performance, survivor-survival self-will, and survivor-survival self-effort urges, tendencies, inclinations, intuitions, impulsiveness, and instincts. Out of which will come survivor-survival acts, actions, deeds, choices and decisions, thinking, believing, and feeling.

Fear wasn't through with you. While you were at your weakest and most vulnerable place and point in your life and while you were busy fighting to overcome, fighting to survive, and fighting for survival, satanic fear would hit you and torture, torment, terrorize, and traumatize you with recurring memories or flashbacks of events that would bring you feelings of guilt and shame. You start to feel like you are on the edge, and you start having a lot of sleepless nights, losing interest, and feeling numb. Overwhelming stress and anxiety show up at will, and when they do, you start to feel anger and rage, and out of those two is birthed and born irritability.

Catering to appetites and impulses

The moment when fear knows it has you and it has gotten you connected to, tied to, linked to, yoked to, bound and limited to, in bondage to, in a stronghold to, and a slave to being led like a sheep for slaughter into survivor-survival self-performances, survivor-survival self-will, and survivor-survival self-efforts, and your mind, mental capabilities and abilities, thoughts, train of thought, thinking, way of thinking, mind-set, and mentality have been detained, delayed, and denied the right to function and flow in and out of and follow overcoming faith logic and overcoming faith laws, fear will keep you catering to survivor-survival appetites and survivor-survival impulses.

What are survivor-survival appetites? They are strong desires or liking for something that a person thinks, believes, and feels with help him or her remain alive or in existence and allow him or her to carry on despite hardships or trauma. They are also desires or a liking for something, an object or practice that has continued to exist from an earlier time, that a person can and will use to help them persevere and remain functional or usable.

What are survivor-survival impulses? They are a sudden strong and unreflective urge (tendency, inclination, intuition, instinct) or desire to act or the influence of a particular feeling, mental state, etc. A sudden, involuntary inclination prompting to action that a person is led to believe will allow them to carry on despite hardships or trauma and will allow them to be in a state where they can continue to live or exist, typically in spite of a terrorizing, tormenting, torturing, and traumatizing accident, ordeal, or difficult situation and circumstance.

Once fear has forced you to function and flow in and out of and live in and out of your carnal or flesh abandoning, overcoming, and more than a conquering faith that can and will help them and lead them into challenging, confronting, conquering, and changing what fear is trying to get them to do, that same person will overwhelmingly be driven into catering to his or her survivor-survival appetites and survivor-survival impulses. Which means that whatever methods, practices, rituals, information, instructions, ingenuity, images, insights, visualizations, secular world theories, religious theologies, etc., that they used the first time he or she was faced with having to survive after his or her initial experience with being tormented, terrorized, tortured, traumatized, and troubled will be the same ones a person will use and utilize as good luck or will use and utilize out of habit and will end up becoming and being their survivor-survival appetite.

And whatever prompted to action reactions, reaction responses, and reactionary response acts, actions, deeds, conversations, communications, conduct, behavior, and ways to handle the trauma, torment, terror, and torture that the person initiated, released, demonstrated, and delivered the first time he or she was being assaulted, attacked, and assassinated by fear, the person will remember, relive, revive, restore, and cater to which will become their survivor-survival impulse. The reason is the person actually, with a convinced conviction, believes, thinks, and believes the impulse he or she was prompted to demonstrate and deliver saved them and helped them survive, be a survivor, and was their survival weapon. They think, feel, and believe if that impulse worked for them the first time, it will continue to work for them and help them survive and be a survivor.

THE SURVIVORS MODE

To cater to survivor-survival appetites and survivor-survival impulses is to provide with what is needed or required for both to have the power and the authority to dominate, manipulate, control, and do what they do without being hindered or held up or stopped. What is provided as the food for survivor-survival appetites and impulses are carnal or fleshly thoughts, feelings, emotions, desires, time, attention, cooperation, energy, willing participation, etc. Every time you are catering to your survivor-survival appetites and your survivor-survival impulses out of your carnal nature, what you are using cannot and will not please or satisfy God or be acceptable to Him.

Fear wants you to be constant, continuous, and consistent in catering to a strong natural desire or liking to a survivor and survival something that you are led to think, feel, and believe can and will satisfy a bodily need and satisfy your survivor-survival needs, and you are to be constant, continuous, and consistent in catering to a sudden strong and unreflective urge or desire to react and act that is sense and reason supported, driven, and motivated and comes out of carnal thoughts and carnal purposes. In doing so, what you will end up doing is allowing fear to keep alive and keep active a mental health condition that is triggered by experiencing or seeing a terrifying, tormenting, terrorizing, torturing, and traumatizing event that you will end up reviving, restoring, remembering, and reliving.

CHAPTER EIGHTEEN

Sensual Survivors

It is these who are agitators setting up distinctions and causing divisions-merely sensual creatures, carnal, worldly-minded people, devoid of the Holy Spirit and destitute of any higher spiritual life.
—*Jude 19*

THE FIRST DANGER with being in and functioning and flowing in and out of a survivor-survival mode, etc., and following survivor-survival principles, processes, and procedures if you consider yourself a Christian, you will be demoted to a sensual Christian; and if you are someone who considers yourself to be spiritual or religious, you will also be demoted to being a sensual religious and a sensual spiritual person. A sensual Christian is someone who is a spiritual being that ends up constantly, continuously, and consistently walking, functioning, and flowing in and out of the natural or the carnal.

The second danger with having a survivor-survival mind, mind-set, frame of mind, state of mind, mental condition and conditioning, and mental state of being and being in a survivor-survival mind-set, mentality, and mode, and being led by survivor-survival tactical feelings, emotions, and desires, and being led by survivor-survival urges, tendencies, inclinations, impulsiveness, and instincts is your thoughts, train of thought, thinking, and way of thinking will end up at some place, point, and time being entangled and entrapped, led and held captive and a slave to seeking to gratify your own selfish, self-centered, self-righteous, and self-justified feelings and emotions.

And then you will begin to (a) seek to gratify your grown, developed, and matured unholy desires; and (b) follow after you own grown, developed, and matured ungodly passions. Both were conceived, birthed, and born the day and the moment when you were in the "survivor-survival" mode, mind, mind-set, frame of mind, state of mind, mental condition and conditioning, and mental state of being and mentality process or incubator.

A person who is sensual is someone who is working and walking in agreement with, on one accord with, and is in sync with and in tune with functioning, flowing, and following the arousing gratification of the senses (see, touch, smell, taste, and hear) and physical, especially sexual, pleasure. If the person is or professes to be a Christian, he or she will end up being a spiritual being walking in the natural and expressing himself or herself through physical means. It is someone who has abandoned his or her spiritual nature and he or she has stepped into his or her physical, carnal, or fleshly nature because of the personal, private, and public trauma, tragedy, and trouble that have brought them sudden hurt, harm, humiliation, pain, and brokenness. The problem is all of what has happened to that person happened without any advance warning, warning signs, and it was unexpectedly experienced or encountered.

Being so deeply wounded and downtrodden and often feeling lifeless, hopeless, destitute, empty, and all alone, a person, who at the beginning was a sensual Christian, was transitioned into a sensual survivor. After being transitioned into a sensual survivor, he or she will begin to see things, say things, do things, handle things, and make choices and decisions that he or she thinks and feels and believes will bring some type of "get even with" gratification. When we look at the photo or the image of a sensual survivor, we are looking at someone who is always needy, wanting, and craving.

And they are drawn, driven, pulled, pushed, persuaded, forced, enticed, tricked, seduced, and deceived into opening themselves up to and allowing themselves to engage in the arousing activities and gratification of the senses (see, touch, smell, taste, and hear) and satisfying the physical, especially sexual, pleasure as a method they are led to think, feel, and believe will help them get past and get over and help them "remain in existence, carry on, cope with, manage to pull through, remain strong, outlive, outlast, and pull through and live through and just make it through" the hurt, pain, brokenness, sudden letdown, and disappointment that came with having their heart and trust broken.

This is what commonly happens when a person has experienced some kind of traumatic, tragic, and troubling unforgettable hurt, pain, betrayal, and brokenness. They will begin to allow their terrorized, tormented, tortured, and traumatic feelings, emotions, desires, needs, wants, and thoughts to be dominated, manipulated, controlled, and dictated to; and in doing so, they would be open and susceptible to everything that can and will challenge, confront, conquer, and change their right and good behavior and behavior patterns into bad, wrong, and negative ones.

A Christian or a spiritual person who has been through a traumatic, troubling, and tragic circumstance, situation, confrontation, and matter will end up being tormented, tortured, terrorized, and traumatized by feelings, emotions, and desires that are not, never have been, and never will be their friends. Satan uses what has happened to them as a way to get them to challenge, confront, conquer, and change their beliefs and belief system, process, procedures, and principles, and even get them to abandon their Christian faith completely. Fear will make sure that same Christian religious or spiritual person never gets linked to, connected to, and tied to trusting God and having faith ever again.

Satan has used fear and the fear of what they have been terrorized, tormented, tortured, and traumatized by as a way to force them out of and away from their faith. Satan suggests to them their faith, their God, and their faith in God have failed them, and neither should never be trusted and relied on again, and then Satan influences you into seeing and perceiving the tactics, methods, mind-set, mentality, and mode you were in that helped you survive and make it through what you were faced with as your "savior," and you should never abandon the methods, principles, processes, and procedures you used and utilized that helped you survive.

The moment when you decided that you would be determined to win and overcome what was supposed to be the natural and normal way to handle and deal with terrorizing, tormenting, torturing, traumatizing trauma, tragedy, and troubled marital and relationships letdowns, disappointments, discouragements, and frustrations, that was the day when Satan began to force you out of being spiritually strong and force you into being a sensually strong person. I can tell you for sure you don't want to be a sensual Christian—you know, someone who was a strong spiritual being that was being forced into walking in and following the suggestions, influences, and lead of your hurt, wounded, brokenness-filled, painful feelings, emotions, and desires.

Getting involved in and engaging in some kind of physical sexual pleasure cannot and will not help deliver, cleanse, purge, heal, and make you whole from and help mend the marital and relationship trauma, tragedy, and troubles you feel. The comfort and consoling you really need has to come from you having the strength to move past what happened to you and being able to move forward from it.

Most people who come out of a marriage and relationship that brought them something bad, negative, and wrong that they never expected end up so weak and vulnerable that Satan easily gets them involved in some kind of sexual activity. After that sexual activity is finished, the hurt person will just lie there in the bed staring into the space still feeling lifeless and empty, still feeling confused, and then feeling guilt and shame. And eventually, they will begin to cry and then not feel anything at all. The reality of what they had just engaged in was not what they really wanted or needed or was looking for; they only wanted someone to listen to them and hear them and maybe even say or do something that would help ease the pain, hurt, and brokenness they were feeling.

The traumatic, tragic, troubling, terrorizing, tormenting, and torturing hurt, pain, brokenness, humiliation, disappointment, etc., has left a hole and an empty place inside of them, and they were left in a weak and vulnerable state and condition. Somewhere in the midst of what happened to them and how they negatively responded, reacted, or demonstrated a reactionary response, along with being caught up in the moment of what shockingly and stunningly happened that caught them completely off guard; they walked away from their spiritual strength, and without them knowing it, they had put on or had entered into a survivor-survival mode, and then they entered into a sensual survivor-survival protective and preventive mind-set, mentality, and mode.

Once in the sensual survivor-survival mode and in the sensual survivor-survival protective and preventive tactic mode, the mission, goal, and objective becomes "to remain in existence, carry on, cope with, manage to pull through, remain strong, outlive, outlast, and pull through and live through and just make it through"; and to say they discovered a survivor state or survivor facts that would help them continue to live and exist, typically in spite of the traumatic, troubling, and tragic marital and relationship accident, ordeal, or difficult circumstances, situation, and confrontation that they came face-to-face with. The fall from being strong spiritual Christians, spiritual beings or persons, to being weak sensual Christians or people who are driven by the terrorizing, tormenting, torturing, and traumatic events that happened to them in the marriage or relationship they were once in will lead them into demonstrating bad behavior and behavior patterns.

What you don't understand and see is the moment when Satan is able to successfully lure, seduce, trick, deceive, entice, and then pull, push, persuade, draw, drive, and pull you out of your spiritual and get you into the sensual by using fear tactics; he has moved you out of your place of power and authority. And when he is able to get you out of your spiritual marriage, spiritual relationships, and spiritual mind, mind-set, and mentality, and also get you over into sensual marriages, sensual relationships, and over into a sensual mind, mind-set, mentality, and mode by using and utilizing those same fear tactics, he knows he has gained a big victory.

If while and when you were in a good relationship and fear got you to perceive something that was said, done, or handled, or a conversation and communication or a person's conduct, behavior, and behavior patterns that "seemed like, felt like, and looked like" it was something that you had heard, seen, and been through before, and you suddenly, immediately, and quickly reacted before you took the time to examine and see what was really happening, fear had forced you out of your spiritual and had forced you into your sensual. You were forced out of following faith and forced into following fear.

THE SURVIVORS MODE

The power of agreement

Being in a sensual mind-set, mentality, and mode and having a sensual attitude instead of a spiritual attitude will always keep you away from seeing the truth when it comes to what is taking place or has taken place in a relationship, and you will be hindered or even disconnected from being confident in your new relationship partner. The other thing that happens will be you cannot and will not be able to show the person you are in that relationship with that you have confidence in them and you trust and believe in the Christ that lives in them.

Fear is the force that forces you into being a sensual Christian. The main thing that Satan does not want you to see and he won't let you see is what the Bible says, which is, "For where two or three gather in my name, there am I with them" (Matt. 18:20). He knows he has broken the power of agreement in that marriage and relationship, and he has damaged, delayed, derailed, dismantled, disconnected it; and he is going to deny the power of agreement to take place between the two people that were in that marriage and relationship, which is the most powerful agreement in the whole world and one of the most powerful places to be.

Nothing becomes impossible when there is a powerful agreement, connection, and bonding between two people. When you and that person . . . two or three . . . came together and got together, unity, harmony, and oneness happened and occurred, and just like a strong chain that is linked together, you and that person became a strong, safe, stable, secure, sound, and solid force that he or his demon spirits could not and would not be able to (1) take down, take over, and take out, and (2) overpower, overtake, and overthrow.

The power of agreement brings about the both of you being able to challenge, confront, conquer, and change anything in your marriage, relationship(s); in your life, love, and living; in your dreams, hopes, desires; in your feelings, emotions, self-will; and in your mind, mind-set, frame of mind, state of mind, mental condition and conditioning, mental state of being, and mentality. You will also be able to challenge, confront, conquer, and change anything and everything in your thoughts, train of thought, thinking, and way of thinking that needs to be challenged, confronted, conquered, and changed without any procrastination, hesitation, questioning, and second-guessing.

What is important for you to clearly see, understand, and know is fear will always force you into being sensual and force you into following your sensual appetites. Fear will also keep you out of the power of agreement by way of forcing you to remember and even relive past and old traumatic, troubling, tragic, terrorizing, tormenting, and torturing events, difficulties, matters, memories, and moments. It will always suggest and influence you into using and utilizing your terrorized, tormented, tortured, and traumatized self-esteem, self-will, self-image, self-worth, self-confidence, and self-respect as a reference point so you will not enter into the power of agreement when there is something in a new relationship you need to sit down with the other person and reason together so that you can have communication and understanding. This is his devised plan, and that is to make sure you have no spiritual power and to make sure you have no present or future spiritual agreement in any relationship you get into and to also ensure you have sensual power only and you continue to get in and stay in sensual survivor-survival agreements.

My conclusion to what I just shared

As you can now see through what I have shared with you, there are and there were so many things that started happening to you all at once the moment you were faced with the traumatic, troubling and tragic circumstances, situations, confrontations, matters and moments you were faced with. The first being was fear seized that moment and pulled, pushed, persuaded, and forced you into being linked to and connected to a survivor-survival mind, state of mind, frame of mind, mental condition, and mental state of being.

Once you were linked and connected, the second thing that took place was you were suddenly and immediately, before you could think about it, transitioned over into being tied to and locked into constantly, continuously, and consistently having survivor-survival thoughts, and tied to being entangled and entrapped into having a survivor-survival train of thought, thinking, and way of thinking.

The third thing that happened was you were quickly in bondage to and bound and limited to a survivor-survival mind-set and mentality. Immediately after you were "in bondage to" and your being "bound and limited" to was in place, the fourth thing that took place was Satan had masterfully used fear tactics, techniques, and methods to complete forcefully getting you yoked to and in a stronghold to a survivor-survival mode.

The entire plot and plan of Satan came together once he had you yoked to and in a stronghold to functioning and flowing in and out of a survivor-survival mode. It would be at that moment, place, point, and time that Satan had used and utilized what was, is, and had been traumatic, tragic, and troubling in your life and what had terrorized, tormented, tortured, and traumatized you enough to make sure you were scared, afraid, and fearful to help bring about, finish, and complete the ultimate master deception of your mind with all its capabilities and abilities.

He had successfully seized, overpowered, overtaken, overthrown, taken over, taken control of, taken down, and then challenged, confronted, conquered, and changed the procedures your mind, with all its capabilities and abilities, would use and utilize when it came to how your terrorized, tormented, tortured, and traumatized past, along with what has been traumatic, troubling, and tragic from your past, was and would be processed. Not only would your thought and thinking, train of thought, and way of thinking patterns be changed, tainted, and distorted, but the principles that they would produce, prepare, and present would also be changed, tainted, and distorted. There would be no right reasoning and right logic, truth, and reality being produced, prepared, and presented.

The fifth thing that would take place is you will always be easily enticed and tricked into being drawn and driven into a survivor-survival attitude and mood, and that would lead to you constantly, continuously, and consistently being a slave to easily and without procrastinating, hesitating, questioning, and second-guessing; release triggered survivor-survival urges, tendencies, inclinations, intuitions, impulses, and instincts anytime and every time you would get into any type and kind of relationship no matter what the reason or reasons would be. And anytime and every time something that is said, done, or handled that "looks like, feels like, seems to be, and appears to be" something that you have seen or been through before that was traumatic, troubling, and tragic.

It would be out of you being yoked to and in a stronghold to a survivor-survival mode that fear would be able to force you out of the spiritual and force you right into the sensual. Satan then would use and utilize fear tactics, techniques, and methods to force you out of faith and force you right into fear, being scared, and being afraid. And the last thing that Satan would do once he has you safe and secure in a survivor-survival mode is he would keep you focused on producing, preparing, presenting, demonstrating, and delivering survivor-survival protective and preventive tactics, techniques, and methods, and he would keep you soundly seduced into self-deception, self-delusion, and self-perception.

CHAPTER NINETEEN

Self-Deception

BEFORE WE GO any further, I want to and I have to take the time to expose some satanic and demonic spirits that many are under the suggestive influence of and they are being led by it, and some are possessed by this spirit. The strength of this spirit is seen and felt every time a person has suffered through something that has been traumatic, troubling, and tragic, and it shows up each time a person is being terrorized, tormented, tortured, or traumatized. It is a spirit that most of us are familiar with, and at some place and point in our lives, in our love for others, and in our relationships, we have had personal, private, and public experiences, encounters, and close encounters with it from time to time when we least expect it and aware of it.

This is a spirit that Satan wants to keep hidden from you so that you cannot and will not challenge, confront, conquer, and change it, so you can be free to receive your total deliverance, cleansing, purging, healing, and be made whole. It is also the same spirit that can and will have you thinking, feeling, and believing you are ready to be in another relationship and you have moved past what has happened to you in your past. This spirit is called *self-deception*, and what this spirit does is gain the right and/or it is given the power and the authority to overpower, overtake, and overthrow a person's "selflessness" and his or her giving heart, mind, mind-set, mentality, and spirit.

Survivor's selfishness

Anytime people have suffered through something in their life that has been traumatic, deeply troubling, or tragic, not only will they end up in a survivor-survival mode if they do not get delivered, cleansed, purged, healed, and made whole from what they been through, but they will also end up being driven and drawn, pulled, pushed, persuaded, and forced into a *survivor selfishness,* and then they will end up being tricked, trapped, enticed, entangled, and entrapped into the spirit of self-deception.

To be entangled and entrapped into a survivor selfishness is to be tricked and trapped and enticed into being a person who survives, especially a person remaining alive after an event in which others have died, and to do so not having or showing concern for the needs or feelings of other people but only for yourself. Because fear has forced you out of faith and has forced you into a survivor mode, everything has become about you and not about anyone else. From the first day you get involved with someone, you start to build your survivor case against protecting the person you are sharing in some type and kind of relationship with just in case something goes wrong or just in case something "seems to be, looks like, or feels like" it is or it might go wrong. You are in a mind-set in which you have made everything about you because of what you have not received out of the last relationship or out of the relationships you were in. The mentality you end up being in is that of "entitlement," and you have the "I deserve" or a "you owe me" mentality.

It's as if everyone that you get into a relationship with owes you something because of what was taken from you in a relationship, because of what you never received even though you were a giver, and because of what happened to you that was traumatic, troubling, and tragic. You only care about your personal survival, and you do not care for the survival of the relationship; nor will you allow yourself to show any care and concern for the person that opened themselves up and allowed themselves to show and demonstrate trust in you when it comes to themselves. And it doesn't matter that they had confidence in your ability to love them just the way they asked you to love them, support them, etc.

It's as if you get into a relationship with your "parachute or life jacket" on anticipating, expecting, and waiting for the moment when you have to bail out of the relationship. Because you are yoked to, bound and limited to and because of, in bondage to, in a stronghold to, and a slave to being concerned excessively or exclusively with oneself; seeking or concentrating on one's own advantage, pleasure, or well-being without regard for others. When you are linked to, connected to, and tied to a survivor-survival mind-set and mentality, everyone else is expendable, and you do not care about collateral damage or damage control of any kind.

You are in that mind-set and you have that mentality and you are in that survivor-survival selfishness mode because the "fear" alone of what happened to you in your past showing up, taking control, taking over, and taking out your present and eventually overpowering, overtaking, and overcoming your future has you are scared and afraid and in a defensive mode as well. There are days when you really feel so nervous and so scared and afraid that the fear you feel can be shocking, stunning, and even stifling to the point where you feel emotionally incapacitated and disconnected and numb.

Not only so, but also you are still being terrorized, tormented, tortured, and traumatized by "what did happen to you" and "what might happen and what could happen to you again" feelings and thoughts. Fear is using and utilizing OCD and PTSD and nervousness and everything else it can to keep drawing and driving and forcing you into the thoughts, train of thought, thinking, and way of thinking where you can only focus on being a person who continues to function or prosper in spite of opposition, hardship, or setbacks being devoted to or caring only for oneself; concerned primarily with one's own interests, benefits, welfare, etc., regardless of others.

Satan wants to make sure you remain a person who copes well with difficulties in their life arising from and out of concern with one's own welfare or advantage in disregard of others. To be in a survivor-survival selfishness is to be in a "me, myself, and I" mind-set, mentality, and mode. Everything in your mind, thoughts, thinking, way of thinking becomes about "you," and you stop being a giver and start being a "taker," or someone who feels like, because of the hurt, pain, brokenness, trauma, troubling, and tragic things that have happened to them, they have a right to "take" what they need from someone because they are fearfully led to think, feel, and believe they better do so before they get "taken." This is one of the things that happen to you when you are in a survivor mode, survival mode, and survivor-survival mode. You are using and utilizing your selfish survivor feelings, emotions, desires, thoughts, train of thought, thinking, and way of thinking as a way to "get them" or "get yours," what you need, want, and never had before and feel you deserve to have and get, just in case other people try to "get theirs" what they can get from you first.

Satan has deceived you into thinking, feeling, and believing, by you constantly, continuously, and consistently using and utilizing survival selfishness, you can and always will survive and you will always be a survivor. Now, let's take a look at what I just shared from a different perspective when it comes to you, out of being scared, afraid, and fearful, believe; your ability to use and utilize *selfishness* as the way, method, motive, and motivation for you being able to survive, be a survivor, and for survival.

- Having or showing concern only for yourself and not for the needs or feelings of other people so that you can continue to live or exist, especially in spite of "what might or could be" or "what looks like is or could be" present or future self-esteem, self-image, self-worth, self-confidence, self-respect, self-will, self-efforts, and self-performance, danger or hardship, accident, or ordeal (survive)
- Being concerned excessively or exclusively with oneself; seeking or concentrating on one's own advantage, pleasure, or well-being without regard for others so that you can remain a person who survives, especially a person remaining alive and cope well with difficulties in life after an event in which others have died (survivor)
- Arising from concern with one's own welfare or advantage in disregard of others; devoted to or caring only for oneself; and being concerned primarily with one's own interests, benefits, welfare, etc., regardless of others that become an object or practice that one allows and has continued to allow and to

THE SURVIVORS MODE

exist from an earlier time; as one's state or fact of continuing to live or exist, typically in spite of "what could be" a traumatic, troubling, and tragic accident, ordeal, or difficult circumstances (survival)

It is a deceptive, deceiving, and twisted thought and a twisted way of thinking that the person believes is real and seems real to him or her. Everything derives from fear, and the mind tricks the person into believing he or she has to be on guard and be on watch and in a "I'm gonna get you before you get me" attitude, mind-set, mentality, and mode; but in all actuality, it is more so a way of thinking, a thought, train of thought, and a thinking process. After fear has driven you into a survivor's selfishness, he then sets you up for being under self-deception.

Self-deception

While being in a survivor selfishness is the first mind-set and mentality, Satan uses fear and you being scared and afraid as a way to draw, drive, and force you into after you have been or you still are being terrorized, tormented, tortured, and traumatized because of a traumatic, troubling, and tragic circumstance, situation, confrontation, matter, or moment in your life; and after he has you linked, connected, tied, and locked into a survivor mode. The second thing he does is use fear to pull, push, persuade, and lead your thoughts, train of thought, thinking, and way of thinking captive into a constant, consistent, and continuous state and condition of being in self-deception.

What is self-deception? It is a process of denying or rationalizing away the relevance, significance, or importance of opposing evidence and logical argument. Self-deception involves convincing oneself of a truth (or lack of truth) so that one does not reveal any *self*-knowledge of the *deception*. What Satan wants you to do is deny, reject, resist, refuse, rebuke, and refute what is rational, real, relevant reasoning that shows, reveals, and exposes what is real and what is right and what is truth. He essentially wants you to see and view the trauma, what was troubling and tragic, and keeps trying to or still is terrorizing, tormenting, torturing, and traumatizing you through the wrong "lens." He wants to keep suggesting to you and influencing you into thinking, feeling, and believing there is something wrong with you, and you are and always will be a target for trauma, troubles, tragedies, and a target for what terrorizes, torments, tortures, and traumatizes. Satan uses and utilizes fear tactics, techniques, and methods to carry out his deception, and he sends those who have hidden agendas and hidden motives as the way to carry out his deceptive, deceiving, deranged, and distorted plan. To do so, he knows he must send something or someone to first *beat* you down so he can *break* you down and get you mentally tired and fatigued to the point where you are receptive to being deceived.

Satan wants to make sure everything that is of significance, that is of importance, that's opposing evidence, that's a logical argument, that can convince you of a truth (or lack of truth) and whatever that can and do reveal any *self*-knowledge is distorted. In doing so, you can't and won't be able to clearly see it or them as they are and see yourself as you really are. Being in and keeping you in a survivor-survival mode and by making sure you always have a survivor-survival selfishness mind-set and mentality, Satan is able to keep you disconnected, detoured, and detained from the truth about yourself that can and will make and set you free (John 8:32).

The art of self-deception

It is the acceptance of the truth about yourself that can and will make and set you free and not the truth about someone else. Self-deception will never work as long as you are accepting and applying the truths about yourself in a positive way. Total and complete deliverance, cleansing, purging, healing, and being made whole will never take place as long as you keep resisting, rejecting, rebuking, refuting, and refusing to accept the truth about yourself, your choices and your decisions, your acts, actions, deeds, and about what really took place when it came to that moment and that day when you ended up being faced with a traumatic, troubling, tragic, terrorizing, tormenting, and torturing circumstance, situation, confrontation, and matter.

THE SURVIVORS MODE

Freedom, victory, power, and authority over what you have been through that "won't let go of you" won't ever show up until you stop telling that "woe is me" story that you keep telling that Satan has tricked you and trapped you into believing is the truth. The moment you can become totally and completely honest with (a) God first, (b) others, and (c) yourself will be the day when you will begin the journey into challenging, confronting, conquering, and changing everything OCD, PTSD, sickness, diseases, infirmities, migraines, nervousness, fear, being scared and afraid, and any other condition has tried to do to you. Accepting and applying the actual "truth" will remove any and every trigger, trap, and trespasser out of your life. But it has to be full-of-living powered God-sent truth and not what you want to believe and keep perpetrating, proclaiming, and pretending is truth.

That is how the art of self-deception keeps manifesting itself in your life. Please understand, it's not about "what you want to believe" that took place that was able to get you into a survivor-survival mode; it's about what actually took place, the truth, that really matters and can and will make a big difference when it comes to you conquering what has been conquering you. Another fact and truth is as long as you keep chasing after "closure" instead of seeking after a "solution" that can and will bring an immediate, quick, and sudden end to your journey with everything that has happened to you that was bad, wrong, negative, and ugly, you will continue to be terrorized, tormented, tortured, and traumatized by fearful feelings and fear-driven thoughts and emotions. It all starts when you be honest with God first; after all, He knows what really took place and He knows what you said, did, or what was it that you handled the wrong way that brought you into what Satan had "set you up for" that you fell for. Please understand, I am in no way whatsoever condoning or cosigning violence and abuse or any bad, wrong, negative, and ugly behavior or conduct any person displays.

What I am trying to get you to do is to get past and beyond "what you want to believe" happened that is derived from you wanting to protect yourself and you wanting to continue to be able "survive" and make it past what took place and not be "overwhelmed" by the moment all over again. I am not trying to get you to restore, revive, remember, and relive those terrible, traumatic, troubling, and tragic moments and events. What you have to do is be honest with God concerning what really took place and let Him, out of His loving kindness that He shows toward you; draw you closer to Him so He can lead you to and get you connected to the truth concerning what actually is truth.

Being honest with God

God really knows the truth about what happened to you, and He knows the truth when it comes to what Satan has been trying to do to keep using fear to do to keep you away from, scared, afraid, and fearful of facing and accepting the truth. Please understand, *everything you give God He will always give you something in return*. What this means is if you give God your pain, He will give you peace; and if you give God your hurt, He will give you happiness. God is not going to show you the truth about yourself, your acts, actions, deeds, and your choices and decisions knowing those areas are still a sensitive sore spot for you and then punish you and make you pay.

He knows how to lead you to "self" truth and reality in a way that you will never have to really restore, revive, remember, and relive the moment, but you will be able to see the truth and the reality and see what it is He wants to show you concerning what actually took place and then empower you and give you His strength so you can release what needs to be released. God will, in that moment when He shows you your "self-deception" truth, will take away the sting, the hurt, the pain, and the brokenness that are associated with and connected to that moment by giving you His perfect peace; in that moment of viewing, you will (1) be at peace, (2) view in peace, and (3) making peace with what actually took place, which will give you the power and the authority to "release."

In that moment of viewing and seeing the truth concerning what actually took place and God showing you what part you played in bringing about what took place, you will experience God's peace, which exceeds anything you can understand. His peace will guard your hearts and minds (so that you can) as you live in Christ Jesus (Phil. 4:7 NLT).

THE SURVIVORS MODE

When God leads you into a sensitive place where He has to show you the real "you" and show you the truth about what has been traumatic, troubling, tragic, terrorizing, tormenting, and torturing, He will, in that moment, guard your heart and mind so what He is showing you cannot and will not have any type and kind of present or future bad, wrong, negative, and ugly effect upon you. The moment when you are being honest with God, the art of self-deception will end in your life. You can't go to God and give Him your version of what you have been and still is being self-deceived into thinking and believing actually took place. He is the all-wise, all-knowing, only true God, and He sits high and He looks low. The only way Satan can continue to master the art of self-deception in your life and keep getting you to accept being self-deceived is to get you to continue to refuse, reject, and resist being honest with God and continue to get you to refuse, reject, and resist, allowing Him to lead and guide you into all truth through the person of the Holy Spirit.

But when he, the Spirit of truth, comes, he will guide you into all the truth. He will not speak on his own; he will speak only what he hears, and he will tell you what is yet to come.
—*John 16:13*

Being honest with yourself

I have discovered that when it comes to the truth about or concerning ourselves, it is much easier to believe a lie than to believe and accept the truth. The reason for that is we always want to think, feel, and believe that we are right and everyone else is wrong. Pride and the spirit of importance are the spirits that show up when self-deception is being introduced so that it can be implemented into your mind, mental capabilities and abilities, thoughts, train of thought, thinking, and way of thinking. To get you to entertain and to endorse that "I'm always right and you are wrong" way of thinking is when and how Satan sneaks in the art of self-deception without you knowing it; and he then uses and utilizes fear tactics, techniques, and methods as a way to create, establish, and build you up in a self-deception attitude, mood, mind-set, mentality, and mode.

Satan wants you to constantly, continuously, and consistently become, be, and end up being scared, afraid, and fearful that by you being found wrong about something, you will not be important and you will not matter, and it will belittle you and take away something from you that you will really need. The other fearful, scared, and afraid mind-set that Satan will draw and then drive and eventually force you into is the self-deceived belief that by someone discovering you were wrong, he or she is going to expose and exploit you, and you will end up being "disrespected," which is another deception. Self-deception is that disguise that is needed and used and utilized to help a person cover up his or her flaws, failures, areas they have fallen in, weaknesses, inadequacies, inabilities, and their insecurities.

So for people to be honest with themselves is for those people to admit, accept, and adapt to the fact that they are not superior, above, and better than everyone else, and it is to also admit that there is something in their past that had damaged, degraded, and hurt them and made them feel less than the way they wanted to feel; as a result, those people decided and determined they would no longer be looked down upon, and they perpetrated a fraudulent portrait of themselves so they could and would feel good about themselves. That perpetrated fraudulent portrait of themselves that they painted and envisioned in their imagination and in their mind would be the image they had decided and determined they would live in and out of and function in and out of.

They basically are hiding from or they are hiding behind or they are running from something about themselves that either they don't like about themselves that made them a target for bullying or some other terrorizing, tormenting, torturing, and traumatizing act, action, or deed, or they are trying to cover up something that they are ashamed and they are embarrassed about. What they are also trying to keep hidden are their self-esteem, self-worth, self-confidence, self-respect, and self-awareness struggles. Pride, the spirit of importance, being arrogant, haughtiness, acting, and being bourgeois, etc., are all self-deception builders. The question I want to ask you is what is it about yourself that you are trying to hide and protect that can, will, and is keeping you from being honest with yourself? Self-deception is not a fantastic and awesome quality that is worth fighting for, and for you to protect it and protect what is terrorizing, tormenting, torturing, and traumatizing you is not something that is worth doing.

Being honest with yourself means you will have to be free of deceit and untruthfulness, and you will have to be sincere and demonstrate you can be morally correct or virtuous when it comes to things about yourself. It is easy to blame others when we have been through something that has been traumatic, troubling, and tragic when, if we would be totally honest with ourselves, we had every opportunity to avoid what happened to us. Once again, please understand I am not condoning or cosigning anyone's bad, wrong, negative, and ugly behavior or conduct, but what I am trying to get you to see and understand is we have to own up to our wrong that was the bait for what brought about what happened to us. It takes two to make something go wrong or right!

If you want to disconnect yourself from self-deception, what you are going to have to do is demonstrate you can be honorable in principles, intentions, and actions; and you can be upright and fair. Whenever you allow yourself to function and flow in and out of self-deception and you allow yourself to follow self-deception principles, processes, and procedures, you are only blocking, hindering, and holding up all the benefits and rewards that you have been praying for and you are stating that you "cannot" be relied upon when it comes to the handling of truth and trust.

Self-deception solutions

The first step toward acquiring a solution for "self-deception" or the first the act of solving a "self-deception" problem, question, etc., so that it will be entered into the state of being solved is to be honest with God. The second step in the solution process that will help solve being under the influence of "self-deception" and even help initiate the elimination process is for you to be honest with yourself. The final step in the "self-deception" solution process will require you to be honest with others.

Being honest with others

This is a very important step in the self-deception solution process. Once again, being honest will require you to be sincere, frank, genuine or unadulterated, and truthful or creditable. If you are going to disconnect yourself from self-deception, also known as self-deceit, or disconnect yourself from the act or fact of deceiving yourself, what you have to do is be honest with others. What this means is you will no longer keep telling your side of the story so you will continue to look good, look innocent, and look like the "victim"; and it will also mean you will stop telling them what you want them to know and think so they will continue to protect and defend you.

In your sharing with others, what was, is, and had been traumatic, troubling, and tragic that keeps terrorizing, tormenting, torturing, and traumatizing you, there were some very important details that you left out concerning what happened. You left those details out so that you could and would appear to be spotless and guiltless, and in doing so, you wanted to make the other person appear to be some horrible, terrible awful person. Now, what the person did to you wasn't right, but my point is Satan used you and your uncontrolled tongue, accusations, assumptions, attitude, and dramatical interpretation of the events that took place, and you pressing and pushing your selfish agenda and hidden motives, as well as your overemotional state and condition, as the "bait" for what took place.

In fact, Satan used you and the unrestrained and uncontrollable you as the "bait," and he set you up for what happened to you. You never told others that you were the bait, and everything you had said and done days, weeks, months, and even years prior to what took place and even moments leading up to what place was the bait Satan "used" to trick and trap the other person. Yes, that's right. Satan *used you* . . . and you let him do so. I have a question for you. Why is it you want to

THE SURVIVORS MODE
313

get even with a human being if and when they use you, but you don't want to get even with Satan when he uses you?

Why aren't you angry with Satan, the one who set you up and used you? You were not completely honest with those who are close to you and those who care about you when it came to what took place. Just like I don't condone or cosign bad, wrong, negative, and ugly conduct and behavior, I also don't and won't condone or cosign a person being deceiving, deceptive, and not completely honest. God will not condone or cosign those methods, motives, and motivation as well. You have made things worse for someone else so that you can protect your bad, wrong, negative, and ugly acts, actions, deeds, conversations, communications, attitude, mind-set, and mentality that set things off in the wrong way.

The fact is Satan used you just like a pimp uses a prostitute, and you let him do it. How does that make you feel? Satan pimped and prostituted your selfish feelings, selfish emotions, and you being emotionally out of control for his personal gain. Not only did he pimp you and them, but also he worked behind the scenes of what he had baited and set you up for, and he got you to push things to the limit and over the limit. How did he do that? He used all kinds of fear tactics, techniques, and methods, and he used every ounce of your out-of-control feelings and emotions; that is how he did it. He made sure you were so deep into self-deception and so consumed with believing your own "woe is me" press release; he would easily be able to distract you and detour you away from being honest with those who are close to you.

Once you were distracted and detoured away from being honest, you were then delayed in being honest, denied being honest, and, finally, disconnected from being honest. You would rather people believe a lie rather than hear and believe the truth. I'm going to share something with you, and I pray you never forget it, and that is.

"God holds you accountable for everything that you say and do to others that is bad, wrong, negative, and ugly, but God will never hold you accountable for what others say and do to you that is bad, wrong, negative, and ugly."

You have to be honest with others because God is holding you personally accountable and responsible for the details that you have left out of and continue to leave out of what really happened that led to you being terrorized, tormented, tortured, and traumatized in a traumatic, troubling, and tragic way. Just tell them the truth! You knew you didn't have what you needed to be in that relationship with that other person, and you knew you had some bad habits and bad attitude and some self-esteem, self-worth, self-confidence, self-image, self-awareness, selfish, etc., struggles. And you heard him every time he said, "Leave me alone and we will talk about it later," but you wouldn't and you didn't. And then you got so emotionally driven and emotionally out of control, you stepped over your "I'm a woman and treat me like a woman" boundaries, and you began to get up in his face and say all kinds of bad, wrong, negative, and ugly things. All along, Satan was there, and he kept pushing and pressing down hard on your emotional accelerator until he drove you right into harm's way.

Were you honest in telling those who are close to you the entire story even if it would make you look bad, wrong, negative, and ugly? I don't think so, because that is not what being locked into self-deception is going to let you do. What self-deception keeps suggesting and influencing you into doing is to keep telling that twisted, distorted, deceiving, and highly deceptive one-sided story that is not the whole truth; it's just your self-deceived truth. And for you to say, "That's not how I remember that happening and I don't really remember it being that way," doesn't make you telling your version of what took place right.

If you really don't remember how things went down that led to you being terrorized, tormented, tortured, traumatized, battered, and abused, just say you don't remember all the details and *stop* telling that deceiving version of what happened. Deformation of character is not something God is going to condone and cosign off on. Be honest with God, be honest with yourself, and be honest with others, and in doing so, you will break and destroy the yokes, strongholds, boundaries, limitations, and bondages of self-deception. Be totally and completely honest with God, yourself, and others no matter what kind

THE SURVIVORS MODE

of self-incriminating implications it may bring you, and you will break every link, connection, tie, and chain that has kept you locked into a self-deception mind-set, mentality, and mode.

Events for self-deception

There are some specific events that have taken place in your life that Satan wants to make sure he uses and utilizes "fear" to isolate, expose, exploit, and make sure there is a strong self-deception placed to help prevent you from receiving your deliverance, cleansing, purging, and healing from everything that has been traumatic, troubling, and tragic in your life. He also wants to prevent you from being made completely whole so that you can move forward and receive personal, private, and even public satisfaction and fulfillment.

Satan is always thumbing and sifting through the pages of your life looking for something that he can use against you, and those terrorizing, tormenting, torturing, and traumatizing moments and memories and matters and events that he has made sure you had close constant, continuous, and consistent experiences and encounters with are what he thrives on using. And this is especially true and a fact once he has driven and pulled and forced you into a survivor-survival mode. Satan wants to make sure there is the following:

1. *The deceiving of oneself as to one's true feelings, motives, circumstances, etc.,* so that you will never get linked to, connected to, and tied to reliving and remembering a time of innocence and love, and you never get back to the way it was for you. Because he knows if you are able to do, so you will be able to clearly see how God is and has always been there for you, and you will be able to see how He has never left you or forsaken you, and He has made sure you have not ever been found begging bread (Ps. 37:25). God has always been there for you long before you went through what you went through, while you were going through, and after it was all over. He is there with you right now, and He loves you.

He doesn't want you to have any contact with your true feelings when it comes to you remembering when life for you was so simple and you did or you didn't and you would and you wouldn't, and that was a choice and a decision you made on your own. And every time you try to get to that place of remembering, Satan says to you, "But it ain't like that anymore." That is what he always suggests that you think and believe, and that is what he tries to make sure he influences you into feeling.

He wants to keep deceiving you and keep you so self-deceived to the point and place where no matter what you try to do you and no matter how many good and positive things that happen, you will stay distracted and detoured away from remembering when life was so easy for you. And you had people in your life who said what they meant they were either for it or against. Every time you try to get back to that kind of thoughts, train of thought, thinking, and way of thinking and that kind and type of people and that kind of times, Satan shows you what has happened to you, and he uses that as a way to draw, drive, pull, push, persuade, trick, seduce, entice, and force you into saying, "But it ain't like that anymore." He knows that each time you say, "But it ain't like that anymore," you are speaking curses upon yourself (Prov. 6:2, James 3:10), and you are entertaining and opening the door for all the "but it ain't like that anymore" to keep showing up in your life.

> "The deceiving of oneself as to one's true
> feelings, motives, and circumstances."

Satan wants to make sure he keeps forcing you into constantly, continuously, and consistently *deceiving your own self as to your true feelings* concerning those days when you could clearly see your way, and seeing the way, and deceiving yourself as to your true and real *motives* when it was up to you to choose whether to win or lose; and, finally, he wants to keep you locked into a state and a condition where you keep deceiving yourself as to how you really perceive and understand the *circumstances* that showed up in your life and challenged, confronted, conquered, and changed those times when it was up to you to see what it was you were to be.

THE SURVIVORS MODE

Fear is the weapon Satan has used to keep your feelings distorted and keep you emotionally detained long enough for him to keep enticing and seducing you into deceiving yourself so that you can consistently get caught up in the mix of complexities.

2. Satan wants to make sure you keep indulging into *the act of lying to yourself or of making yourself believe something that isn't really true,* so you will never remember when your life was so simple, and you will not remember your parents were a light, and through them, you were to see what was right. He wants you to indulge in constantly, continuously, and consistently believing and thinking and feeling the opposite so that you can continue indulging in the "blame game" and never accept or own up to the warnings they gave you through the way they lived and what happened in their relationship or through the things they said to you that you that were to help you when you grew up that you rejected, resisted, and refused to listen to, hear, and heed. Their instructions and information were simple and easy, but the fear of accepting, adopting, adapting to, and applying the truth, the truth they spoke to you, pride, and the fear of them being right and you being wrong give place to Satan being able to keep you yoked to, bound and limited to, in bondage to, in a stronghold to, and a slave to you quickly and immediately *lying to yourself and/or making yourself believe something that isn't really true.* And to help justify and appease you doing so, out of a rebellious heart, mind, and spirit, you say things like, "Oh, well, that's the way it is, but it ain't like that anymore. I'm not that person anymore, and I wish I would have, should have, could have," etc.

As long as Satan can keep you quickly, immediately, suddenly, instantly, and automatically *lying to yourself and/or making yourself believe something that isn't really true,* you will continue to be seduced, enticed, entangled, and entrapped into his deceptive, deceiving, distorted, and tricked-out twisted way he wants you to think, perceive, understand, feel, believe, articulate, and analyze remembering when life was really so easy and little boys grew into men and little girls grew into women; but it ain't like that anymore, and you ain't like that anymore. It's all because you got into a comfort zone, you became complacent, you got contented, and you compromised, and in doing so, you allowed your creation to be challenged, confronted, conquered, and changed.

You made comfort zone, complacent and contented and confused compromises instead of you standing up and fighting for your right to be the person and creation God created you in the image of. Please understand, "God doesn't make any mistakes," and God is not and was not and never will be confused when it comes to your creation (Gen. 5:2). I know those who introduced you to being comfortable with your complacent, contented, comfort zone, confused, and compromised "compromise" made it and made you feel good, real, right, positive, and pretty, and they "turned up" and tuned out truth, and they then "turned you out." And now you are "into something that you can't shake loose."

Those compromises have challenged, confronted, conquered, and changed your self-image, self-worth, self-esteem, self-confidence, self-perception, self-will, and self-awareness so much so that your world has been shaped wrong, and your opinion of men and your approach to life, how you have built your own life, and your view of the world have also been challenged, confronted, conquered, changed, and altered. And to make that right, you say things like life has happened and you are just being who you really are. As long as you keep allowing Satan to use the fears, doubts, worries, cares, and concerns you have when it comes to yourself to keep you away from self-truth and creation truth, "your creation truth," you will continue to allow Satan to "set you up" for failure, falling, sickness, disease, and infirmities.

For every second, minute, hour, day, week, month, and year you keep allowing Satan to use fear tactics, techniques, theories, methods, arguments, reasoning, and what appears to be high and lofty creation ideas as the way in which he keeps you indulging into *the act of lying to yourself or of making yourself believe something that isn't really true,* you will never know where you belong, and you will never know what is really right and what is really wrong. You won't ever be able to give a simple yes or no, and everything that has to do with you will demand and require an explanation and an excuse, and there will always have to be a justified conversation and communication held when it comes to your choices, decisions, conduct, behavior, and behavior patterns.

THE SURVIVORS MODE

As long as you continue to allow yourself to be terrorized, tormented, tortured, and traumatized because you keep indulging into *the act of lying to yourself or of making yourself believe something that isn't really true*, you will continue to be in a traumatic, deeply troubled, and tragic state and condition, and you will continue to be someone who is halt between two opinions, two minds, hesitating, dubious, and irresolute. You will constantly, continuously, and consistently be fearfully drawn and driven and forced into being a person who is unstable and unreliable and uncertain about everything you think, feel, and decide, and as a result, you will continue to function and flow in and out of procrastination, hesitation, questioning, and second-guessing.

For each moment that you continue *lying to yourself or making yourself believe something that isn't really true*, you will continue to also allow yourself to be terrorized, tormented, tortured, and traumatized by "should I stay or should I go" questions and thoughts and thinking because of your "what seemed to be right, but I'm not really sure" choices and decisions. The mere fact that you keep *lying to yourself or making yourself believe something that isn't really true* will ensure your life will continue to become so selfishly advanced that you will one day wish you had a second chance to go back if you could and see what was bad and what was good that you missed.

And one day after years of allowing yourself to be terrorized, tormented, tortured, and traumatized by a past and old traumatic, troubling, and tragic circumstance, situation, confrontation, matter, moment, and memory, you will wake up and come to your senses after *lying to yourself or making yourself believe something that isn't really true* when it came to it all, and the only thing you can and will be able to say is "Now I'm here, and what I feared the most has come true." And what that is and was that you feared most that finally came true would be "All you ever wanted for was yea and nay, and when you tried to search for it until you would find it . . . you are still left looking for a yea or nay."

3. The final event or important moment that has taken place in your life that Satan wants to keep having the power and the authority to dominate, manipulate, and exercise control over is your father-daughter relationship experiences and encounters or the lack thereof. By keeping you driven into *the action or practice of allowing yourself to believe that a false or unvalidated feeling, idea, or situation is true* that had to do with your father-daughter moments or the lack of there being any, Satan is able to make sure you never understand and have any concept of what it means to have a father's influence in your life so that your self-esteem, world, self-image, self-worth, self-respect, self-confidence, etc., are shaped in the right way.

He wants to make sure you stay so overwhelmingly terrorized, tormented, tortured, and traumatized because of the one you had and what took place in it that was bad, wrong, negative, hurtful, and painfully traumatic, troubling, and tragic that you forever continue to punish every man for his sins and you continue to push men away regardless as to what the price and the penalty will be for committing such an act and action. The other thing that Satan does not want you to see and know is you continuing to function and flow in and out of *lying to yourself or making yourself believe something that isn't really true* when it comes to what you did get out of your father-daughter relationship that was either too extreme or not enough, or what you didn't get out of one because there was an absence of one, or the one you had just couldn't and wouldn't be enough to help shape your confidence and opinions of men in the right way.

Satan was hiding behind the scenes of your life and watching God create you, and he saw God pour into you His perfect "creation," will, and perfect plan, which was for you to have a father and have a father-daughter relationship and go on father-daughter dates, and for you to grow, develop, and mature into the right woman. He also knew that how your dad approaches life will serve as an example for you to build off in your life, even if you chose a different view of the world; so he had to make sure when and "if" something happened in that relationship that would end up being distracting and it brought about some kind and type of disconnection, you would end up being so traumatically and tragically troubled, hurt, and broken that you would spend all your life *lying to yourself or making yourself believe something that isn't really true* when it came to what brought about the disconnection. With all this being said, let us now take a power prayer break!

POWER PRAYER BREAK

You will know the truth

> *You will know the truth, and the truth will make you free.*
> —*John 8:32*

And one of those truths is "The LORD your God is the one who goes with you. He will not fail you or forsake you" (Deut. 31:6). Do you feel hemmed in by circumstances? The truth is circumstances have no power to bind you. The truth is the true power of God is with you; you can surmount circumstances. Do you feel inhibited by self-doubt and lack of confidence? The truth is you can do all things, be all things, and accomplish all things through the power of God with you. The truth is God has created you with abilities and talents that are unique in you. The truth is that as you express your divine God-given gifts, as you think and act like a child of God, you become more assured and confident daily.

Do you feel that it's too late to begin again? Do you feel that you are too old to change? The truth is, with God, the time is always in "the now." The truth is, in spirit, you are ageless and eternal.

The truth is, at any time you desire to change, at any time you want to have a different kind of life, God is ready to help you. God sets an open door to success before you. One of your greatest assets is your open line to God right now. In any time of need or when faced with a problem or challenge, you can go to God in prayer. You can turn to the One who is your all-sufficiency in all things. You can keep in constant contact with God. God is your source of all good.

When you are in constant contact with God, you receive an outpouring of love and blessings in every area of your life. You are strengthened by prayer. You take time every day, in your new day and in your new beginning, to become still and to become aware of the presence of God that is always with you. In the presence of God, you become aware of all love, all peace, and all fulfillment. You release *all* doubt and fear. You release all limited beliefs about yourself to God. In 1 Chronicles 16:11, the Bible states, "Seek the Lord and God's strength, seek God's presence continually!" You will be filled with new power as you open your mind to God's light and wisdom. You will receive a continual flow of inspiration. You become refreshed physically, mentally, and spiritually. Your activities will take on new God-given energy and vitality. You will be filled with the joy of living. God is so good in your life every day and all day. So be strong and courageous! Do not be afraid, and do not panic.

DAILY POSITIVE POWER PRAYER

Dear God, with Your help, I am ready to do new things.

There is something new to learn each day of my life, and I am ready and teachable.

I may begin some days anxious about my responsibilities or decisions needing to be made, but I let these thoughts be dissolved in the Truth of who I am, a child of God.

I know that I *can do* whatever I am called upon to do, for the all-knowing mind of God is within me to teach me and guide me.

I meet this year with the assurance that its activities are opportunities for me to express the joy of life, the joy of God, and to use my God-given talents and abilities.

I know that You are teaching me everything I need to know and remember, and I am open to Your instruction.

Whatever there is to be learned, I am serene in the awareness of You as my all-knowing Guide and Teacher.

In Jesus Christ's name, amen!

THE SURVIVORS MODE

CHAPTER TWENTY

Accountability and Responsibility

I CAN TELL you for sure that one of the things the spirit of self-deception cannot and will not allow you to see or accept is personal accountability and responsibility for anything that you have personally said or done that led to the traumatic, troubling, and tragic things that have been said and done to hurt you, hinder you, and bring you brokenness and that have led you to being in the state of mind and in the mental condition that you are in. Fear wants to make sure you constantly, continuously, and consistently think, feel, and believe you are the "victim." My question to you is why would you want to continue to think, feel, believe, and conduct yourself, function and flow in and out of being a victim, and want to follow a victim's script, processes, procedures, and principles when you can become a "victor," someone who is more than a conqueror over what the devil meant for evil?

Everyone wants to be a "victim," and no one wants to be a "victor" and have victory. A victor is a person who defeats an enemy or opponent in a battle, game, or other competition. Isn't that the type and kind of person you want to be? Or are you addicted to the attention you have been getting as a result of you sharing your "woe is me, I'm a victim" story? Maybe you are addicted to the attention, pity, gifts, offerings, help, etc., that you receive each time you share your "victim story," and you in the back of your deceived mind know that if it were not for your "woe is me, I'm just a victim" story, you would not receive the attention you have been getting, and you would not be receiving the sympathy that you have been getting as a result of your "I'm a victim story."

Fear has you addicted to getting attention and getting sympathy. Fear has tutored, trained, and taught you, out of self-deception, how to play and prey upon the sympathy, pity, care, concern, loving and giving heart, and spirit of people, and how to play upon and prey upon the feelings, emotions, and compassion of others. Are you so scared and afraid and fearful that without your "woe is me, I'm a victim" story, you would go back to being the person you were before what was traumatic, troubling, and tragic happened to you? You would go back to being someone who would not be recognized, and the fear of thinking and believing that you would go back to not feeling you are not important and that you matter really and truly scares you so much so that you want to continue your "woe is me, I'm just an innocent victim" routine.

Fear has you scared and afraid that you would go back to being "scared and afraid and fearful"! Fear is the weapon being formed against you and used to draw, drive, pull, push, persuade, force, trick, trap, entice, entangle, and entrap you into fear. Please understand, satanic fear driving and motivation force that is behind the spirit of self-deception, and the mission, goal, and purpose for self-deception is to make sure you cannot, will not, and do not see or accept the truth about yourself, and see and accept the truth and reality about your acts, actions, deeds, conversations, communications, conduct, behavior, behavior patterns, attitude, accusations, assumptions, beliefs, traditions, mind-set, mentality, mode, moods, choices, decisions, etc., that may have, could have, and really was the reason that you ended up being tortured, tormented, terrorized, and traumatized.

Self-deception keeps suggesting, influencing, and telling you to blame everyone or someone for what has happened to you and never ever accept any type and any kind of personal accountability and responsibility for what happened to you. That spirit of self-deception keeps seducing you into saying, "It wasn't my fault, and I didn't say and do anything wrong," for that to happen to me. In some cases, yes, that may be the truth; but in most cases, no, that is not the truth. Why would I say this? In many and in most cases, the people who ended up being faced with something that was traumatic, troubling, and tragic heard "something" telling them not to make the choice and decision they made before they came face-to-face with what ends up terrorizing, tormenting, torturing, troubling, and traumatizing them long after what was traumatic and tragic happened to them.

THE SURVIVORS MODE

There was some kind and type of prompting, or there was some type and kind of bad and negative "feeling" people got long before what happened to them happened, and they, "of their own free will," made the choice and the decision to ignore the prompting, and they ignored and ran past that "something told me" voice, and they continued to say, do, and handle things in the way they, out of being selfish, self-centered, self-righteous, and of self-justification, wanted to. Self-deception is not going to let you see what I just shared with you. My point is, with everything that has happened to you that was traumatic, tragic, and troubling that held you hostage to being terrorized, tormented, tortured, and traumatized by what took place, there are three things I know to be true, and that is you either

A. caused what happened to you,
B. created the atmosphere for what happened to you, or
C. contributed to what happened to you.

I know this is a hard harsh truth and reality because you have become addicted to "blaming someone else" for something that was traumatic, deeply troubling, disturbing, and tragic that happened to you. In most cases, and *not* "in all cases," people had the opportunity to take a different route or course of action long before they ended up facing what they faced and they chose not to do so. The spirit of self-deception will keep deceiving you into thinking, feeling, and believing that what happened to you wasn't your fault or you had no control over what happened to you, and bad, wrong, negative, and ugly things are always said and done to you; that is the way your life has always been, and that is the way your life will always be.

Self-deception will try to suggest and influence you into accepting bad, wrong, negative, ugly, traumatic, troubling, and tragic things happening to you as your "lot in life," as a "part of your life," and that is the way it has been and always will be, which are all deceptive and deceiving lies, lies, lies, wiles, trickeries, schemes, devices, and deceptions of the devil, who is also Satan. The spirit of self-deception wants you to accept, adopt, and adapt to you being terrorized, tormented, tortured, and traumatized as the way your life will always be. The spirit of self-deception will always be constant, continuous, and consistent in deceiving you into saying, "I can't and won't ever get over what was said and done to me!"

Yield to He

Yes, the truth is you caused what happened or you created the atmosphere for it to happen or you contributed to it happening to you by not controlling your feelings and emotions. You allowed yourself to become, be, and end up being emotionally driven in what you had said and done and in the way you handled matters. You didn't "yield to He who has the right of way"! What does that mean? Let me illustrate it or let me paint the picture so you can see what I'm saying. You are driving your car, and you come up to an intersection where there is a yield sign in front of you because there is merging traffic. Instead of you coming up to that yield sign and "yielding," you approach the sign and tap your brakes really quick not enough to stop or slow down your vehicle; but you keep moving in a forward progression not really seeing "what was coming," and you merge into the oncoming traffic and, in doing so you, end up causing, creating the atmosphere for, and/or contributed to others being affected by the selfish, self-centered, self-righteous, and self-justified choice and decision you made.

When you don't "yield to He who has the right of way," which is the leading and the prompting of the Holy Spirit of God, which is that still small voice of God, and you continue to run past and ignore the prompting to "yield," wait on God, be still, be patient, slow down, don't be anxious, and don't keep pressing and pushing your own self-deceived survivor-survival "sensed" selfish, self-centered, self-righteous, self-justified agendas and motives. The reason is you will end up being headed for a traumatic, troubling, and tragic crash. And that crash is one that you caused, created the atmosphere for, and contributed to by not "yielding" and not waiting to receive divine instructions, information, guidance, and direction before you acted.

THE SURVIVORS MODE ~327~

Flowing in self-deception

Instead of doing so, you allowed yourself to become emotionally impacted and then emotionally driven and motivated, and you did not "yield." Of course, Satan took advantage of that highly emotional moment, and he put his foot on the "gas pedal" of that emotion, causing it to speed up to its highest deadly, destructive, damaging, self-destructive, and detrimental speed. Once self-deception had you emotionally charged, emotionally entangled, and emotionally entrapped, it then seduced, enticed, entangled, and entrapped you into the hands of some kind and type of fear that you had already been entertaining, yielding, submitting, and surrendering to.

And that same fear you had been entertaining forced you into having the urge, tendency, inclination, intuition, impulse, and instinct of wanting to survive after you had said what you had to say, and that led to you wanting to make and prove your point out of being emotionally charged, changed, and challenged by because of a self-deceptive or a self-deceiving fear. Fear had deceived you into getting into a fight that was already fixed, and it was not in your favor. You were set up for what was so traumatic, troubling, and tragic that terrorizes, torments, tortures, and traumatizes you. You were "set up for failure," and you were "set up to take the hit and the fall."

Once Satan had used and utilized something that was said or done or handled that you had already survived through as a way to seduce you emotionally into self-deception and into self-deceived selfish, self-centered, self-righteous, and self-justified acts, actions, deeds, conversations, attitudes, moods, etc., he knew he had you, and then he "set you up for" feelings that felt right that were in all actuality, all the way wrong. Satan hated and still does hate you so much that he would make sure he "sets you up" for a *beating* that he wanted to use to *break* you so he could *build* you up in a type and kind of fear that can, would, and will keep you fearful, scared, and afraid all your life. That whole traumatic, troubling, and tragic moment that you walked into that terrorized, tormented, tortured, and traumatized you, Satan had "set you up for," and all he had to do was get you to continue to do what you had already and always had done before, and that was to make sure you continued to not "yield to He who has the right of way." You always did the opposite of what Philippians 4:6–7 instructed you to do, and that was.

Don't fret or worry (be anxious). Instead of worrying, pray. Let petitions and praises shape your worries into prayers, letting God know your concerns. Before you know it, a sense of God's wholeness, everything coming together for good, will come and settle you down. It's wonderful what happens when Christ displaces worry at the center of your life (Phil. 4:6–7 MSG).

God, in that moment before you, of your "own free will," disregarded His prompting and disconnected yourself from Him leading you and then you said, done, and handled things your way, had given you His peace, which is far more wonderful than the human mind can understand. His peace will keep your thoughts and your hearts quiet and at rest as you trust in Christ Jesus. The spirit of self-deception used your own survivor-survival mode and your survivor-survival selfishness as a way to distract you and then detour you away from receiving "a sense of God's wholeness; everything coming together for good [that] will come and settle you down. It's wonderful what happens when Christ displaces worry at the center of your life."

God was there in that moment before you, out of self-deceived selfish feelings and emotions and out of a self-deceived attitude, mindset, and mentality, reacted in a bad, wrong, negative, and ugly way. His Holy Spirit was there before you delivered and demonstrated a self-deceived reactionary response, and in both moments and times, He was there trying to prompt you to receive His peace and He was prompting you to make peace with that matter and He was prompting and trying to get you to step back and let Him handle it for you, but you didn't and you wouldn't let it go, and you rejected, resisted, and refused to "yield to He who has the right of way." And in doing so, you, "of your own free will," through your personal and private wrong motives and wrong motivations, caused, created the atmosphere for, and contributed to what happened to you.

THE SURVIVORS MODE

Self-deception wants to keep you blind, ignorant, and deceived to this truth, reality, and fact. Self-deception keeps telling you to continue in the "blame game" and continue to think, feel, believe, and conduct yourself just like you are a "victim"; because "it's not your fault" what happened to you, and "you didn't say and do anything wrong to deserve what happened to you." After all, you had a right to say what you had to say, do what you had to do, and handle things the way you did. It didn't matter if you were so self-deceived, so into your selfishness, so into your survivor-survival mind-set, mentality, and mode, and so into being so emotionally charged that your "delivery" and what you "demonstrated" in the process of and the way in which you "expressed" yourself and your points was bad, wrong, negative, hostile, and ugly.

The spirit of self-deception does not want you to accept and see your personal accountability and responsibility for what happened to you. God, somewhere in the midst of what you went through and even before what happened to you took place, prompted you "to leave, get out, don't go back, don't say and do that"; but you didn't yield, submit, and surrender to what God, through that "something told me" still small voice, was telling and leading you to do. You were being led to "respond" in the right way, but you were self-deceived into "reacting" in the wrong way. When you are under the suggestive influence of the spirit of self-deception, it will not let you see this truth that says, "Don't be misled—you cannot mock the justice of God. You will always harvest what you plant" (Gal. 6:7 NLT). The manner, tone, delivery, attitude, mind-set, mentality, mode, spirit, etc., in which your "delivery" and "disobedience" were demonstrated in were what you sowed and you had to reap.

My point is there was a prompting and a "something told me"or a "I just felt something wasn't right" and many other "yield" signs and stop signs that showed up before what happened to you came about. But self-deception and you being self-deceived had to disregard the warnings, prompting, leading, and yielding. My second point I will make is in the form of a question, which is, are you and did you "reap" something that you needed to remember or relive, or are you "reaping" something that you need to repeat until you learn your lesson and get the message God is trying to tell you?

Self-deceived

Wherever a person is up under the suggestive influence of the spirit of self-deception, he or she will be held hostage and held captive to the spirit of being self-deceived. When a person is self-deceived, he or she is holding an erroneous opinion of oneself, one's own effort, or the like. This is the spirit that Satan uses and utilizes to stop, block, and hinder you from seeing what you have said or done and seeing how you handled a matter, circumstance, situation, confrontation, or challenge that led to you causing, creating the atmosphere for, and contributing to the trauma, troubles, and tragedy that you came face-to-face with and had to endure.

Being yoked to, bound and limited to and because of, in bondage to, in a stronghold to, and a slave to the spirit of self-deception is not the same as being linked to, connected to, tied to, and trapped in being self-deceived. They both sound like they are the same, but they are different in what they do and in how and when they manifest themselves. Self-deception is defined as the act of lying to yourself or of making yourself believe something that isn't really true, while being self-deceived is defined as holding an erroneous opinion of oneself, one's own effort, or the like. There has to be a self-deception first before you can be self-deceived. Self-deception affects how you perceive and see yourself, and being self-deceived affects what you think about yourself.

Whenever there is self-deception and a person is self-deceived, there will always be some type of bad, wrong, negative, and ugly effect. Being driven and motivated by the spirit of self-deception leads to you being drawn, driven, pulled, pushed, persuaded, forced, seduced, enticed, and tricked into being self-deceived, and when those two are working together and in cahoots, they will bring with them self-pity; false care, concern, and compassion; addictive and compulsive disorders; distorted self-image, self-awareness, self-perception, self-esteem, self-confidence,

THE SURVIVORS MODE

and self-worth; along with a bad, wrong, negative, and ugly opinion of men.

Being overpowered, overtaken, and overthrown by the spirit of self-deception and the spirit of being self-deceived will also disconnect you from and detour, delay, and even deny you from having the right to have the right approach to life, knowing how you should build your own life, and will ensure you have a very different view of the world, and that view is also distorted and tainted with terrorized, tormented, tortured, and traumatized feelings and emotional perspective. Every time you give place to and heed to allowing your understanding and interpretation of traumatic, troubling, and tragic circumstances, situations, confrontations, matters, memories, and moments in your life to end up being mistaken, you will start forming an erroneous judgment, etc., in your own mind, as from careless or wishful thinking.

Escapism

Once again, truth and reality will continue to escape you, and fear will drive, push, and force you into the practice of escapism. When you are locked into escapism, you are locked into the avoidance of reality by absorption of the mind in entertainment or in an imaginative situation, activity, etc. What happens when escapism has seized, taken control of, taken over, and taken out your right reasoning mind, frame of mind, state of mind, mental condition and conditioning, and mental state of being is your thoughts, train of thought, thinking, and way of thinking will begin to function and flow in and out of the avoidance of reality by absorption of the mind in entertainment or in an imaginative situation, activity, etc., and this will eventually become your mind-set, mentality, and mode.

Self-deception will blind your mind, and mental capabilities and abilities, being self-deceived will hinder and handicap your train of thought and your way of thinking, and escapism will seriously impair and distort, and then detour your thoughts and thinking. As you can see everything I am sharing with you all started the moment when you were linked, connected, tied, trapped and then yoked, bound and limited to, in bondage to, in a stronghold to and a slave to a survivor mode, survival mode and a survivor-survival mode. Your whole mind-set and mentality, thoughts, train of thought, thinking and way of thinking ended up being challenged, confronted, conquered and changed and captured and held captive opening the door for survivor's selfishness, self-deception, being self-deceived, and the practice of escapism which opens the door for a person being entangled and entrapped into a self-delusion.

Self-delusion

A self-delusion happens or occurs when a person's mind-set and mentality have been constantly, continuously, and consistently tricked and then trapped in being involved in, entangled in, and entrapped and locked into the action of deluding or imposing a misleading belief upon oneself that deceives and fools oneself in a way that it causes, creates the atmosphere for, and contributes to a failure to recognize reality. This is not the same as being self-deceived, which once again is holding an erroneous opinion of oneself, one's own effort, or the like. Let me now break all of what I have been sharing with you down so that you can clearly see the difference between them:

- ➤ Being locked into a self-delusion can only happen when you "impose" and keep imposing a misleading something that you shouldn't have when it comes to yourself.
- ➤ And being linked, connected, tied, and trapped into being self-deceived can only occur when you have accepted, adopted, and adapted to and start *applying and keep applying* a wrong and erroneous "opinion of yourself."
- ➤ To find yourself yoked to, in bondage to, and a slave to a self-deception or self-deceit stronghold can only take place when you have already *implemented* and have made an active part of the "action or practice" concerning yourself that brings about you lying to yourself or making yourself believe something about

THE SURVIVORS MODE

yourself that is false and/or it is an nonvalidated feeling, idea, situation, or belief that isn't really true that looks and feels like it is real and true to you.

The point I want to make when it comes to you being a slave to a self-delusion as a result of you being in a survivor-survival mode is Satan has used fear to force you into the action of deluding or imposing a misleading belief upon yourself that basically states,

"For you to survive, remain alive, and continue to live and exist and cope well with the trauma, troubles, tragedies that consistently, constantly, and continuously torment, torture, terrorize, and traumatize you that come into and show up in your life whenever they want to, you have to allow a practice that has continued to exist from an earlier time, which has been survivor selfishness and escapism, to be your way or manner in which everything that has to do with you occurs or is experienced, expressed, or done even though it will end up deceiving and fooling yourself and lead to your having a failure to recognize reality."

What I just described to you in the statement above is the attitude, mood, mind-set, and mentality of someone who is in a survivor-survival self-delusional mode. In the end, fear wants to force you to yield, submit, and surrender to escapism being what you constantly, continuously, and consistently allow yourself to experience and express and be done without you resisting, rejecting, refusing, rebuking, and refuting. In you doing so, you will end up with a distorted self-perception.

Self-perception

If and when Satan is able to distort your self-perception, what he is able to do is pull or twist out of shape and give a misleading or false account or impression of the idea that you have about the kind of person you are. And that self-perception is always derived from survivor selfishness, self-deception, being self-deceived, self-delusion, and escapism. Once your self-perception is distorted, Satan makes sure your self-perception is detained long enough for him to ____

When you are a slave to self-perception, you are being misled and deceived by Satan and fear into giving and having a misleading and false account or impression of "where you are" as a person in relation to what has been traumatic, troubling, and tragic in your life, what you have been through, and what has been terrorizing, torturing, tormenting, and traumatizing when it comes to you. Satan wants to distort the "lens" you look through to view your life, yourself, and what you have been through and what actually happened and took place. Once it is distorted, he can then detain your mind, mental capabilities and abilities, thoughts, train of thought, thinking, and way of thinking; and finally, he can detain your mind-set and mentality long enough to force all of them into the mode he wants them to function and flow in and out of.

And out of that kind and type of functioning and flowing will arise having the urge, tendency, inclination, intuition, impulse, and instinct to follow distracting, distorted, and detained self-perception processes, procedures, and principles. Not only so, but you will also end up having a distorted idea about the kind of person you are as a result of everything that has been traumatic, troubling, tragic in your life and what has terrorized, tormented, tortured, and traumatized you. The idea that you are led to have, the view that you see, and the lens that you end up looking through can only give you a survivor-survival image, reflection, and view.

The self-perception theory puts in position, place, assumes as a fact, and puts forward as a basis of argument that people determine their attitudes and preferences by interpreting the *meaning* of their own behavior. Every self-perception statement or theory that Satan uses and utilizes and works through fear to draw, drive, pull, push, persuade, force, trick, entice, and seduce you into accepting, adopting, adapting to, and applying and releasing is made on the assumption that it will prove to be true.

THE SURVIVORS MODE

My conclusion to these matters

What I want to say to you is, as long as you are locked and yoked into a survivor-survival mind-set and you continue to be bound and limited and in bondage to having a survivor-survival mentality and you keep yielding, submitting, and surrendering to you being in a stronghold to a survivor-survival mode, you will continue to function and flow in and out of (1) survivor selfishness, (2) self-deception, (3) being self-deceived, (4) self-delusion, (5) self-perception, and (6) escapism.

And in doing so, you will constantly, continuously, and consistently remain a slave to delivering and demonstrating (a) self-willed, (b) self-effort, and (c) self-performance acts, actions, deeds, handlings, and interpretations. You will never get to the point and place where you are functioning and flowing in and out of faith, and you will not get to the place and point where you are following faith-delivering, cleansing, purging, healing, and make-you-whole processes, procedures, and principles. You won't ever get to the place and point where you are permanently disconnected from thinking, feeling, and believing you are a survivor, you have to survive, and you need to stay in a survival mind-set, mentality, and mode.

You will continue to be fear driven and motivated and continue to be fearfully locked into having and demonstrating "I'm a victim" reactions, reactionary responses, urges, tendencies, inclinations, intuitions, impulses, and instincts. You will also continue to be scared and afraid to live again, love again, trust again, believe again, have hope again, have confidence again, have faith again, and open yourself up to getting into a relationship again. And last but not least, you will continue to struggle and strain in your self-esteem, self-worth, self-image, self-confidence, and self-awareness, and you will continue to have a distorted view of your opinion of men and how you are to approach life. You will never find and have a good, right, and positive "approach to life" example for you to build off in your own life.

And, finally, if you continue to function and flow in and out of a survivor mode, survivor selfishness, self-deception, being self-deceived, self-delusion, and self-perception and practice escapism, not only will

~336~　　ANTHONY MCMARYION

you end up being constant and consistent having to demonstrate and then deliver and express yourself out of your self-will, self-efforts, and out of self-performance acts, actions, and deeds, but you will also continue to choose a different view of the world because you have not let go of the trauma, troubles, and tragic events that had happened to you, and you are still oversensitive to those same events and finally because you continue to allow yourself to be a terrorized, tortured, tormented, and traumatized to the point and place where you are scared, afraid, and fearful. Let us now take another power prayer break.

POWER PRAYER BREAK

LOVE LIFE!

This is the day which the Lord has made; let us rejoice and be glad in it.
—Psalms 118:24

Power thought: No life is perfect until you fall in love with it.

Every day provides you with another opportunity to praise God for the gift of life. It is good to be alive. Every day, there are manifold joys and an endless array of blessings. This is crowned by the ever-present spirit of God as your illumination, your strength, and your help in every need. The presence of God fills your life and your world with good. There is no room in your thinking for regret, fear, or depression. God has and is fulfilling every good desire of your heart. Jesus constantly gave thanks, and you have much for which to give thanks. You put love into your daily tasks and into all your relationships. You give of your time and you share of your faith. As you give to life, you are filled with a spirit of joy and love.

No matter what has happened in the past, the spirit of the Christ is with you and waiting to give you all the help and support you need. So you can put the past behind you and get on with living your life. Love your life with enthusiasm and a sense of renewal in your mind and heart. Today is the first day of your new life, a life that you will love.

THE SURVIVORS MODE

Can you see the unlimited possibilities that await you? Rejoice at all that you have to be grateful for and claim it now. None of us can say exactly what the future holds for us. But as we move forward with God as our guide, we can be certain that the future will be full of phenomenal experiences. And although the future is uncertain, perhaps we can begin to influence the possibilities that abound by establishing a permanent bond of harmony and love in the world around us.

Like a seed planted in the ground, this unbridled sense of peace and harmony will soon grow and spread on its own, from person to person, from city to city, until your whole world is infused with God's goodwill. Yes, the future holds great things for you, and you can look forward to it with the expectation of unlimited joy. I ask you to read aloud this prayer.

DAILY POSITIVE POWER PRAYER

I love life!

I love my life right now!

My joy is complete, for I abide in God and God abides in me.

Good morning, God!

I am glad to be alive!

I welcome this new day and all the good it holds.

I know that You are with me in this day and that Your love accompanies me wherever I may go.

Because You are with me in all things, this will be a day to remember, to enjoy, and to happily bask in.

I place all my plans for this day in Your loving care, knowing that all things will go smoothly and well.

I will feel Your loving presence with me.

Because You are with me this day, this will be a day of divine order.

You bring happy experiences of blessed fulfillment to all my relationships this day.

This will be a day when harmony prevails, when peace is felt by me and by those around me.

This will be a day when I know that Your loving protection is with me, my family, and my friends, guiding us and making our way safe.

Thank You, God, for this day.

I will make it Your day following Your actions of love.

In Jesus Christ's name, amen!

CHAPTER TWENTY-ONE

Secular Sense and Reason Ministers

I NOW WANT to ask you to focus your attention on marriage, love, life, yourself, and relationships. In doing so, what I want to do is give you a preview of coming attractions when it comes to all five as long as you continue to hide in, function, and flow in and out of a survivor-survival mind-set, mentality, and mode. And you continue to allow yourself to make choices and decisions out of that traumatic, troubled, tragic place, state, condition, and moment in your life that you are still being terrorized, tormented, tortured, and traumatized at. The future of your love, marriage, and relationships is still in harm's way, still at stake, and still at risk as well as everything that you are still praying will happen in your life.

What is important for you to know is all the present and future choices and decisions you will make and end up making will still derive from not only your survivor-survival attitude, mood, mind-set, mentality, and mode but also survivor selfishness and self-deception mode that Satan has used fear to ensure you linked, connected, tied, trapped, and held hostage to. In doing so, you will not be able to move forward in the way you want to, and as a result, at some place, point, and time, you will constantly, continuously, and consistently run into and hit that invisible relationship ceiling. And when you do, you will not have what you need within yourself to sustain and maintain the right relationship with God, with yourself, and with others, as well as not having what you need to sustain and maintain and help grow, develop, and mature a good, health, strong, prosperous, productive, and successful relationship.

Inadequacies and inabilities

The first reason for you having "sustain and maintain" inadequacies and inabilities is and will be due to you are and still will be struggling and straining to get and move past those traumatic, troubling, and tragic moments in your life that have left you still scared, afraid, and fearful of being terrorized, tormented, tortured, and traumatized again. The second reason is you personally are and still will be in a struggling-and-straining-to-survive mind-set, mentality, and mode; and your self-esteem, self-worth, self-respect, self-confidence, self-awareness, and self-image will still be in a struggling and straining state and condition. The final reason is and will be you will also continue to struggle and strain when it comes to your confidence and opinions of men because both still have not been properly shaped and you still do not and have not had the right example to build off when it comes to how you should and how you are to approach life, even if you chose a different view of the world.

Where you go to for help and whom you turn to for help with everything in your life that is and have been traumatic, troubling, tragic and that terrorizes, torments, tortures, and traumatizes will also derive from you being scared, afraid, and fearful that you will have to relive and remember and then struggle and strain to survive the process and procedures. And when that happens, you are fearfully being led to believe, think, and feel you will also end up having to struggle and strain because you would be wanting to make sure you can and will still survive the reliving and remembering and the "releasing" process and procedures alone. The only way Satan is going to allow you reach out for help, turn to someone for help, and accept help is you do so out of and from a self-deception perception and perspective.

Secular world healers and healings

With that being said, let me move forward by stating, "You have been in the survivor-survival mode too long," and it is time for you to stop having past and old traumatic, troubling, and tragic terrorizing, tormenting, torturing, and traumatizing root cause reactions, responses, and reactionary responses, and it also time for you to stop going to secular world ministers, pastors, prophets, teachers, evangelists, apostles, bishops, elders, "life coaches," etc., who keep giving you secular world surface healing solutions. If you don't you will continue to be someone who is new marriage, love, life, and relationship "unstable," and your new marriage, love, life, and relationships will continue to be past and old marriage-, love-, and relationship-gone-wrong disease infected and affected to the point and place where you will demonstrate you are marriage, love, and relationship unreliable and uncertain.

And everything that you think, feel, and decide when it comes to marriage, relationship, life, views, yourself, love, and opinion of men will end up deriving from an irresolute perspective and point of view. Secular world ministers can only give you "fake it till you make it" healing processes, procedures, and principles that make you look good on the outside but leave you really in a bad inner "ability to love and live" shape, state, and condition.

Only God can forgive all your past and old marriage, love, and relationship sins, mistakes, and errors; and He is the one who brings deep-rooted core inner healing into all our traumatic, troubling, and tragic marital, love, and relationship diseases and experiences. He is the only one who can keep us from present and future marriage, love, and relationship graves (Ps. 103:2–4). Secular world healing solutions can only produce, prepare, and present secular world "look like and feel like" they are deep-rooted core inner healing, but that is only a distorted appearance or a distorted image that ends up becoming a "figment of your imagination" healing image and not the real thing.

Secular world ministers specialize in drawing, driving, pulling, pushing, persuading, tricking, seducing, and enticing you into their secular world ministers' healing proposals and propositions by using secular world healing sayings that you and a lot of others have been attracted to and have accepted, adopted, adapted to, and applied as part of your daily marital, love, views, life, and relationship practices and procedures.

And you follow what their sayings are, and you listen to and hear what they have to say when the only thing they are doing and can do is provide a temporary healing fix and repair to what has been a deep-rooted core past and old marriage-, love-, and relationship-gone-wrong permanent problem. Secular world ministers can only give you traumatic, troubling, and tragic past and old marriage, love, relationship, self-esteem, self-image, self-worth, self-confidence, self-respect, self-perception, etc., healing solutions and remedies that instruct you to "remove" and "replace," but full-of-living powered deep-rooted core inner healing words, messages, instructions, information, ideas, and insights that come from the Master Healer Himself give "relief" so you can "release" and never remember, relive, or repeat. When you follow secular world healing minister's solutions, they can only make it appear like you are all right and you have made it. Your outer may be clear and clean and free, but your inner is still residue entangled and entrapped in the past and old.

Secular world healing ministers and secular world healing methods and methodologies, processes, procedures, and principles followed cannot and will not allow you to disconnect you from a survivor-survival mode, and they will not allow you to put on the new deep-rooted core inner healed self, which is constantly, continuously, and consistently being renewed in the image of its Creator, who is God. You must remember and never forget it was and it is God who protected you and saved you from everything that was traumatic, deeply troubling, and tragic in your life that was once and still is terrorizing, tormenting, torturing, and traumatizing. He did so not because of the righteous marriage, love, life, self, and relationship things you had said or done; but it was because of His love for you, His grace, and His loving kindness that He showed toward you and because of His relationship and marriage mercy.

He is now, in this very same hour as you are reading this book, wanting to save you from secular world ministers' surface healing solutions, and the only way He can do so will come through you responding in the right way and manner to the washing of your marriage, self, love, relationship, opinions, and views and allow there to be a renewal of them all that comes only through and by the Holy Spirit. You didn't make it this far because of practiced secular world ministers' healing solutions that were, in all actuality and in all reality, nothing more than a trick of the enemy to get you to believe, think, and feel that way.

Let's be clear on something, and that is you made it through and you have been able to keep making it through what you went through because God's grace and mercy kept you safe from being further drawn, driven, pulled, pushed, persuaded, seduced, tricked, trapped, deceived, enticed, entangled, and entrapped into those distorted, damaging, deceptive, and deceiving secular world ministers' healing solutions and remedies. You made it through it all because God wanted to make sure you would be able to hear and to read the truth and realities written in this book. Please don't get it twisted!

Let me ask you this question. Why would you want a temporary surface healing fix for what has been a permanent and long journeyed past and old traumatic, troubling, and tragic marriage-, love-, and relationship-gone-wrong problem? Secular world surface healing ministers solutions applied can and will only suggest and influence you into imitating the world's ideas, concepts, precepts, and practices when it comes to healing. And once applied, you will end up being conformed in your mind, thoughts, train of thought, thinking, way of thinking, and in your frame of mind, state of mind, mental condition and mental state of being to those same secular world surface healing solution ideas, concepts, precepts, and practices.

And in doing so, you will, in the results, end up (1) being distinguished as someone who is a good, acceptable, and perfect will of a secular world ministers' surface healing solution "protégé," and in doing so, you will also (2) become prosperous, productive, and successful at accomplishing, achieving, acquiring, and accumulating secular world ministers acceptance and accolades and occasional recognition and rewards, blessings, and benefits.

Transformation change

On the other hand, when you accept, adopt, adapt to, and apply full-of-living powered deep-rooted core inner healing remedies and solutions that cannot and will not, in no way whatsoever, imitate the secular world ministers' healing remedies and healing solutions, you will end up in a moving forward into a past free, present, and future marriage, love, and relationship state and condition where you will begin to not only experience but also have encounters with being transformed and changed by the renovation of your "relationship, love, views, marriage, and opinions of men" mind.

As that transformation-change-renovation is happening to your personal, private, and public views, it is happening to your views on marriage, love, relationship, and opinions of men along with what you have been through; that same transformation-change-renovation is also taking place in every way, manner, and method you use to articulate, analyze, and come to conclusions. Not only will what I just shared with you end up being transformed, changed, and renovated, but also you, the person and individual, will personally end up being transformed and changed and set apart, and in doing so, your thoughts, train of thought, thinking, way of thinking, attitude, mood, mind-set, mentality, and mode shall be released from being survivor-survival entangled and entrapped, and they all will be transformed and changed and will be set apart.

Once your thoughts, train of thought, thinking, way of thinking, attitude, mood, mind-set, mentality, and mode have been transformed, changed, and renovated and set apart, they all will end up becoming and end up being distinguished as being ready to function and flow in and out of and ready to follow the right type of marriage, love, self, self-esteem, self-image, self-worth, self-confidence, self-respect, opinion of men, suggestion and influence, and relationship processes, procedures, principles, and practices that are God good, God acceptable, and perfect will of God ordained, grown, developed, matured, created, built, established, and powered.

After which, you can and will have what can and will do the right kind and type of "shaping," and you will be in the right state, condition, mind-set, mentality, and mode where you can receive being accurately inspired in the right way so you can receive the right examples for you to build your approach to life off. And the final thing that will happen

THE SURVIVORS MODE

is for whatever different reason or reasons you choose to view the world through and your world through, they will end up being accurate reasons and views. Please understand and be clear on this fact and truth—that all of what I just described and shared can only take place, occur, and happen when you abandon secular world healing solutions and get permanently linked to, connected to, tied to, yoked to, bound and limited to, in bondage to, in a stronghold to, and a slave to receiving and being a constant, continuous, and consistent recipient of a full-of-living powered God truth-filled healing.

Secular minister healing remedies

Secular ministers, pastors, preachers, teachers, evangelists, prophets, apostles, bishops, and elders base their healing faith or the faith in healing on secular world ministry healing remedy theories and reasoning that bring about or that produce, prepare, and present a proud and lofty healing mode, mind-set, and mentality. Every secular minister's healing faith or their faith in their healing methods, techniques and tactics are conformed to this world's customs, ideas, information, insights, image, and fashions, and it is conformed according to the peculiar state of healing and the present state of healing that is in the world; all of which is as much opposed to the spirit of genuine deep-rooted core inner healing.

Secular Christian ministers and secular world minister and secular ministers "inner healing" practitioners use a lot of techniques that are most commonly used in mysticism. One of those techniques that are used is "prayer journeys." What prayer journeys do is encourage people to remember past hurtful situations and moments in their life and then visualize Jesus being there with them at the moment when those hurtful and painful moments of brokenness occurred. This all sounds good and right, but it is not accurate. Their second and most commonly used is "visualization," and when you subject, submit, and surrender yourself to secular world Christian ministers' "inner and emotional healing" visualization solutions and remedies, there are some potential dangers that are inherent in visualization techniques and mystical New Age methods. Three of those are

- the harm that comes from prolonged dwelling on occurrences that evoke hurt, anger, etc.;
- the danger of basing our ideas of God upon an image in our mind instead of the truth of who He is as revealed in biblical scripture; and
- opening the doors of our minds to demonic interferences, suggestions, and influences.

Yes, it is true that God wants to make and set us free from the wrong we caused, created the atmosphere for, or contributed to, or we had no personal accountability and responsibility for that happening, for that came about as a result of us being in past and old marriage, love, and relationships that were traumatic, troubling, and tragic that keep tormenting, torturing, terrorizing, and traumatizing us. But God has no need for visualization concepts, precepts, theories, and techniques, and He does not need prolonged emphasis being made on past and old bad, negative, ugly, wrong, traumatic, troubling, and tragic marriage, love, relationship, choice and decision fallacies, failures, and flaws to make and set you free from them.

Mind's eye

This is what you have to know and be clear in your understanding of when it comes to how secular world healing ministers and secular world healing "life coaches" are able to, in a sneaky way, draw, drive, pull, push, persuade, seduce, entice, and force you into the grips of their secular world "healing concepts and precepts." Please note that every secular world healing technique, tactic, and method has to first appeal to the "what makes sense" or appeal to the "that makes sense" part of your analytical reasoning. And once that "appeal" has "captivated" your thought, train of thought, thinking, and way of thinking, it will

THE SURVIVORS MODE

produce, prepare, and present an appeal to your "process" being put in place and put in motion.

The next thing that happens after the "sense" part of you has done its evaluation of the secular healing ministers' healing solution arguments, theories, and reasoning and has decided and determined it has the "appeal" that it needs is the "there is a good reason" or the logical assumption and conclusions part of you shows up. And what that "there is good reason" part of you does when it shows up is validate the need for you needing and wanting what is and has been appealing. What has been appealing has projected a reflective image or a selfish reflective "imagination image" of what you possibly can and will look like after you have accepted, adopted, adapted to, applied, released, and received secular world healing and secular world "life coach" healing solution processes, procedures, and principles into your attitude, mood, mind-set, and mentality, causing all of them to end up being "captured" and then end up being held "captive" to that distorted, deceptive, and deceiving projected image of what you could or might look like.

And once that distorted, damaging, deceptive, and deceiving what could or might be your "appearance" has "captivated" and has held "captive" your attitude, mood, mind-set, and mentality, that same "there is a reason" that is logical part of you will begin to, out of the wrong "lenses," sense, see, perceive, and project secular healing ministers' healing solution images, ideas, inspirations, ingenuities, instructions, and information that are supposed to bring about a visible manifestation of that "captured" and held "captive" distorted, damaging, deceptive, and deceiving appearance.

Out of which will end up being conceived, birthed, and born logical "appearance" procedures that have a reason for being put into effect. My point with sharing with you all of what is above is secular world ministers and secular world "life coaches" use clever slogans, methods, techniques, tactics, and methods that "appeal" to the "appearance" that is already living, dwelling, abiding, and lying dormant within your "mind's eye." And that appealing appearance that is lying dormant within your "mind's eye" relies on an image that, in your opinion, makes sense for you to desire, and, therefore, you will have a logical, reasoned explanation, excuse, and justification for wanting, accepting, adopting, adapting to, and applying those secular world healing principles, processes, procedures, and methods.

The phrase "mind's eye" refers to the human ability to visualize (i.e., to experience visual mental imagery; in other words, one's ability to "see" things with the mind). Secular world healers and secular world healing "life coaches" always will administer secular world "mind's eye" healing solutions and remedies that appeal to the appearance that you, for selfish reasons, are wanting and you are visualizing. They are selfish envisioned healings and selfish visualizations because they give a deceptive and deceiving projected image of who you are; when deep down on the inside, you have not been totally and completely delivered, cleansed, purged, healed, and made whole from what has been traumatic, troubling, and tragic, and what still haunts, terrorizes, torments, tortures, and traumatizes you.

CHAPTER TWENTY-TWO

Secular World Ministers' Healing Solutions

SECULAR WORLD MINISTERS and secular world life coaches use and utilize healing solutions that thrive on and are based and built on, count on, and depend on keeping your past traumatic, troubling, and tragic marriage, love, and relationship feelings and emotions alive and active in their healing processes, procedures, and principles. They will continuously, constantly, and consistently play and prey upon those feelings and emotions so they can continue to profit and prosper off your past and old marriage, love, and relationship hurt, pain, and brokenness. That is their intent, and that is their motive and motivation. God is the only true minister of healing and deep-rooted core inner healing of any kind.

Let's take a look at Isaiah 53:4–5 in from a different perspective. It would read as thus:

- Surely He has borne your self-esteem, self-image, self-respect, self-confidence, self-worth, self-determination, etc., your wrong approach to life, and wrong opinion of men griefs, sicknesses, weaknesses, and distresses, and He carried your father-daughter sorrows and pains (of punishment), yet you (ignorantly) considered Him stricken, smitten, and afflicted by God (as if with leprosy).
- In fact, He was pierced for your past and old, present and future traumatic, troubled, and tragic marital, love, and relationship transgressions.

- He was crushed for your past and old, present and future traumatic, troubling, and tragic marital, love, and relationship iniquities that would constantly, continuously, and consistently terrorize, torment, torture, and traumatize you.
- The punishment that brought you past, present, and future terrorizing, tormenting, torturing, and traumatic marriage, love, relationship, and choice and decision peace was on Him, and by His wounds, you can, will be, and are deep-rooted core inner healed.

We have been given the power and the authority and the right to accept, adapt to, apply, and receive deep-rooted core healing. Satan can't and won't be able to stop you from doing so unless you give him the power and the authority to do so. The moment you give place, yield, submit, and surrender to following secular world ministers, pastors, prophets, teachers, evangelists, apostles, bishops, elders, life coaches healing processes, procedures, and principles that are needed for their healing solutions and healing remedies to be put in motion and put into effect, you can expect the following:

A. To stay addicted to your past and old traumatic, troubling, and tragic marital, love, and relationship pain, rejection, heartache, etc., and to say addicted to your marriage and love and relationship gone wrong story, which will keep you from believing you deserve deep-rooted core inner healing and believing you can freely have it without having to earn it or work for it.

B. You will stay locked into the mind-set and mentality and mode where you want to receive, accept, adapt to, adopt, and apply deep-rooted core inner healing processes and procedures on your own terms.

C. You will want Jesus to compromise with you when it comes to deep-rooted core inner healing and let you receive, have, and apply His deep-rooted core inner healing your way and when you choose to.

THE SURVIVORS MODE
351

D. You will easily let *C* above happen because you will reject, resist, refuse, and refuse to be tutored, trained, and taught how to receive, accept, adopt, adapt to, and apply deep-rooted core inner healing truth and reality processes, principles, and procedures.

E. As well as being tutored, trained, and taught why you should and how you should and how to receive, accept, adapt to, and apply deep-rooted core inner healing truths and realities.

F. Satan will keep you deep-rooted core inner healing blind, ignorant, and deceived so you will never know deep-rooted core inner healing can and will bring you hope in your outcome.

G. You will continue to settle for less in your healing and in any new marriage, love, and relationship you get into.

H. You will constantly, consistently, and continually "limit" yourself to anticipating and expecting and receiving the bare necessities and the bare minimum out of your healing and out of a marriage, love, and relationships and never the maximum.

I. You won't ever accept any kind of personal accountability and responsibility for seeking out and finding and discovering and then humbling yourself to receiving deep-rooted core inner healing. You will always try to find and come up with ways, reasons, and excuses to make It someone else's responsibility to find and discover it for you, while you just sit back in your "I'm all right where I am" in this marriage, love, and relationship and when it comes to myself, comfort zone, contentment, complacency, and compromise. You will even go as far as holding someone else accountable for you finding, discovering, and having the deep-rooted core inner healing principles, processes, procedures, solutions, and remedies you need.

J. You will continually, constantly, and continually yield, submit, and surrender your deep-rooted core inner healing power of choice over to satanic and secular world ministers' suggestive influences.

ANTHONY MCMARYION

Don't continue to empower the devil to destroy your life, and don't let him continue to take away and rob, cheat, bamboozle, swindle, kill, steal, destroy, trick, and deceive you so he can take your deep core inner healing power of choice from you. You gave your best to the wrong person, and now you have nothing left for the right person whom you are in a new marriage, love, and relationship with, and/or you are struggling and straining when it comes to giving them your best and giving them all your relationship, love, and marriage committed, dedicated, and loyal heart.

Applying secular world healings

Every time you apply secular world healing solutions and remedies, you will still be harboring and hiding and holding hostage inside of you that same past and old "just in case" something goes wrong in this new marriage, love, and relationship survivor-survival clause in the back of your mind. You still will be experiencing "residue" past and old traumatic and tragic marriage, love, and relationship gone wrong thoughts, train of thought, thinking, and way of thinking. What you have to realize and understand is if you continue to be in a "residue relationship reserve" mind-set and mentality and mode, you will keep accepting, adapting to, applying, functioning, and flowing in and out of residue relationship reserve standards, and you will continue to have head-on collisions with residue relationship reserve boundaries and limitations.

When you finally wake up and decide to go get your deep-rooted core inner residue marriage, love, self, and relationship healing, it will end up being a "too much, too little, and too late" moment. That moment will happen and take place because the person who was with you and who waited on you to change and get rid of your past and old traumatic and tragic marriage and love and relationship gone wrong terrorized, tormented, tortured, and traumatized behavior, behavior patterns, conduct, attitude and mood, mind-set, mentality, and mode will have gotten tired of waiting on you, and he or she would want to be free of having a marriage, love, and relationship with you.

THE SURVIVORS MODE   353

In the flow with secular healing ministers

How you articulate and analyze your need, want, and desire for healing is very important because there are only two forces in this world, and they are God and Satan, and the healing words you use will bring either God's deep-rooted core inner healing processes, procedures, and principles or satanically suggested and influenced secular world surface healing principles, processes, and procedures. Secular world healing ministers, pastors, prophets, teachers, evangelists, apostles, bishops, elders, and life coaches are waiting on you.

They are more confident you will receive, accept, adopt, adapt to, and apply their "good idea and good-intentioned" misguided, misdirected, deceptive, and deceiving healing remedies and solutions as long as you are so past and old bad, negative, wrong marriage, love, and relationship distracted and deceived because of you still being terrorized, tormented, tortured, and traumatized. While you are in that state and condition and you have that mind-set and mentality, they can detour you away from deep-rooted core inner healing that comes from and through God's full-of-living powered deep-rooted core inner healing truths and realities. They don't want you to have any type and kind of personal and private or public encounters with God's healing ministers who know how to help you get to true and real deep-rooted core inner healing that He died for you to have.

As long as you are and you stay distracted and detoured away from deep-rooted core inner healing, those secular world healing ministers and secular world life coach healers can dismantle any desired openness you have to receiving and pursuing after deep-rooted core inner healing, and then they will find and create ways to derail your deep-rooted core inner healing thoughts, train of thought, thinking, and way of thinking and disconnect you from having any desire to pursue and have it.

And when that is completed, they will then stir up enough past and old traumatic, troubling, and tragic flashbacks that in turn bring about a flaring up of terrorized, tormenting, torturing, and traumatizing feelings that you thought you had gotten past and had gotten over. All those flashbacks and flare-ups that end up showing up came from your unresolved past and old marriage, love, and relationship troubles, traumas, and tragedies that were able to drive, push, force, and put you into a desolate and destitute marital, love, and relationship mind-set and mentality and mode.

And once in that mode, you would begin to heed and follow your urged impulsiveness and your urged instincts that would seduce and entice you into willingly denying good, right, happy, and positive feelings, and you will begin to once again feel so empty and feel so all alone.

Once you are in that place and at that point again, those secular world healing ministers and secular world life coach healers will begin to cause, create the atmosphere for, and contribute to you having a lust, crave, hunger, thirst, and desire for their interpretation of healing, their image of healing, their instructions for healing, their healing insights and healing inspirations, their healing information, their healing ideas, their healing ingenuity, and their healing intellect.

Appealing appearance

Which healing performance you will eventually end up demonstrating and delivering will ultimately decide and determine which healing conduct, behavior, and behavior patterns you will demonstrate. When you are functioning and flowing in and out of secular ministers' healing theories, concepts, and precepts, you will need the assistance of and have to use and utilize surface self-willed healing, surface self-performance healing, and surface self-effort healing techniques, methods, acts, actions, and deeds. The reason is no matter how "healing appealing" your "healing appearance" looks and seems to be, all your past and old traumatic, troubled, and tragic relationship and marriage and love residue is still there with you and within you lying dormant and waiting for the moment when it can be sparked into action.

And because of that, you are still in an emotionally desperate mind-set, mentality, and mode. You have not moved forward, and you have not moved on from those emotionally destitute and emotionally draining days. Every day, you are filled with the anticipation and the expectation that the secular world healing you have received can and will bring about and stir up within you a real, right, good, and positive new relationship, marriage, and love desire; all because you followed the secular healing ministers' healing advice and instructions for your healing. You are also thinking and believing you will also become emotionally alive and alert again and you will want to willingly participate in love, marriage, and relationship dialogue again.

Which cannot and will not happen, and the reason is there are some secular ministers healing and some secular life coach healing truth and reality-filled facts that they want to keep hidden and kept secret from you and everyone that come to them. Remember, "He, Jesus was pierced for our rebellion, crushed for our sins. He was beaten so we could be whole. He was whipped so we could be healed."

CHAPTER TWENTY-THREE

Secular Ministers' Healing Facts

THERE ARE SOME key facts that you need to know when it comes to the secular ministers' and secular life coaches' surface healing that you have received and you are protecting with your survivor-survival mode, mind-set, and mentality, and those facts are the following:

1. Secular ministers' healing processes, procedures, and principles and standards, solutions, and remedies are derived from (a) secular healing arguments, (b) secular healing theories, and (c) secular healing reasoning, and they are derived from (d) proud and lofty secular healings; all of which are driven, motivated, and powered by and through carnal thoughts and carnal purposes, which are hostile to God. The reason is secular ministers will not allow or permit carnal healing thoughts and carnal healing purposes to be yielded, submitted, and surrendered to God's deep-rooted core inner healing law and to God's deep-rooted core inner healing principles, processes, procedures, and standards.

2. Secular ministers' and secular life coaches' healing processes, procedures, principles and standards, solutions, and remedies are constantly, continuously, and consistently processed through sense and reason without the help and the assistance of the Holy Spirit. Secular healing ministers, pastors, prophets, teachers, evangelists, apostles, bishops, elders, and life coaches suggest that their healing methods, healing tactics and techniques, healing theories, healing reasoning, and their proud and lofty healings must make *sense,* and there must be some type or kind

~357~

of visible *reason(s)* and reasoning for a person needing and wanting healing.

a. To say that deep-rooted core inner healing that comes from and through the presence and power of God is needed because of there still being past and old traumatic, troubling, and tragic marital, love, and relationship residue that needs to be removed and released from the person's feelings and emotions; secular world healing ministers *suggest* to the person's mind, frame of mind, state of mind, and state of mind such a healing is unnecessary and it doesn't make *analytical sense* and there is no *analytical reason or reasoning* for such.

b. And then analytical sense and analytic reason and reasoning *influence* the person's thoughts, train of thought, thinking, and way of thinking into rejecting, resisting, refusing, and refuting deep-rooted core inner healing because it is analytically unnecessary and unproductive.

3. Secular ministers' and secular life coaches' healing processes, procedures, principles and standards, solutions, and remedies cater to carnal analytical healing appetites and carnal analytical healing impulses that derive from a carnal analytical healing nature. And none of them can please or satisfy or measure up to God's methods and measure of full-of-living powered deep-rooted core healing virtue; nor are secular ministers' analytical healing appetites and secular ministers' analytical healing impulses acceptable to God.

4. Secular ministers' and secular life coaches' healing solutions and remedies remove deep-rooted core inner healing logics and truths and realities and replace them with make sense and have a visible reason(s) and reasoning that can make a person feel proud and lofty when it comes to themselves because of their surface "I look good and I feel good" about myself healing appearance.

The bottom line is, if you are living the life of a person who has received a secular minister's healing package, with its processes, procedures, and principles along with its promises, Satan has you deceived if you are expecting long-term secular ministers' healing out of a short-term secular ministers' surface healing solutions and remedies.

Secular ministers, pastors, preachers, teachers, evangelists, prophets, apostles, bishops, elders, and life coaches base their healing faith or the faith in healing on secular world ministry healing solutions and healing remedy theories and reasoning that bring about or produce, prepare, and present a proud and lofty healing attitude, mood, mind-set, mentality, and mode. Their healing faith or their faith in healing is conformed to this world's customs, ideas, information, insights, image, and fashions, and according to the peculiar state of healing and the present state of healing that is in the world; all of which is as much opposed to the spirit of genuine deep-rooted core inner healing.

CHAPTER TWENTY-FOUR

Overpower, Overtake, Overthrow

F OR YOU TO *overpower, overtake, overthrow, overcome,* and disconnect fear, OCD, PTSD, depression, cancer, stress, high blood pressure, migraines, addictions, lust, envy, doubt, worry, unbelief, fear of being raped, molested, battered again, fear of something that has happened to you in the past showing up again, etc., you are going to have to start by

Solution one

a). Admitting you have a fear addiction

You see, the devil is defeating you in areas that you are showing weakness in. He knows that fear is a weakness for you and fear is an addiction for you. Yes, I said it. You have become addicted to fear, OCD, PTSD, depression, cancer, stress, high blood pressure, migraines, addictions, lust, envy, doubt, worry, unbelief, fear of being raped, molested, battered again, fear of something that has happened to you in the past showing up again, etc., so much so that you want to protect them and prevent them from being exposed, revealed, and cast out.

You got addicted the day and the moment you claimed them as your own—you know, when you said, "The doctors said I have," and you fed off that by saying, "I have been dealing with 'my' fear, PTSD, OCD, etc.," issues, matter, or however you said it. You claimed all of what you were diagnosed with as yours, and the moment you did, you were locked into a survivor-survival mode, mind-set, and mentality, and that led you to, without you even knowing it, protect fear and all its friends,

.360.

and then you started protecting them by not yielding, submitting, and surrendering them to being cast out.

The truth be told, fear, OCD, PTSD, depression, cancer, stress, high blood pressure, migraines, addictions, lust, envy, doubt, worry, unbelief, fear of being raped, molested, battered again, fear of something that has happened to you in the past showing up again, etc., have a place of weakness for you. Most people spend all their time working on their strengths or working on the areas and things they are strong at, but they never work on their weakness or the areas and places they are weak at or are showing weakness in. That's the place where the devil is constantly, consistently, and continually defeating you.

To get rid of fear, OCD, PTSD, depression, cancer, stress, high blood pressure, migraines, addictions, lust, envy, doubt, worry, unbelief, fear of being raped, molested, battered again, fear of something that has happened to you in the past showing up again, etc., you are going to have to turn the table on the devil, stop working on your strengths, the areas you are strong in, and start doing something you have never done, and that is to focus all your attention, time, energy, prayers, and efforts on working on your weakness.

You have to *get rid of* that weakness to fear, OCD, PTSD, depression, cancer, stress, high blood pressure, migraines, addictions, lust, envy, doubt, worry, unbelief, fear of being raped, molested, battered again, fear of something that has happened to you in the past showing up again, etc., and not *cover them up* or continue to "band-aid" them or continue to coexist with them and try to get along with them. Not only has fear and all its friends become your *weakness,* became a place of weakness for you, and has become your weak place and point, but also that same fear, along with all its friends, OCD, PTSD, depression, cancer, stress, high blood pressure, migraines, addictions, lust, envy, doubt, worry, unbelief, fear of being raped, molested, battered again, fear of something that has happened to you in the past showing up again, etc., you have become *addicted* to. Stop living in denial!

And just like a drug addict or an alcoholic, you won't and haven't admitted you have a fear, OCD, PTSD, depression, cancer, stress, high blood pressure, migraines, addictions, lust, envy, doubt, worry, unbelief, fear of being raped, molested, battered again, fear of something that has happened to you in the past showing up again, etc., addiction. You can't and won't ever receive help and deliverance from them until you admit you have a fear, etc., addiction and weakness.

Power thought: You can't and won't be able to accept help until you admit you have a fear, OCD, PTSD, depression, cancer, stress, high blood pressure, migraines, addictions, lust, envy, doubt, worry, unbelief, fear of being raped, molested, battered again, fear of something that has happened to you in the past showing up again, etc., addiction and you ask for help. The moment you wholeheartedly do so, that is the moment when you can get the help and healing you need.

Are you of your own free will ready to admit you have a fear addiction or an OCD, PTSD, depression, cancer, stress, high blood pressure, migraines, addictions, lust, envy, doubt, worry, unbelief, fear of being raped, molested, battered again, fear of something that has happened to you in the past showing up again, etc., addiction?

The picture of a fear-addicted person

When you look at someone who is addicted to fear, you are looking at someone who is physically and mentally dependent on an unpleasant emotion caused by the belief that someone or something is dangerous, is likely to cause pain, or is a threat, and he or she is unable to stop talking about it, thinking about it, and taking it without incurring adverse effects. Fear is just like a particular substance that the person is unable to stop taking and he or she can take doses of fear without incurring adverse effects. They are used to being and living in and being tortured and tormented by fear to the point and place where they become numb to its effects and numb to how it will eventually affect them.

Photo 2: The second photo image of a person who is addicted to fear and all its friends is someone who is enthusiastically devoted to being afraid of OCD, PTSD, depression, cancer, stress, high blood pressure, migraines, addictions, lust, envy, doubt, worry, unbelief; being raped, molested, battered again, something that has happened in the past showing up again, or someone or something from their past or present or future as the thing or activity that is likely to be dangerous, painful, or threatening.

Whatever that particular story, thing, or OCD, PTSD, depression, cancer, stress, high blood pressure, migraines, addictions, lust, envy, doubt, worry, unbelief, fear of being raped, molested, battered again, fear of something that has happened to you in the past showing up again, etc., activity is, the person has been tutored, trained, and taught how to struggle, strain through it, and rely on, depend on, and get into a survivor-survival mode, mind-set, and mentality until they make it past the heart and soul of the addiction and they are "coming down" from it.

Addicted to your story

I have a question for you. Are you addicted to your story? Are you so addicted to what has happened to you that has driven, pulled, pushed, persuaded, enticed, seduced, tricked, and forced you to accept, adopt, and adapt to fear, OCD, PTSD, depression, cancer, stress, high blood pressure, migraines, addictions, lust, envy, doubt, worry, unbelief, fear of being raped, molested, battered again, fear of something that has happened to you in the past showing up again, etc., and in doing so, you are and have been applying fear, OCD, PTSD, depression, cancer, stress, high blood pressure, migraines, addictions, lust, envy, doubt, worry, unbelief, fear of being raped, molested, battered again, fear of something that has happened to you in the past showing up again, etc., processes, procedures, and principles?

Are you addicted to telling your fear, OCD, PTSD, etc., story so much so that you are not able to receive deliverance, cleansing, and purging from them so that you can be healed and made whole? A person who is addicted to their story is someone who is physically and mentally dependent on a particular substance, story about their life, and they are unable to stop taking it or talking about it without incurring adverse effects. Whatever it is that you are physically and mentally dependent on and upon you will *protect*. You just can't stop talking about what happened to you as if it is a valued treasure or it is something that you are proud of that has happened to you and in your life; and you have learned when to cry, when to feel sorry for yourself, and how to draw others into your addiction so you can get what you want out of them.

You have been tutored, trained, and taught how to use what has happened to you as a way to get the attention you may or may not have ever had. And you use your story as a way to draw attention to yourself so that you can and will feel like you are important and you matter. The fact is you are important and you do matter, and that is without your tormenting and torturing fear, OCD, PTSD, depression, cancer, stress, high blood pressure, migraines, addictions, lust, envy, doubt, worry, unbelief, fear of being raped, molested, battered again, fear of something that has happened to you in the past showing up again, etc., story.

Are you addicted or enthusiastically devoted to a particular thing, activity, or part of your fear, OCD, PTSD, depression, cancer, stress, high blood pressure, migraines, addictions, lust, envy, doubt, worry, unbelief, fear of being raped, molested, battered again, fear of something that has happened to you in the past showing up again, etc., story? Whatever it is you are enthusiastically devoted to, you will *prevent* from being removed or cast out.

Are you addicted to telling your fear, OCD, PTSD, depression, cancer, stress, high blood pressure, migraines, addictions, lust, envy, doubt, worry, unbelief, fear of being raped, molested, battered again, fear of something that has happened to you in the past showing up again, etc., story? You are because you have gotten addicted to receiving empathy and sympathy and you know you can get and gain special privileges and special considerations and special attention because of your story. You know how to tell your story in a way that it will pull upon the heartstrings of loving, caring, concerned, compassionate, and giving people.

Fear once again has you fearful in thinking and feeling and believing that if you do not have the fear, OCD, PTSD, etc., story you are addicted to telling and holding on to, no one will listen to you, hear you, see you, help you, or pay you any attention, and you will go back to be what you once was and never wanted to be. Just like Linus in the cartoon *Charlie Brown,* you carry your addicted story around like it is a security blanket for you. Linus would cry and scream and throw a temper tantrum when someone took his addicted-to blanket, or he lost it because he felt like he couldn't make it or survive without it. That is the same way and the same type and kind of attachment you feel when it comes to your addicted-to sad story and when it comes to your fear, OCD, PTSD, depression, cancer, stress, high blood pressure, migraines, addictions, lust, envy, doubt, worry, unbelief, fear of being raped, molested, battered again, fear of something that has happened to you in the past showing up again, etc., story.

Are you ready to give up that addicted-to story of yours and admit you have a fear, OCD, PTSD, depression, cancer, stress, high blood pressure, migraines, addictions, lust, envy, doubt, worry, unbelief, fear of being raped, molested, battered again, fear of something that has happened to you in the past showing up again, etc., addiction? Every time you tell one or both of your addicted-to stories, Satan keeps you addicted to struggling, straining, and being connected to an addicted-to survivor-survival mode, mind-set, and mentality. Without you knowing it, Satan sneaks in an addiction to you trying to survive, even when surviving is not an issue, and just being open and honest and telling the truth and facing reality is the issue at hand.

Are you someone who is addicted to rejecting, resisting, refusing, rebuking, and refuting self-truth and self-reality information, instructions, ideas, images, etc.? This is where you must start if you want to be made and set free; you have to be willing to admit you have a fear, OCD, PTSD, depression, cancer, stress, high blood pressure, migraines, addictions, lust, envy, doubt, worry, unbelief, fear of being raped, molested, battered again, fear of something that has happened to you in the past showing up again, etc., addiction.

Practice the principle: You have to also be willing and sincere when you admit you have a fear, etc., addiction. It must come from your heart. Let's do it. Repeat after me:

- "Jesus, I, of my own free will, admit that I have a fear, (name whatever else you want to) addiction, and

- today, of my own free will, I have decided that I will no longer be addicted to my fear (name whatever else you want to) addiction.
- Jesus, please take the taste, desire, thought, feeling, emotions, and the urges, tendencies, inclinations, intuitions, impulsiveness, and instincts and everything that connects me to me being addicted to fear (name whatever else you want to).
- I ask in Jesus's name, I receive my freedom from fear (name whatever else you want to) addiction, and I thank you for doing so."

God has heard your heartfelt sincere prayer, and you have now opened the door for God to do the next things for you. It is important that you be honest with (1) God first and then be honest with (2) yourself and, finally, be honest with (3) others, those who genuinely love and support you and believe in you. The next thing you are going to have to do is this:

Solution two

b). Ask God to strengthen you where there has been fear weakness/ weakness to fear

"Three times I pleaded with the Lord to take it away from me. But he said to me, "My grace is sufficient for you, for my power is made perfect in weakness." Therefore I will boast all the more gladly about my weaknesses, so that Christ's power may rest on me" (2 Cor. 12:8–9).

There is no need for you to get into a battle and a war with fear, OCD, PTSD, depression, cancer, stress, high blood pressure, migraines, addictions, lust, envy, doubt, worry, unbelief, fear of being raped, molested, battered again, fear of something that has happened to you in the past showing up again, etc. God has given you power and authority over all of them.

Being addicted

As I stated earlier, when a person has an addiction or he or she addicted to fear, he or she is physically and mentally dependent on an unpleasant emotion caused by the belief or the thought that someone or something from the past or present, and OCD, PTSD, depression, cancer, stress, high blood pressure, migraines, addictions, lust, envy, doubt, worry, unbelief, fear of being raped, molested, battered again, fear of something that has happened to you in the past showing up again, etc., is dangerous, likely to cause pain, or a threat, and you are unable to stop talking about it, thinking about it, and taking it without incurring adverse effects.

The second thing about being addicted to fear is you can and will, at some place, point, and time, end up being enthusiastically devoted to being afraid of someone or something from your past, present, or future as likely to be dangerous, painful, or threatening, and instead of you trying to stop being fearful and stop having fearful feelings, emotions, desires, urges, tendencies, inclinations, intuitions, impulses, and instincts, you basically start to, out of being fearful, mentally plan and prepare and position yourself for whatever particular fearful thing or fearful activity or fearful condition that is needed for whatever particular fearful substance, situation, circumstances, and confrontations that could show up.

Fear weakness factors

When you have a weakness and that weakness is fear or for fear what that will look like, you will end up with a mind, frame of mind, state of mind, mental condition, and mental state of being that is in the state or condition of lacking the strength you will need to reject, resist, refuse, rebuke, or refute an unpleasant emotion that's caused by the belief that someone or something past and old, present or in the future is dangerous, is likely to cause pain, or is likely to cause a threat. Your *mind, frame of mind, state of mind, mental condition, and mental state of being* will not have the strength to refute arguments and theories and reasoning and lofty things and proud things that set itself up against you that oppose you and want to bring you hurt, harm, and danger or want to steal and then kill and then destroy your faith, hope, belief, confidence, self-esteem, self-will, self-effort, will to win, and ability to try for the first time or try again.

You don't have the strength within yourself to fight against fear-driven and motivated arguments, fear-driven and motivated theories, fear-driven and motivated reasoning, fear-driven and motivated tactical lofty things, and fear-driven and motivated proud things. And your mind, frame of mind, state of mind, mental condition, and mental state of being are not stable, secure, solid, safe enough; they are not strong enough to stand up against an unpleasant emotion caused by the belief that someone or something is dangerous, likely to cause pain, or a threat, and against OCD, PTSD, depression, cancer, stress, high blood pressure, migraines, addictions, lust, envy, doubt, worry, unbelief, fear of being raped, molested, battered again, fear of dying, fear of something that has happened to you in the past showing up again, etc.; all of which are satanic and demonic wiles, trickeries, schemes, devices, deceptions, delusions, distorted images, etc., and they are also satanic and demonic fearful strategies and deceits that he tries to suggest and influence you into opening up your mind, frame of mind, state of mind, mental condition, state of mind, thoughts, train of thought, thinking, and way of thinking to receiving them.

The second thing that grows, develops, and matures out of a weakness to fear or out of a fear weakness is you will become, be, and end up being a person who will be dominated, manipulated, and controlled by the thoughts, train of thought, thinking, and way of thinking that you have a quality or feature regarded as a disadvantage or fault when it comes to being afraid of someone, something, OCD, PTSD, depression, cancer, stress, high blood pressure, migraines, addictions, lust, envy, doubt, worry, unbelief, fear of being raped, molested, battered again, fear of something that has happened to you in the past showing up again, etc., as likely to be dangerous, painful, or threatening and will happen again.

Your *thoughts, train of thought, thinking, and way of thinking* will lead you to believe, think, or feel that if you touch or start challenging, confronting, trying to conquer and you force an unpleasant emotion caused by the belief that someone or something from your past, present, or future is dangerous, it is likely to cause pain; or a threat when being forced to change, it will become worse and do more personal and private damage and destruction. What you have to know is when you think, feel, or believe like that, you are and will be making any and all choices and decisions out of an unpleasant emotion caused by the belief that someone or something is dangerous, likely to cause pain, or a threat mode, mind-set, and mentality.

The final thing that happens when you have a fear weakness or a weakness to and for fear is you will suddenly and immediately be drawn, driven, pulled, pushed, persuaded, easily tricked, enticed, seduced, led, and forced into an attraction and into a relationship with a person that is someone whom you are unable to resist, or you like excessively someone that you have a mixed feeling of dread and reverence for and you get a feeling of anxiety concerning the outcome of something or anything he or she says and does, the choices and decisions he or she makes, and the way he or she handles things, matters, circumstances, situations, and confrontations. You know what he or she is saying and doing can and will jeopardize and put in harm's ways the safety and well-being of others and someone you really love and care for.

You are unable to resist or you like excessively someone that you know, sense, feel, and even believe he or she is making choices and decisions and what he or she is thinking, feeling, contemplating, and wanting to do is something that has the likelihood of something unwelcome happening. And no matter how hard you try to get away from that person you can't because they have somehow got you into a *mode, mind-set and into a mentality* where you like them so much that you can't resist them and you are locked into a unpleasant emotion caused by the belief that the person is dangerous, is likely to cause you pain, or they are a threat to yourself and to those you love and care about. You are locked into, connected to, linked to and you are yoked, in bondage to, bound and limited by, in a stronghold and a slave to that kind of twisted, torturing and tormenting reverential *mind-set, mentality and mode.*

These are your fear factor weaknesses, and you have been tutored, trained, and taught by fear, OCD, PTSD, depression, cancer, stress, high blood pressure, migraines, addictions, lust, envy, doubt, worry, unbelief, fear of being raped, molested, battered again, fear of something that has happened to you in the past showing up again, etc., to accept them, adopt them, adapt to them, and apply them to all areas of your life. You demonstrate you have been tutored, trained, taught, and you have learned what they want you to do and say every time you yield, submit, surrender, and practice reverencing and respecting them, reacting to them, having and demonstrating reactionary responses to them, and every time you give way to and give place to fearful urges, fearful tendencies, fearful inclinations, fearful intuitions, fearful impulsiveness, and fearful instincts.

Every time you are functioning and flowing in and out of and you are following fear weaknesses or out of and following a weakness to fear, you are working in cahoots with fear factor weaknesses. And every time you do so, you are giving your strength, the strength you will need to overpower, overthrow, and overtake them to fear and to all its friends. You are also giving your strength to fear-filled feelings, fear-filled emotions, and fear-filled desires. Having, heeding, and entertaining fear-filled desires will draw, drive, pull, push, persuade, force, trick, trap, entice, entangle, and entrap you into "what looks like" is the right way to get out from under the grips of fear, OCD, PTSD, etc.

Don't give in to those "what looks like" moments because they are dangerous, deadly, damaging, and self-destructive. You can't and won't ever receive help and deliverance from fear weakness or weakness to fear until you ask for the strength to overpower, overtake, and overthrow them. The strength you will need is not your strength but a strength that is stronger than your strength, that is more solid, safe, secure, and more sound than your strength is and will ever be. Having a weakness to fear is just like a person who has a sweet tooth. And they will get up at any time of day or night, or they will do crazy and unusual things just to satisfy that sweet tooth urge. It doesn't matter if eating too much sweets will make them sick or bring serious hurt, harm, and danger to them; they don't care, and they don't think about the risk involved. Their whole mode, mind-set, and mentality are locked into the thought, train of thought, thinking, and way of thinking of they just have to have something sweet and they go after it.

Fear facts

Please understand that fear is not your friend; it is you foe, your enemy, and it is a trespassing spirit that loves to violate you and degrade, humiliate, scare, bully, and badger you. It is also a spirit that loves to "punk you" and watch you cringe and crawl up into a corner or watch you ball up in a knot and shake and tremble and cry and have fear convulsions and do whatever else you do. Every time you do so, fear and all its friends, OCD, PTSD, depression, cancer, stress, high blood pressure, migraines, addictions, lust, envy, doubt, worry, unbelief, fear of being raped, molested, battered again, fear of something that has happened to you in the past showing up again, etc., all stand around and applaud their success. They high-five one another, and they move around in the darkness, bragging on what they had done to you and bragging on how they were able to torture and torment you.

Just like you would be proud of something that you have accomplished, achieved, acquired, or accumulated, and just like you would tell others about your prosperity, successes, and how you were productive, you need to see that nasty demon spirit called fear, OCD, PTSD, depression, cancer, stress, high blood pressure, migraines, addictions, lust, envy, doubt, worry, unbelief, fear of being raped, molested, battered again, fear of something that has happened to you in the past showing up again, etc., doing the same thing. They are proud of how they beat up on your "faith," your mind, your heart, your dreams, hopes, and desires, and your God-given "will to win." Fear loves to brag on how it punked your faith and how you stood back watched it do it over and over again and time after time, and you did absolutely *nothing* to prevent it or prepare yourself to fight against it.

THE SURVIVORS MODE

Let me tell you what fear is

Fear is a spirit, and it is not a physical opponent, something that you can physically see or touch. It is a spirit that thrives on ruling in darkness, and it thrives and feeds on truth and facts about yourself and your life that you choose to disregard or pretend is not real; truths and realities that you deny, etc. It thrives and feeds off dark places, such as family-inherited generational curses that you choose to ignore. It feeds off everything that you choose, of your own free will, not to challenge, confront, conquer, and change that is bad, wrong, negative, ugly, fowl, etc. Fear thrives and feeds off whatever it is you are running from, hiding from, don't want to look at, face up to, etc., those dark, hidden, vicious cycle areas that keep causing, creating the atmosphere for, and contributing to you falling and failing at that keep you flawed and producing the wrong kind of character, conduct, conversation, communication, personality, integrity, intellect, behavior, behavior pattern, etc., fruits.

Fear loves ruling over, thrives, and loves having power and authority over some part of you, your life, where there is darkness or where there is some part of you and your life that is error plagued and is weak that you have not worked on, dealt with, you keep avoiding, protecting, and ignoring. Fear is a "pimp" spirit, which means it loves to use any part of you that it can for its own profit and personal gain. And the funny thing is you allow that spirit to use any part of you, and you give it the right, power, and authority to prostitute some parts of or all of you. A pimp cannot be a pimp if he cannot do what a pimp does unless he has someone who is weak and vulnerable that he can dominate, manipulate, control, rule over, and get into their mind and convince them of something that is not true about themselves, and that is totally the contrary to what the person may think and feel when it comes to themselves. That pimp has to get into that person's head, mind, etc., and that person whose head or mind he has found his way into has to "let" that pimp and his pimp processes, pimp procedures, and pimp principles mess with his or her head. It is a free will choice and decision that the prostitute makes because of some weakness and dark areas from their childhood, teenhood, or adulthood that are bad, negative, wrong, ugly that they have not been challenged, confronted, conquered, and changed. It can be a past and old or present bad, wrong, negative, ugly circumstance, situation, confrontation, matter, and moment in his or her life that the person doesn't want to address.

The same applies to fear. It can only pimp and prostitute some part of you that you are weak to and you refuse, reject, and resist dealing with, cleaning up, and releasing. Fear can only pimp and prostitute areas in you and areas in your life that have to do with where you, of your own free will, refute self-truth and self-reality information, insights, instructions, ideas, and images. Anything that is fear-filled arguments, theories, reasoning, and a proud and lofty fear messages and anything that set itself up against the true knowledge of God fear are trying to get you to accept them.

You are, of your own free will, allowing fear, OCD, PTSD, depression, cancer, stress, high blood pressure, migraines, addictions, lust, envy, doubt, worry, unbelief, fear of being raped, molested, battered again, fear of something that has happened to you in the past showing up again, etc., to pimp you and prostitute the "real" you that is scared and afraid for its personal, private, and public gain. You are, of your own free will, allowing fear to prostitute your fear-filled feelings, fear-filled emotions, and fear-filled desires. Every time you give into fear, OCD, PTSD, depression, cancer, stress, high blood pressure, migraines, addictions, lust, envy, doubt, worry, unbelief, fear of being raped, molested, battered again, fear of something that has happened to you in the past showing up again, etc., and you allow them to do whatever it is that they do to you, what's really happening is you are giving them the right to prostitute and use you in anyway fear deems necessary.

Fear, OCD, PTSD, depression, cancer, stress, high blood pressure, migraines, addictions, lust, envy, doubt, worry, unbelief, fear of being raped, molested, battered again, fear of something that has happened to you in the past showing up again, etc., were able to get into your head, mind, mental capabilities and abilities, thoughts, train of thought, thinking, and way of thinking, and now you have to get it out. The same way you let it in, you are going to have to get it out, and that is

THE SURVIVORS MODE
373

of your "own free will." Fear didn't force itself into your head, and it didn't make you open up your mind and accept it. All of what happened to bring you into being fearful, Satan used something or someone to initiate the fear factor contact, and you either not knowing what it was the person was saying or doing or you being "childhood," teenhood, and even adulthood weak and vulnerable to something you did or didn't get, you opened yourself willingly and voluntarily up to what fear was presenting.

Let's stay on the "truth path and let's keep the different perspective" point of view. Fear, OCD, PTSD, depression, cancer, stress, high blood pressure, migraines, addictions, lust, envy, doubt, worry, unbelief, fear of being raped, molested, battered again, fear of something that has happened to you in the past showing up again, etc., cannot, will not and did not force themselves upon you and into your head, mind, etc. Fear and all its friends can only (1) suggest and (2) influence you into accepting, adopting, adapting to, and applying its processes, procedures, and principles. The ultimate choice and decision as to whether to accept them or reject, resist, refuse, rebuke, and refute them and their arguments, theories, reasoning, thoughts, and purposes was and still is yours.

Fear is a principality spirit, which means it can dominate, control, manipulate, and rule however it chooses to, and it has powers and it is a world force of this present darkness, and it is a spiritual *force* that is wicked, and it hides in the heavenly (supernatural) *places*. OCD, PTSD, depression, cancer, stress, high blood pressure, migraines, addictions, lust, envy, doubt, worry, unbelief, fear of being raped, molested, battered again, fear of something that has happened to you in the past showing up again, fears of all kinds, etc., are fears imps or foot soldiers. They are carrying out fear's orders in the earth realm and in your life. Don't let them continue to reign and rule over any part of you. When a spirit such as fear is a principality, what that states or signifies is it has a state, territory, area of your life that is ruled by a prince; satanic fear is a demonic prince (the Bible says Satan is the prince of the power of the air, Eph. 2:2).

Fear usually has a relatively small state (area of your life) or a state (area of your life) that falls within a larger state (area of your life) such as an empire. When we say satanic and demonic fear is a principality, what we are describing is the position or authority of a prince or chief ruler; its sovereignty; its supreme power.

Back to the fear facts

Now, let me get deeper into what I have to tell you. Not only is fear not your friend, but also it is and has become a weakness for you. Anytime you accept, adopt, adapt to, and apply the vicious cycled processes, procedures, and principles of fear, or something else, you are willingly or unwillingly, knowingly or unknowingly doing the following:

A. Accepting that something, that fear, as your quality or feature that prevents you from being effective or useful.

B. Every time you feed into your fear and give it what it wants and you don't challenge, confront, conquer, and change it, you are basically stating that it, fear, is something that you like so much that you are often unable to resist it.

C. Giving the person who tutored, trained, and taught you that fear is a "standing ovation" and you are thanking them for taking the time out of their "dark" schedule to help you learn how to be fearful, fear driven, and motivated, you are giving them the glory, honor, and praise for doing so.

D. Every time you run and hide in fear, cringe, are jumpy, and you shake, tremble, and everything else you do out of fear, you are honoring and reverencing the person who tutored, trained, and taught you what fear is and how you are to react to it.

E. Every time you are so scared of "what might or can or could happen" that hasn't and in all actuality wouldn't happen, etc., you are honoring the moment when the first person that tutored, trained, and taught you how to live in fear, when to live in fear, why you should live in fear, where you should live in fear, you are not only honoring that moment, but you are engaging in a dedicated, committed remembrance ceremony of that moment. Just like a person who goes religiously to a cemetery to remember his or her gone past and old loved ones, that is what you are doing.

F. When you are so frightened and you procrastinate, hesitate, question, second-guess, and stay halt between opinions because you are so frightened, you have learned from your "fear, OCD, PTSD, depression, addiction, etc., " tutor, teacher, and trainer" how, when, where to, and the reasons why you should deliver and demonstrate a fear reaction and fear reactionary response, fearful urges, tendencies, inclinations, intuitions, impulses, impulsiveness, and instincts you are honoring and "bowing down" to that person in deep humility and with a deep love for them doing so.

G. For every second, minute, hour of the day, and for every week, month, and year you, of your own free will, allow yourself to stay connected to, linked to, tied to, yoked to, in bondage to, in a stronghold to, bound and limited to and because of, on high alert because of, and a slave to fear urges, tendencies, inclinations, intuitions, impulsiveness, and instincts, you are giving *your* strength to fear and you are making it strong and you are making it stronger than your faith.

H. You are making your faith a subordinate to your fear, and you are taking and making the God of your faith and the God who has and is still protecting and providing for you a second-class subordinate to the God of your fear.

I. Anything that you treat as a subordinate is something or someone you treat or regard as lesser importance than something else. Each time you give in to fear and say and do what it wants you to, you are saying with your fearful acts, actions, deeds, your fearful reactions and reactionary responses, and with your fear-driven and motivated urges, tendencies, inclinations, intuitions, impulses, instincts, choices and decisions, etc., your *faith* is under the control and the authority of fear, OCD, PTSD, depression, cancer, stress, high blood pressure, migraines, addictions, lust, envy, doubt, worry, unbelief, fear of being raped, molested, battered again, fear of something that has happened to you in the past showing up again, etc.

J. When you try to coexist, get along with, accept, try to be at peace with, live with fear with all its friends, and make fear and faith equal partners with you and give them ample quality or quantity time, not only are you saying and you are stating and validating you believe that your faith is weak and beggarly and it is lower in rank than your fear, but you also, through your faithless actions and through your fearful actions, render your faith that is powerful; you render and make it powerless. Is that what you want to do?

K. Fear is a bully and badgering spirit, and as long as you let it continue to rule over you and take what belongs to you from you it, with all its friends, you know them, OCD, PTSD, depression, cancer, stress, high blood pressure, migraines, addictions, lust, envy, doubt, worry, unbelief, fear of being raped, molested, battered again, fear of something that has happened to you in the past showing up again, etc., they will continue to take from you.

L. Not only is fear a bullying and badgering spirit, but also what you have to know is it cannot and will not be successful with its tactical wiles, trickeries, schemes, devices, deceptions, delusions, distorted view points, tricks, traps, enticing, entanglements, entrapments, etc., without the willing cooperation of your thoughts, train of thought, thinking, way of thinking, and your urges, tendencies, inclinations, intuitions, impulsiveness, and instincts.

M. They have to willingly cooperate for fear, OCD, PTSD, depression, cancer, stress, high blood pressure, migraines, addictions, lust, envy, doubt, worry, unbelief, fear of being raped, molested, battered again, fear of something that has happened to you in the past showing up again, fears of any kind and to any degree, etc., to accomplish their mission, goal, and purpose.

N. Fear is a "shadow spirit," which means it is not a living human being. It is a "spirit" that must have a body to live in and work through. Anything that is a shadow is of something or that exists as a shadow is something that is a dark area or shape produced by a body coming between rays of light and a surface. Anything that is the shadow of something is something that is not really there; it just gives off the appearance of it being there. You take away its rays of light, its reflection, or you take away its reference to proximity, ominous oppressiveness, or sadness and gloom, and you have taken away its mystique, madness, and mystical magic. Fear is a shadow, and it is a shadow sprit. It can only exist where it can be reflected onto, into, and revealed in and through. You are running and hiding from something that is afraid to and cannot and will not manifest itself in a physical form and manifest itself in who and what it is so that you can physically challenge it and fight it. Fear is a shadow spirit!

What I want you to know and clearly understand is you can bring shame to that shadow spirit, and you have the right, power, and authority to embarrass it. You do so by allowing and bringing the light of God-sent truth and reality to the forefront and let it shine and expose the "shadow" of death that fear tries to cast and project. You can fight fear, and you can flee fear not by physical means and with physical or canal weapons and words.

You do so by standing in who God says you are, and staying in, functioning, and flowing in and out of what God says you can do, and striking, damaging, and destroying every fear tactic with the weapons of faith. I want you to know and understand, be clear on this, fear cannot do no more and not less than what you "willingly" allow it to say and do. My point is you have control over fear, and it does not have control over you. Fear, OCD, PTSD, depression, cancer, stress, high blood pressure, migraines, addictions, lust, envy, doubt, worry, unbelief, fear of being raped, molested, battered again, fear of something that has happened to you in the past showing up in your present or future are something you have control over.

Let's do it

It's time for you to actively engage in some corrective acts, actions, and deeds. It is time for you to get rid of your weakness to fear or get rid of your fear weakness. Paul, in 2 Corinthians 12:8–9, had a weakness just like you have a fear weakness or a weakness to fear; his weakness wasn't the same as yours, but it was still a weakness. God didn't take his weakness away, but He did something that I found was so wonderful and unique and is just like God. He gave Paul something that was even greater and more rewarding and fulfilling than Paul's request. God gave Paul something he didn't even know he didn't have and he had the rights to.

Paul probably felt powerless over his weakness just like you feel and have felt, and he probably got tired of dealing with it and having his weakness take from him what he knew, felt, and believed he had a right to, and that was the right to live his life to the fullest until it would overflow in richness and in abundance, increase, and overflow. God could have pampered Paul and taken that weakness away, but God knew Paul needed to know he had access to something even greater and more powerful than he could have and use every day of his life and he could use and apply to whatever it was he would be faced with in the present and in his future. Let me say something right here. You have not been able to defeat and destroy fear, OCD, PTSD, depression, cancer, stress, high blood pressure, migraines, addictions, lust, envy, doubt, worry, unbelief, fear of being raped, molested, battered again, fear of something that has happened to you in the past showing up in your present or future is something you have control over, etc., and everything else not only from your past but also what could, can, or will show up in your present and future. God was not about to give Paul a "temporary fix" for something that quite possibly could have been a long-term problem, battle, war, or issue, matter, circumstance, situation, or confrontation. Paul was human just like we are human, and we will make mistakes and open ourselves up to some things that we don't want to and we are not trying to willingly do. God delivers permanent solutions to part-time, full-time, seasonal, temporary, or permanent past, present, and future problems, flashbacks, setups, matters, and moments.

God wanted Paul to know he had access to something that was even greater, and he wanted Paul to know it was and would always be available to him whenever he needed and wanted it. Ignorance and having a lack of knowledge and truth are what is keeping you living in fear and is keeping you living with OCD, PTSD, depression, cancer, stress, high blood pressure, migraines, addictions, lust, envy, doubt, worry, unbelief, fear of being raped, molested, battered again, fear of something that has happened to you in the past showing up in your present or future is something you have control over, etc. If God had not shown or revealed to Paul what he had always had access to, God would have had to over and over help Paul with his weakness.

That is not something God wants to do. He wants to empower you to defeat your weakness. He wants to empower you to be an armed and dangerous "weakness weapon." Check out the conversation God had with Paul and Paul had with God:

Paul: *Concerning this I implored the Lord three times that it might leave me.*

God: *And He has said to me, "My grace is sufficient for you, for power is perfected in weakness."*

Paul: *Most gladly, therefore, I will rather boast about my weaknesses, so that the power of Christ may dwell in me . . . (2 Cor. 12:8–9).*

God wasn't going to nor did he ever have endless conversations with Paul concerning his weakness, nor did they enter into debates and negotiations concerning them. God wasn't going to beg and plead with Paul to give up his weakness, and God would not consistently babysit Paul and his weakness because God knew that would be a never-ending occurrence, and He knew if it wouldn't be the weakness he had, it would be something else because he, just like you and me, is human, and we are not perfect in the human and fleshly sense.

God showed Paul he had a permanent solution to any and all his past, present, and future weaknesses, and that was "His strength, power-made perfect in weaknesses." That is what you do not need, and that is some temporary secular ministers, secular healers, secular world solution that is surface and temporary fix. You need a permanent "solution," not a "fix" to what has been and will and could quite possibly become, be, and end up being a continuous, constant, and consistent permanent, past, present, and future weakness.

Paul asked God to remove it, his weakness, and God didn't do that, but He gave Paul a vision of what his life could and would be like, and He showed Paul he needed something greater. Paul accepted what God had said to him, and he didn't reject, refuse, resist, rebuke, refute, try to argue and wrestle with God over them, and make all kinds of excuses for not accepting; nor did he try to justify why he couldn't and wouldn't accept what God's permanent solution was. He didn't refute the answer, information, and instructions God gave them; instead, he opened up his heart and mind to what God was saying even though he didn't know what it all meant and he didn't know what would be involved in the process and procedure. That wasn't his concern, and neither should it be yours.

Whatever it is that you have to give up, fear, with all its friends, is where your focus should be and not what's going to happen to them and you. Stop trying to analyze and be analytical about this process. You don't have to analyze and try to figure out what God is saying what God is going to do, how He is going to do it, what's going to happen, what you are going to have to give up, and what will you have to go through. I can tell you that whatever God does to get rid of your fear, OCD, PTSD, depression, cancer, stress, high blood pressure, migraines, addictions, lust, envy, doubt, worry, unbelief, fear of being raped, molested, battered again, fear of something that has happened to you in the past showing up in your present or future is something you have control over, etc., can and will and should be all right with you.

THE SURVIVORS MODE

Welcome to the exchange

I can tell you it will be painless, and you will feel a whole lot better than you ever have since the day fear and all its friends took over your life. Don't analyze; just accept and be delivered, cleansed, purged, healed, and made whole. Do what Paul did—open up your heart and mind and accept, adopt, adapt to, apply, and receive what God is about to give you in exchange for what you are about to give up, which is fear. This is your time and this is your moment. Don't let this moment pass you by.

I want to welcome you to the exchange. Here's how the exchange work. Everything you give God, He will give you something in return. For example, you give God your pain, and He will give you peace; give Him your hurt, and He will give you happiness; give God your fears, and He will give you His full-of-living powered faith; and give Him anything and everything, OCD, PTSD, depression, cancer, stress, high blood pressure, migraines, addictions, lust, envy, doubt, worry, unbelief, fear of being raped, molested, battered again, fear of something that has happened to you in the past showing up in your present or future is something you have control over, etc., and He will give deliver you from all of them, cleanse you, purge you, heal you, and make you ever wit whole.

Give God an open heart and an open mind and a willingness to receive and accept, and He will make and set you free indeed. Just remember when you enter into the exchange zone or the place of exchange with God, remember and never forget "anything you give to God, He will give you something in exchange." It's free, and you don't have to beg, plead, tarry, or go through any unnecessary, humiliating, shameful, etc., changes and acts. Just ask Him to do it, and He will. That is what you are going to have to do, and that is exactly what you are going to do, and that is what I'm going to help you do.

Practice the principle: Open up your heart and be sincere when you say or ask the following:

o   Jesus, I come to You right now and I lay my fear weakness before You.

o   I know You know what they are and where they came from and how they ended up in my life.

o   I don't want any kind of fear, and I don't want those fear weakness. I don't want to have a weakness for fear (name everything else).

o   I ask You to take my weakness to fear and give me Your strength made perfect in my weakness to fear (name everything else).

o   Give me Your strength in my weakness so that my weakness to fear will turn into a place of strength, power, and authority over fear.

o   I ask for Your strength that will help me resist, reject, refuse, and refute any and all weaknesses I have had to fear and for fear in Jesus's name.

o   I release walking in my strength, and I receive and release myself to walk in your strength so that I can overpower, overtake, overthrow, and overcome my weakness to fear (name everything else) in Jesus's name.

o   Fear and any weakness to fear, get out of my life. I will not serve you anymore in Jesus's name.

Now, rejoice and thank Him and praise Him and worship Him for answering your prayer.

Moving forward to the next step

Now that you have accepted that solution and it is now a part of you, use any of the solutions I am giving you as often as you need them. There are no boundaries and limitations and time frames attached to them. When the devil tries to tell you they didn't work and there isn't anything happening and he tries to tell you nothing has changed with you and you are the same, know that he is a *liar,* and all he can do is lie to you. His lying to you is a reverse psychological trick and deception. Things are exactly the opposite of what he is saying. He is a liar, and that is all that he can do (John 8:44). The devil *can't and won't be able to tell the truth!*

Important information: The way to release, set yourself in agreement with, and put into motion and put into effect the first two solutions, you can do so by way of making them a daily part of your faith confession. Make solution one and solution two a daily part of your day and life by confessing or reciting them as often as you may need to do so. You can even go as far as making out a confession sheet for yourself and begin to speak positive and good things over yourself, into your life and day, and confess then daily.

While you are assaulting, attacking, and assassinating fear, OCD, PTSD, depression, cancer, stress, high blood pressure, migraines, addictions, lust, envy, doubt, worry, unbelief, fear of being raped, molested, battered again, fear of something that has happened to you in the past that was traumatic, troubling, and tragic showing up in your present or future is something you have control over, etc., by putting solutions one and solutions two into motion and putting them into effect in your life and day, you must stay focused on doing the following:

c) gain and keep a tight grip on your *power of choice,* and you will need to

d) be in and stay in control over your self-will and not allow them both to be seized and under control of fear filled urges, tendencies, inclinations, intuitions, impulsiveness, and instincts.

In the flow with fear

With that being said, I want you to know that the playmates for fear and its best friends are your feelings and emotions and desires. The first place or target fear strikes or hits is your feelings, emotions, and desires because he knows they are not your best friends even though you treat them as though they are.

Once fear is able to make an impressionable hit or dent into your feelings, emotions, and desires, the next leaving you tormented, tortured, dominated, manipulated, controlled, and driven by fear-filled feelings, fear-filled emotions, and fear-filled desires, the next target is your sudden and immediate reactions, responses, and reactionary responses. Once a successful hit has been made and you are running around out of control, you are making or you are demonstrating fearful reactions or fear reactionary responses without thinking you are ready for fear's next move.

After those two have felt the blunt force trauma and wrath of fear, the next target for fear is to assault, attack your urges, tendencies, inclinations, intuitions, impulsiveness, and instincts, and get them excited and in control. The result is your fear-filled feelings, your fear-filled emotions, and your fear-filled desires will have and get you quickly over into releasing uncontrollable fear-filled reactions and into releasing fear-filled reactionary responses and heavily being led into and led by fear-filled urges, fear-filled tendencies, fear-filled inclinations, fear-filled intuitions, fear-filled impulsiveness, and fear-filled instincts.

What I just described will end up becoming and being your everyday behavior pattern for every circumstance, situation, confrontation, or matter, be those positive or negative. That pattern after repeated practice will end up being your every day survivor-survival mode pattern of behavior and conduct. Your mind, mind-set, and mentality will lock it in as your fear mode.

As I stated before, fear's best friends are your feelings, emotions, and desires, and the only way to disconnect fear from your feelings, emotions, and desires and the only way to eliminate fear making a connection with your reactions, reactionary responses, and the only way to make sure fear does not get linked and tied to your urges, tendencies, inclinations, intuitions, impulsiveness, and instincts is to arm yourself with the following information and knowledge:

THE SURVIVORS MODE

Solution three

(1). "And having disarmed the powers and authorities, he made a public spectacle of them, triumphing over them by the cross" (Col. 2:15). Jesus, on your behalf, disarmed fear, and He disarmed the power that fear has, and He disarmed the authority fear can have over your life. After doing that, He went even further on your behalf. Jesus made a public spectacle of fear, OCD, PTSD, depression, cancer, stress, high blood pressure, migraines, addictions, lust, envy, doubt, worry, unbelief, fear of being raped, molested, battered again, etc. He then triumphed over all of them and everything else that could and would bring you fear by the cross or by dying on the cross for you.

- ❖ ***Power exercise-****say this out loud and mean it:* "Fear, Jesus disarmed you."
- ❖ Jesus disarmed the power you have had over my life, OCD, PTSD, depression, cancer, stress, high blood pressure, migraines, addictions, lust, envy, doubt, worry, unbelief, fear of being raped, molested, battered again, etc.
- ❖ Jesus disarmed the authority you have had over me and over my life, fear, OCD, PTSD, depression, cancer, stress, high blood pressure, migraines, addictions, lust, envy, doubt, worry, unbelief, fear of being raped, molested, battered again, etc.
- ❖ Jesus made a public spectacle of you, fear, OCD, PTSD, depression, cancer, stress, high blood pressure, migraines, addictions, lust, envy, doubt, worry, unbelief, fear of being raped, molested, battered again, etc.
- ❖ Jesus triumphed over you, fear, OCD, PTSD, depression, cancer, stress, high blood pressure, migraines, addictions, lust, envy, doubt, worry, unbelief, fear of being raped, molested, battered again, etc.
- ❖ Jesus did all this for me, and I receive His gift and because of what Jesus has already done to you on my behalf, fear, OCD, PTSD, depression, cancer, stress, high blood pressure, migraines, addictions, lust, envy, doubt, worry, unbelief, fear of

being raped, molested, battered again, etc. (call by name what you are fearful of).

❖ I command you to get out of my life *in Jesus's name.* You are a trespasser and a violator. I won't serve you, and I won't bow down to you anymore, and I loose and release my faith to conquer you, fear, OCD, PTSD, depression, cancer, stress, high blood pressure, migraines, addictions, lust, envy, doubt, worry, unbelief, fear of being raped, molested, battered again, etc.

That felt really "good," didn't it? Make this your everyday confession and do it as often as you need. Remember not only is the devil afraid you will wake up and begin to take authority over him and you will realize he is afraid of you, but you will also realize Satan and fear are *afraid of your faith.*

Solution four

(2). "The weapons we fight with are not the weapons of the world. On the contrary, they have divine power to demolish strongholds. We demolish arguments and every pretension that sets itself up against the knowledge of God, and we take captive every thought to make it obedient to Christ" (2 Cor. 10:4–5). The only way you will be able to disconnect yourself from fear and all its friends and the only way you can and will be able to defeat them is through God's word and through the releasing of your faith.

The first thing this particular scriptural text tells us is the secular world ministers, secular world healings, and secular healings do not get to the core root of what is causing you to be tormented and tortured by fear. The reason is their methods and methodologies are carnal physical weapons of flesh and blood that cannot and will not have any power or authority over demonic spirits. You can't fight and win a spiritual battle with carnal means. It just won't happen and you will never win. Fear, OCD, PTSD, depression, cancer, stress, high blood pressure, migraines, addictions, lust, envy, doubt, worry, unbelief, fear of being raped, molested, battered again, etc., are spirits that you can't physically see. What we see are the aftereffects of it and what we see if how they affect people.

With that being said, we are also told in verse 5 that we have the power and the authority and the right to challenge, confront, conquer, change, and right to

    a. refute fear, fear arguments and fear theories and fear reasoning and every proud and lofty fearful thing that sets itself against the true knowledge of faith and truth. And we have the power and the authority and the right to

    b. lead every fearful thought and fearful purpose away captive into the obedience of Christ, the Messiah, the Anointed One.

When you refute something, you prove (a statement or theory) to be wrong or false and you disprove it. Yes, you have the right to prove fear, OCD, PTSD, depression, cancer, stress, high blood pressure, migraines, addictions, lust, envy, doubt, worry, unbelief, fear of being raped, molested, battered again, and repeated acts, actions and deeds, etc., do not belong in your life and they do not have a right to dominate, manipulate, and control you. They do not have a right to just show up in your life and day whenever they want to.

You have a right to prove fear, OCD, PTSD, depression, cancer, stress, addictions, high blood pressure, migraines, addictions, lust, envy, doubt, worry, unbelief, fear of being raped, molested, battered again, repeated acts, actions, and deeds, etc., showing up and happening to you again to be wrong or false. You have a right and the authority to disprove what the doctors have diagnosed as the reason(s) why you will always need fear, OCD, PTSD, depression, cancer, stress, high blood pressure, migraines, addictions, lust, envy, doubt, worry, unbelief, fear of being raped, molested, battered again, etc., drugs and medications and treatment for the rest of your life.

Jesus died on the cross, defeated death, hell, fear, OCD, PTSD, depression, cancer, stress, high blood pressure, migraines, addictions, lust, envy, doubt, worry, unbelief, fear of being raped, molested, battered again, etc., the grave, and He was resurrected with all power over all of them and any others that show up in this world and in your life in His hands. And the Bible says in Matthew 16:19, "I will give you the keys of the kingdom of heaven; whatever you bind on earth will be bound in heaven, and whatever you loose on earth will be loosed in heaven."

That's right. You have the right, power, and authority to bind, tie, or fasten fear, OCD, PTSD, depression, cancer, stress, high blood pressure, migraines, addictions, lust, envy, doubt, worry, unbelief, fear of being raped, molested, battered again, etc., tightly so they cannot get loose in your life and day anymore. When you do so, you are literally placing restraints, restrictions, boundaries, limitations, yokes, and strongholds on all of them, and then you need to "loose" something. Binding is t*he* way you refute anything that the devil is trying to trick and deceive you with and strike fear into.

- o ***Power exercise**-say this out loud and mean it:*
- o "Fear, in the name of Jesus, I bind you," and I reject you, I resist you, I refuse you, I rebuke you, and I refute you, and I "loose" my more than a conquering faith.
- o OCD, PTSD, depression, cancer, stress, high blood pressure, migraines, addictions, lust, envy, doubt, worry, unbelief, fear of being raped, molested, battered again, etc., I bind you in Jesus's name, and I command you to desist in your maneuvers against me and I loose my faith.

You have the right to refute, resist, reject, rebuke, and refuse fear and all its friends. Don't just let that power you have go unused. If you don't take authority over fear, you will continue to be driven into a survivor-survival mode, mind-set, and mentality. God has given you everything you need for you to overpower, overtake, overthrow, and overcome fear, OCD, PTSD, depression, cancer, stress, high blood pressure, migraines, addictions, lust, envy, doubt, worry, unbelief, fear of being raped, molested, battered again, fear of something that has happened to you in the past showing up again, etc.

THE SURVIVORS MODE

Redeployment

Just as the military deploys a lot of soldiers to help protect any military interest weak spots and they never send or deploy a lot of soldiers to protect places where they are strong at, you are going to have to take that same kind of approach and have that same kind of mindset. You have to understand the devil is not attacking you at where you are the strongest; he is using fear as a weapon to assault, attack, and assassinate where you are the weakest. In any military conflict, the goal of the opposing enemy is to seek out and find its enemy's weakest link or its weakest point and place and assault, attack, and try to assassinate that weak place or point.

When Satan knows he can use fear as a way to distract, detour, damage, destroy, delay, derail, deny, etc., you long enough for him to move in and kill, steal and destroy some part of you that you are going to need, he is going to do so without your permission. Most people never work on their weaknesses; they spend all their time working on what they are the strongest at while they keep failing and falling at where they are the weakest at. That is exactly how Satan is getting to you; he knows you are not going to work on the areas and places he has direct access to you at, and he knows you are going to dedicate and commit all your time working on what you are good at and you are at your strongest. He knows you are not going to work on turning your fear(s) into faith, and he knows you are not going to turn your weakness to fear into a place of strength, power, and authority.

He knows he can easily torture and torment you with fear because you are weak to it, and rather than you work or turn that weakness to fear into a strong place where you easily reject, resist, rebuke, and refuse fear and you can easily refute all fear tactical messages, images, ideas, ingenuity, information, and instructions, he knows he has you afraid to come face-to-face with your fears. He knows not only does he have you afraid to face up to your fears because you are scared to do so, but he also knows you have not and you are afraid to challenge, confront, conquer, and change that fear into faith, that weakness into a strength. Work on your weaknesses! Whatever you are weak to, you need to turn that weakness into a place of power, authority, and strength. You will need God's strength in that place of weakness, and you will need to redeploy your soldiers to that weak area and move them from the place you are the strongest.

Once you have completed solutions one through four, the next thing that you have to do is redeploy. What that means is you are going to have to reassign your troops, employees, or resources to a new place or task. What are your troops, employees, and resources? Your troops are your mind, frame of mind, state of mind, mental condition, and mental state of being. Your employees are your thoughts, train of thought, thinking, and way of thinking, and your resources are your mode, mind-set, and mentality. All these perform at your command, and they protect and prevent as you command them to do so.

It is time that you issue a redeployment order and send it into your mind, mind-set, mentality, mental capabilities and abilities and send them into your mentality and transfer their focus from one theater of operations to another. They all need to be too moved or allocated to a different position, use, function, or the like; reassigned to protecting and preventing you from having a weakness to fear, OCD, PTSD, depression, cancer, stress, high blood pressure, migraines, addictions, lust, envy, doubt, worry, unbelief, fear of being raped, molested, battered again, etc.

Solution five

You have already issued a redeployment order when you engaged in and continued to confess and profess solutions one through four on a daily basis. Now, let me help you get your soldiers, which are your militant mind, mental capabilities and abilities, thoughts, train of thought, thinking, way of thinking, mind-set, and mentality into the right protecting and preventing position. Let me also tell you your resources hat you need to protect and prevent fear and OCD, PTSD, depression, cancer, stress, high blood pressure, migraines, addictions, lust, envy, doubt, worry, unbelief, fear of being raped, molested, battered again, etc., from gaining access to are your feelings, emotions, and desires.

The assets that you need to redeploy your militant soldiers or your mind, mind-set, mentality, mental capabilities and abilities, and your mentality to protect and prevent from being stolen, destroyed, and killed are your God-given dreams, hopes, desires, visions, and destiny. Redeploy them so that they can protect your most valuable treasured asset, which is the plans that God has for you, plans for welfare and peace and not for calamity to give you a future and a hope and an expected end to all your praying, believing, trusting, and hoping (Jer. 29:11).

Fear has been trying to kill, steal, and destroy that asset from you. OCD, PTSD, depression, cancer, stress, high blood pressure, migraines, addictions, lust, envy, doubt, worry, unbelief, fear of being raped, molested, battered again, fears all kinds of fears of any kind or type, etc., have been working overtime in an effort to keep you distracted, detoured, delayed, and denied the right to know what you have been reading in this book. Up to this point and place in your life, you have deployed your mind, mental capabilities and abilities, mind-set and mentality, thoughts, train of thought, thinking, and way of thinking to protect your weaknesses and weakness to fear, and you have given them the order to prevent them from being exposed, revealed, dealt with, and rid of.

How have you done that? Every time you refuse, reject, and resist talking about your fears and OCD, PTSD, depression, cancer, stress, high blood pressure, migraines, addictions, lust, envy, doubt, worry, unbelief, fear of being raped, molested, battered again, fears of any kind to any degree etc., in the context of you wanting to get rid of them, you are protecting them and preventing them from being removed out of your life. It's time that you get rid of fears, OCD, PTSD, depression, cancer, stress, high blood pressure, migraines, addictions, lust, envy, doubt, worry, unbelief, fear of being raped, molested, battered again, etc., and stop working with them.

Are you ready to issue a redeployment? Are you ready to get the reassignment going and moving forward? You are your mind's, mental capabilities and abilities, thoughts, train of thought, thinking, and way of thinking "commander in chief," and they will obey any strategic order or demand that you issue.

Let's get it done

"Casting down and demolishing imaginations, arguments, and every pretension, speculations and every lofty thing and every high thing that exalteth itself against the knowledge of God, and bringing into captivity every thought to the obedience of Christ" (2 Cor. 10:5).

- *Power exercise-say this out loud and mean it:*
- In the name of Jesus, I cast down and demolish fear-filled imaginations, fear-filled arguments, and every fear-filled pretension, fear-filled speculation, and every fear-filled lofty thing and thought
- that exalteth itself against my peace of mind, against me having peace in my heart, peace in my spirit, and against me having peace all around me.
- In the name of Jesus, I cast down every fearful thought and thing that exalteth against me having the knowledge of God's peace.
- I bring into captivity every fear-filled thought, feeling, and emotion to the obedience of Christ in Jesus's name.
- In Jesus's name, I command and I place a demand upon my mind, with all its capabilities and abilities, to guard and protect me having peace of mind, and I command and demand my mind with all its capabilities and abilities to prevent fear of any kind and type from penetrating my God-given peace.
- I command and demand my mind, with all its capabilities and abilities, to bring into captivity every fearful thought to the obedience of Christ.
- And I "loose" the peace of God, which transcends all understanding, to guard my heart and my mind in Christ Jesus (Phil. 4:7).

THE SURVIVORS MODE

Now, rejoice, worship God, and thank Him for giving you His peace that can and will overpower, overtake, and overthrow fear and all its friends.

You can and should make this your daily confession of faith until you feel and know fear does not have power, authority, and dominion over your mind with all its capabilities and its abilities.

Remember, when I say or speak of fear with all its friends, I am referring to OCD, PTSD, depression, cancer, stress, high blood pressure, migraines, addictions, lust, envy, doubt, worry, unbelief, fear of being raped, molested, battered again, fears all kinds of fears of any kind or type, etc., and everything that can and will and do cause you to fear.

And *remember,* when I say or speak of your mind with all its capabilities and abilities, I am referring to your mind, mind-set, thoughts, train of thought, thinking, way of thinking, frame of mind, state of mind, mental condition/conditioning, mental state of being, and mentality. You no longer have to accept fear and none of its friends.

Every day you are going to have to resist, rebuke, reject, and refuse fear, and you are going to have to refute fear arguments and fear theories and fear reasoning and fear thoughts and fear purposes and every proud and lofty fear thing that sets itself up against the true knowledge of God's peace. You cannot and should not let up or take a break from using the weapon you were just armed with because Satan is not going to try and find some way to strike you with fear. It's a fear fight, war, and battle that you have already won because Jesus has already disarmed fear and its powers and authorities and He made a public spectacle of fear with all its friends triumphing over them by the cross (Col. 2:15).

My conclusion to this matter

Stop asking God to do something (1) He has already given you the power and the authority to do and (2) He has already done. When Jesus died on the cross and He said, "It is finished," everything that you need victory, power, and authority over, everything you will need deliverance, cleansing, purging, healing, and to be made whole from, "it is finished"! Whatever it is that you need, want, and even desire when it comes to you having long life, good health, you prospering, you being in good health, and when it comes to your soul prospering, "it is finished."

God is not going to come down off the cross to do something He has already done for you, me, and anyone. It's time for you to stop being a coward and show some courage and rise up and challenge, confront, conquer, and change what Satan has been doing to you. When Jesus said, "It is finished" (John 19:30), that means everything that have to do with you having victory, power, and authority and with you winning is already done.

Here it is

Are you ready? Here it comes. Get ready, get ready, get yourself ready! You win! That's right! God has given you power and authority over

- ✓ sophisticated fear arguments,
- ✓ fear imaginations,
- ✓ fear arguments,
- ✓ fear-filled pretension,
- ✓ fear-filled speculations
- ✓ lofty fearful thing
- ✓ high fearful thing
- ✓ fear-filled theories
- ✓ fear-filled reasoning
- ✓ fear-filled thoughts
- ✓ fear-filled purposes

God has given you the right to have power and authority by and through the shedding of His blood on the cross and through Him defeating death, hell, all types and kinds of fear, and the grave on your behalf. You have to see your fears as defeated and treat them as defeated foes.

You don't have to revere and respect fear, OCD, PTSD, depression, cancer, stress, high blood pressure, migraines, addictions, lust, envy, doubt, worry, unbelief, fear of being raped, molested, battered again, fears all kinds of fears of any kind or type, etc. You have been given the right, the power, and the authority to overpower, overtake, overthrow, and bring into captivity every fearful thought to the obedience of Christ.

You can overpower, overtake, and overthrow and bring every fearful exalted and fearful proud thing that sets itself up against the (true) knowledge of God and the peace He gives you. Jesus gave you the right, power, and authority to overpower, overtake, overthrow, and take every fearful thought and fearful purpose captive to the obedience of Christ. You win! And because you win and because you are the "commander in chief" of your mind, you have the right to deploy them, speak, declare, and decree this:

Solution 6

"Do not conform any longer to the pattern of this world, but be transformed by the renewing of your mind. Then you will be able to test and approve what God's will is—his good, pleasing and perfect will" (Rom. 12:2).

- My mind, frame of mind, state of mind, mental condition/ conditioning, and mental state of being, you are no longer conformed to the pattern of the fear that is in this world and the fear that has been in my life.
- I command and demand right now that you disconnect yourself from fear and be renewed according to processes, procedures, and principles of more than a conquering faith in Jesus's name.
- My thoughts, train of thought, thinking, and way of thinking, you are no longer conformed to the pattern of the fear that is in this world and the fear that has been in my life.
- I command and demand right now that you disconnect yourself from fear and be renewed according to processes, procedures, and principles of more than a conquering faith in Jesus's name.

- My mind's mind-set, mentality, and mode, you are no longer conformed to the pattern of the fear that is in this word and you are no longer to be conformed to the fear that has been in my life.
- I command and demand right now that you disconnect yourself from fear and be renewed according to processes, procedures, and principles of more than a conquering faith in Jesus's name.
- From this day forward, I command and demand my mind with all its capabilities and abilities to accept, adopt, adapt to, and apply, test, and approve what God's faith will is—His good, pleasing, and perfect faith-filled will is for me in Jesus's name, amen.

I am proud of you and I am happy for you. Stay on top of this confession as with the others and never forget "whatever it is that you give you focus to and pay attention to the most, you give strength and power to."

CHAPTER TWENTY-FIVE

Take down, Take over, and Take out

I WANT TO start out by telling you Satan's master deception and his master delusion is "it looks like." He wants to keep you reacting to, having reactionary responses when, and he wants to keep your reaction-driven and your reactionary response motive, urges, tendencies, inclinations, intuitions, impulses, impulsiveness, and instincts on a high "it looks like" alert. What this means is something or someone may just look like or have said or done something or appear to be something that you have seen or been through, and you have had to fight hard to get to where you are today, but what it looked like it really isn't and wasn't.

Faith response

Fear had you overreacting the moment when it just "looked like" OCD, PTSD, depression, cancer, stress, high blood pressure, migraines, addictions, lust, envy, doubt, worry, unbelief, fear of being raped, molested, battered again, fears all kinds of fears of any kind or type, etc., "appeared to be" trying to show up again and instead of you responding in "faith":

1. Because responding and right responses is a "faith" response or it is the right response to a faith act, action, deed, choice, decision, and moves.
2. You reacted and had a reactionary response, which is a "fear" reaction or the right reaction and reactionary response to fear acts, actions, deeds, choices, decisions, and moves.

And the moment when you did so, fear reaction and fear reactionary responses called up and made active and alive fearful reactionary and fearful reactionary response urges, tendencies, inclinations, intuitions, impulses, impulsiveness, and instincts. Those fearful reactionary and fearful reactionary responses began to take down, take over, and take out right faith responses, and when that took place, a reactionary and a reactionary response survivor-survival mode was connected. And your whole character, conduct, conversation, communication, attitude, personality, integrity intellect, etc., suddenly and immediately began to change.

You begin to demonstrate "what looks like" reactionary behavior and behavior patterns and "what looks like" reactionary response behavior patterns and behavior. But in all actuality, what "it looked like" it really wasn't and isn't, that was the perception and the perspective Satan wanted you to see and interpret what you saw through. He knew you wouldn't challenge, confront, conquer, and change what you saw to make sure what you saw was "as it is" and it wasn't just a fearful figment of your imagination. When Satan shows you something that "looks like" something that you have seen before and it is not the thing itself, what you are seeing is a "shadow" of something.

He wants to take down, take over, and take out your right, power, and authority to challenge, confront, and conquer whatever it is that you are seeing that "looks like and even feels like" something that you have seen and been through. What you may be looking at and what you may be feeling may "feel like and look like" it is OCD, PTSD, depression, cancer, stress, high blood pressure, migraines, addictions, lust, envy, doubt, worry, unbelief, fear of being raped, molested, battered again, fears all kinds of fears of any kind or type, etc., showing up again, but it really isn't. And instead of Satan allowing you the time to look at and examine that "what it looks like and feels like" so you can change your bad, wrong, negative, and ugly reaction to a right faith response, he has quickly, suddenly, and immediately driven, drawn, pulled, pushed, seduced, tricked, enticed, and forced you over into a reactionary response survivor mode, mind-set, and mentality; a survival reactionary and reactionary response mode, mind-set, and mentality;

and a survivor-survival reactionary and reactionary response mode, mind-set, and mentality.

You see, what happened is that "what looks like and what feels like" took over, took down, and took out any and all kinds and types of faith responses. Faith was forced out of the driver's seat, and fear was placed in the driver's seat of your life, day, choices, and decisions. Anytime you keep a OCD, PTSD, depression, cancer, stress, high blood pressure, migraines, addictions, lust, envy, doubt, worry, unbelief, fear of being raped, molested, battered again, fears all kinds of fears of any kind or type, etc., survivor-survival "backup" plan in the back of your mind "just in case" something or someone says, does, handles a matter, demonstrates an act, action, deed, feeling, emotion, has a conversation or communication, etc., that "looks like and feels like," what you are doing is expecting and anticipating and getting ready to "welcome" fear when it shows up.

You are also giving place to and you are preparing yourself for the moment when fear shows up take down, take over, and take out faith responses and your overcoming mode, so you can and will be able to survive. Once Satan has you in a "just in case" and in a "what looks like and what feels like" reactionary and reactionary response survivor-survival mode, mind,-set and mentality, he is basically keeping you in a place at a point where he can easily take down, take over, and take out any type and kind of resistance, rejection, refusing, rebuking, and refuting you will try to put up when fear is trying to dominate, manipulate, and control you.

In the flow of it all

Once a fear-driven and motivated "take down" mode is turned on, the next thing that happens is a fear "takeover" mind-set kicks in, and, finally, a fear "takeout" mentality finishes the flow. How this all flows is a fear's mode main objective is take down any kind of faith responses and modes, and then open the door for a hostile fear takeover mind-set to set in and settle in, and after that happens, a fear takeout and take control mentality grows, develops, and matures. The results is fear can and will and do have access to totally dominating, manipulating, and controlling the person's responses, reactions, and reactionary responses and the person's feelings, emotions, desires, thoughts, train of thought, thinking, and way of thinking.

To continue to allow fear to take down your faith mode and take over your faith mind-set and, finally, to continue to allow fear to take out your faith mentality is to be in a self-destructive mind, frame of mind, state of mind, mental condition, and mental state of being where you are giving fear the right, power, and authority to seize, rule over, and take control of faith and place your faith in a yoke, stronghold, in bondage, and place boundaries and limitations upon your faith and make your faith a slave to fear. I don't think this is what you want to do. It is important that I tell you right now, fear is not your friend, and fear is waiting for the moment when it can seize, take down, take out, take over, and take control. When fear speaks, what it does is tell faith, "I have been handling things this long, and I really don't need your help because I have the help of a protector and a preventive defense called a survivor-survival mode, mind-set, mentality, and the help of survivor-survival tactical weapons."

Fear fighting against faith

Fear when fighting against faith and is in its takedown, takeover, and takeout mode. It wants to be prosperous, productive, and successful at accomplishing and achieving at the following:

A. Torturing, tormenting, dominating, manipulating, controlling, and dictating to your faith.
B. Getting you to think and feel and believe your faith is weak and beggarly and it is powerless and insignificant.
C. Fear wants you to also think, feel, and believe your faith is filled with a lot of bad, negative, wrong high "risks" that can and will distract, detour, damage, destroy, hurt, and hinder you in some kind of way.

D. Fear wants you to think, feel, and believe your faith can't, won't, and don't work, and fear wants to convince you there is no need for faith.

E. Fear wants you to think, believe, and feel that by exercising your faith, something is going to be taken from you and faith is not going to give you something.

F. Fear wants you to think, feel, and believe faith is going to handicap and hurt you and not help you.

G. Fear wants you to see the need for it because it has provided you with a survivor-survival mode, mind-set, and mentality, and fear wants you to think, feel, and believe faith wants to take away something that has provided, protected, and prevented and been the reason why you have survived.

H. Fear wants you to think, feel, believe, and be in the mode, mind-set, and the mentality when it comes to faith where you don't and won't have time to wait for the assurance (title deed, confirmation) of things hoped for (divinely guaranteed), and the evidence of things not seen (the conviction of their reality— faith comprehends as fact what cannot be experienced by the physical senses because you need to be prepared, protected, and prevented from "faith falling and failures and flaws," and you need to survive right now and not one day soon when faith decides to show up or be made manifest).

I. Fear wants you to challenge, confront, and conquer faith and change faith into fear because fear wants you to think and feel and believe it has always been there for you and it is your best friend and your protector.

There is so much more that I could share with you when it comes to fear fighting against faith. I can tell you this fight is constant, continuous, and consistent. I can also tell you fear is going to wage a good warfare against your faith. Whatever it is that fear has to do to take down, take over, take out, and take control of your faith and yourself, it will not waste any time in doing so. Fear is a seizing spirit, and it doesn't have any kind of love and respect or appreciation for you.

Reaping from sowing fear

It would be tragic and a tragedy for you to be in a new faith relationship, marriage, and love and have an old fear mode, mind-set, and mentality. Each time you allow and give place to and way to a fear-driven, motivated, and take down, take over, take out, and take control survivor-survival mode, mind-set, and mentality being in control, you will end up pushing the right person and people away from you, and you are opening the door for and to you being on a feeling and emotional roller coaster.

"⁷ Do not be deceived, God is not mocked [He will not allow Himself to be ridiculed, nor treated with contempt nor allow His precepts to be scornfully set aside]; for whatever a man sows, this and this only is what he will reap. ⁸ For the one who sows to his flesh [his sinful capacity, his worldliness, his disgraceful impulses] will reap from the flesh ruin and destruction, but the one who sows to the Spirit will from the Spirit reap eternal life" (Gal. 6:7–8).

The most important thing you have to realize, recognize, and understand that if you keep sowing, having worldly and disgraceful fear reactions, reactionary responses, urges, tendencies, inclinations, intuitions, instincts, and impulses is you will continue to reap those same ones. It is time for you to stop sowing or planting fear seeds by scattering them on and into all areas of your life or in the earth by way of your words, what you speak, say, and do, how you react, and how and what you think and feel. It is time for you to stop planting the seeds of fear, OCD, PTSD, depression, cancer, stress, low self-esteem, diabetes, high blood pressure, migraines, addictions, lust, envy, doubt, worry, unbelief, fear of being raped, molested, battered again, fears all kinds of fears of any kind or type, etc., reactions and reactionary responses as if they were and are a plant or crop.

It is time for you to stop planting the seeds of fear-driven and motivated OCD, PTSD, depression, cancer, stress, high blood pressure, migraines, addictions, low self-esteem, lust, envy, doubt, worry, unbelief, fear of being raped, molested, battered again, diabetes, fears all kinds of fears of any kind or type, etc., urges, tendencies, inclinations, intuitions, impulses, impulsiveness, and instincts just like they are a plant or crop.

It is time for you to stop planting the seeds of a fear into your mind, mental capabilities and abilities, and sowing seeds of fear into your thoughts, train of thought, thinking, and way of thinking. It is time for you to stop sowing seeds of fear into mind's mode, mind-set, and mentality.

It is time for you to stop sowing the seeds of fear, OCD, PTSD, depression, cancer, stress, low self-esteem, diabetes, high blood pressure, migraines, addictions, lust, envy, doubt, worry, unbelief, fear of being raped, molested, battered again, fears all kinds of fears of any kind or type, etc., into your mind, frame of mind, state of mind, mental condition, state of mind, into your thoughts, train of thought, thinking, way of thinking, and into your mind's mode, mind-set, and mentality as if you were planting them in a piece of land and fear is the seed.

What you sow, you will reap. It is time for you to start sowing faith, hope, belief, and confidence and victorious, challenging, confronting, conquering, and changing faith words that will cause, create the atmosphere for, and contribute to you taking down, taking over, and taking out fear and you reaping those same words. It is time for you to totally and permanently disconnect yourself from fear and the fear of OCD, PTSD, depression, cancer, stress, low self-esteem, diabetes, high blood pressure, migraines, addictions, lust, envy, doubt, worry, unbelief, fear of being raped, molested, battered again, fears all kinds of fears of any kind or type, etc., symptoms, side effects, reoccurrences, flashbacks, etc., because Jesus has already *disarmed* all of them.

And because He has done so, you can disconnect them from your life, and you can disconnect yourself from functioning, flowing in and out of it and them, and from following fear, OCD, PTSD, depression, cancer, stress, low self-esteem, diabetes, high blood pressure, migraines, addictions, lust, envy, doubt, worry, unbelief, fear of being raped, molested, battered again, fears all kinds of fears of any kind or type, etc., patterns, patterns of behavior and conduct.

In the flow with the fear principles, processes, and procedures

Fear can't and won't be able to do no more to you than you allow it to do. You don't have to accept, adapt to, and adopt fear, and you don't have to apply fear principles, processes, and procedures. Fear has only one speed and one mode, motive, mind-set, and mentality, and that is to kill, steal, and destroy some part of or all of you. What are the fear takedown, takeover, and takeout processes, procedures, and principles? Let me break down the fear process, fear procedures, and fear principles for you, but I want you to see them from a different perspective other than yours:

> ➤ The fear process is a series of actions or steps taken to achieve a particular end, which is to *steal some part of* you and "take down" that part of you.
> ➤ The fear procedure is a series of actions conducted in a certain order or manner or an established or official way of doing something to *kill some part of* you and "take over" that part of you.
> ➤ The fear principles are a fundamental truth or proposition that serves as the foundation for a system of belief or behavior or for a chain of reasoning or a fundamental source or basis of something that will ultimately *destroy* some part of you and "take out" some part of you.

"For God did not give you a spirit of fearfulness; but of power and love and discipline" (2 Tim. 1:7 ASV).

Shadows of fear

Throughout this book, I have been endeavoring to tutor, train, and teach you how to challenge, confront, and conquer fear and how to change fear into faith. I have been showing you how to go about overpowering, overtaking, and overthrowing fear with all its friends, a.k.a. OCD, PTSD, depression, cancer, stress, low self-esteem, diabetes, high blood pressure, migraines, addictions, lust, envy, doubt, worry, unbelief, fear of being raped, molested, battered again, fears all kinds of fears of any kind or type, etc.

And now let us take fear with all its friends, which were once friends of yours, all the way out. Let's step up now and take down, take over, and take out fear, OCD, PTSD, depression, cancer, stress, low self-esteem, diabetes, high blood pressure, migraines, addictions, lust, envy, doubt, worry, unbelief, fear of being raped, molested, battered again, fears all kinds of fears of any kind or type, etc. Let's suddenly and immediately aggressively *dismantle* fear, OCD, PTSD, depression, cancer, stress, low self-esteem, diabetes, high blood pressure, migraines, addictions, lust, envy, doubt, worry, unbelief, fear of being raped, molested, battered again, fears all kinds of fears of any kind or type, etc.

And let us now, with Holy boldness and with the power and the authority Jesus has given you, me, and us, seize, overpower, overtake, overthrow, take down, take over, take out, and *disconnect* fear, OCD, PTSD, depression, cancer, stress, low self-esteem, diabetes, high blood pressure, migraines, addictions, lust, envy, doubt, worry, unbelief, fear of being raped, molested, battered again, fears all kinds of fears of any kind or type, etc., remainder residue and *residue* symptoms, residue flashbacks, and residue effects. The way we are going to do so is by taking and using the scripture below and bringing it to life.

> "Yea, though I walk through the valley of the shadow
> of death, I will fear no evil: for thou art with me; thy
> rod and thy staff they comfort me" (Ps. 23:4 KJV).

> "Even when I walk through the darkest valley, I will
> not be afraid, for you are close beside me. Your rod and
> your staff protect and comfort me" (Ps. 23:4 NLT).

The moment when you learn the truth about something or someone, you will know how to approach it and them, and you will know what to say and do to it and them; you will also know how to handle it or them, am I right? What accepting, adopting, adapting to, and applying truth do is bring you into the reality where you are made and set free. Our truth and your truth is Jesus has already "dismantled" fear and OCD, PTSD, depression, cancer, stress, low self-esteem, diabetes, high blood pressure, migraines, addictions, lust, envy, doubt, worry, unbelief, fear of being raped, molested, battered again, fears all kinds of fears of any kind or type, etc., strengths and symptoms and residue flashbacks.

Jesus has already disarmed the fear and OCD, PTSD, depression, cancer, stress, low self-esteem, diabetes, high blood pressure, migraines, addictions, lust, envy, doubt, worry, unbelief, fear of being raped, molested, battered again, fears all kinds of fears of any kind or type, etc., rulers.

Jesus has already disarmed fear and OCD, PTSD, depression, cancer, stress, low self-esteem, diabetes, high blood pressure, migraines, addictions, lust, envy, doubt, worry, unbelief, fear of being raped, molested, battered again, fears all kinds of fears of any kind or type, etc., authorities.

Jesus has already disarmed all those supernatural fear forces of evil that was operating against you, me, and us, and Jesus made a public example of fear and OCD, PTSD, depression, cancer, stress, low self-esteem, diabetes, high blood pressure, migraines, addictions, lust, envy, doubt, worry, unbelief, fear of being raped, molested, battered again, fears all kinds of fears of any kind or type, etc. Jesus, on your behalf, went about exhibiting them, fear with all its friends, as captives in his triumphal procession, and having triumphed over them, fear, OCD, PTSD, depression, cancer, stress, low self-esteem, diabetes, high blood pressure, migraines, addictions, lust, envy, doubt, worry, unbelief, fear of being raped, molested, battered again, fears all kinds of fears of any kind or type, etc., through the cross. Yes, he did!

Jesus wanted to make sure you would be able to or be empowered to dismantle and disconnect fear arguments, fear theories, fear reasoning, high and lofty and proud hidden agenda, and hidden motive fear techniques, wiles, trickeries, schemes, devices, deceptions, delusions, and strategies. He wanted to make sure that you could and would be able to overwhelmingly overpower, overtake, overthrow, take down,

THE SURVIVORS MODE

takeover, and takeout fear-driven and motivated images, ideas, insights, inspirations, ingenuities, information, and instructions.

Jesus loved you so much that He wanted to make sure you would not ever have to be a slave to, yoked to, in a stronghold to, bound and limited by and because of, and in bondage to fear and OCD, PTSD, depression, cancer, stress, low self-esteem, diabetes, high blood pressure, migraines, addictions, lust, envy, doubt, worry, unbelief, fear of being raped, molested, battered again, fears all kinds of fears of any kind or type, etc., not today, tomorrow, or in the future.

Jesus shed His blood so that you would not ever have to yield, submit, and surrender to fear, become complacent, contented, in a comfort zone with, and compromise with fear; subject yourself to being tutored, trained, and taught by fear, and have fear dictate to, decide, and determine for you. Jesus went down into the grave, and He defeated fear urges, tendencies, inclinations, intuitions, impulses, instincts, fear-filled doubts, worries, stresses, and fear-filled unbeliefs, choices, and decisions.

Jesus knew long before your mom and dad met and got together, and long before you were even thought of, conceived, birthed, and born, when, where, and how fear would be introduced into your life, and He knew what fear and OCD, PTSD, depression, cancer, stress, low self-esteem, diabetes, high blood pressure, migraines, addictions, lust, envy, doubt, worry, unbelief, fear of being raped, molested, battered again, fears all kinds of fears of any kind or type, etc., would try to do to you.

He knew fear would always try to draw, drive, pull, push, persuade, force, trick, trap, seduce, swindle, bamboozle, entice, entangle, entrap, hinder, hurt, distract, detour, dismantle, derail, delay, and deny, damage, destroy, destitute, desolate and distance you. He knew fear would not give up at trying to get you to accept, adopt, adapt, apply fear-filled emotions, fear-filled feelings, fear-filled desires, fear-filled processes, fear-filled procedures, fear-filled principles, fear-filled senses, fear-filled sensibilities, and fear-filled sensitivities.

Jesus looked down, through, and into the pages of your life long before you had a life, and He saw generational inherited curse fears and OCD, PTSD, depression, cancer, stress, low self-esteem, diabetes, high blood pressure, migraines, addictions, lust, envy, doubt, worry, unbelief, fear of being raped, molested, battered again, fears all kinds of fears of any kind or type, etc., working all the time and working overtime at trying to get you to open yourself up to engaging in fear remembrances, fear reliving, fear releasing and releases, fear-filled frustrations, fear-filled discouragements, fear-filled disappointments, fear-filled links, fear-filled ties, fear-filled connections, and into fearful repenting, fearful repeating, and fearful resenting.

He knew and saw how fear and OCD, PTSD, depression, cancer, stress, low self-esteem, diabetes, high blood pressure, migraines, addictions, lust, envy, doubt, worry, unbelief, fear of being raped, molested, battered again, fears all kinds of fears of any kind or type, etc., would work while you would be asleep at trying to come up with ways it could get you to cause, create the atmosphere for, contribute to, produce, prepare and present, function, flow, and follow fearful and fear-filled entitlements, fear-filled assumptions, and fear-filled accusations.

He knew Satan would not let up and he would not give up on trying to get you to fearfully analyze, fearfully articulate, fearfully procrastinate, hesitate, question, and second-guess fearful struggles, fearful straining, fearful surviving, fearful fighting, fearful resisting, fearful rejecting, fearful rebelliousness, fearful commitments, fearful compliments, fearful comments, and fearful completions. God knew Satan would send every demon spirit he had and he would charge them with making sure never abandoned fearful behavior, behavior patterns, fearful conduct, conversations, and communications.

He knew Satan would charge them with launching constant, continuous, and consistent fear-filled assaults, attacks, and assassinations and fear-filled weapons against you as well as launching fear-filled addictions, fear-filled afflictions, fear-filled tests, trials, tribulations, and temptations at you; as well as fear-filled aggravation, fear-filled agitation, fear-filled irritation, fear-filled destiny, fear-filled disasters, fear-filled deaths, and fear-filled drama at you.

Jesus knew He had to conquer death, hell, the grave, on your behalf so that fear and fear-filled OCD, PTSD, depression, cancer, stress, low self-esteem, diabetes, high blood pressure, migraines, addictions, lust, envy,

THE SURVIVORS MODE

doubt, worry, unbelief, fear of being raped, molested, battered again, fears all kinds of fears of any kind or type, etc., fear-filled experiences, fear-filled encounters, fear-filled deceptions, fear-filled delusions, fear-filled unseens, unknowns, unexpected, unforgettable, unbelievable, unwanted, unthinkable, unfair, unaware, unsure, uncertainty, etc., that would represent death, hell, and the grave for you could not and would not have the power over you.

When Jesus got up out of that grave with all power in His hands, He took away and stripped Satan of his power over you, He took away and stripped the powerful effect fear could and would have over you, and He made sure Satan did not have the power over you and he could not and would not have the power to keep you living in and out of fear-filled self-effort, fear-filled self-performance, fear-filled self-will, fear-filled personality, fear-filled integrity, fear-filled intellect, fear-filled public life, fear-filled private life, and fear-filled personal life. I could go on and on, but I know you get the picture; I know you are seeing what Jesus has done for you.

You seeing and having *disarmed* fear and the fear powers and the fear authorities, He made a public spectacle of them, fear, OCD, PTSD, depression, cancer, stress, low self-esteem, diabetes, high blood pressure, migraines, addictions, lust, envy, doubt, worry, unbelief, fear of being raped, molested, battered again, fears all kinds of fears of any kind or type, etc., and He, Jesus, went a step further on your behalf because He knew what kind and type of fear was going to take place and show up in what would be your past, present, and future; so He, Jesus, triumphed over them, fear and OCD, PTSD, depression, cancer, stress, low self-esteem, diabetes, high blood pressure, migraines, addictions, lust, envy, doubt, worry, unbelief, fear of being raped, molested, battered again, fears all kinds of fears of any kind or type, etc., by the cross.

Jesus "disarmed" fear so that you can dismantle and disconnect it. So what you sometimes sense or feel is not fear itself; what you sense or feel is just a "shadow" of fear. That's right. It's just "shadows" of fear, or it's just an image or mirage of fear lying in the shadows of what it once was. Jesus disarmed fear, OCD, PTSD, depression, cancer, stress, low self-esteem, diabetes, high blood pressure, migraines, addictions, lust, envy, doubt, worry, unbelief, fear of being raped, molested, battered again, fears all kinds of fears of any kind or type, etc., and the only thing that can be left over from what He has disarmed and stripped of its power and authority is a remnant, residue, or leftover that "feels like and looks like" fear, etc., but it isn't fear itself.

You have been running from and you have been scared and afraid of something that is only a "shadow" of what it once was. What you have been afraid to challenge, confront, conquer, and change is the "shadow," or the silhouette, outline, shape, contour, or profile of what fear was and used to be before Jesus (a) *disarmed* fear, (b) stripped fear of its power, (c) stripped fear of its authority, (d) made a public spectacle of fear, and (e) triumphed over fear.

What has kept you shaking and trembling and having nervous reactions and reactionary responses is something that is an unpleasant emotion caused by the belief that someone or something is dangerous, likely to cause pain, or a threat-proximity, ominous oppressiveness, or sadness and gloom feeling, emotion, thought, sense, but it isn't what you think and thought it was and is. And that proximity, ominous oppressiveness, or sadness and gloom is not what Satan wants you to believe it is, and it can't do what you think and thought it can, could, or would do to you because Jesus "disarmed" what fear gave the impression it was, gave the impression it was big and bad enough to do whatever it wants to and how it wants to, gave the impression it could, at will, continue to do what it wants to do to you as often as it wants to, and gave the impression it still had the rights and freedoms it once had to do to torment and torture you as it always had.

Jesus "disarmed" what fear, OCD, PTSD, depression, cancer, stress, low self-esteem, diabetes, high blood pressure, migraines, addictions, lust, envy, doubt, worry, unbelief, fear of being raped, molested, battered again, fears all kinds of fears of any kind or type, etc., once were, and now it's time for you to dismantle fear with all its friends and disconnect yourself forever from it and what it does. You are only going to dismantle and disconnect a "shadow" of what fear was and is. Fear itself in the totality of what it once was and what it once had the freedom, power, and authority to do in your life has been "disarmed" by Jesus.

THE SURVIVORS MODE

Let's make "disarmed" do what it does

When something is disarmed, what has happened is what has made that something a weapon has been taken away along with its presence and force, power, and authority. It's like what seems like and feels like and looks like is a big ferocious lion that is roaring and making all kinds of what looks like is scary growling and roaring, but that lion has no teeth, and it doesn't have the lion's "strength," power, and authority it once had. The only thing that lion has to work with is its "presence" and its once known influence and distinctive and pervasive quality or character, air, atmosphere, aura of respectability, aura of fierceness, and subtly pervasive quality or atmosphere seen as emanating from a person, place, or thing.

What you are seeing looks like, feels like, and sounds like it is a lion, but it really isn't the lion that it once was. What you have been running from, trembling and shaking and afraid and scared of, is a distinctive and pervasive quality or character, air, atmosphere, aura of respectability, aura of fierceness, and subtly pervasive quality or atmosphere seen as emanating from the shadow of what fear once was before Jesus "disarmed" it and stripped fear of its power and authority. The only thing fear has left to use to try and torment and torture you is what it once was, its past aura, and the shadow of what it once was. Let's dismantle and disconnect that shadow of fear and that fear shadow right now. As I said before, fear has already been "disarmed" or it has already been deprived of the power to injure or hurt.

The hostility and suspiciousness of fear, OCD, PTSD, depression, cancer, stress, low self-esteem, diabetes, high blood pressure, migraines, addictions, lust, envy, doubt, worry, unbelief, fear of being raped, molested, battered again, fears all kinds of fears of any kind or type, etc., have already been allayed by Jesus when He "disarmed" fear and fear tactics. And the highly dangerous, destructive, damaging, deadly fiery fuse that fear once had that so many was fearful of lighting has been removed and made an open spectacle of and it has been triumphed over by Jesus.

It's time to seize, overpower, overtake, and overthrow what fear was and isn't, and it's time to take down, take over, and take out the "shadows" or the remaining residue of fear that has enveloped, cast a shadow, or overshadowed you and your life. Are you ready? All right, then, let's get it on in the name of Jesus.

Solution 7

- *Power exercise-say this out loud and mean it:*
- Jesus, I come before You, and I stand on the authority of Your word.
- In Colossians 2:15, You stated that You have already disarmed fear, its powers, and its authority over my life and in my life.
- You said in Your word that You have already, long before I came into this world, made a public spectacle of fear (name everything else).
- You triumphed over fear (name everything else) by the cross.
- Today, right now, in Jesus's name, I bind, reject, resist, refuse, and rebuke all "shadows" of fear (name everything else).
- I loose and release my faith, and I thank you that I have divine protection from fear.
- I speak, declare, and decree that from this day forward, when I walk through the darkest fear valleys, I will fear no evil, for You are with me.
- I thank You that Your rod and Your staff, they comfort me.
- I, of my own free will, command fear (name everything else) to get out of my life.
- You are trespassing spirits, and I will serve you no more by shaking and trembling and being afraid and scared.
- I "loose" my walk in faith, and I will, from this day forward, walk through the shadows of fear in faith because Jesus dismantled faith, its power, and its authority, and He made an open spectacle of fear, and he triumphed over fear on my behalf.
- I believe what Colossians 2:15 says Jesus did to fear (name everything else).

THE SURVIVORS MODE

- I receive this Colossians 2:15 gift from God, and I call forth a visible manifestation of it in my life and day in Jesus's name, amen.

Now praise and worship God and thank Him for the Colossians 2:15 and the Psalm 23:4 gift.

You no longer have to be afraid and scared of fear "shadows" or afraid and scared of shadows that give the impression of being fear. You don't have to receive, accept, adopt, adapt to, and apply, react, or have any kind of reactionary responses to fear. Jesus has disarmed fears power and authority, and He made an open spectacle of fear, and He triumphed over fear by the cross!

Fear face-off

"Surely goodness and mercy shall follow me all the days of my life: and I will dwell in the house of the LORD forever" (Ps. 23:6 KJV).

Just like shame and embarrassment knows how to shadow your life, fear is just a "shadow" spirit that does the same. It is a spirit that lurks around in the dark, unrestrained, uncontrolled, uneducated, unforgiven, unrepentant, compromised places in your life. Wherever there is a shadow of fear, there is horror, alarm, panic, agitation, trepidation, dread, consternation, dismay, and distress. Now that God has brought you to this place and point, I want you to know fear is not going to just go away. You are going to have to have face-offs with fear, but you won't have to engage in a fear fight, battle, and war as long as you stay committed, faithful, and true to your solution 1–7 confessions.

Your solution 1–7 confessions are the way to eliminate your fear weakness or your weakness to fear tactics of Satan. I want you to picture yourself waking up every morning and you go about your morning getting ready to walk out of your house and go and face your day. And throughout your day, all types and kinds of circumstances, situations, even confrontations and matters that you didn't expect nor did you plan and prepare for. And somewhere in the midst of all that, Satan sneaks in some of his fear tactics, and before you know it, you have found yourself reacting and having reactionary responses to what he has done. You didn't prepare yourself like you should have for your day.

Fear is not going to stop fighting you, and it is warring against you; and fear is not going to just let you walk away delivered, cleansed, purged, healed, made whole, and free from fear. You are going to have to arm yourself with the weapons that can and will help you face fear and challenge, confront, and conquer it. We get so caught up in life that we forget to live, and that is what fear wants to do, and that is to keep you so caught up in life that you become, be, and end up being fearful of living.

Fear tells us what we need to do, what we have to do, but fear is not going to allow us or let us do what you want to do. Fear is not going to let you do something that is "simple." Fear wants to keep you living a complicated and complex life. Fear wants to be the driving force behind your life and in your life. Fear is so bold now that it tells us what is important, and fear wants to dictate what our priorities are and should be, and in doing so, fear can dominate, manipulate, and control our lives. Fear does two things, and that is "suggest and influence," and when we heed to what it suggests and we give into what fear influences us into thinking, believing, and feeling is important, we allow it to get into the driver's seat in our lives and we allow fear to drive us into total oblivion. We have allowed fear to tell us what is and what isn't important.

Into the fear process and procedures

Fear "suggests" something is important, and then fear "influences" us into believing, thinking, and feeling what it has suggested is important. And once we take the fear "suggestion" and the fear "influence" bait, Satan makes sure we make what fear has suggested as important, and he then makes sure we make what fear has suggested we say and do as very important. When we give in and give place to the fear suggestions and influences that fear has made sure what it has suggested we say, do, and how we handle matters, has suggested how we should think, feel, and believe is real and right and good to us and for us; and when we give in to the behavior, behavior patterns, conduct, conversations, communications, personality, integrity, and intellectual influences of fear and we endorse them as real and right and good to us and for us, fear then eases its foot on the gas pedal in our lives and fear drives us into a mode, mind-set, and mentality where we become obsessed and possessed with accomplishing, achieving, acquiring, and accumulating.

Fear only has two paces, and that is the "fast lane" in life, love, and living, or all the way in the "slow lane" in live, love, and living. Fear uses the power of suggestion and the power of influence as its way of getting us to do what he wants us to do. We have allowed and we have given fear the right, the power, the authority, and the place to tell us or to suggest to us what is important in life and what our dreams, goals, objectives, and focus should be, and it then knows we are open to listening to and hearing and heeding to and obeying what it influences us into accepting, adopting, and adapting to what is important in our life, world, choice, and decision making.

Fear has told us that if we do not accomplish, achieve, acquire the dreams, hopes, and desires it has told us and has suggested to us is important to us and for us, then something is wrong with us and we will end up dying "a nobody" with nothing that went "nowhere." Fear influences us into making what we should be passion driven over into being what we feel like we have to pursue and never let up no matter what it cost us. Fear tells us what we have to have, what we have to do, what we should do, what we can't and won't and shouldn't do, and where we can and can't, should and shouldn't go. In some kind of way and in some kind of shape, form, or fashion, fear is involved in suggesting and influencing and in being the driving force in our lives and in our day.

Fear has us afraid to win and afraid to lose. Fear has us afraid to relax and afraid to live the one life we have to live. Fear tells us what we should focus on, what we should fight for or against. Fear takes the good and the real and the right that we set out to do, and it will find a way to suggest something to it, and fear will find a way to influence that good, real, and right that you have set out to say and do. And when he can successfully do so, he will draw, pull, push, persuade, seduce, entice, force, and drive what you set out to do as good, real, and right into something you are obsessed into having, saying, and doing, and fear will then make that obsession something that you make urgent and a vital necessity. What I'm trying to get you to see is fear can even be the driving force behind what you say and do that is good, real, and right. What you have to remember and never lose sight of is whatever it is that fear suggests and influences you will become obsessed and possessed by and with, that is fear's procedural process.

Fear can and will find a way to send its suggestions into your thoughts, train of thought, thinking, and way of thinking, and when fear has done that, it will get you to cause, create the atmosphere for, and contribute to fear influences finding and getting into your mind, frame of mind, state of mind, mental condition/conditioning, and mental state of being. Once the suggested and influenced parts of your mind have been compromised and have been seized, overpowered, overtaken, and overthrown, fear's next move is to make sure its suggested and influenced obsessions and possessions become, be, and end up being a dominant, controlling, and manipulative active and persuasive part of your mind's mode, mind-set, and mentality.

Face-to-face with fear

Fear will tell you it is important that you are prosperous, productive, and successful and anything less than that is unacceptable, and when you take this suggestive and influential "fear bait" and allow it to take down, take over, and take out your faith balance, fear once again is able to get into the driver's seat of your thoughts, train of thought, thinking, and way of thinking, and it will put its foot on the accelerator in your adrenaline and fear will drive and push and force you over into a mode, mood, attitude, mind-set, mentality to where your mind and your mental capabilities and abilities are so overworked that you come home tired and exhausted.

You will be mentally worn out because fear was in the driver's seat of your mind with all its capabilities and abilities and fearful suggestions and fearful influences that have been the fuel that your mind with all its capabilities and abilities have been running on all day and you didn't even know it. Fear still believes it is your bestie, or your best friend, and every day, you will, in some kind of way, in some manner, and in some place and point in your day and in your life, come face-to-face with fear. It will always be waiting on you, and what should happen is you shouldn't let fear handle you. Rise up and you handle fear and deal with it like it needs to be.

Fear will have you too afraid to live and too scared to die. Somewhere in your day, fear is going to try and railroad you, and it is going to try and find a way to suggest and influence you into being "led" into it, and then you will be driven by it. Fear does not want you to fight against it; fear wants you to think, feel, and believe and accept, adopt, and adapt to it as if it was and is your friend. That is why it is a "shadow" spirit. It is a shadow spirit with badgering, bullying, tormenting, and torturing presence and power. Anything that remains or stays in the "shadows" is not something that wants to be seen, challenged, confronted, conquered, dealt with, and changed. The trick and the delusion and the deception here is fear doesn't want you to fight against it, but it will constantly, continuously, and consistently fight against you.

Fear stays and remains in the "shadows" of your life and day, and fear hides in the shadows of your shame and embarrassment, and it makes a mockery out of the OCD, PTSD, etc., and out of everything else you have been through. So when you come face-to-face with fear again, remember it is not your friend; it is your foe, and it wants to make sure you never move forward and you never get past and you never get over. If you give fear a chance and an open door and an opportunity, it can and will have you running, reacting, thinking, and reactionary responding at a rapid pace. Fear's job is to frighten you and intimidate you and make you seem like you are weak, insignificant, and powerless and you are not important and you do not matter.

Footsteps in the dark

Fear wants to punk you into believing, thinking, and believing you cannot and will never win and gain a victory over everything from your past and old and from your present that has been causing the hair to stand up on your body, causing you to feel like something in the dark is following you and is chasing after you, and causing you to feel like your life will end before its time and you will leave this life a loser. Fear's power over you lies in it being able to get your mind into playing tricks on you, and it lies in getting you to thinking, feeling and, believing you are hearing footsteps in the dark. Fear is the master of "shadow" illusions and delusions and deceptions. Why do you seemingly keep hearing footsteps in the dark? It's because your mind is playing tricks on you. Fear has to get into your head before it can get to your heart.

I want to say something to you right now, and that something I want to say is "Don't let your past become your present and your future." Whatever "shadows" of fear that are from your past, don't let those same shadows stand in the way and block, hinder, and hold up the present and future God has for you. The only way to get rid of a shadow is to turn or shine light on it and it will disappear. The same applies to the "shadows of fear" that you walk through. You won't ever have to fear "fear" if you turn the light of truth on and shine that light of truth on it. Fear loves to sneak up on you, and it thrives on trying to get you to procrastinate, hesitate, question, and second-guess.

Fear wants to turn any urge you get and turn that urge into an urgency by suggesting and influencing it into one, and when that happens, fear knows your heart rate can and will increase, and your adrenaline will get stirred up and it will increase, and you will feel like you just have to fulfill and satisfy that urge, need, want, desire, or fantasy; and fear will then have you think, feel, and believe you just "have to" have and you "have to" see that urge, need, want, desire, and fantasy met, and that is when fear steps in and puts its foot on the gas and becomes the driving force behind that urged urgency.

Fear will then have you drive past faith, drive past any yield and stop signs, and drive past any and all signs that say, "Slow down. You are headed for a crash." Fear does not want you to have faith and have any facts, and fear does not want you to do truthful rational reality thinking. Fear wants you to live on the edge of self-destruction and on the edge of self-demise. When you give into fear, it can and will have you looking

THE SURVIVORS MODE

like or appearing to be crazy and border line schizophrenic. Fear is the driving force behind schizophrenia. When a person is schizophrenic or has schizophrenia, the "shadows of fear" that lie in his or her darkness have that person interpreting reality abnormally.

Fear-filled schizophrenia

When a person's mind is playing tricks on him or her, that person is afraid to challenge, confront, conquer, and change something from his or her past and old or present. The person is so afraid they choose to downplay and ignore what's shadowing them and their life, or he or she chooses to pretend like nothing is wrong and has happened, and he or she sweeps that traumatic, torturing, and tormenting something, moment, memory, matter, circumstance, situation, and confrontation "under the carpet" as to say.

Schizophrenia may result in some combination of fearful hallucinations, fearful delusions, and extremely fearful disordered thinking and behavior. Contrary to popular belief, schizophrenia isn't a split personality or multiple personality. The word "schizophrenia" does mean "split mind," but it refers to a disruption of the usual balance of emotions and thinking. Fear is always that force that brings about that disruption of the usual balance of emotions and thinking. Fear-filled emotions and fear-filled thinking heeded and given place to can and will always keep a person mentally out of balance in their emotions and in their thinking. Fear traumatize, tortures, and torments that person's emotions, feelings, thinking, and ability to bring about frame of mind, state of mind, mental condition, and mental state of being balance.

When there has been traumatic fear experiences and encounters that have traumatized, tortured, and tormented a person's mode, mind-set, and mentality and their ability to function and fear has brought about a range of problems with thinking (cognitive), behavior, or emotions, a person most likely will end up with some or all of the following:

- **Fear-filled delusions.** These are unpleasant emotions caused by the belief that someone or something is dangerous, likely to cause pain, or a threat that are false beliefs that are not based in reality. For example, you're being harmed or harassed; certain gestures or comments are directed at you; you have exceptional ability or fame; another person is in love with you; a major catastrophe is about to occur; or your body is not functioning properly. Fearful delusions can occur in as many as four out of five people with schizophrenia.

- **Fear-filled hallucinations.** These usually involve unpleasant emotions caused by the belief that the person is seeing and hearing someone or something or things that are dangerous, likely to cause pain, or a threat that doesn't exist. Yet, for the person with schizophrenia, he or she has the full fear force and fear-filled impact of a "normal" fearful experience. Fear-filled hallucinations can be in any of the senses, but hearing fearful voices is the most common hallucination.

- **Fear-filled disorganized thinking (speech).** This is an unpleasant emotion caused by the belief that someone or something is dangerous, likely to cause pain or a threat that causes the person to engage in disorganized thinking inferred from disorganized speech. Fear being the driving force can bring about and lead to effective communication being impaired, and answers to questions may be partially or completely unrelated. Rarely, fearful speech may include putting together meaningless words that can't be understood, sometimes known as word salad.

- **Fear-filled extremely disorganized or abnormal motor behavior.** This may show in a number of ways, especially when there are unpleasant emotions caused by the belief that someone or something is dangerous, likely to cause pain, or a threat that draws, drives, pulls, pushes, persuades, seduces, entices, and forces the person into behavior and behavior patterns that are ranging from childlike silliness to unpredictable agitation. When fear is the driving force behind the behavior, a faith-filled right behavior is not focused on a goal, which makes it hard to perform tasks. Fear traumatizing, torturing, and tormenting abnormal motor behavior can include resistance to instructions, inappropriate and bizarre posture, a complete lack of response, or useless and excessive movement.

- **Fear-filled negative symptoms.** This refers to reduced ability or lack of ability to function normally because of an unpleasant emotion caused by the belief that someone or something is dangerous, likely to cause pain, or a threat. For example, the person appears to lack or be scared and fearful of emotion, such as not making eye contact, not changing facial expressions, speaking without inflection or monotone, or not adding hand or head movements that normally provide the emotional emphasis in speech. Also, the person may have a reduced ability to plan or carry out activities, such as decreased talking and neglect of personal hygiene, or have a loss of interest in everyday activities, social withdrawal, or a lack of ability to experience pleasure because of being scared or afraid.
- **Fear-driven delusions.** These are an unpleasant emotions caused by the belief that someone or something is dangerous, likely to cause pain, or a threat that is an idiosyncratic belief or impression that is firmly maintained despite being contradicted by what is generally accepted as reality or rational argument, typically a symptom of mental disorder.
- **Fear-driven hallucination.** This is an unpleasant emotion caused by the belief that someone or something is dangerous, likely to cause pain, or a threat that is an experience involving the apparent perception of something not present.

Walking through the shadows of fear

As you move forward and go about your day and when you have a fear faceoff and when you come face-to-face with fear while you are walking out your deliverance, cleansing, purging, healing, and being made whole from fear, know that (a) God has already worked things out for your good. Fear cannot draw you and drive you anymore because (b) God has disarmed it, and you have and will continue to (c) dismantle and disconnect and destroy fear with all its friends from your life though and by way of your faith solution 1–7 confessions. The other things I want to tell you are the following:

1. "Surely God's goodness and unfailing love will pursue you all the days of my life, and you will live in the house of the LORD forever" (Ps. 23:6 NLT).
2. "Be alert and of sober mind. Your enemy the devil (fear) prowls around like a roaring lion looking for someone to devour" (Ps. 23:6 NIV).
3. The angels of God are camped around you, and they are protecting you from fear and they are preventing fear from gaining any place or ground in your life.

When you wake up and you start to prepare for your day, I want you to stop at your door and do the following before you leave out of the door of your home:

- ***Fear power exercise-**say this out loud and mean it:*
- Fear, I bind you and I restrict you from showing up in my day and life today.
- God's grace, God's goodness, and God's mercy, I release you and I invite you to come and get into my vehicle with me.
- I release you to go before me.
- I release you to follow me around all through my day.
- In Jesus's name.

Divine fear protection

All right, now, you are free to go about your day. Grace, mercy, and goodness are your new "faith" friends. Make sure you invite your new friends to get in the car with you and to be a part of your day. Every time you sense, see, or feel fear is trying to show up, repeat your fear power exercise in faith and be adamant about it. Keep releasing God's goodness and God's mercy to follow you around. They will have your back, and fear cannot and will not be free to stab you in the back. Keep declaring and decreeing and speaking God's grace has and is gone *before you* and God's goodness and God's mercy is *following* you.

You now have divine protection because God's grace in front of you and God's goodness and God's mercy are following you (Ps. 23:6). Rejoice and be exceedingly glad! Fear can remain in your shadow, and it can remain a shadow because you are not having or entertaining fear thoughts, train of thought, thinking, and way of thinking. Remember what you think about the most you give power, strength, and authority to. You can walk in the victory, power, and authority over fear and your weakness to fear that God has given you. Once again, I want to say to you,

"Surely God's goodness and God's unfailing love, and mercy and loving kindness will follow and pursue, will stay close to, YOU all the days of your life, and YOU will dwell, live in, remain in, will rest in the house of the LORD forever, as long as YOU live, for the rest of your life, to the length of your days, and for days without end" (Ps. 23:6). Hallelujah and to God be the glory!

CHAPTER TWENTY-SIX

Run for Your Life

I F YOU ARE in an abusive circumstance, situation, confrontation, and relationship, I want to encourage you to "run for your life." Don't make excuses. *Stop* procrastinating, hesitating, questioning, and second-guessing yourself. You are in harm's way, and so are your children and even your family members that are standing up for you. Run . . . for . . . your . . . life! This is not a test . . . It's not going to get better . . . Stop defending that person and making excuses for their bad and wrong behavior . . . Run for your life.

You have heard those lies before, you have seen the tears, and you have heard the empty apologies that have no feelings and have no fruit. How long has it been now? How many scars and bruises have you had and do you have? How many broken bones, black eyes, swollen faces, and hurt and pain in your body? The question is not whether your abuser loves you; the question is do you love yourself and do you love your children? Do you want to live? Pack your bag *now!* Have your emergency bag packed and be ready to leave in a hurry! Do it now, move quickly, and do the following:

1. ***Pack in the bag:*** a change of clothes for yourself and child/ children, toiletries (toothpaste, toothbrush, and deodorant, whatever you think you may need), money, bank account numbers (so you can put a stop to bank accounts that have your name on them. It may very quickly go into overdraft). You will be unable to think what you need if and when that time comes to flee.

   > You will not be able to think about what you
   > need if and when that time comes to flee.

425

2. ***Hide your emergency bag.*** Hide it in a place where the abuser will not find it because when you are in a desperate situation, nothing else matters except getting out with your life and your children's lives. Time will not wait on you, and time will not be on your side.

3. ***Do not tell your abuser you are going to leave then, and do not tell anyone else what you are going to do and where you are going to go.*** The only people you can and should tell are the people who are going to help you *run for your life.* The people you confide in have to be those you absolutely know you can trust.

4. Plan and prepare and continue to go about your daily routine and never give any hint or indication that you are going to leave.

Fight the feeling

"For God hath not given us the spirit of fear; but of power, and of love, and of a sound mind" (2 Tim. 1:7 KJV).

You can leave and you can get out and you can fight the fear feeling. It's your life, and your life does not belong to anything and anyone else. Satan and fear did not purchase your life. They are not your friends, and they are not on your side; they are trying to steal your life, kill your life, and destroy your life. Satan is afraid your "faith" is going to be "awakened" and you will discover you have and always have had power and authority over fear. You are a winner, and you win in Jesus's name. However, you know that you have a responsibility in demonstrating your faith. It is up to you to believe completely and to trust wholeheartedly in God's will of good in your life. When you release your faith, you cooperate with the demonstration of God's good. You rejoice in the knowledge that your prayers are heard and answered. God has the power to bring forth, through you, the needed good in the midst of every challenge. How do you release your faith? You say and do something that you had not been able to do and you would not normally do.

When you do so, let me tell you what is going to take place. God's strength is going to show up, and it will overpower, overtake, and overthrow your weakness and turn your weakness, fear, and being scared and afraid into a supernatural strength, His supernatural strength. His power and His strength work best in your weakness (2 Cor. 12:9). The only thing you have to do is *act* and not react, *respond* or give the right response, and don't reject, resist, and refuse. *Stop* thinking and overthinking what you have to do. Just *do it!*

Act and give the right response in God's strength and in Jesus's name. Those days of you having low and no self-esteem, self-worth, self-image, and self-respect, and those days of feeling lonely and believing you are all alone and all by yourself are *over!* You are no longer a slave to feelings of being tortured, tormented, terrorized, and traumatized. Those days of you having recurring memories or flashbacks of events that would bring you feelings of guilt and shame are *over.* You will no longer start to feel like you are on the edge, and you will no longer start having a lot of sleepless nights, a loss of interest, and numb feelings. I speak God's strength into your weaknesses right now in Jesus's name.

All those overwhelming stress and anxiety days and moments that used to show up at will are disconnected and destroyed in Jesus's name. I bind the spirit of stress and anxiety, feelings of anger and rage and irritability in Jesus's name, and I loose God's strength into all areas where you think, feel, and believe you are overwhelmed in Jesus's name. Jesus shed His blood on the cross so that you can be free from overwhelming and overwhelmed feelings and emotions. Be free in Jesus's name!

I speak God's strength and power into your self-esteem, self-image, self-confidence, and self-worth, and I speak God's strength into everything that is to shape your world and shape your confidence and opinion. I plead the blood of Jesus against every negative, bad, and wrong thought and feeling that has kept you yoked, bound, limited, and in bondage in Jesus's name!

THE SURVIVORS MODE

STOP! LOOK! AND LISTEN!

Each time he said, "My grace is all you need. My power works best in weakness" (2 Cor. 12:9).

God's strength is moving within you right now. Receive it! Yield, submit, and surrender to His strength right now! God's overpowering, overtaking, and overthrowing *strength* is upon you right now, and His strength and power are overpowering, overtaking, and overthrowing

- reexperiencing the trauma symptoms;
- Intrusive memories that interrupt your everyday life;
- flashbacks that bring about acts and you acting or feeling like you're still in the middle of the event again;
- reoccurring nightmares about the trauma;
- intense distress or irritability when reminded of the event;
- physical reactions, like rapid breathing, sweating, or nausea, when remembering or being reminded of the trauma;
- increased distress as the anniversary of the event approaches;
- avoidance symptoms;
- feeling emotionally detached from others;
- experiencing hopelessness about the future ("No one will ever love me" or "I know I'm going to die young");
- inability to remember important aspects of the traumatic event;
- arousal or anxiety symptoms;
- bouts of moodiness or anger;
- insomnia or difficulty staying asleep;
- a sense of being "on alert" or "on guard" (also called hypervigilance);
- developing a destructive addiction to alcohol, drugs, or even gambling; and
- suicidal thoughts or actions.

Receive what Jesus is doing in you and for you right now . . . *Respond* in the right way by putting your hands up, and begin to praise and thank Him for touching you and making and setting you free! You have a right to be free from PTSD, and you have a right to be free to live your life. God's presence and God's anointing is right in the room where you are. Open up your mouth and your heart and begin to thank Him for loving you and for touching you right now in Jesus's name!

Be free in Jesus's name . . . be cleansed and purged in

Jesus's name . . . be made whole in Jesus's name!

"No weapon formed against you will prevail" (Isa. 54:17).

As you are reading this book, God's presence is there with you, and everything within you is responding to God's truth and God touching you . . . Receive His touch . . . Receive His love for you. The anointing is there in the room with you, and it is upon you and it is *destroying* the weapons of you

- having repeated thoughts or images about many different things, such as fear of germs, dirt, intruders, acts of violence, hurting loved ones, sexual acts, conflicts with religious beliefs, or being unduly tidy;
- doing the same rituals over and over such as washing hands, locking and unlocking doors, counting, keeping unneeded items, or repeating the same steps again and again;
- not being able to control the unwanted thoughts and behaviors;
- not getting pleasure when performing the behaviors or rituals, but getting brief relief from the anxiety the thoughts cause; and
- spending at least one hour a day on the thoughts and rituals that cause distress and get in the way of daily life.

Be free in Jesus's name! You have a right to be free, and you no longer have to be a slave to OCD. God is giving you His strength that will empower you to release OCD. I plead the blood of Jesus against you being yoked to, in a stronghold to, and in bondage to OCD thoughts, feelings, emotions, and desires. Despite all the things OCD has tried to do to you, receive the *overwhelming* victory that is yours through Christ, who loves you (Rom. 8:37).

THE SURVIVORS MODE

My conclusion to this matter

Please understand that Jesus's teachings on deliverance, cleansing, purging, healing, health, and complete well-being are true for you and family and friends today. Therefore, you do not become anxious when symptoms appear, for the ever-present love of God abides with you and within you all. Right now, God is pouring forth perfection throughout your mind and body, and you will begin to express health and well-being. Your heart beats in perfect rhythm. Your body is revitalized and renewed. Your mind and body are governed by God's perfect order.

Wait on it! Healing can manifest itself in an instant or over a period. If you are going through a time of healing, take heart. Remember that Jesus prayed more than once for a blind man. Right after Jesus's first prayer, the man could see but not clearly. Jesus prayed again, and the man's sight was restored; he saw clearly.

My prescription for you

Daily and monthly, you claim your deliverance and claim your healing. You claim you are mentally healthy and whole, you are of sound mind, and you have a healthy heart and strong bones. You claim freedom from OCD and PTSD discomfort and freedom to move about effortlessly with no flashbacks. You speak blessings upon your mind, mind-set, and mentality, upon your mental capabilities and abilities, upon your thoughts, train of thought, thinking, way of thinking, and upon the joints and muscles of your body, as you envision yourself in the warm glow of healing light.

You can claim your healing knowing that every day and in every way, you are growing healthier and stronger. Deliverance from OCD and PTSD is your heritage, or part of your possession that you inherited when He purchased your life through Him dying on the cross and shedding His blood for you (Eph. 1:14). Receive your special or individual possession, your allotted portion, your deliverance, and your inner healing. It's your inheritance, and it is free. You don't have to earn it, beg for it, or bargain for it. You were made "worthy" of it because of what Jesus did for you when He gave His life for you. It is your heritage, and you are a rightful heir to deliverance, cleansing, purging, healing, and being made whole!

> "This is the heritage of the servants of the LORD
> and this is their vindication from me,'
> declares the LORD"
> (Rom. 8:37).

Thank you for reading my book. I would like to hear from you. Please e-mail me at authormack@yahoo.com.

Printed in the United States
By Bookmasters